LIFE'S PICTURE HISTORY OF WESTERN MAN

LIFE'S PICTURE HISTORY OF WESTERN MAN

TIME INCORPORATED • NEW YORK • 1951

BOOK TRADE DISTRIBUTION BY SIMON & SCHUSTER, INC.

TABLE OF CONTENTS

The glory that was Greece was revealed to the mind of Western Man in the awesome relics of Greek drama and in the living body of Greek philosophy, but nowhere so thrillingly as in the lovely remnants of Greek sculpture. This art gave Western Man a simple, noble concept of the human form, which is still the ideal of most members of his civilization. The horseman above, a fragment of a frieze, was carved in the fourth century B.C. by an unknown sculptor who caught and held in everlasting stone "a moment's life of things that live."

INTRODUCTION

WESTERN MAN'S ANCIENT HERITAGE

WESTERN Man—who is he and where did he come from? When did he step out on the stage of human civilization and what was his performance there? How did the onward roll of history affect his beliefs and actions and how did they, in turn, guide the course of large events?

The purpose of this book is to answer some finite aspects of these infinite questions about the most wonderfully dynamic creature ever to walk this earth. In a sense, this book is a spiritual biography of Western Man, recording in terms of his own genius what he thought and felt and did about himself and the world around him. It is not a formal history, with dates and dynasties. Nor does it attempt to provide any startling new answers to the great riddles of the past or to develop any novel thesis with which to confound the experts and make all things clear to all men in a single flash.

It does, however, proceed on these historical assumptions: 1) Western Man was the architect of the modern world, the chief contributor to its patterns of thought and action; 2) he was a most interesting, instructive and colorful individual whose manifold activities through the centuries elevated the human spirit and ennobled the human heart; 3) he was a Christian (and may still be one today) and his faith served as a mighty engine of civilization which not only produced works of art that remain the wonder and the admiration of posterity, but also evolved a set of moral standards which are the very bedrock of his heirs' society today.

Western Man, by any definition, is a product of western Europe. He was born in the murk of the Dark Ages, just as the morning of Christianity was breaking over the land. His wild pagan ancestors had hunted the German forests, pirated the North Sea, fished the salty outlets of the Rhine and fought the Romans everywhere. His youth was a hard daily scrabble for survival. He educated himself. He worked to shape his world more to his liking. His identity as Western Man, distinct and different from his predecessors, became historically clear about 800 A.D. (earlier in some places, later in others) and he was ready to set out on his bright-starred mission of creating a new civilization for the world. Thereafter his progress can be clearly followed in the homes he built, in the altars he raised to his one God, in the songs he sang and the pictures he painted to celebrate the glory of himself and his soaring spirit. He had a vast talent for reflecting himself and in this book he proves to be his own best portraitist. He was mixed up in a great deal of history and generally gave a good account of himself, either by name or in the mass. Under Martel he fought the Moors at Poitiers. He saw Charlemagne crowned emperor of the West by the Pope. He was with the Norman William at Hastings. ("Twenty thousand thieves," Emerson called him and his fellow invaders.) He went on the Crusades because "God wills it."

His body was like ours, with less height and more jaw perhaps, but otherwise the same, and his feelings and appetites were understandably similar. He was fair of skin, hardy of limb, brave of heart, and he believed in the eternal salvation

On the Acropolis the Greeks erected the most splendid monument of their civilization, the perfect Parthenon, which sheltered the great statue of Athena by Phidias, and the Erechtheum, to which the delicate little porch of the Caryatids, shown above, is affixed.

of his soul. He gradually developed a sense of political action, the institutionalization of self-interest, and, through politics, he worked toward freedom, first for his own person, then for his own mind and spirit, and finally for others in equal measure. Human, he had sorry lapses into deceit, treachery and debauch, but gradually he tempered his cruelest instincts, disciplined his crudest lusts and eventually achieved an elegance of manner and a refinement of intellect of which his descendants could well be proud. By enormous effort this Western Man created a civilization which this book takes as its theme—from his first emergence in the Middle Ages to his contemporary position of world leadership in the United States of America.

WESTERN Man was obviously not born into a cultural vacuum. Behind him, as part of his natural heritage, lay a vast store of world history of which no adequate record can be given here. His roots reach back into the ancient worlds of Greece and Rome, and upon their treasure he has drawn prodigiously for his own enlightenment. Together they contributed substantially to his language, his esthetics, his methods of thinking, his ideas of organization, his concept of justice But their history is not his. In his maturity, Western Man was inclined to look back fondly upon this lost world as upon some bright dream he had dreamed long ago in an earlier incarnation. He could never be sure about separating fact from beautiful fancy, but he took them both, and they gave him a sense of history when he needed it most.

Civilized history, however, had not as yet turned on the stage lights for even this prelude to Western Man when the first herdsmen filtered down from some northern forest into that dry, dusty, chopped-up corner of Europe called Hellas. There these tribesmen found an older civilization under foot; they crushed it and replaced it with one of their own—the finest masterpiece of its kind. Why such a miracle should occur when, where and how it did is impossible to explain. It was, perhaps, partly because of Greece's topography; isolated valleys between barrier hills dipped on down to a ragged shore line and to that great civilizer, the sea. As these early Hellenes ventured out into the Aegean in their crude, rudderless rowboats and coasted among its islands, they met and mixed with older cultures already there—the Cretan, Egyptian, Lydian, Persian. Ideas and goods were exchanged between East and West in this warm incubator of civilization. A good thousand years before Christ, Western Man's ancient antecedents sailed with Agamemnon the wine-dark sea to fetch Helen home from Troy and wreak vengeance on Priam's city. Homer may have been a blind myth and the *Iliad* nothing but a singsong version of some primitive economic struggle, but no poet, no poetry, has so stirred the hearts of more men for more centuries.

GREEK SOLDIER

While they sang epic songs of their epic past, the Greeks were amply busy with their lively present. They built themselves trim city-states and grew rich and refined. But they had an inordinate passion for individual liberty. Their patriotic loyalty was to their native city—Athens, Thebes, Sparta or Corinth—and not to Hellas as a whole. Never could they federate or coalesce into a nation for peaceful purposes. In great emergencies they would pool their fighting forces—for example, to defeat the invading Persians under Darius at Marathon (490 B.C.) or Xerxes at Salamis (480 B.C.)—but, with victory, they would promptly fall out again and exhaust their physical and spiritual strength in long, local wars.

APHRODITE

It is not this bloody record of war that causes these city-states to survive so brightly in Western Man's memory, but rather their ways of peace. From them all, except martial Sparta, Western Man fell heir to a standard of beauty that has never deserted him—an idea of proportion and simplicity, of form and line which he has tried to re-create again and again without ever matching the lost original. This beauty reposed not only in visible relics like the Parthenon (440 B.C.) and the remnant works of Phidias and Praxiteles, but also in the very language of the Greeks. Borrowing their alphabet from the Phoenicians and adding vowel signs to limber it up, the Hellenic dramatists, poets, historians and orators bequeathed to Western Man a literature of breathless beauty—still a glowing treasure even though Greek is no longer culturally fashionable. Today's science would be mute and inglorious indeed without this priceless tool chest of philology to work with.

TO complement this beauty, a nobility of spirit and a freedom of mind were likewise born in Athens. Socrates, Plato, Aristotle first taught mankind *how* to think. They harnessed the mind and made it work by asking the right questions, the eternal questions of mankind's universal destiny. The fact that their metaphysical answers were often wrong is quite irrelevant to the intellectual contribution they made to civilization. They made *mēden agan*—moderation in all things—a practical virtue. Excessive pride (*hubris*) was brought low by the watchful gods who peopled Mount Olympus. The rich Athenian was a man of good taste. He did not indulge himself in private splendor or dazzling ostentation. His family life was relatively modest and decent, though the position of his women was low and hetaerism was openly accepted. He did not make a drunken glutton of himself at public banquets. (Pericles dined out only once in thirty years.) Even his slaves he treated with a mildness notable in a cruel age. In his youth he served his city as a soldier and in his old age he was ready to serve again as judge or counselor.

Take Aeschylus as a sample Greek of his day. Father of Hellenic drama, he added the second character to the traditional choral cast and thereby opened up the whole range of human relationships for the stage. He wrote ninety plays, of which only seven survive in full and, with his enormous genius for poetry, was a steady winner for years in Athens' drama contests. Almost forgotten, though, is the equally pertinent fact that as a young man he fought at Marathon and was present at Salamis. Largely from personal knowledge, he composed *The Persians*, that magnificent historical drama reciting, for the glory of Athens, only eight years after the event itself, the Greek defeat of Xerxes at Salamis and the bedraggled return of that Persian ruler to Susa. When Aeschylus died in Sicily (456 B.C.), the epitaph on his tomb accented a martial career ("Of his noble prowess the grove of Marathon can speak, or the long-haired Persian who knows it well.") but was silent about poetry.

The poetry of Athens was better than its politics. In fact Hellenic politics contrasts darkly with all the nobility and exaltation exhibited in other fields. The Greeks coined many of the right-sounding political words—*politēs*, *dēmokratia*—but their use of them was crass, deceitful and often bloody. *Dēmos* (the people) became the governing power of the city, and *dēmos* would assemble by the hundreds and thousands to express its common will and execute public business. But it was not the *people* of Athens as we think of the broad American electorate, but only the *politēs*, or citizens, of Athens who operated these levers of political power. And citizens composed a very exclusive core of the population. (Both parents had to be Athens-born before a man could qualify.) When Athens, at its prime, had a population of nearly half a million, less than ten per cent were citizens. The rest were foreigners, slaves, transients and women and children—all politically zero.

The same violent passion for individual liberty—unbridled particularism, it would be called today—that kept the Greek city-states incurably divided kept domestic politics seething with confusion. *Dēmos* despised the elite. Pericles, as honest and honorable a "tyrant" as ever lived, was continuously besmeared and traduced—for his relations with Aspasia if the mob could find nothing better to carp about. Phidias died in prison. Aristides was ostracized because some bumpkins were tired of hearing him called "The Just." Private interest regularly won out over public good. While the philosophers theorized about the ideal state and freedom and justice in the groves of learning, the bosses who actually ran the political show made a sorry spectacle of public business.

"Greatness in Greece," remarks Gilbert Murray, "comes out only in the art and literature and thought, and not in the political or social history—except in dim flashes." But, like lightning on some far horizon, such dim flashes suggested a sense of struggle toward political freedom which glowed in an otherwise dark world and grew through the ages into one of Western Man's greatest ideals.

THEATER SEATS

Hellenism—that marvel of creative culture which blossomed in many Greek city-states before 350 B.C.—had no more ardent admirer than handsome, young Alexander of Macedon. Aristotle was his private tutor. Homer he knew by heart; he slept with the *Iliad* under his pillow. His military genius carried him and his thirty-five thousand soldiers through Persia to India to found a huge empire, which crumbled away when he died at thirty-three. More worthy and lasting was his export of Hellenism to his Asiatic domain. He built some seventy cities (many of them named Alexandria) and staffed them with Greek governors and scholars to Hellenize the conquered. While Alexander himself was parading around in Persian clothes and playing the passionate Oriental despot, Greek literature and art and architecture and dress and manners were being deeply planted throughout his empire. The results were not Hellenic in the old sense but rather, as the historians say, Hellenistic—moonlike reflections of a sun that had set.

PERICLES

After Alexander, Hellenistic civilization grew into the great natural conservator of the original Hellenic heritage. An age of criticism succeeded an age of creation. Alexandria, in Egypt, with its huge library, served as the central treasure house of Hellenistic culture. There, for example, grammarians unwittingly saved from oblivion a few sample plays of Aeschylus, Sophocles and Euripides by converting them into textbooks for schools. At Byzantium developed another island of Hellenistic scholarship, to be taken over by Constantine six centuries later and perpetuated for a millenium. From Greece itself diluted cultural currents curled around Sicily and lapped up to Rome where they were absorbed and preserved. Christianity was floated out of small Judea to the larger world on the tides of Hellenistic pessimism. But the spring of true Greek learning had dried up long before, and Athens was left an abandoned temple looming darkly over Greece's desert.

Greece in somewhat more than a century gave the Western world its heritage of beauty and diversity; Rome in somewhat less than a millenium supplied it with a concept of order and unity. Here, for the first time, was an expanding political universe based on constitutionalism and law. The distinction between Athens and Rome, Edgar Allan Poe sensed with poetic intuition: Greece was *glory*, the glory of the human spirit free to create, to speculate, to believe what it would; Rome was *grandeur*, the grandeur of power and discipline and conformity. Athens was sovereign only a few miles out from the city walls; Rome's dominion ran clear to the rim of outer darkness. Rome never succeeded in creating a culture comparable to Greece's, but it did provide other kinds of genius.

From Romulus' first mythical furrow (over which Remus skipped and was killed for his impertinence) Rome was unique in spirit and action. It possessed a sense of destiny. Its story is the story of a whole people moving forward together, rather than the story of leaders and their feats. The early Romans were a breed apart—vigorous in action, simple in taste, obedient to command. They were the toughest kind of warriors. They were master politicians. They were family folk, with the father as the iron-fisted boss. They were animated by a high sense of public spirit and public service and they loved Rome to the death. They had a misty mythology devoid of Greek beauty, their religion was replete with turgid ceremony and they drove hard bargains with their gods. But they did live by inflexible codes and a moral sense of right and wrong. Brutus, the first consul, never flinched when he sentenced his own sons to death for conspiring with enemies and then calmly watched the lictor cut off the boys' heads. Virginius stabbed his maiden daughter to death rather than see her falsely declared a slave by a crooked decemvir who lusted for her. Cincinnatus left his plow, became dictator, routed a hostile army from the walls of Rome and returned to his farm, all within sixteen days. And Horatius, according to Macaulay's verse, perfectly summed up his Roman patriotism as he strode out to single combat on the Tiber bridge:

ALEXANDER THE GREAT

> And how can man die better
> Than facing fearful odds,
> For the ashes of his fathers
> And the temples of his gods?

These Romans were hard and coarse and often cruel, but they were destined to conquer the world and be a credit to the human race. Centuries later, when virtue was ebbing out of the Empire like blood from a wound, it was the custom of Roman orators to invoke "the old morality" and call for a mass return to the simple and self-sacrificing spirit of the legendary days of the republic.

Politically, Rome got rid of its own kings early in its career (before 500 B.C.). It drove out the Tarquins, those riddlesome Etruscan usurpers who imported the toga and other gadgets of civilization, and settled down for a long run as a patrician republic. It was not a democracy in any Greek sense. It had popular assemblies in which the plebeian tribes were herded into sheep pens to vote, but it was the Senate and the two consuls who actually governed. The Senate was a council of elders, and not any system of representative government. "SPQR," the legions' standards proclaimed—*Senatus Populusque Romanus*—the Senate *and* the Roman People.

Roman citizenship was a prized possession of large advantages, but to vote, a man had to fight. With the consuls leading the army and rich patricians marching in its front ranks, Rome conquered its Latin neighbors and neatly organized them into the Roman system. That system was based on the principle of divide and rule. Defeated enemies enjoyed much local freedom as "allies" of Rome but they were rigidly prohibited from any intercourse or confederacy among themselves. Rome literally became the hub of a wheel, with each spoke isolated from all the others. Here began Rome's genius for external government.

The republican Roman had a greedy eye on his own commercial advantage and advancement. He spotted his real rivals promptly and laid them low with a cruelty that still makes some historians shudder. It took him a hundred years and three long wasteful wars to achieve the final murder of Carthage (146 B.C.), spurred along by the vengefulness of that censorious old prig, Cato. This Punic conflict, people against people, race against race, forever fixed the fate of the Mediterranean, and so of Western Man. Thereafter, all the known world from Britain to Mesopotamia fell easy prey to the Roman legions.

THE Roman legion was a demonstration of Rome's military genius and a major explanation of its expanding conquest. This heavy infantry unit of five or six thousand men was the finest fighting force of its epoch. The republican army was originally manned by Romans drafted for local defense or short-range conquests. Gradually, as the perimeter of conquest expanded beyond Italy and ordinary citizens found it irksome to go on long campaigns, the legion became a professional outfit, with full-time soldiers paid in cash and the promise of loot. These troops were heavily equipped with helmet, shield, spear and sword. Their discipline was ruthless. Moving as a compact mass into battle, they conquered Greece and Gaul (all three parts) and met their match only on the Rhine against the Germans. Before too long, to pace Rome's advance with fresh manpower, the legions began enlisting the non-Roman provincials and finally "barbarians" only recently subdued.

The legion was a mighty instrument of conquest, but it soon proved to be an even mightier instrument of politics. The legionary's loyalties shifted from the Senate and the people to his own commander. When Caesar, Pompey, Crassus and Antony, together or separately, were contesting for political supremacy and the final death of the republic, it was the loyal legions of each which settled the issue. Later, by mere sword-rattling, the legions, which numbered about twenty-five at Augustus' death (14 A.D.), made and unmade emperors with an utter disregard of qualifications or public good.

ROMULUS AND REMUS

A more wholesome result of the legions set on guard around the Empire's borders was the Pax Romana. It was not real peace, since the frontiers were forever in turmoil with skirmishes and sorties. But it did serve to keep down general warfare in order that Roman civilization could root and grow and flower.

What saved Rome from being a blind mass of brute force, what guided it on its upward way from kingdom through republic and dictatorship to empire, was *jus*—the right, the law—the rounded idea behind our word "justice." Without Roman law there would probably not have been a Roman

Empire, and without a Roman Empire, Christianity might have died aborning. Evolving out of old tribal and religious customs, *jus* developed into an original system of civil jurisprudence unmatched anywhere in the ancient world. Step by step it tracked Rome's political and economic progress. It reflected the plebes' long uphill fight for equality. It detailed every possible human relationship from paterfamilias to the meanest slave. It established and maintained all the rights and privileges of a Roman's citizenship. It provided a whole set of special rules and regulations for foreigners within Rome's gates. It covered all aspects of trade and commerce, of contracts and torts. At its close it included even the natural law universally applicable to mankind. A magnificent sweep of human thought, it stretched from the Law of the Twelve Tables (450 B.C.), erected in the Forum so the lowest Roman could know his own community imperatives, to the Code of Justinian (529 A.D.), which became not only the cornerstone of most medieval jurisprudence, but also the sire of Catholic canon law.

ROMAN SOLDIERS

The Romans took great pride in their law. It was practical and rational—and held good anywhere in the Empire. Its aim was justice and equity, with due consideration for the facts and the precedents. It probably did more than any other single factor to hold the overblown and wheezy Empire together and postpone its inevitable collapse. Its far-off echo can still be heard today in many a legal phrase uttered casually in any American court.

The West is inclined to look back in indulgent admiration on some of the finer aspects of old Rome—the political talent which organized and institutionalized eighty million people, the language of Caesar and Cicero, the colossal engineering of aqueducts and amphitheaters, roads and baths and vast public structures. But imperial Roman life, on close inspection of its rich and important leaders, provides scant moral or cultural inspiration to Western Man.

Wealth rotted out the best in the Roman character. As the city grew rich on tribute and trade, its upper classes grew lax and lazy. They indulged themselves in every ostentatious luxury. Family life went on the rocks of unbridled sexuality and the birth rate fell precipitately. (Ovid's *The Art of Love* has been authoritatively labeled "the most immoral book ever written by a man of genius.") Eating became a sort of stuffing match, with *vomitoria* handy where any contestant could disgorge and start afresh.

Rome nurtured a cruel system of slavery. The slave market was constantly replenished by fresh conquests; thousands of cultivated foreigners captured in battle found themselves in the vilest servitude. Some were used as scribes, translators and accountants to do Rome's mental chores, but most were assigned to do farm work like the lowest animals. When the servile rebellion led by Spartacus the Gladiator was finally put down, some six thousand slaves were crucified along the Appian Way. Rome's rulers pandered to the people's basest and bloodiest instincts by providing them with great arenas where captive gladiators fought to the death and high-born ladies shrilled their delight at the spectacle of gore and guts on the white sand.

Pagan Rome took over Greece's literary and artistic heritage as part of its conquest and proceeded to imitate this Hellenistic culture, but it added little that was new or creative. Greek remained the language of the intellectual few; Plutarch, that great Greek, lived for years in Rome and never found it necessary or worth while to learn Latin. The mass population of Rome matched its unhappy poverty with the blackest ignorance. Anything like popular education was unheard of. Gossip and rumor provided the usual means of general communication.

The Roman mind never rose to the challenge of the natural sciences. The cumbersome system of Roman numerals is a fair indication of its stunted thinking in this direction. Superstition and magic—animal entrails and bird flights—still guided and controlled public and private doings, though all intelligent Romans recognized these ceremonials as pious nonsense. For all their far-flung commercial travels, Romans knew little or nothing about geography, and their art of navigation, once they had defeated the seagoing Carthaginians, stood still for centuries. Rome was the political center of the world, but the cultural capital was at Alexandria, whither scholars journeyed to complete their education.

Thus had Roman civilization set the world stage for destiny to plant a sublime seed in the dry, barren soil of the negligible Jewish province of Judea. In Rome, Augustus Caesar was emperor, turning the city from brick into marble. Virgil had just completed the *Aeneid*, his epic to give Rome a heroic ancestry, at the price of invidious comparisons with Homer ever after. Livy was approaching the end of his 142 books of a heroic *History of Rome* ("the chiefest people of the world") and Horace had just died on his farm, leaving a legacy of satiric verse to tantalize all future translators. It was, in fact, the very heyday of Rome—the Golden Age.

FORUM AT ROME

About 4 or 5 B.C.—the year is unclear—a boy was born in the town of Bethlehem and named Jesus. At Nazareth he grew up to be a carpenter by trade. When he was about thirty he began to preach in Galilee a new and revolutionary gospel. This gospel concerned the one God and the Kingdom of Heaven and everlasting life. It was a doctrine of charity, humility, faith and the brotherhood of man for the righteous and penitent. It was also vastly disturbing to the Jews. Jesus bowed to civil authority—"Render unto Caesar" (Tiberius was then emperor)—but because he often spoke in parables

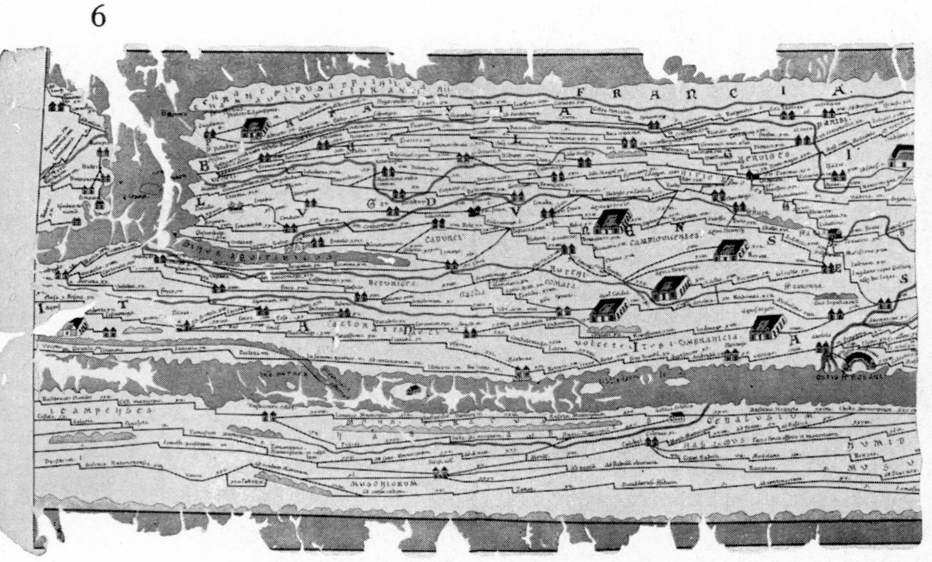

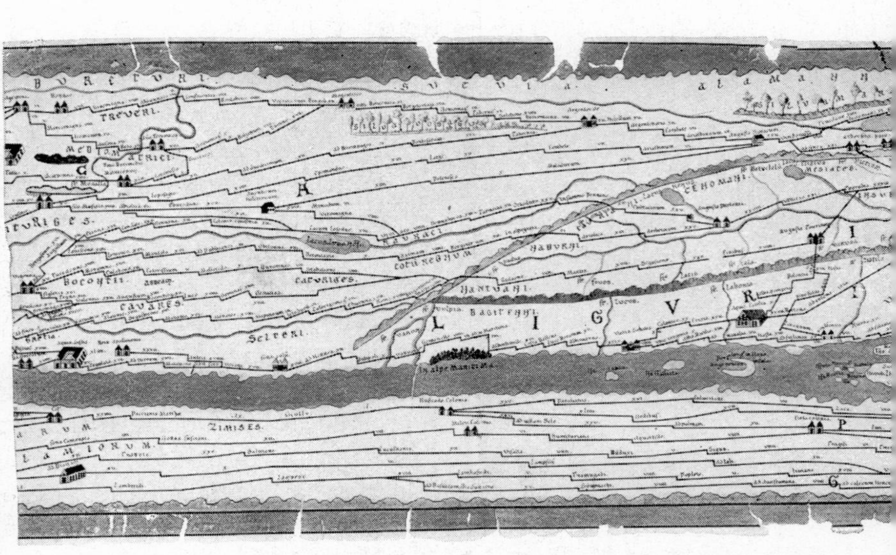

This fourth century Roman road map of western Europe, deliberately elongated, shows a part of the Empire's fifty-one thousand miles of paved highway. The Mediterranean Sea runs lengthwise through the middle, with Africa below. In the first section, England appears at upper left, Paris at upper right. Two ridges of the Alps divide the second section. The third panel shows northern Italy,

his words could be twisted to have political meanings. At the demand of the Jewish high priest, Jesus was arrested in Jerusalem and tried before Pontius Pilate ("What is truth?") for his claim to kingship and was crucified. No Roman scribe in Judea bothered to make a written record of this trivial incident in the affairs of a turbulent and troublesome people in a remote Roman province.

Jesus left about a hundred and twenty faithful followers behind in Jerusalem. They were baffled and dispirited by his tragic end. His body had disappeared from its tomb and they comforted themselves with the belief that he would return to them soon, as he had promised, and in some miraculous way establish the Kingdom of Heaven on earth. His first disciples, plain men with plain minds, seem never to have apprehended in full the new and mighty implications of Jesus' gospel which they continued to preach to the same Jews he had addressed.

It is historically arguable that the whole mission of Jesus would in time have been reduced to a minor sect of Judaism and thus lost to the Western world, had it not been for a very remarkable Jew named Saul who lived at Tarsus in Asia Minor. He was a Roman citizen. He had a brilliant mind, well-sharpened in Hellenistic culture and Jewish law. He was bitterly antagonistic to the early Nazarenes and joined in persecuting them as violators of that law. Then one day on the road to Damascus he had a radiant vision of the resurrected Jesus. Instantly he was converted. He recognized him as the Christ and his whole outlook was reversed. He had never seen Jesus, so he hurried to Jerusalem to consult with Peter and the other disciples there and learn all he could of his earthly life from those who knew it at first hand. In the next thirty years, under his Roman name of Paul, he performed a miracle of his own by organizing a fullfledged, world-wide religion out of Jesus' moral and mystical teachings about the Kingdom of Heaven.

Into this religion went much Jewish tradition and belief, including monotheism, the Ten Commandments and priestly offices. But Paul forever separated Christianity from Judaism by explaining the crucifixion as God's sacrificial redemption for sinful man. He gave the new faith its everlasting symbol —the Cross. He carried Christianity to the non-Jews, and became known as the Apostle of the Gentiles. A profound theologian, he expounded the deep mysteries of the new faith, provided it with a specialized language and a distinctive ritual. The first and greatest of Christian missionaries, he preached, founded churches, traveled thousands of miles, wrote letters and revealed himself as a personality of extraordinary talent and energy. In Corinth hostile Jews had him indicted but the Roman governor dismissed the charge. In Ephesus he was booed down by skeptical Greeks and his meetings were dissolved. In Jerusalem he was roughed up by a mob and arrested as a disturber of the peace. As a citizen of the Empire, he appealed his case to Rome. There he waited two years for Nero to hear him. The outcome of his trial is not historically certain but there is evidence that he was acquitted—or at least given a suspended sentence. Later a great fire swept Rome and the Christians were accused of starting it. In the persecution that followed, Paul was beheaded on the same day, tradition says, that Peter was crucified upside down.

Solid Christian history fades out here in Rome about 67 A.D. for a lapse of two centuries. No contemporary documents were kept to chart the growth of doctrine and creed and the record is as dark as the catacombs of Rome where the primitive Christians supposedly assembled in secret. Something called tradition developed during this obscure period and later became an integral part of the Church's ceremony and dogma, but it had to be accepted on faith, not fact.

Christianity meanwhile was spreading fast and far through the Empire. Its appeal was particularly to the poor and humble, the desperate and the disinherited in the decaying Roman social system. It touched men's hearts and gave them hope in a hopeless world.

These first Christians were in constant trouble with the Roman authorities. Because they believed only in God the Father, God the Son and God the Holy Ghost, they refused to recognize the emperor as a deity. Roman governors in the provinces began exchanging anxious letters about the eccentric behavior and subversive conduct of the members of a new cult called "Christians" who would not worship the emperor like all other good Roman citizens. Emperors issued edicts to the effect that Christianity was a crime against the state, punishable by death. Sometimes the decrees were

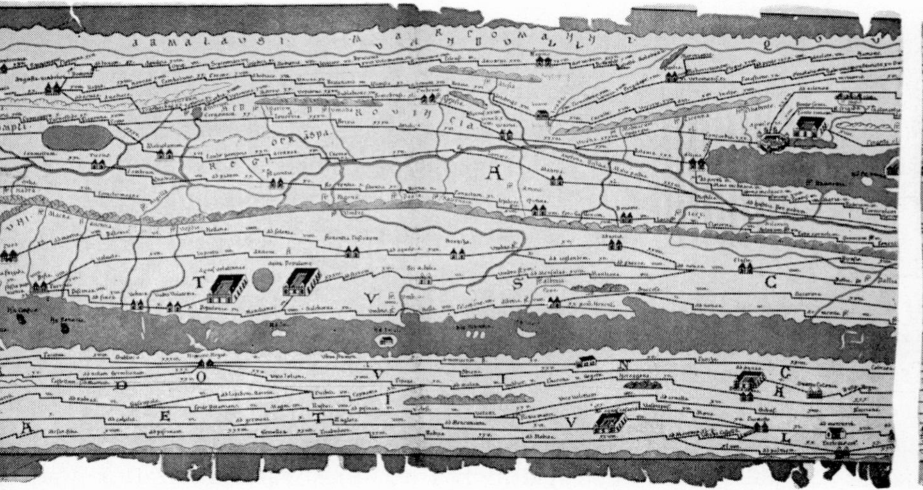

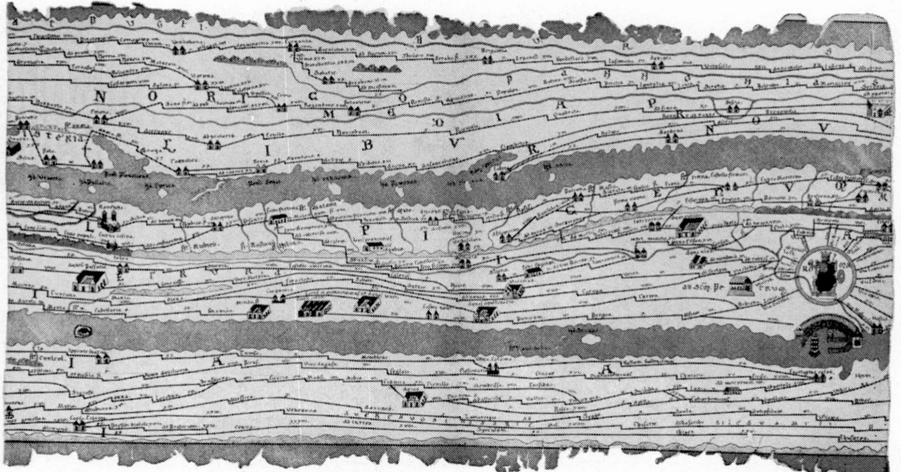

with the upper Adriatic. The big square buildings mark famous baths, the twin houses important towns. In the fourth section, the Appian Way leads to Rome at the far right. Every ten miles along the roads there was a stable, every thirty miles a brothel. On these roads a chariot could average five miles an hour, the same speed Napoleon made across Europe in a coach fifteen hundred years later.

enforced in a blood bath of Christian martyrdom; sometimes they were not, and furtive conversions reached up into the imperial family itself. The number of martyrs and the degree of their torture remains uncertain. Gibbon estimates two thousand put to death for their inflexible faith—a figure far too low to satisfy Church historians who harp on the "furies of hell" inflicted by Roman authorities.

In 303 A.D., under Diocletian, began the last great persecution. The Christians resisted extermination so stoutly that Constantine, the next emperor, put the cross on his legion standards, more for luck than faith, before he went into battle outside Rome in 312 A.D. When he won the battle, he almost immediately issued his edict of toleration for Christian faith throughout the Empire and Christian worship was never menaced seriously thereafter during Roman rule. Constantine, as a personal footnote, allowed himself to be baptized a Christian on his deathbed twenty-four years later.

St. Paul

While their religion was a proscribed underground affair, the Church Fathers in Rome did their best to keep its stream of doctrine pure and undefiled by the muddy crosscurrents of other religions then popular among the irreligious Romans. They fought off Gnosticism (Matter is evil, only spirit is good), Montanism (Christ's second coming is at hand) and lesser brands of heresy. But modern scholars believe that Christianity, during this blank period, absorbed a variety of beliefs and expressions from other contemporary creeds to which its followers were constantly exposed in everyday life—a process of religious osmosis. The sun-god Mithras killed a bull and in its blood his adherents were born anew; Christians at this time first conceived of themselves as being "washed in the blood of the Lamb." In the Alexandrine cult of Serapis-Isis-Horus, the gods Serapis and Horus were father and son, yet both one, and Isis was the mother of each; Christians developed the concepts of the Trinity and the Virgin Mary. These parallels are profitless to pursue too far, except to establish the great ferment of religious thought and action which marked the latter days of the Roman Empire and provide Western Man with some of his greatest theological mysteries.

Meanwhile, the Empire was rolling slowly downhill to its doom and the rise of Christianity was only one of many complex causes for its final fall. Too vast and loose-jointed to be managed by one man, it had been split in two—the Western Empire of Rome and the Eastern Empire of Constantinople. The latter, Greek in language, in thought and faith, went on for a thousand years as a sort of protracted aftermath of Alexander the Great's imperial dream, but its influence on Western Man dwindled to the vanishing point. Not until the Turks finally captured Constantinople in 1453 and sent its scholars scurrying off to Europe did Western Man receive in full the classical heritage of the Revival of Learning.

ROME suffered a shorter, swifter fate as the tides of tribal invasion lapped over the rim of its European provinces. Yet its fall was no sudden catastrophe. Rather was it like some super-slow-motion movie on the dim screen of time. The old-time light of patriotism had flickered out. The army had disintegrated. Broken and neglected roads brought Empire commerce to a standstill. To support the tottering imperial machinery, taxes were raised and raised again until landowners deserted their fields in despair. Food grew scarce and poor people starved. Riots and revolts festered and burst in the cities. Roman life sank to the bottom of human misery.

Any detailed record of the northern and Asiatic tribes that now rode down upon Italy and later swamped Europe adds nothing but confusion to the history of Western Man. For centuries they go by like flights of birds against a darkening sky. The first of these wild peoples, constantly pressed from the rear by other fiercer tribes in mass migration, had been allowed to cross the imperial frontiers and settle down among the older population. Others had been bought off from their depredation by huge ransoms. But behind came a torrent of invaders who were not to be denied by reason or riches. They seemed bent on nothing but conquest—pillage and loot, fire and sword, murder and mayhem. Beneath the swirling fury of their assaults, political history becomes unintelligible chaos.

Sometimes they did recognize the nominal authority of a remote emperor; more often they set up their own crude sovereignty. Huns and Vandals—their very names have passed into the common language of Western Man as ruthless wreckers and destroyers.

By 400 A.D., the imperial city of Rome was imperial no longer. The emperors of the West had deserted it as their seat of government soon after Constantine had moved his capital to Byzantium. They set up their courts in Milan, in Treves or in Ravenna to be closer to their soldiers struggling to dam the flood from the north. In 476 at Ravenna an emperor ironically named Romulus Augustulus was imprisoned and deposed by the invaders and, as no successor was named, had the distinction of being the last of his imperial line. Here, the historians say, was the final end of the Roman Empire, though in fact it made no difference in the turmoil of the times.

Early Christians in Rome

The so-called "barbarians" who demolished the Roman Empire politically are victims of a large injustice at the hands of history. Illiterate, they left no records of their own and so have come down to us only through the distorted writings of the hostile Romans, who depicted them as wild beasts bent on the wholesale destruction of a beautiful civilization.

The Asiatic invaders were probably as bad as they were painted, but many Germanic tribes—Goths, Burgundians, Lombards, Franks, Saxons—were far from being the unmitigated savages Romans described them. Their warfare was ruthless, their manners were rough and they lacked culture and refinement. But they did possess an innate dignity of character, a faithful sense of honor and a hearty hospitality toward friend and foe. By Roman standards they were uncivilized but they were endowed with a capacity for civilization destined to outshine Rome's.

MANY of these invaders were herdsmen, coveting fresh fields for their stock. With the warriors came their families as colonists and settlers, large, docile populations ready to be Romanized. They brought along their rudimentary political organizations and their crude system of tribal law. The best warrior was usually the chief, surrounded by his loyal companions whose descendants eventually became the nobility of feudal Europe. A mixing and a mingling of local populations and customs and ideas ensued. The results were beneficial to mankind and the wreckage of the Roman political system was a fair price to pay.

These invaders, though unlettered and without taste, were fascinated by the moldy splendors of Roman civilization. They did not want to destroy it; they just wanted to take it over for their own. But in the take-over, like hoodlum kids in a fancy toy store, they broke a great deal of it. When the Vandals up from Africa rampaged through Rome's smoking ruins in 455 they first carted off all the treasure their ships would hold, only to lose it when their homing fleet sank in a Mediterranean storm. One rough, rugged chieftain was so enthralled by a lovely white swan in a floor mosaic that he crashed his battle-ax into it to see if it was real and then broke into tears when it disappeared in rubble. The Roman world gasped in horror at such wanton destruction, but it was the politics of Rome rather than its mosaic swans that the barbarians' battle-axes really annihilated.

By the time Rome had ceased to be the political capital of the world, it was well on its way to becoming the religious capital of Christendom. The bishop of Rome, claiming direct succession from St. Peter, was supreme in the hierarchy of the Western Church. His see had the prestige of tradition and power and wealth. His ecclesiastical organization was fleshed out on the skeletal remains of the Roman Empire and Latin was the language of his court. In the absence of local authority, he long supplied Rome with what civil government it had. (Leo I persuaded Attila, "the scourge of God," to spare the city one more devastation.) The bishop of Rome was elected by the city's population, then down to a ghostly fifty thousand from nearly a million at the time of Augustus Caesar. Thus the papacy became a political prize among the noble families of Rome, with its consequent degradation.

CHRISTIAN orthodoxy was a prime concern of the Pope. The faith seemed to need constant supervision and interpretation. Its divine mysteries challenged the human mind. What was the nature of God? Was Jesus Christ one with God or of lesser divinity? The Council of Nicaea, held in 325 A.D., declared overwhelmingly for the Trinity and the equal and same divinity of Father, Son and Holy Ghost. This was the first great doctrinal split in the early Church. Arianism (the lesser divinity of Christ) was outcast, but the struggle to define the true faith continued for seven hundred years and resulted only in the final and irrevocable rupture between the Catholic Church of Rome and the Orthodox Church of Constantinople. In all this long controversy over creed, with its violent language and bitter temper, the authority and position of the papacy were enhanced as the one Christian force that held the Christian world together in its darkest age.

Somehow the simple spirit of Jesus survived these fierce doctrinal debates, and his gospel—"the good news"—was carried by brave and faithful souls to the pagans of Europe. Missionaries from Rome brought Trinitarian orthodoxy; missionaries outlawed by the Eastern Church at Constantinople sowed the seeds of Arianism—and fresh fights over heresy bloodied the land. The process of Christianization was rarely accomplished by soft persuasion. Local chieftains soon realized the advantages of an alliance with the Church and whole tribes were baptized for political reward or put to the sword for refusing the benefactions of the new religion. A great turning point in the conversion of Western Europe to the Roman faith occurred on December 25, 496, when Clovis, a Germanic heathen, was baptized at Reims with three thousand of his Frankish warriors. Monasteries were

Barbarian Invader

founded and churches were built and gradually, in the dim light of this ecclesiastical culture, the stage was being set for the birth of Western Man.

The violent ebb and flow of tribal tides across the face of Europe began slowly to subside. A settling-down process could be detected here and there. All concept of state had been lost in the debacle. Out of this mist of confusion and insecurity emanated something that looked like a rude form of order—the kingdom of the Franks. Here at last was a ladder on which civilization could climb back out of the mire.

The Franks were Germans and Germans were the principal ancestors of Western Man. Tacitus describes these remarkable tribesmen beyond the Rhine: "They have stern blue eyes, ruddy hair, bodies large and robust, but powerful only in sudden efforts. They are impatient of toil and labor. Thirst and heat overcome them, but from the nature of their soil and climate they are proof against cold and hunger." For four centuries these German tribes held the Roman legions at bay; hence the influence of Roman civilization made far less impress on them than on the Gauls and the Britons. But when they finally flooded out of their forest glades and crossed the Rhine, they carried all Western Europe before them.

They were frenzied fighting men and to them a warrior's death was the sweetest of all. But they were also something much more; they were people with a pride in their own individual liberty. Life might be a melancholy mystery to them, but while they lived it each man was personally responsible for his own conduct. From long communal experience the Germans had a worthy sense of local political action. The tribes met in large assemblies ("Mayfields") and disapproval on important issues was expressed by grunts and groans while the clash of javelins recorded assent. They had a complete system of tribal law, personal in nature and serving a German wherever he went. They did not have trial by jury but they did use original methods to arrive at the truth. One was compurgation, based on the sanctity of an oath. The defendant and his friends would swear to his innocence—hence our "cross my heart and hope to die." Another was trial by ordeal, in which the defendant risked death by burning or drowning—hence our "through fire and water."

The Germans worshiped gods who gave their names to the days of the English week—Woden's day, Thor's day, Frigga's day. They had no written literature, but they left wonderful ballads like those found in the song of *Beowulf.* They ate and drank too much, slept a lot, quarreled just for the fun of it, but they treated their women with a courtesy and respect unknown before.

The Frankish Germans established an empire from mid-Germany to Spain, from the Atlantic to Hungary. Their tribal cousins to the north, the Jutes, the Angles and the Saxons, swarmed over Britain after the Romans' withdrawal and made it so thoroughly Germanic that it had to be Christianized a second time. And even farther off and later in history were the Norsemen, with their brightly painted ships and rousing sagas, who would supply Western Europe with a seafaring tradition.

The greatest contribution these Germanic peoples made to Western Man was themselves—new blood in new bodies. Christianity was established in Western Europe. The Germans had replaced the Romans as the continent's rulers. Vigor and hope stirred again in the air. Throughout Western Europe, Western Man was being born.

A superior sample of Western Man in his early youth was Charlemagne, Charles the Great, the rugged monarch who became king of the Franks and first Holy Roman emperor. His large and well-run empire was less important to Western Man's growth than was his beneficent attitude toward scholarship and culture and the human spirit. In and out of the Church, he was the energetic promoter and prodder of education in his day. Not learned himself, he yearned to create a civilization of grace and wisdom. He foregathered with scholars in private to discuss the mysteries of heaven and earth. He brought back the color of gold and silver art work to his court. And when he died, at the age of seventy-two, he became the subject of countless legends and songs and miracles that remain to this day as great folk literature.

Light and learning were breaking through the clouds of the Dark Ages. An Age of Faith was dawning. The human spirit rose on the wings of a mighty Christian emotion—the first mass movement of this budding civilization—the Crusades. It is here that this book picks up the story of Western Man and carries it forward a thousand years.

IN his delightful essay, "Everyman His Own Historian," the late Carl Becker says that "every generation, our own included, will, must inevitably, understand the past and anticipate the future in the light of its own restricted experience. . . ."

"Restricted" is hardly the word this mid-century generation of Americans would apply to their own experience. Our experience has been, to use a word of the hour, global. The names of even the most obscure Pacific islands—Tarawa, Kwajalein, Iwo Jima, Bikini, Okinawa—have become current coins in our daily language. Our experience includes such strange and fantastic things as guided missiles, supersonic flight, wonder drugs, and the obsolescence of man's old acquaintance, the plague. Beyond the endless catalogue of such wonders, our awareness stretches out from Mount Palomar to clusters of galaxies rushing away from where to whither at the rate of billions of miles per year (or is it per second?). "Restricted" may sound wrong for the experience of our generation, but nevertheless Becker's thesis stands.

Our generation is confronted as none before it by the size and scope of time and space. It is confronted also by the massiveness of Evil, whether its symbol be the destructiveness of the Bomb or the hideousness of the concentration camp. In the face of these confrontations, and of the perhaps even more perilous abyss of the irrational "subconscious" of the human psyche, the supreme question of our time is whether anything can have any meaning. Beyond the range of Palomar and at the bottom of the well of consciousness, can any one of us speak to any other one of us with the tiniest certainty of conviction and intelligibility?

Against these doubts and fears we put, in gage of battle and in good hope of victory, the story of man on this little flick of whirling rock called Earth and in this minuscule fraction of time called History. In particular we put against all doubt the story of Western Man because this is a story we know, as children know the stories they heard at their mothers' knees, and as older children know from the historians who, to quote Becker again, belong to "that ancient and honorable company of wise men of the tribe, of bards and storytellers and minstrels, of soothsayers and priests. . . ."

We have undertaken to retell the story of Western Man for a reason and a purpose. It is because, once again, Western Man is face to face with a crisis so huge and terrible that he feels, rightly and intuitively, that his very survival is at stake. And it is because, for the first time in our history, a sense of critical responsibility for overcoming the crisis rests upon the hearts and minds of Americans.

So, while we Americans have always enjoyed at our ease the story of Western Man, feeling free to applaud and criticize, to joke and laugh and weep, at the various passages of romance and melodrama, now it is different. More than a heritage which we abandon or defend, it is now a question of whether we save the meaning of our lives as individuals in saving the meaning of the whole drama of Western (and, inescapably, Christian) civilization.

WE began to tell this story of Western Man in a series of picture-and-text articles in LIFE in 1947. The instant and hearty response on the part of millions of Americans was proof enough that all of us today, regardless of our private eccentricities of thought, are bound together by a feeling of responsibility to the past *for* the future. After the articles had been published, it was apparent that they contained more than passing interest. And so we set out to make this book.

The basic principle of the series has been maintained: to illuminate with contemporaneous drawings and paintings one great era after another in the progress of Western Man, rather than to try to tell a connected historical narrative. Even so, the editors early decided that much new material in picture and word was needed to give rounded coherence. New chapters were written, new illustrations were uncovered and the number of color pages almost doubled to include a generous selection of the greatest art created by human genius.

We have told the story in our own way. But who are we? We are the Editors of LIFE and our interested and painstaking associates. We are, that is, journalists. As journalists we have gone to all the primary sources we could reach. We have gone to the stored-up treasures of museum and library, to learned men, historians, philosophers, art critics, theologians. All this search and study has not made us either learned or expert. We remain journalists, attempting as always to be honest brokers between the men of learning and the ordinary citizen who is eager to learn and to understand.

Our interpretation of the history of Western Man is our own. Not that we have attempted any "new" interpretation; rather we have tried to express as best we could the consensus of generations of scholars whose philosophy of history accords transcendent significance to human affairs.

The book is the product of the Editors of LIFE in that many members of LIFE's staff have had a part, large or small, in it, and that the Editors of LIFE take responsibility for the whole. But in the division of labor, greatest responsibility has been assigned to a few individuals and contributions of special value have been made by a few. Thus it is proper that we should record the names of those who have had the largest share of responsibility or who made special contributions:

¶ Joseph J. Thorndike, Jr., managing editor of LIFE when the series was originated and printed in 1947–48. He returned to LIFE temporarily from his own book publishing business to take charge of this project as chief editor.

¶ Joseph Kastner, of LIFE's board of editors. In direct charge of the original magazine series, he performed the same invaluable service in the editing of this book.

¶ Charles Tudor, LIFE's art director. To the graphic creation of this book, he gave unsparingly of his talents.

¶ Whittaker Chambers, formerly a senior editor of *Time*. He wrote many of the original articles in the LIFE series and, with some revisions, they appear here.

¶ Louis Kronenberger, *Time* editor. He drew on his deep scholarship of eighteenth century England for the chapters on that subject and the rise of Parliamentary government.

¶ Lincoln Barnett, formerly a LIFE editor. He contributed the chapters on the Dawn of Modern Science and the Rise of Bourgeois Man.

There are others whose work on this book deserves special mention. Crane Brinton, professor of history at Harvard, dealt with his specialty in the chapter on the Age of Revolutions. Henry Bradford Darrach, Jr., wrote much of the material to illuminate and explain the pictures in various chapters. Credit must also go to Tom Prideaux, Margit Varga and Dorothy Seiberling, all members of LIFE's staff, whose work on the original magazine articles has been incorporated in this book.

The series in LIFE was never completed with a capstone article on the United States as the ultimate heir to Western Man's civilization. To remedy this omission, John Knox Jessup, whose scholarly editorials are well known to the readers of LIFE and *Fortune*, wrote the climactic chapter of this book—The American Experience.

Toward the end of the eighteenth century, the history of Western Man comes to a great forking. After the American Revolution a new and distinct branch appears in the United States where, under fresh and different circumstances, Western Man, American style, proceeds to meet his own problems and solve his own destiny. It is the thesis of our final chapter that this American branch holds greater importance for the future of the human race than the European parent culture. For this reason this book bypasses almost entirely the nineteenth century in Europe and develops the American story through a century of national growth to maturity. Only then in the twentieth century does Western Man, American style, reverse the historic trend and return to Europe as a mighty new force dedicated to the defense of Western civilization.

—JOHN SHAW BILLINGS

THE SPIRIT OF THE MIDDLE AGES

For the greater glory of God, the wealth and artistic skills of the Middle Ages were lavished on religious objects. This jeweled cover of a ninth century Gospel is of hammered gold encrusted with 327 gems, including sapphires, rubies, emeralds, topazes and pearls.

I

THE SPIRIT OF THE MIDDLE AGES

ONE day in the early Middle Ages, St. Scothinus, having purged himself by severe chastisement from all molestations and imperfections of lustful desires, commenced to walk across the sea to England. By chance he met a ship that carried St. Barry the Bishop, who, beholding and recognizing this man of God, inquired of him wherefore he thus walked on the sea. To whom St. Scothinus answered that this was a flowery field whereon he walked, and presently, stretching his hand down to the water, he took from the midst of the ocean a handful of vermilion flowers which, in proof of his assertion, he cast into the bishop's lap. The bishop for his part, to maintain his own truth, drew a fish from the water and cast it toward St. Scothinus; whereupon, magnifying God in His marvelous works, they departed with blessings one from the other.

Such an encounter might well startle a twentieth century American to whom the miracle of electric light is nevertheless a commonplace. It would scarcely have startled a medieval man. For, as the American knows that all things are possible to science, medieval man knew that all things were possible to faith.

Moreover he had read (or had heard, if he was one of the millions who could not read) scores of such testimonies from one of the Middle Ages' most popular anthologies, the *Golden Legend*. The spontaneity with which both saints magnified the miracle of God's works demonstrated the faith in which all Christian men, according to their degrees of understanding, were at one. And their casual parting there in mid-sea rang true to the sweetness of the medieval mind. This same sweetness would soon soften the rigors of Catholic orthodoxy with the cult of the Virgin, the loving Mother of Christ, and the rough-and-tumble of secular life with the cult of chivalry.

THIS singular sweetness, at once childlike and virile, is the unique quality of the medieval mind. It characterizes every achievement of the Middle Ages. Stern Dante, the man who, his contemporaries said, had been in Hell, felt it in Paradise when he once more saw Beatrice, his dead but lifelong love, and she turned to him and said, "Direct thy mind to God in gratitude, who hath united us with the first star." And it stirred Geoffrey Chaucer, poet, politician and civil servant, to write at the touch of the English spring:

> Whan that Aprille with his shoures soote,
> The droghte of March hath perced to the roote;
> And bathed every veyne in swich licour
> Of which vertu engendred is the flour. . . .

This sweetness is in the name which transfigures the obese and disputatious Thomas of Aquino, greatest of medieval minds—the Angelic Doctor. It humanizes the austerity of those superearthly figures that guard the west portal of the cathedral of Chartres. And it rings from the Middle Ages' characteristic epic, the *Song of Roland*, in the sound of the paladin's horn, winding, indomitable in disaster like medieval man himself, from the lost battlefield of Roncesvalles.

For the edification of their patrons, the artists who illustrated manuscripts put Bible stories in medieval settings. Here, outside a castle, King David leads an orchestra of vielle, trumpets, flute, tambourine and castanets to the delight of the castle's chatelain.

Through the early Middle Ages, popes fought to keep the Church and their own power intact. John VII, whose mosaic portrait was found among the graves of popes beneath St. Peter's in Rome, ruled in the eighth century when Christendom was swept by a wave of Moslem invasions. He was much interested in the construction and restoration of church buildings and erected on Vatican Hill a chapel to the Virgin, a model of which he holds in his arms. The square halo signifies that he was still alive when this portrait was made.

In the deepest sense, this sweetness is an aspect of that *caritas* (St. Paul's loving charity) which St. Thomas Aquinas declared to be inseparable from the right understanding of God. And it redeems from historic horror a blood-soaked, brutal, riotous, lustful and chaotic age.

For the miracle of medieval man is that he began not, for the most part, as a barbarian, but as the heir of a fallen Roman civilization, struggling to keep alive in the centuries following Rome's collapse. His historic task was to infuse into the total ruin a new life and spirit. In six centuries, thought by groping thought, stone by heavy stone, from the ground up, by faith and works, he created a new Christian civilization. Then, in an incomparable outburst of creative energy, he made all succeeding men his heirs in the architecture of the Gothic cathedrals, in the splendor of their stained-glass windows, in the all but flawless structure of St. Thomas's philosophy, in the *Divine Comedy* of Dante Alighieri and the scientific insights of Roger Bacon.

The light of civilization burned lowest in the centuries of chaos, before and after the official "fall," when the great imperial structure of Rome, the universal state, was crumbling slowly into ruin. These were Europe's darkest ages. Through their monumental night thudded the onrushing feet of barbarians and other marauding war bands, drowning the shuffle of fugitive populations. Like intermittent beacons of despair, burning strongholds and burning crops lit up the coast and countryside. Towns were sacked. Families fled for safety into remote valleys where they clumped apart in communal distrust.

Here and there, in little communities far from one another, the precious flames of civilization were kept burning. These were the houses of the monastic orders, chiefly of the Benedictines whose center was at Monte Cassino in Italy. The monasteries were built low, thick-walled and almost windowless for safety, in the new Romanesque style. They opposed to the hazards of the outer world their stony carapaces and the harshness of monastic discipline.

Not all the hazards were human. Hell and its legions were also abroad. Incubi, succubi, sylphs, undines, witches and the hierarchies of devils, spirits of seduction and malefaction romped through the night. They would never quit the world, or the medieval mind, as long as the Middle Ages lasted.

As the fusion of Roman and barbarian cultures brought the grey dawn of medieval civilization, the landscape of a new Europe was revealed. The bones of the dead civilization were still there, immense and mute, in the form of Roman aqueducts, baths and amphitheaters, many of which now served as lairs for local strongmen. But a new architectural feature dominated the new Christendom—the tower. It had a twofold use. Militarily it answered the need of ever vigilant defense. Religiously it symbolized the fact that the Church, which spoke to the minds and souls of its believing multitudes, was the center of men's lives; the bell tower was its convoking voice.

For Rome, in dying, had bequeathed two mighty legacies to medieval man of Christendom—a common Catholic faith and the Latin tongue. This common tongue would bind together literate men of all national stocks and keep alive a

At the height of its power in the thirteenth century, the Church was beset with philosophical conflicts, which were largely resolved by the great Thomas Aquinas. Here St. Thomas conducts a discussion among monks while a disputatious devil (*bottom*) argues a point.

The Christian king Charlemagne, ruler of the Franks, supported the Church and fought its enemies. As his reward he was crowned emperor of the West by Pope Leo III on Christmas Day in 800.

Charlemagne vigorously fostered Church reform and ordered the repair and building of holy edifices all over his kingdom. Here, wearing his crown, he directs masons at work putting up a church.

sense of unity amid the hodgepodge of medieval political divisions and the babble of newly emerging national languages.

Men were obsessed with salvation and, therefore, with God. For when the world had been destroyed there had been nothing left but God. And to restore the world, there was no unifying principle but God. They enshrined their obsession in a creed of majestic simplicity:

Credo in unum Deum, Patrem omnipotentem, factorem caeli et terrae, visibilium omnium et invisibilium . . . "I believe in one God, the Father Almighty, Maker of heaven and earth, and of all things visible and invisible. And in one Lord Jesus Christ, the Only-begotten Son of God, and born of the Father before all ages. God of God; Light of Light; true God of true God; begotten, not made; consubstantial with the Father, by whom all things were made. Who for us men, and for our salvation, came down from heaven. . . . I confess one Baptism for the remission of sins. And I look for the Resurrection of the dead, and the life of the world to come."

This creed medieval man exalted in the thrusting spires of the Gothic cathedrals. He gave it elevation in the Gothic ribbed vault. He gave it illumination in stained glass. He gave it intonation in the *Alleluia*, the *Gloria*, the *Kyrie eleison*, the *Agnus Dei*, the *Requiem*, the *Te Deum*, and the great medieval hymns like the *Dies Irae*. He flooded it with the light of reason and gave it the strength of logical structure in the works of St. Thomas Aquinas.

Medieval man carried his creed into secular life. He embodied it in his political system, feudalism, in which every man held his rank and obligation in descending order from the sovereign whose right proceeds from God. Medieval man converted his creed into economic terms in the guild system. He denied himself many profitable practices (for example, usury) because his religion prohibited them. He implemented his creed in law and, insofar as erring man can, practiced it in his civic conduct. With it, he sanctified the indissoluble union of the family. And when medieval man's faith waned, the Middle Ages died.

THE emperor Charlemagne (742–814), a great patron of learning, kept a writing tablet under his pillow and practiced pothooks in bed. But he never learned to write. In the early Middle Ages man began to go to school, doggedly studying Latin grammar and the other rudiments of learning. By 1150 there were famous schools in all corners of Christendom, and the grand medieval debate on theology and philosophy had begun.

To the twentieth century mind, the problems that bedeviled medieval schoolmen, their obsession with allegory and symbolism, with abstruse definition and dialectic, are arid and irrelevant. The din of their theological disputations, mounting to a clamor after the great universities were founded at Paris, Oxford, Bologna, seems a boring babble. Twentieth century man may be absorbed in the all but mystical motions of the atom, for science is power. But he cannot feel the passionate concern of medieval man in the burning question: can angels move from one point to another without passing through the intervening space? To medieval man, faith was power since it was the way to God, and angels were a concept as important as atoms.

The great men connected with the debate were William of Champeaux, Peter Abelard, Bernard of Clairvaux, Albertus Magnus, Duns Scotus—whose name has been twisted into the word "dunce." Their names have lost their historical resonance and intellectual identity, as have the great issues they debated. But in the thrust and flashing snicksnack of such dialectics the medieval mind was honed to a trenchancy and rigor never since equaled. Since all opponents fought under the same banner, one Catholic faith, the struggle to

A mighty warrior, Charlemagne extended Frankish rule from the Atlantic and the Pyrenees to the Elbe, defeating the Lombards and the Saxons and bringing many pagan tribes into the Church.

Charlemagne's worst defeat came at Roncesvalles where Saracens ambushed the great Roland. Dying, Roland wound three blasts on his horn, which brought Charles back to mourn his fallen paladin.

the modern mind seems to lack drama. Yet it was a theological epic staged between heaven and earth; for the struggle was forever for the human soul and its goal was God.

While the struggle to know God raged in men's minds, life for the mass of medieval men was hard and often brutal. The cities were close-built and dark. The Black Death ravaged the Continent. Such conditions have caused the popular impression that medieval life was universally ugly and harsh.

But medieval man was a magnificent craftsman and the creator of great art. He wove Europe's most superb tapestries. He made stained glass of a beauty that modern man has failed to imitate. His book-making surpassed anything that twentieth century book designers and manufacturers have done. His hymns, like Adam of St. Victor's hymns to the Virgin, are still unexcelled. The universities, a medieval creation that the classical world had not known, have come down to us in the same form. In countless ways modern man is the heir of the Middle Ages.

He is, romantically, the heir of the medieval idea of love. Medieval man was a great lover. He dedicated himself to love in the cult of chivalry in which a knight plighted his troth to a lady. He devoted his life to her and sometimes died for her. But, as with almost everything else, medieval man sought to transfigure love, in the cult of the Virgin, whom the Middle Ages exalted to the post of guardian of superabundant grace and intercessor for the souls of men with God.

FOR two hundred years medieval men built their churches in modified Romanesque style. Then in the twelfth century a new surge of faith and power flowered in a new style, the Gothic. The cathedrals of Chartres, Amiens, Notre Dame at Paris, Laon and others rose from the earth. In one century alone, the thirteenth, it is estimated that the equivalent of one billion dollars was spent in France on the cathedrals. The nobility contributed heavily. But money came from all men, and all men came to help in the building, contributing their time to the great work of glorifying God. It was a labor anonymous and communal. Until scholarship dug them out from archives, the names of the master builders were unknown. These men worked with simple tools, compass, level, plumb line, square. Like them the workmen were capable and filled with the same faith. Under God, man and master worked as one, for one purpose.

The Gothic cathedral is a prayerful uprush of stone. It is as solid as the earth it stands on. At the same time it seems to float in the air. In Romanesque churches the walls had been thick. It was the inspiration of the medieval master builder to make the walls skeletal enough to achieve space and elevation but strong enough to sustain the weight of spires and roof. For the same purpose he set the flying buttress, a bridge between earth and air, to resist the thrust of superabundant mass. The rest is an expanse of stained glass whose function is not to exclude but to enhance light.

To medieval man, the Gothic cathedral was rich in allegorical symbols. The plan of the cathedral copied the Cross and pointed east to Jerusalem, the center of the Christian world. All meanings that the medieval mind had found in life and faith were gathered here, as delicate and as unbreakable as the embodying stone. When the scaffolds were cleared away medieval man perceived that he had magnificently created his need of God in stone.

A comparable achievement was meanwhile being effected for medieval theology. St. Thomas Aquinas was born about 1225 in Italy near the abbey of Monte Cassino, now a twentieth century ruin. He defied his family by entering the Dominican order. In Paris he became the pupil and friend of Albertus Magnus, the weightiest theologian of his time. In manner St. Thomas was heavy and slow, which earned him the name of the "big dumb ox of Sicily." But in matters of thought he was an irresistible and subtle force. He composed more than sixty works, of which the most important are the *Summa contra Gentiles* (*Summation of Doctrine against the Unbelievers*) and the *Summa Theologica* (*Summation of Theology*). The *Summa Theologica* is still the most complete and explicit assertion of Roman Catholic doctrine.

What man loves he seeks to possess. What the soul loves it seeks to exalt. What the mind loves it seeks to know. When twentieth century man switches on his electric light, he cares little about the nature of electricity. He does not love electricity. Medieval man loved God and sought with his whole mind, for hundreds of years, to know Him. But the more medieval man sought to know God, the less he seemed able to agree as to what God is. By the thirteenth century theology had become a complicated feud among philosophies.

INTO this strife of the God-seeking mind Thomas Aquinas brought clarity, order, harmony. The *Summa Theologica* was intended as a simple manual of Christian doctrine for the use of students. Its method is the application of reason to all the activities of man in the light of religion. But reason and the knowledge that results from the use of reason are not enough. Revelation is also necessary, for reason unaided by revelation cannot enable men to know the supernatural end —salvation—toward which their acts of faith will lead them. It is necessary first to accept revealed truths so that the mind can explain them and draw conclusions from them. This process is called theology, which is a science because it proceeds from principles which are certain, having been revealed by God. The subject of this science is God and His relation to His creations. The function of reason is not to prove the facts of faith, which are accepted on the authority of God, but to defend, develop and explain the revealed doctrines.

The great *Summa* is divided into three parts and arranged in the form of question and answer. Part I (God in Himself and as Creator) treats of the nature of God. Part II (God as the End of all Things) treats of man, the rational creature, and his advance toward God. Part III (God as Redeemer) treats of Christ, "who, as man, is the way by which we tend to God." The work was immense, the achievement unsurpassed, for its field was all that had existed, might have existed or ever could exist. It treated of many things—the world, science, medicine, incubi, succubi, beatitude. It answered once for all the question of whether angels can move from one point to another without passing through the intervening space. They can.

This vast work was based primarily on the philosophy of Aristotle, the great body of whose thought had at last reached medieval Europe in Arabic translation by way of Moslem Spain. The *Summa* might not fully satisfy theological extremists of any school. But like a Gothic cathedral it was spacious enough to include them all. And as the cathedral, embodying in stone man's need for God, soared above the medieval town, the *Summa*, embodying man's need to know God, soared above the invisible landscape of the mind.

These were the twin spires of medievalism. A third was to be added—Dante's *Divine Comedy*. When Dante, around 1300, started to write his poem he was a political refugee from Florence. Dante rejected Latin in favor of Italian for the *Comedy*. This first great literary use of a national language was also an expression of the new popular stirrings that were to burst out in the Renaissance.

DANTE was the last great medieval mind: The *Divine Comedy* is the ordeal of medieval man's love of God. Its ending is salvation. To achieve it Dante, in the three books of his masterpiece, *Inferno*, *Purgatorio* and *Paradiso*, took the Middle Ages through hell, purgatory and heaven. All the Middle Ages are in this poem. It crowns and ends them.

The *Divine Comedy* is the *Summa* in poetic form. Its theology and philosophy are St. Thomas's. But modern men do not read the *Divine Comedy* with delight simply because it dramatizes the *Summa*. They read it for its poetry and for its evocation of the whole medieval mind. For here is chivalry and the cult of love, expressed in terms of Dante's pure and personal love for his childhood sweetheart, Beatrice, merging in heaven into the cult of the Virgin. Here is much that was cruel, vengeful and monstrous in medieval life and thought. And here is medieval sweetness, touching us even after six centuries, like winds blown across pools of melting snow.

"*Come i gru van cantando lor lai*" (As the cranes fly singing their lays), writes Dante. And we see against the medieval sky, with the simple vividness of the earliest primitive paintings, the line of birds which, in their seasonal flight from the darkness of the barbarian north to the ruins of Egypt, had crossed and recrossed for hundreds of years the darkness of Europe.

Here is more of God than any later man has put into a secular book. And hell is here—not the hell whose devils had terrified medieval man in superstition and darkness, but a more terrible hell fixed for eternity in the terms of rational Aquinian theology. Above its gates is set its awful charter:

> Justice moved by great Creator,
> Divine Power made me—
> The summation of Wisdom and Primal Love. . . .
> Abandon all hope, ye who enter.

It might have been a legend for the darkest ages. But there is pity, too, in hell. As early medieval man turned for enlightenment to classical culture, Dante turns to his guide Virgil, the pagan poet, for consolation. And in words that might have applied to the Middle Ages, Virgil replies, "Here must all distrust be left; all cowardice must here be dead."

LIGHT had been the supreme craving of medieval man —light after historical darkness, light in ignorance, light in human despair, light as God. It was given to Dante to see this light in heaven: "O supreme Light, Who liftest Thyself so high above mortal thought, lend me again a little of that which Thou didst seem; and give my tongue such power that it may leave even a single spark of Thy glory to all men to come."

Medieval man could do no more. And as he looked back, in the evening of the Middle Ages, at the darkness from which he had come and the heights which he had achieved, he could say with Dante, climbing out of the pit of hell, "*E quindi uscimmo a riveder le stelle*" . .

And thus we emerged again to see the stars . . .

Poet at the Gates of Hell

THE Florentine Dante Alighieri, who described himself as one "to whom the world is native country, just as the sea is to the fish," stands before the walls of his native Florence, from which he was long exiled, holding in his hand a copy of his masterpiece, the *Divine Comedy*. At the far left is shown the beginning of Dante's preview of immortality, where devils drive damned souls behind the gates of hell down into the eternal pit below:

> Here sighs, with lamentations and loud moans . . .
> Horrible languages, outcries of woe,
> Accents of anger, voices deep and hoarse,
> With hands together smote that swell'd the sounds,
> Made up a tumult, that for ever whirls
> Round through that air with solid darkness stain'd. . . .

Behind Dante is the hill of purgatory, where souls not permanently damned work out their salvation. The angel marks with his sword on each soul's forehead the number of sins it has to expiate. Climbing its penitential rounds the soul arrives purified at the earthly paradise symbolized by the presence of Adam and Eve. Over all is stretched the empyrean, heavenly paradise of saints, of which Dante wrote:

> And I beheld, shaped like a river, light
> Streaming a splendour between banks whereon
> The miracle of the spring was pictured bright.
> Out of this river living sparkles thrown
> Shot everywhere a fire amid the bloom
> And there like rubies gold-encrusted shone. . . .

Reims Cathedral, probably the most generally admired example of the Gothic style, was begun in 1211 and finished almost a century later. This is the west façade, showing the elaborate stone carving and the great stained-glass rose window over the doors. Carved above the center arch is the baptism of Clovis, the first Christian king of the Franks, who was baptized on the cathedral site in 496.

Religious life in many communities was quickened by the presence of a nearby monastery. Here a procession of monks, led by St. Bernard, takes over the famous Cistercian monastery at Clairvaux.

The pilgrimage season in England began in April when people set out for the cathedral at Canterbury or at York. At left, Chaucer's Canterbury pilgrims hear a tale told by the rider on the white horse.

Cathedrals and Pilgrims

TO the plain medieval man the cathedral was not only a tribute to the glory of God. It was also a symbol of his town's importance. The abiding faith which moved people to give time and strength to the task of building a cathedral was reinforced by home-town booster spirit, by the knowledge that a cathedral lent to a place something of the same prestige that a big new courthouse lends to an American town today.

Like the courthouse, the cathedral was a government building—a center of administration for that powerful ruler and landlord, the Church. It was a dispensary of alms, advice and sometimes of medical care. It was also a feat of architecture, engineering and executive ability, of transportation, financing, mining, quarrying and all the arts. To build it, kings, nobles and bishops vied in making large donations. Church collections and the sale of indulgences provided substantial sums. Those who could give no money helped haul the huge blocks from the quarries. The cathedral enshrined in beauty the toil and hopes of all who had labored to erect it, not with the work of a few months or years or even of a lifetime, but with the work of centuries.

For everyone the cathedral was an encyclopedia of holy stories and churchly lore. In its stained-glass windows, which are among the world's most magnificent works of art, the scenes of the Bible were displayed so vividly that unlettered churchgoers walked from window to window as if reading the pages of a book. In its sculpture they grew familiar with great prophets, martyrs, saints and heroes. And there was perpetual amusement in the thousand grimaces and contortions of the little stone heads and figures girdling the capitals of columns or hunched down in the corners of great arches.

The cathedral dominated not only the town but the countryside around. Its bells, which could be heard for many miles, announced disasters like war or fire and proclaimed such events as feast days or visits from royalty. To peasants working in outlying fields as well as to hustling townsmen, the rhythm of life was marked by the bells, ringing for Mass and the Angelus, ringing again for christenings, weddings, funerals.

Inside the cathedral the people got their most spectacular entertainment. Brilliant processions and elaborate ceremonies filled its vast dimness with life and color. The modern theater originated there in the old miracle plays which dramatized Bible stories and the life of Christ. Until the fifteenth century, Church authorities even permitted parodies of holy services to be held in the churches. During the annual Feast of Fools sacred ceremonies were richly burlesqued and sometimes a donkey was led to the altar in mock solemnity. The priests themselves were seldom aloof and ascetic holy men. They lived close to their flocks, playing, joking and drinking with them. While this policy led sometimes to abuses in the priesthood, it strengthened the hold of the Church.

NOT every medieval town boasted a cathedral, which was built only in a place designated as a bishop's seat. Most of the towns had unpretentious churches or chapels. To atone for their sins, many pious people went on yearly pilgrimages, traveling on foot or on horseback to some distant cathedral or shrine, like Chaucer's Canterbury pilgrims (*above, left*). Such journeys were thrilling adventures. To the pilgrims a medieval cathedral appeared at its greatest glory when, after a long journey, they first beheld its spires soaring into the heavens, higher than any building they had ever seen, and they knew that they soon would share in God's grace.

In Bourges Cathedral, French stonecutters achieved one of their greatest triumphs. The scene over the central portal depicts the Last Judgment. At the bottom, resurrected kings, bishops and commoners struggle up from their graves to the weighing of souls. Above, the figure of Christ the Judge dominates the scene. Arching over all, angels, saints and prophets join the celestial company.

Stone Saints and Demons

One inexorable fact that haunted the daily life of every medieval man was the certainty of divine judgment after death. The relief above, from the Abbey of Vézelay, France, shows blessed souls borne heavenward by three angels accompanied by St. Peter, while the Virgin Mary looks back toward the weighing of souls (*opposite page*).

Another certainty ever present in the minds of the credulous was that the devil was out to trap them at every turn. Atop this column at Vézelay, two horned devils with wings and cloven hoofs torment a venerable patriarch of the Church. Not content with pulling his beard, they tear his cloak and brandish hatchets over his head.

Here, on the Vézelay façade, the Archangel Michael weighs souls in his eternal balance, as a devil tries to tip the scale to get one more. At right those already damned march with woebegone expressions toward hell, represented by the open mouth of a jagged-toothed monster with a snake for a tongue and breathing realistic flames.

The golden calf was the favorite symbol for heathen idolatry or heresy. On this Vézelay capital, a stern Moses (*left*) raises the tablets with the Ten Commandments to confound the golden calf and the snaky-haired devil astride him. Both are aghast at the sight. The peasant at right, bringing a sacrifice to the calf, looks on in deep awe.

Stories of the Virgin's miracles were plentiful. When the thief Ebbo was hanged, Mary kept him alive by supporting his weight on her finger to give him enough time to repent his sins and save his soul.

An artist was painting a fresco of Mary trampling on an ugly devil. Enraged, the devil broke the ladder on which the artist stood. But the Holy Mother reached out of the fresco to hold the artist up.

In Cologne, devils tried to seize the soul of a monk who had died unshriven. St. Peter, his heavenly patron, made an appeal to Mary, who intervened and had the dead man's soul returned to his body.

The text over this miniature from a fifteenth century manuscript reads: "Mary is the mediator between God and men." She is shown shielding sinners with her cloak from the arrow of divine wrath.

The Queen of Heaven

TURNING from the figures of God the Father and of Jesus, who were stern reminders of the righteous judgment which awaited all mortals, medieval worshipers sought a warmer, more personal object of adoration. In the gentle, compassionate Virgin Mary they found one who could promise pity as well as justice, and they worshiped her almost as a deity in her own right, taking her into their hearts and daily lives even more than they did the heavenly Son she had borne.

The cult of Mary grew and its signs were visible everywhere. In the Holy Mother's honor, the magnificent cathedrals of Reims and Chartres were reared. Great pilgrimages were made to her shrines. Most cathedrals had their own chapel of Our Lady and the Virgin's praises rose night and day in two of the world's great hymns, the *Salve Regina*—"Hail, Queen of Heaven"—and the *Ave Maria*—"Hail Mary, full of grace . . ."

Sinners begged Mary to intercede for them at the Court of Heaven. Noble ladies and peasant women prayed for her help in time of family sickness and travail. Knights made her their lady and proudly wore her insignia into battle. All Christendom rang with testimonials of her miracles and Mary stories became the chroniclers' favorite theme. One of the best known of these tales, "Our Lady's Juggler," is given here in an abridgment of Anatole France's version:

IN the days of King Louis there lived in France a poor juggler named Barnabas, who traveled from town to town performing tricks of strength and skill. At first people would look upon his performance with indifference. But when, standing head down on his hands, he would throw in the air and catch with his feet six copper balls which shone in the sun, or when, arching back until his head touched his heels, he made his body into the shape of a perfect circle and, in this position, juggled with twelve knives, a murmur of admiration would rise from the onlookers and pieces of money would rain on his carpet.

On an evening he met along the road a monk and saluted him.

"Friend," said the monk, "how is it that you are dressed all in green? To play the part of the fool in some mystery?"

"Father," replied Barnabas, "I am called Barnabas and I am a juggler by trade. It would be the finest trade in the world if it provided me with food every day."

Medieval men-at-arms bore pictures of Mary when they went into battle against the infidels. Here Christian knights fighting under the Virgin's aegis rout a troop of bearded and turbaned Moors.

"Friend Barnabas," answered the monk, "take care what you say. There is no finer estate in the world than that of the monastic. The life of a monk is a perpetual hymn to the Lord."

Barnabas answered, "Father, I would willingly abandon the art for which I am known in more than six hundred towns and villages, to enter monastic life."

The good monk, touched by the juggler's simplicity, answered, "Friend Barnabas, come with me and I will have you enter the monastery of which I am prior." This is how Barnabas became a monk.

The prior, as his work, composed books which dealt with the virtues of the Mother of God. Brother Maurice copied those treatises on parchment. Brother Alexander painted fine miniatures on them.

There were also poets in the monastery who composed Latin prose pieces and hymns in honor of the Most Blessed Virgin Mary.

Witnessing such wealth of praises and such a rich harvest of works, Barnabas bemoaned his ignorance and artlessness.

"Alas," he sighed. "It makes me very unhappy to find myself unable to praise worthily the Holy Mother of God."

One evening he overheard one of his brothers telling the story of a monk who could only recite the Ave Maria. This monk had been looked upon with contempt because of his ignorance; but when he died five roses grew out of his mouth in honor of the five letters in the name of Maria and his holiness was thus made manifest. On hearing this story Barnabas once more admired the goodness of the Virgin, and he wanted to celebrate the glory of His Lady.

One day when Barnabas was closeted in the chapel as was his habit, the prior came, accompanied by two old friars, to observe through a crack in the door what he was doing inside.

They saw Barnabas, before the Holy Virgin's altar, head down and feet up, juggling with six copper balls and twelve knives. He was performing his tricks in honor of the Holy Mother of God. The two old friars cried sacrilege. The prior knew that Barnabas was pure of heart but thought he had become insane. All three were about to drag him from the chapel when they beheld the Virgin descend from the altar and with the edge of her blue mantle wipe the sweat which poured from the juggler's forehead.

Then the prior, throwing himself face to the ground, intoned these words: "Blessed are the pure in heart for they shall see God."

"Amen," responded the friars, kissing the ground.

The Virgin Mary's character as a loving and helpful mother is reflected in the radiant face and graceful posture of this thirteenth century woodcarving of the Madonna holding the Infant Jesus.

Saints in Stained Glass

The Ascension of Christ was done in the twelfth century for a window in the cathedral of Saint-Julien at Le Mans. Like most work of the earlier medieval stained-glass artists, it has a simpler design than later masterpieces (*opposite page*). Here figures of the Virgin Mary (*top center*) and the Twelve Apostles stand on pinnacles of rock on the Mount of Olives looking up with adoration toward heaven.

Three apostles, Peter, Paul and John, stand in narrow windows at the cathedral of Bourges. Peter holds a cross and the keys of heaven; Paul, the sword with which he was beheaded; and John, a book symbolic of his Gospel. These devices, as well as Peter's bald pate and hoary locks and John's youthfulness, were put in to help the many worshipers who could not read the names beneath the figures.

Monastic scribes who set out to preserve knowledge by reproducing texts also created new beauty, in the delicate ornaments and miniatures with which they embellished their work. On this page from a thirteenth century French manuscript, a clerk in a monastery scriptorium (*bottom, left*) directs the copying and illuminating of the text in his hand. Holding a knife in one hand, the copyist sketches decorations with a pen. At top are shown King Louis IX and his mother, Blanche of Castille, for whom the book was made.

Scribes in Monasteries Took on the Task of Education

AT the end of his day's work some eleven hundred years ago, the monk Cairbre, an Inch-madoc man, left off the laborious copying of the text of Priscian's Latin grammar in the scriptorium of an Irish monastery and scribbled on the margin: "Oh, my hand! May Saints Patrick and Bridget move Maelbrigte [the supervisor] that he be not angry with me for the writing writ this day." There is no record of the stern Maelbrigte's reaction to this plaint, and Cairbre's other querulous jottings about the cold, the quality of his pen and the parchment. But it could not have been too harsh; Cairbre went on to finish the manuscript, which served as a schoolbook for generations of students before ending in the library of a Swiss monastery.

The scriptorium in which Cairbre worked was one of hundreds attached to monasteries throughout Europe. Like a schoolroom, it had individual desks for the writers and illuminators and supplies of inks, quills, powdered paints, brushes and parchment. As in a schoolroom, silence was imposed. The scriptorium was medieval man's publishing house. It issued missals, Bibles and works of the Church fathers as well as grammars and editions of the classic authors for the use of students in the cathedral and monastic schools. The scholar's first instruction in Latin usually came from the pedantic works of Donatus and Priscian, containing just enough quotes from the pagan poets to illustrate grammatical points. The grammar mastered, he was fitted to wander in the perilously attractive fields of Virgil, Horace and Ovid. But grave abbots discouraged their charges from too much tasting of such heady stuff; at Cluny, monks desiring to read a profane author in the hour of silence were required to make the motion of scratching behind the ear, like a dog.

For centuries, Europe's richest source of scholarship was Ireland. In the sixth century the Irishman St. Columban and his disciples established more than a hundred monastic strongholds of learning on the Continent. Later, Irish foundations spread east as far as Nuremberg, Vienna and even Prague. The wandering Irish carried with them not only the traditions of scholarship but precious manuscripts as well.

Like all scholars, the Irish found a ready welcome at the court of Charlemagne. Gathering learned men from Spain, Italy and England, as well as Ireland, the emperor ordered the collection and copying of documents and fostered the development and spread of the clear round Caroline minuscule which became the model for all modern Western typescripts. He also revised the language of the Latin Bible and the liturgy. Under Charlemagne's peace there was constant interchange between Church foundations all over Christendom. The Englishman Alcuin, master of Charles's Palace School at Aachen, took two years' leave to work in York. Writing back to a friend at court, he passed on the latest gossip from Ireland and complaints about British beverages: "Woe is me! There is death in the pot, Oh man of God! . . . The wine is gone from our wineskins, and bitter beer rageth in our bellies." Alcuin asked his friend to ship him some good French wine.

AFTER Charlemagne's death and the split-up of his empire, disaster hit the monastic schools. As Northmen sacked the monasteries near the coasts and rivers of Ireland, England and France, scholars streamed to the inland safety of Liége, St. Gall and Reichenau. For decades an educated society almost ceased to exist. Small groups of monks huddled together behind thick monastery walls and, lacking fresh parchment, made palimpsests by erasing classic texts on old manuscripts, or merely wrote between the lines to record their chronicles and accounts. In the eleventh century scholarship began to recover again, and its center shifted back to France and Italy. Henceforth it was the cathedral schools, especially those in the growing cities, which were to take the lead.

Monasteries were also centers of instruction. Here, at Tavara in Spain, scholars work in an outdoor scriptorium while colleagues ring the bells. The man seated at left works with pen and knife while the student facing him solves a geometric problem with a compass.

At the University of Paris, in the later Middle Ages, higher education was conducted in comparative luxury. At right, seated scholars are led in discussion by their teacher while three others stand ceremoniously around with scepters containing holy relics or the Blessed Sacrament. Through most of the Middle Ages, university students had neither benches to sit on nor texts to read. Classes were held in the corners of churches where the students squatted on straw laid over the floor. Too poor to buy texts or parchment and ink for taking notes, students had to rely largely on their memory of what the teacher told them. All instruction was oral, the master reading from the text, then making detailed comments, which were called "glosses." After a class, the students would usually rush to a tavern to go over the lecture and to spend long hours in discussion and argument.

Universities Flourished In the Revival of Learning

LATE in the twelfth century, matters had become very disorganized at the University of Bologna and the students laid down the law to the faculty. Henceforth, they said, teachers must hold classes at regular and frequent intervals, be conscientious and punctual in attendance, cover all necessary ground in their courses, and not leave town without student permission.

The disorganization which prompted this stern, and successful, student action at Bologna was not uncommon at medieval universities. The university, an entirely new kind of educational institution, had grown up quickly and haphazardly in the revival of learning after 1000. The increase in cathedral schools, where promising boys were trained for the priesthood, had stimulated interest in higher learning and the demand for teachers. Often a university began with a few masters settling in a town and attracting students. Occasionally a rich noble or a civic-minded town would contribute some money. But the university had no classrooms, no dormitories, no organized faculty or curriculum. Gradually either students or masters began to organize, set standards and give the university form. At the University of Paris in 1257, Robert de Sorbon gave a building to house some students and masters and thus founded the oldest academic college, the Sorbonne. By 1291, Paris had a student body of twenty thousand, more than the combined enrollment at Yale and Harvard today.

For a bachelor of arts degree a student worked four or five years, studying rhetoric, logic, mathematics and Aristotle's philosophy. The students were usually earnest, irrepressible and short of money. They fought with townspeople, hazed newcomers, consorted with low women and irritated their teachers. His students, complained Master Gilbert de la Porrée of Paris, would make better bakers than scholars. A chronicler of the university at Freiburg in Breisgau depicted student life in incidents (*below*) which look familiar today. And the most universal of medieval student songs is still the most widely sung of college songs—*Gaudeamus Igitur*—which goes:

Let us live then and be glad While young life's before us!
After youthful pastime had, After old age hard and sad,
Earth will slumber o'er us.

The Middle Ages' most impressive school buildings were built for Winchester College in England in 1394. Winchester was a "public school," so called because it was intended for poor students who could not afford private tutoring. Its graduates went on to Oxford.

The students at Freiburg spend a dull Sunday listening—but only barely—to a long sermon.

In class, students oppose one another in "disputation," debates which went on for hours.

In his cell-like room, a student makes his own bed. Being poor, students did their own chores.

A quarrelsome bunch, students liked to fight—each other (*above*), townspeople, authorities.

An irreverent bunch, students gambled in university rooms, which was strictly forbidden.

An immoral bunch, students broke the cardinal school rule: don't ask a girl up to your room.

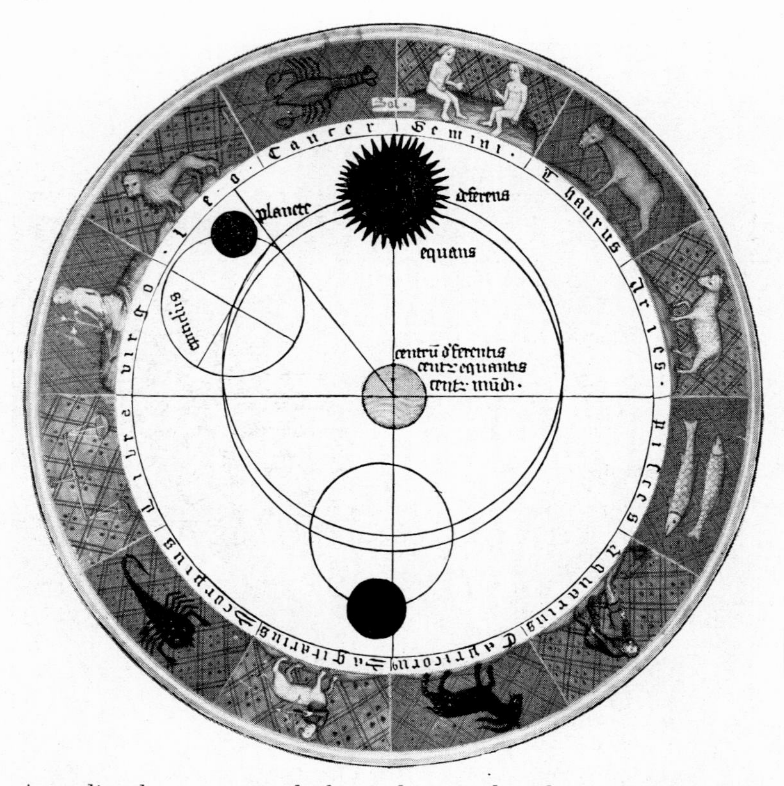

A medieval astronomical chart, decorated with astrological symbols, had the sun moving in regular circles around a stationary earth while the moon and planets revolved in complex double orbits.

Science and Pseudo Science

THE medieval scientist was handicapped by his dependence on a mass of Biblical legends and inaccurate Greek and Arabic manuscripts, by a tradition which bound him to accept without question the statements of Aristotle and by a preoccupation with bogus sciences. Believing that human destiny was governed by the stars, he studied astrology; trying to transmute base metals into gold, he practiced alchemy, a misguided kind of chemistry. But a few men had the basic requisite of the scientist, the urge to ask questions. The most important among them was a peevish, abusive British monk named Roger Bacon who observed spiral nebulae through a primitive kind of telescope, peered at cells through a forerunner of the microscope, wrote a recipe for crude gunpowder and speculated on the possibility of flying machines. Above all, he foresaw the importance of mathematics and firsthand observation as tools for research and paved the way for modern scientific method.

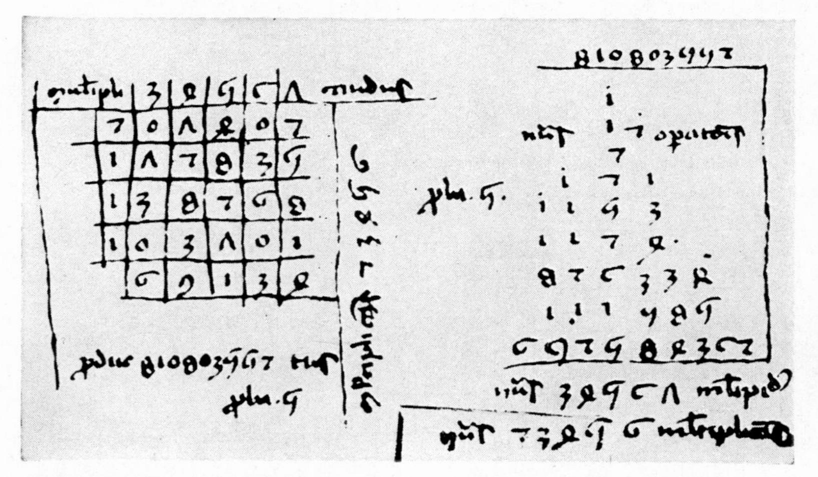

Arabic numerals came to Europe from India by way of the Spanish Moors. In this thirteenth century calculation, 34,567 (*top left*) is multiplied by 23,456 (*center*) to give 810,803,552 (*top right*).

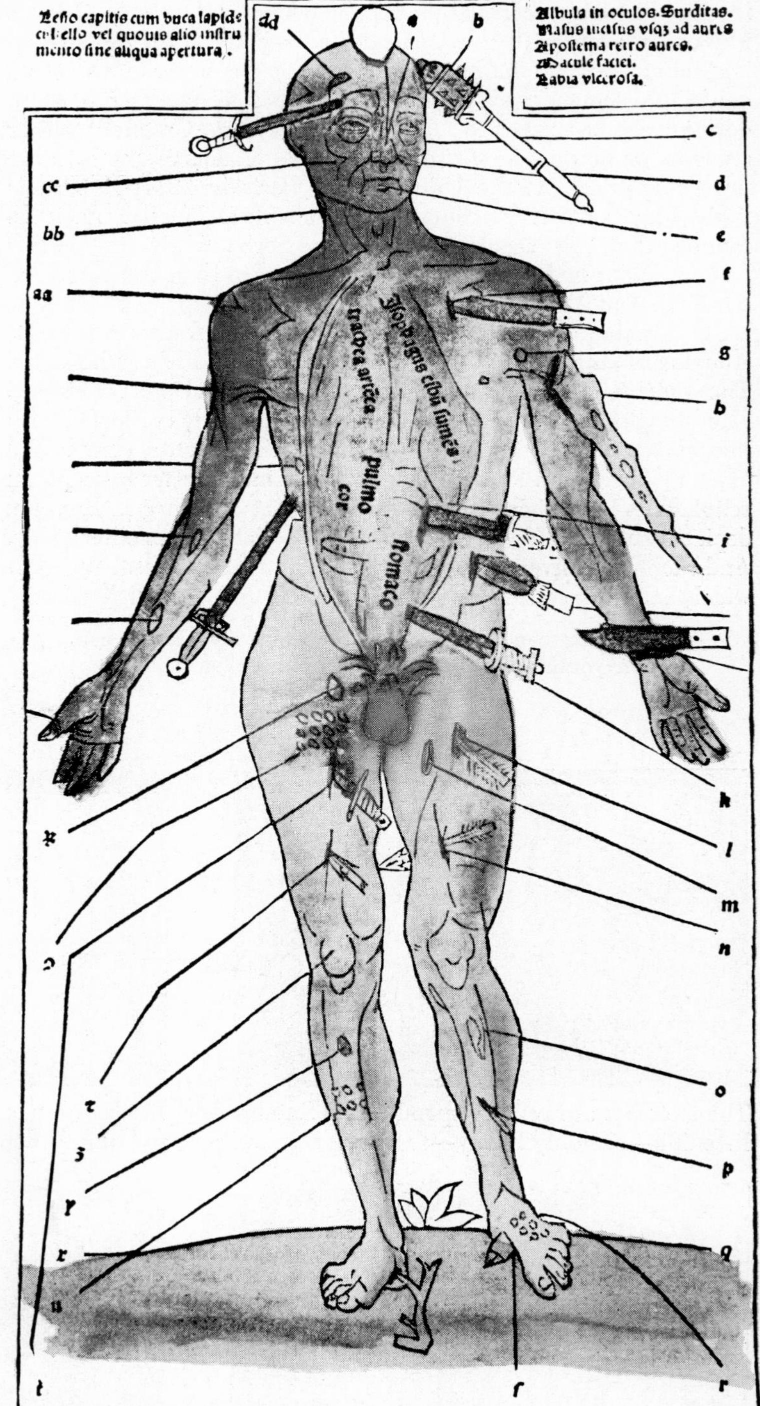

Johannes de Ketham's handbook of medicine, a compendium of medieval knowledge, supplied this chart of common battle wounds, described typical aftereffects and gave handy hints for first aid.

The Alchemist was drawn by Pieter Bruegel, the elder, to give a detailed picture of how the early chemists performed their labors. The alchemist (*left*) mixes his ingredients under the direction of the learned scholar (*right*). As the hungry children raid the cupboard, their mother shakes the last coins from her purse for one more experiment. In back can be seen the probable outcome: the poorhouse.

Personality was said to be governed by body fluids called humors. Each humor corresponded to one of the four supposedly basic elements of matter: air, fire, water, earth. From left to right are: the sanguine man (air), who has plenty of blood; the melancholy man (earth), full of dark bile; the hot-tempered man (fire), who has a surplus of choler; the sluggish man (water), with too much phlegm.

The World in 1280

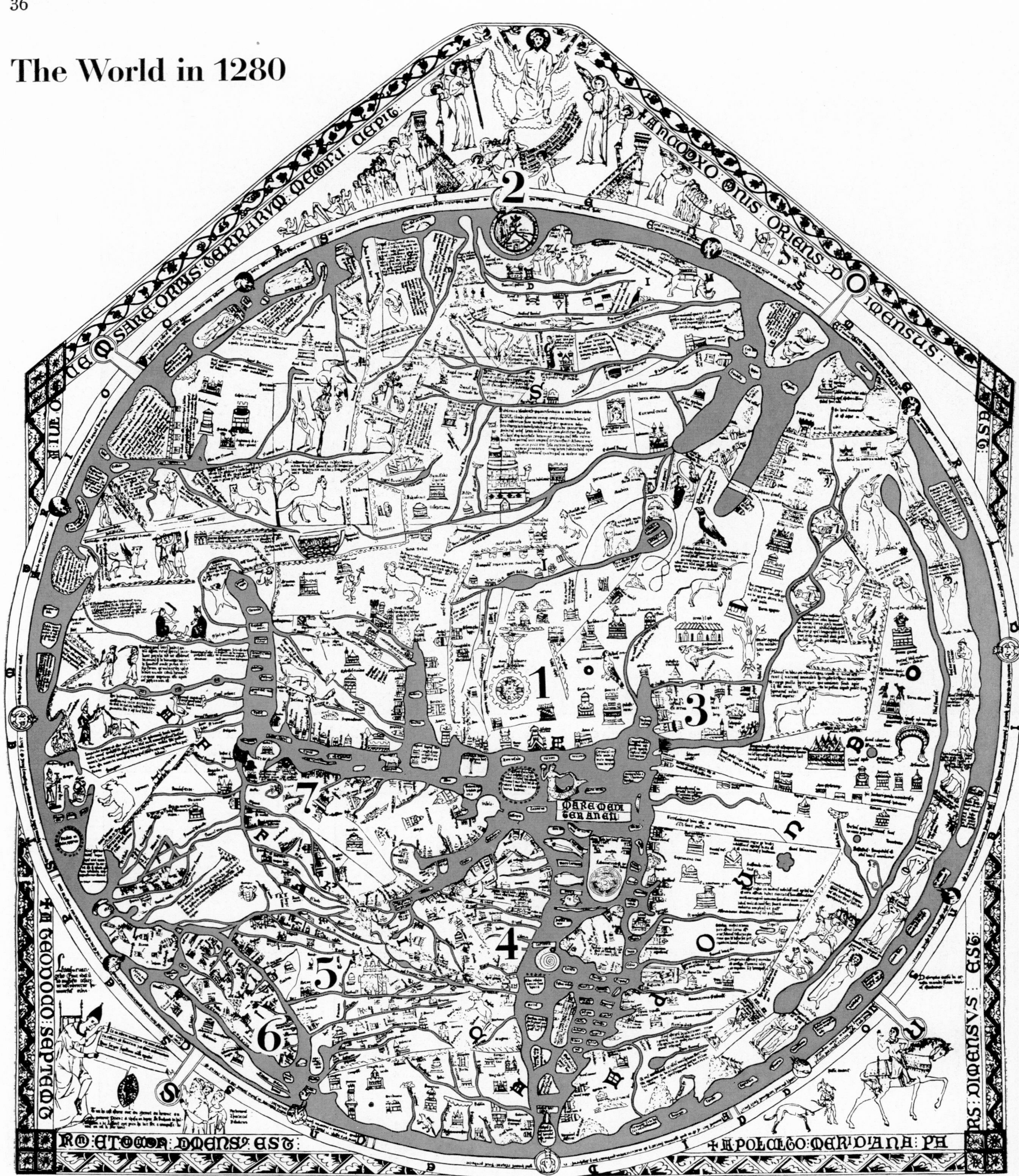

Though some learned folk were aware that the world was round, most medieval men believed that it was flat as a pie and surrounded by a bottomless sea. This view was shared by an English clergyman and scholar named Richard de Haldingham, who drew his famous Hereford map around 1280. With only a hazy knowledge of geography, de Haldingham tried to cram all known features of the world into his circle, including fanciful beasts, freaks, Biblical landmarks, medieval lore and semi-scientific conjecture. By mistake he reversed the labels of Europe and Africa in the lower right and left sides. In the map west is at bottom, south at right.

In accordance with Christian belief, Jerusalem was placed in the center of the world (*1*). At the top of the map is the Garden of Eden (*2*). The large building halfway between them is the Tower of Babel. Other more or less recognizable spots are Alexandria (*3*), Rome (*4*), Paris (*5*), London (*6*), Constantinople (*7*). The body of water branching through the lower half of the map is the Mediterranean Sea (labeled *Mare Mediteranea*), with the Strait of Gibraltar and Pillars of Hercules at the bottom. De Haldingham's map did not disseminate accurate knowledge of geography, but it aroused great excitement and interest concerning the world.

MEDIEVAL LIFE

The medieval castle guarded its people behind heavy stone walls which were pierced at intervals by narrow, deep-set embrasures. From these openings the castle's defenders could drop stones, shoot arrows, throw spears or pour boiling pitch and lead on attackers. To keep scaling parties from getting in, the openings were set with spiked mullions whose sharp points would tear up a man's body. This is an embrasure in the room used by the captain of the guard at Gradara Castle, built in central Italy in the eleventh century.

II

MEDIEVAL LIFE

ON the wall of the castle of Melun, the Bastard of Mareuil stood watching the siege of his fortress by the army of the duke of Normandy. He saw a stout knight come rushing through a storm of bolts from the castle crossbowmen, lay a ladder against the wall and start climbing it. "See how short and square he is," marveled one of the defenders, "big and bulging like a hog in armor. It is Bertrand du Guesclin." The knight looked up and cried, "Ho, Bastard! Come down into the alder grove and we will fight with a right good heart." But Mareuil seized a herring barrel full of stones and rolled it over the parapet onto Bertrand's head. The ladder broke and the knight plunged into the moat, where his head stuck in the mud. Seeing his plight, the duke of Normandy cried, "Succor my Bertrand!" Whereupon a squire pulled him out by the feet and laid him on a warm dungheap to bring him to. In a little while the knight arose from the dungheap and with his battle cry of "Guesclin!" rushed back to the battle, driving the attack as far as the castle drawbridge. It was then nightfall and the assault was stopped for supper, after which the two captains met and made a treaty, lifting the siege.

The feats of Bertrand du Guesclin were told at many a banquet table in the stony castles which studded the landscape of medieval Europe. For Bertrand was a perfect knight, a classic model for that order of men whose function was to defend feudal society.

In that society, knighthood was the goal of almost every highborn boy whose ancestry and property made him eligible for the noble estate. He commonly entered the service of a lord at seven or eight as a page and began a long apprenticeship in the arts of war and the practice of the chivalric code. When he was judged ready for knighthood he underwent the solemn ceremony of adubment, in which the lord gave him a stunning buffet on the back of the head, the last affront he might ever accept without taking redress. Thenceforth he was entitled to be called "Sir" and to bear the arms and armor that gave his class a monopoly of military power. And thenceforth he was obliged to live by the code of chivalry. The code had come originally out of the customs of the German forest tribes, in which the young men formed a military band, or comitatus, to follow and defend a tribal leader. Under the influence of the Church and the patronage of noble ladies, this barbarian institution was gradually made over into a grand and intricate structure which gave warfare a moral sublimity it has never had before or since. But beneath its splendid façade, chivalry was simply the power basis of the feudal order.

NOBODY planned feudalism. It grew. In the anarchy that followed Rome's fall, feudalism gave an answer to the desperate need for a social order in which a man could plant a crop and live to reap it. It did not take exactly the same form in all parts of Europe. Even in the same region it did not remain the same from century to century. But its main features were simple. Its chief idea was to offer something

The castle of the counts of Flanders was built about 1180 along the River Liève in Ghent by Philip of Alsace, who constructed the stronghold in his rebellious possession to "restrain the pride of the men of Ghent." The building with a peaked roof (*left*) was the count's house.

that almost anybody could give—loyalty and service—in exchange for something that only a powerful few could give—protection and land.

The basic economic fact of feudalism was the relationship between a lord and his serfs. In return for his protection and a piece of land to work, the serf performed specified services and paid specified fees. Subject to the moderating force of the Church and of ancient custom, the lord made laws and dispensed justice.

Politically, the basis of feudalism was the relationship of the nobles among themselves and to the king. Every medieval man was another man's vassal. The king was God's vassal. The moral sanction of feudalism was the belief that the king received his right divinely from God. Thus all other men in descending order received their rights from God through the king. To the medieval mind vassalage was not humiliating. A man became a vassal by placing his hands between those of his superior and swearing fealty to him as long as either lived. In return the vassal received a fief, usually a grant of land but sometimes the right to levy a toll on a road or a bridge. Vassalage obliged a man to pay his lord a regular fee, to follow his lord in war, to betray his lord's enemies, to defend his lord's person. A man might be the vassal of more than one lord, in which case he owed allegiance to his liege lord. As feudal society grew more complex, lords and dukes, even bishops and abbots, might be vassals of other nobles. Indeed, bishops and abbots, who were usually the sons of great lords, often led their retainers into battle.

Feudalism's touchstones were loyalty and service. The feudal system spun a web of human relationships from the king down through the secular and Church lords to the lowest serf. It was ideally organized to further the Middle Ages' three chief activities—fighting, farming and praying.

Contrary to general belief, the world of feudalism was one of fresh hope and surging vitality. Having stood off the fierce barbarian raids of the ninth and tenth centuries, men sensed that the worst was over and their spirits rose with the new walls that were turning the face of twelfth century castles from wood to stone. Hope flashed from the bright banners snapping in the wind from the castle watchtowers. Hope gleamed from the armor of jousting knights. Hope echoed from the cries of ladies and squires following the hunt with their falcons. It rang from the songs of strolling minstrels and shone in the bright costumes of parties swarming the wretched roads in pilgrimage to holy shrines.

Medieval roads were muddy cart tracks. It took all the power of pulling horses and pushing peasants to get this cogwheeled cart up a hill. These horses are wearing the new style collar, invented about 1000 A.D., which relieved the pressure of the harness strap on the windpipe and increased a horse's pulling power four times.

Even the peasant had his hopes. The collapse of Rome, terrible for all classes, had been most terrible for the poor. But the Church gave every medieval man, however lowly, the promise of a life everlasting, while feudalism gave him a basic security in this world.

THE castle, surrounded by serf-worked lands, was the hub on which medieval life turned. Its central tower, the donjon, was surrounded by a chain of other towers connected by the wall, and outside this by a moat, crossed by a drawbridge. In summer the moat was a hunting ground for frogs (then, as now, a delicacy) and a breeding ground for mosquitoes. Inside the donjon was a vast hall, almost pitch dark without candles, where the whole castle garrison could assemble if necessary in time of siege. From its tower jutted a beam from which malefactors were sometimes hanged as a stern reminder of the lord's justice. Its deepest chamber, black, dank and rat-ridden, was the jail, which in later times took the name of the whole tower, or dungeon.

The donjon was the lord's house and its great hall was the scene of constant activity. Here the lord received homage from his vassals and managed the business of his domain. Here he dined with his family and guests on a dais, perhaps beneath his tapestries and armor. Here, on wet or wintry days, the whole castle population crowded around long tables, on backless benches, to eat, gossip, play jokes or dice, listen to jongleurs sing ballads and love songs or watch them perform acrobatic tricks. Here at night mattresses were laid on the floor and the whole household slept in the same room, masters and servants together. Except on great occasions most castle folk retired with the birds (medieval lamps and candles shed little light) and, except in winter, when bed was the warmest spot in the castle, got up with them.

When not encased in iron clothing, a well-dressed lord wore linen underdrawers and undershirt. Fashion decreed staid stockings, though dashing dressers sometimes affected black hose with red stripes. The chief outer garment was a fur-trimmed pelisse, or woolen tunic, and over this a pull-on shirt. For outdoor wear, a tasseled cape, fur-lined even in summer, was in vogue. Men's hair was done in bangs and fetching curls. The Church had long inveighed against beards, which it associated with the devil, and by the thirteenth century lords endured the ordeal of shaving at least twice a week.

Medieval woman's main business was marriage. Elaborate specifications governed her appearance and conduct. Blondes were preferred. They should be tall and slender. They should not trot or run, scold, overeat or drink too much in public. Aniseed was recommended for bad breath. And ladies were advised to wipe their greasy fingers (forks were unknown in the Middle Ages) on a napkin rather than on the tablecloth or the dog. Because a castle was a military encampment, medieval women were accustomed to coarse talk and jokes and could take, and give, broad banter. They spoke with men on

the most intimate subjects with a freedom that might make even modern women blush.

The splendor of the feudal achievement and the vivid hurly-burly of noble life were only a merry din or a martial menace on the daily horizon of the serf. The serf was bound to the land but he did not own it. Not a slave, he usually had, by custom if not by law, the right to live on the land of his fathers and to pass on that right to his sons. In some regions he could throw off his serfdom by escaping for a year and a day (hence the modern expression). If he made good his escape he might become a freeholder in one of the frontier settlements where the German forest was being slowly pushed back.

THE peasant lived in a wooden cottage with one or two rooms, a dirt floor, a thatched roof and no chimney but a hole in the roof to let the smoke escape. He wore a cloth or sheepskin blouse and trousers, covered by a knee-length mantle. Women wore much the same, but with skirts instead of trousers. Unlike the lord, who had leather shoes, the peasant went barefoot or wore wooden clogs. Much of the peasant's time was spent not in working but in walking, for peasants' strips of land were scattered all over the lord's manor. Wooden plows were drawn by oxen and a crude form of crop rotation was practiced, but the science of farming in feudal Christendom was far below that of the Roman estates in Marcus Aurelius' time or that of Moslem Spain in the Middle Ages. A signal advance in agriculture occurred about 1000 when the modern horse collar was invented. Before that time farmers had tried harnessing horses to the plow in place of oxen but had failed because the harness strap pressed on the horse's wind-pipe and cut off his breath. The unknown inventor of the horse collar, which left the animal's windpipe free, increased fourfold the motive power at the peasant's command.

The serf paid tribute to the lord through an intricate system of fees and dues. The share of his produce, from a tenth to a third, which he turned over to the lord's collector, was but the beginning. The serf's sheep had to be driven into the lord's pen so that he could have the manure. When the peasant's wife baked she had to bake in the lord's oven and pay

For peasants, the lord's word was law, his justice terrible. For infractions of the lord's orders, a peasant might be blinded (*top left*) or decapitated out of hand (*center*). Because the lord's needs were paramount, peasants reaped his grain, worked in his vineyard and plowed his land—and, as youngsters, sometimes stole his grapes.

Knighthood In Full Flower

THE medieval knight was a romantic figure and a hard-working warrior. As a lover, he might be hoisted up to his ladylove's towered chamber (*top left*). As a chivalric hero back from war, he would be welcomed with a stiff drink and rose-petal bath (*top right*). But there was a less flowery side of knighthood (*below*). In training, a squire practiced on a device called a quintain. If his lance missed the center of the target, the hanging weight smacked him. In tournaments, a knight's glory passed when a better fighter unseated him. In battle, his career had an ignoble aftermath when, lying dead, he was stripped of his valuable armor and left naked on the ground.

a fee in loaves. There was a fee if the peasant's daughter married a man on another estate, and even a fee when a peasant died. Besides paying fees the serf had to give a certain number of days' labor, as many as three a week, to till the lord's lands, mow his hayfields, keep up the roads and repair the castle walls. In some places the lord enjoyed the *droit du seigneur*, or right of the first night, with the serf's bride, and only by the payment of another fee could the serf forestall the exercise of this right.

THE battle trumpet sounded the theme of the secular Middle Ages. War was a normal condition, peace an unnatural pause between battles. When, toward the end of the eleventh century, the turmoil of warring lords, jousting knights and rebellious peasants had reached such a tension that it seemed as though medieval society must fly apart, the Church summoned medieval man to his most dazzling adventure—the Crusades. His response rang out in the shout of the eager knights who in 1090 answered Pope Urban II's call at Clermont with *Deus vult*—God wills it!

There were eight major Crusades. They occupied two hundred years and much of the energy of western Europe. In them were involved the great and colorful figures of the Middle Ages, from Peter the Hermit to Richard Coeur de Lion. Their proclaimed purpose was to free the Holy Land from the Seljuk Turks, but men were moved also by the desire to see new places, find new opportunities and perhaps renew fading fortunes. For all who went on the Crusades the Church promised remission of sins.

The first crusaders set up a string of shaky feudal states in Syria and Palestine. Later Crusades were sent to save them. Politically, the Crusades were a costly failure. They ended with Mohammedanism overrunning great parts of the Christian empire of Byzantium and thrusting into Europe. By the end of the thirteenth century nothing was left of the crusaders' kingdoms but the ruins of their feudal fortresses and a surprising number of fair-haired children among the dark natives of the Holy Land.

But the influence of the Crusades on western Europe was immense. Before the Crusades Europe had been shut off from the rest of the world as by the walls of a medieval castle. The Crusades brought Europe and Asia face to face again. New goods, new ways and views of life, new knowledge seeped back into the West. From the East, in the train of the returning crusaders, came sugar, melons, lemons, muslin and damask cloth, lilac and purple dyes, the use of powder, glass mirrors and even the rosary.

More important, the Crusades changed the institutions of Europe. They brought closer the end of feudalism by putting masses of property on the market (crusading was an expensive business) and by disturbing the validity of titles. They introduced modern taxation when Louis VII of France, to finance the Second Crusade, levied the first general tax. And though the Christian knights eventually lost the Holy Land, the merchant fleets that supplied them, especially the Venetian, opened up the Mediterranean to a rich commercial traffic. Both the goods and the ideas that poured into southern Europe planted in medieval life the seeds of change that would soon flower in the Renaissance.

The way the early Middle Ages waged war was described in this thirteenth century Spanish manuscript telling the story of Nebuchadnezzar's siege of Jerusalem. The stone walls around the massive city gate, which the attackers would try to force, are surmounted by spiked parapets. Manning them are unarmored soldiers carrying early medieval round shields, wearing primitive helmets and brandishing spears and rocks. The pensive figure at the right is the Biblical prophet Jeremiah who predicted the destruction of the city.

The Conquering Normans: 1066

The most important conquest of the Middle Ages was made by William, Duke of Normandy, who in 1066 invaded and conquered England. The event was commemorated about twenty years later in the Bayeux Tapestry, commissioned by William's half brother, Odo, Bishop of Bayeux. A strip of embroidered linen 231 feet long and 19 inches high, the tapestry tells its dramatic story in Latin text and vivid pictures. Here workmen fell trees and plane boards, while shipwrights construct the vessels for William's invasion fleet.

At the height of the Battle of Hastings, men and horses tumble to the ground in wild confusion. The English are usually depicted with long hair and mustaches, and using the deadly two-handed English battle-ax as well as lances and swords. Going into battle, the Normans shouted: "*Dex Aie!*" (God help us!). The laconic English replied: "*Ut!*" (Get out!). In the section at left, a mustachioed English knight bashes the head of a Norman's horse with his ax, just as another Norman lunges at him from behind with his sword. In the

William's fleet of Viking "dragon ships" arrives at Pevensey, on England's Channel coast. The duke's flagship, in the center, flies a banner with a cross given him by the Pope, and bears on its sternpost an effigy of his son Rufus carrying a pennant and a trumpet. The horses William took with him, some of which are seen in the ships before and behind his own, gave the invaders a great advantage over the English, who lacked well-trained cavalry. They rode their horses up to the battle lines, then dismounted to fight on foot.

section at right a group of English yeomen make a stand on a hill. At far right, under his name ODO, is the bishop himself, wielding a Norman war mace. The upper border is filled with heraldic beasts, the lower with corpses. The long Latin text reads: "Here English and French fell together in battle." The remainder of the tapestry describes the death of Harold, last of the Saxon kings, and the ragged English rout. William was crowned in London on Christmas Day but it took five years before all England acknowledged his rule.

Arthur, the Chivalric King

THE figure who towers above all others in the legend of medieval chivalry is King Arthur—Christian ruler, wise soldier and model of knighthood. The historic Arthur was a Celtic chieftain who, after the Romans left Britain in the fifth century, led his countrymen against the invading Angles and Saxons. In the Battle of Mount Badon in 500 he defeated the Saxons so badly that they let the Britons alone for nearly fifty years. Centuries after his death, chroniclers began weaving fanciful tales about Arthur and the knights of his Round Table. Wandering troubadours endowed him with supernatural majesty in secular ballads, and the Church claimed him as the embodiment of the perfect Christian king. This King Arthur tapestry, woven toward the end of the fourteenth century, is one of the earliest representations of Britain's hero. He is enthroned in a cathedral, surrounded by bishops and archbishops with croziers. At the far left are two of his knights.

The hunt begins (*left*) when the hunter, probably the future King Francis I (*second from left*), and his companions hold their hounds at the forest edge. In a tree at upper right a lookout beckons that he has sighted the unicorn.

Hunted down (*left*), the unicorn kneels and dips its horn in a stream flowing from a fountain, the symbol of the waters of eternal life. Hunters marvel at the sight. The "A E" in the tapestry are the first and last letters of Anne.

Surrounded (*right*) near the king's castle, the unicorn is threatened by the hunters' spears. The letters "F R" at top center were added later, probably when the set of tapestries was presented to King Francis I (*Franciscus Rex*).

The Capture of a Unicorn

THE springtime splendor of the noble's life in the Middle Ages is nowhere expressed more joyously than in the famous series of sixteenth century tapestries known as *The Unicorn Hunt.* In elaborate and realistic detail they show three plumed hunters setting forth with their servants and hounds to capture the mythical one-horned beast in a flowery forest. Every face is a small gem of portraiture. Every bird, plant and animal is bursting with life.

For medieval men, with their love of symbolism and hidden meanings, the unicorn had both a religious and an erotic significance. In one sense it stood for the wounded and risen Christ. In another, it was a swift and unconquerable beast which could be tamed only by a virgin. When it was captured and chained it stood for a consummated marriage—an appropriate allusion in these tapestries, which were originally woven as a gift for Anne of Brittany when she married King Louis XII of France. Two tapestries were added fifteen years later to honor Francis I, who succeeded Louis.

At bay (*right*), the unicorn flails the air with its hoofs and gores one of the eager hounds with its long sharp horn. The spearmen stand ready, poised for the kill.

The unicorn (*shown twice in the scene at left*) is slain, then draped over a horse to be brought to Louis and Anne. From the castle, servants watch the excitement. Resurrected (*above*), the philosophic unicorn rests in a flowery pasture under the shade of a pomegranate tree, symbol of fertility.

Queen of Two Lands And of the Courts of Love

THE first grand lady of the Middle Ages, the only woman ever to be queen of both England and France and the richest heiress of her day, was Eleanor of Aquitaine. Her two husbands were kings, two of her sons were kings and two of her daughters were kings' wives. But though Eleanor made history as easily as some women make quilts, she is remembered mostly as a patron of the troubadours, of the courts of love and of the courtly styles which the unicorn tapestries on the previous pages exemplify.

Eleanor was born in 1122 in southern France, where the climate is friendly to lovers. Her father, Duke William, ruled the rich province of Aquitaine. Upon his death Eleanor at the age of fifteen fell heir to twice as much land as even the king of France could boast. That same year she herself became the queen of France as the bride of King Louis VII. Her husband, then sixteen, was a pious, rather monkish monarch who loved his passionate young wife so dearly that he took her with him on the Second Crusade to the Holy Land.

In the East, Eleanor was the center of wild parties and, later, of considerable gossip about her relations with her uncle, Prince Raymond. Whatever the truth, Eleanor's husband was distressed both by her reputation and by the fact that she had borne him one daughter, no sons. The Pope himself had a sober talk with the royal couple. Back in France, Eleanor gave birth to her second child, but it was again a daughter.

PERHAPS the greatest mistake Eleanor made was that she took being a queen too seriously. She had a queenly instinct to found a strong dynasty and this led her to look with favor upon the bull-necked young duke of Normandy, Henry Plantagenet. Henry in his turn was impressed by Eleanor's worldly charms and worldly possessions, which still included Aquitaine. After a bewildering amount of intrigue King Louis was persuaded in 1152 to divorce Eleanor on the grounds that they were distant cousins whose marriage could not be sanctioned by the Church. Eleanor, once a child bride, now at thirty married a youth of nineteen. Her husband added further to his fortune by inheriting England's throne. In 1154, at Westminster Abbey, Henry II and Eleanor were crowned king and queen of England.

As Europe's leading queen, Eleanor was the special patroness of the poets and troubadours who had enlivened her court in Aquitaine and had followed her to Paris and London. The troubadour was a mixture of knight, sycophant, gigolo and poet. He was usually recruited from the ranks of poor knights' younger sons, but his anomalous position as a court hanger-on was not dishonorable. He was a product of French logic: in a country where most marriages were made strictly for business it was sensible for a woman to take a lover of her own choosing. Since it was unthinkable that affairs be carried on with unseemly haste, there were four fixed stages which a troubadour must traverse before he won his lady:

Stage 1. Worship from afar: The lover claimed that a mere glimpse of her turned winter's ice into rosebuds.

Stage 2. Declaration: He confessed his love openly, saying, "You have put me in a fire."

Stage 3. Self-praise: "My valiance and my superiority are things known. . . . I kiss the ladies and overthrow the knights."

Stage 4. Acceptance: Says he, "I have given myself. . . . Her beauty is as gold refined in the fire."

When the troubadour was not engaged in an active campaign for love, he entertained the court by relating problems of a lover and his lady, setting his little stories to music. His musical debates were so fascinating to Eleanor's courtiers that they invented their own debates and thus started the famous courts of love, which convened either in a garden or around the fire in the big hall. Eleanor herself, as the queen of the courts of love, was the presiding judge.

The noble face of Eleanor of Aquitaine (*left*) looks out from the capital of a medieval pillar. Next to her is her second husband, Henry II.

The courts discussed such questions as whether a young man should reject the love of an older woman, or whether a lover, having been repudiated by a lady, should be welcomed back in her embrace. At first the cases decided by the courts were theoretical, but sometimes a confused lover would anonymously submit a real question in writing and wait for trial. In her verdict, Eleanor gave advice as if she were running a modern newspaper column for the lovelorn.

FOR all her amorous wisdom, Eleanor could not hold her own husband and, though she lived in a society that encouraged infidelity, she took Henry's philandering bitterly. Nevertheless, she bore him three daughters and five sons. One daughter became queen of Sicily, another, queen of Castile. Two of her sons were among England's most renowned monarchs—Richard I (The Lion-hearted) and John I, who granted the Magna Charta. Eleanor urged her sons to revolt against their father, and Henry was forced to imprison and restrict his wife for fourteen years.

After her release Eleanor showed no disposition to retire from medieval history. When her favorite son, Richard, was captured after the Third Crusade, Eleanor tried to free him by challenging the Pope. She wrote, "Two sons yet survived to my solace, who now survive only to distress me. . . . King Richard is detained in bonds, and John, his brother, depopulates the captive's kingdom with the sword and lays it waste with fire. . . . Restore my son to me then, O man of God, if indeed thou art a man of God, and not a man of blood. . . ." The Pope persuaded Richard's captors to release him, but for a large ransom.

Old age—she lived far beyond the normal medieval span—had little effect on Queen Eleanor's energy. When she was eighty-one she successfully directed the defense of her castle against the attacks of one of her grandsons. Only after that did Eleanor finally retire at Poitiers in Aquitaine. Here in her ancestral province, having outlived her husband and most of her children, she died at eighty-two.

Carcassonne in southern France is a perfect medieval walled city. The counts of Carcassonne around 1100 made it into one of the most modern bastions of the day. They withstood the king and northern barons, who finally took the town by treachery and proceeded to fortify it further. In the past century the town has been much restored.

The game of *lourche* was much like the modern game of backgammon. The loser was left "in the *lourche*."

A wandering peddler shows a noble lady his wares, including such items as mirrors, girdles, belts and purses.

Dancing was a prime diversion in the castles. Here an elegant lord and his lady step into a stately pavan, accompanied by the decorous but dissonant music of two primitive flutes and an ancient bagpipe.

Walled Town and Castle

THE castle was medieval man's refuge from a hostile world. Crude early castles were built in the ninth century when powerful nobles began to establish their own local strongholds. At their bases huddled the villages whose peasants tilled the nobles' land. With increased knowledge of fortification, battlements became more elaborate and sometimes whole cities were enclosed within their walls (*above*).

With its livestock and crops, its ovens and mill, the castle was a self-sufficient unit that could hold out for months against siege. Inside, it was far from comfortable. Rooms were dark and drafty. Floors were strewn with rushes, which gathered dirt and vermin, though for special events they might be sweetened with sprigs of mint. Privies, which were not uncommon, were over the moat. Fowl had the run of the place, and grand ladies often had to shoo hens from their chambers. There was little privacy, maids often sharing a lady's room. But the castle was an exciting place. Dancing and feasting enlivened its halls. Peddlers came to its gates and travelers stopped for shelter, bringing welcome news of the world.

In this manuscript illustration, a walled town is besieged by an army camped all around in tents. If a city refused to be starved out and if direct attack failed, besiegers often dug tunnels under the walls.

Two levels of lawmaking are described in a fifteenth century calendar. The scene at the left shows the duke of Normandy in session with his nobles, handing down a verdict. The other scenes give the sequence of a less august case. Reading down from top center: two men argue about a pot, get into a fight over it and are arrested by the duke's officers. At top right, a magistrate swears in witnesses.

Torture was used to punish or to force confession. On the rack a prisoner has his limbs broken by a wheel. Others are boiled in oil.

A king's charter gave special rights. Here a ruler hands charters to deserving barons. The greatest of all charters was Magna Charta.

Law Courts and Parliament

THE development of law during the Middle Ages was a painfully slow process, but it brought man closer to his present concept of justice and representative government. Trial by ordeal and combat gave way to the court trial based on sworn evidence and, by the end of the Middle Ages, to trial by jury. The first juries were meetings of local elders, or doomsmen, who assisted the judge. English kings developed the concept of a grand jury to indict criminals, and later, a petit jury to try them.

In the twelfth century, English and French rulers appointed specialized ministers to advise them and work at the expanding tasks of government. This greatly strengthened the king's administration and created the forerunners of modern cabinets. Parliaments got their start when English kings began to call assemblies of great nobles to give advice and sanction taxes. Later, minor knights and townsmen were added and by the fourteenth century, parliament had become an effective check on the king's power. The parliament shown was called by Edward I, probably in 1279. Seated around the outer benches are Church dignitaries and secular peers. In the center, the judiciary sits on woolsacks, while at the bottom, behind two clerks holding scrolls, are the representatives of the commons.

Commerce was heavy along the rivers. Here townsmen load a boat with goods while guards stand nearby to protect them against robbers.

Merchants and Manufacturers

As growing political stability permitted the opening up of new areas and production of food increased, a surplus became available to feed people who did not spend their time in agriculture. Nourished by this surplus, the medieval cities grew and, along with them, the tradesmen's guilds.

Originally all merchants belonged to one guild. Later, separate guilds were established for tanners, millers, bakers and for every other trade or profession. Each guild worked out its own system of price control and stabilized workmanship and materials used in its products. It determined the number of years an apprentice must work before he became a full-fledged member and settled on fair wages and working hours.

In commercial towns like Ghent the guildsmen were influential in government and Church. Meetings were held in guildhalls like those at the right. Regularly the guild threw a wine-drinking party at which the brothers were asked to check their arms and wooden shoes at the door lest, warmed by wine, they use them as weapons.

A medieval illustrator describes the making of glass: digging for fine sand (*top*); blowing hot glass (*bottom*); testing finished product (*left*).

Guildhalls (*right*) in the Belgian town of Ghent still stand along the Lys River. From right are: the House of the Free Boatmen; the House of the Grain Measurers; the tiny customs house; the Staple House; the guildhall of the masons.

The great stone keep of the Duc de Berry's château at Vincennes still stands, almost as it was when painted for the December scene of the Book of Hours (*see p. 70*).

The Book of Hours

IN 1409, the Duc de Berry, possibly the wealthiest man in all of France, announced that he wanted the most handsome book of hours ever created. Since the duke was accustomed to getting what he wanted, nobody thought his announcement presumptuous. His favorite court artist, Pol Malouel, called de Limbourg (after his birthplace in Flanders), set right to work.

A book of hours was a kind of illustrated calendar for the pious, containing devotions for every week of the year, religious texts, prayers to the Virgin, psalms of penitence, litanies of the saints, along with the signs of the zodiac and charts of the moon's phases. What the duke required, in addition to all these, was a work of art which would celebrate the kind of life he had lived. De Limbourg gave him both in fullest measure, creating one of the world's most exquisite art treasures and glorifying the life of the Middle Ages at its most sophisticated peak.

The man whose court and times are perpetuated in this book, the Duc de Berry, is seen on the opposite page at his banquet table. As a brother of King Charles V of France, he owned most of northwestern France and his many palaces are painted on the pages of his book. Like an American tycoon shuttling across country from one branch office to another, the duke was forever moving among his estates, hunting at Vincennes, boating at Poitiers, overseeing the construction he had ordered at Bourges or Riom. Building was a passion with the duke. His distracted architect was always in hot pursuit of his peripatetic patron and scarcely had time to organize the materials and craftsmen at one château before he was forced to supervise a job at the next royal residence.

Besides being a notable patron of art, the duke was also an inveterate collector of natural oddities, who assembled a whale's tooth, a porcupine quill, ostrich eggs, "the jaw of a giant" (probably an elephant's molar) and a "horn" from the mythical unicorn. His menagerie, which included a special aviary for nightingales, was stocked with swans, dogs and a favorite bear that followed its master from castle to castle in a small chariot. Ailing pets were treated with ointments and plasters and any dog suffering from rabies was treated by being plunged into sea water.

The staff of the ducal household was big enough to fill a town. At the château of Mehun alone was Simonet Garnier, keeper of greyhounds; Simonet Besançon, keeper of dogs; the abbess of Villiers, keeper of little dogs; Jean d'Espagne, keeper of the chamois; Henri Bar, keeper of the dromedary; and Guillaume Merlin, keeper of the ostrich. The ducal retinue also included bands of musicians, gardeners, tailors, embroiderers, clockmakers, glassmakers and a character pleasantly called "Jehannet le Fol, hermit of the lord."

To maintain such a unique assemblage, the duke was constantly conniving for money and constantly in debt. He even denied his daughters a proper dowry in order to make life easy for his nightingales. In the duke's last years, the Paris rabble, who had hated him for his profligacy, pillaged his château and howled at his gates.

THE arrogant duke did not live long enough to see his precious book of hours completed. De Limbourg had finished ten and a half pages (all but November and half of September) when, in 1416, the duke died. His heirs, appalled at his extravagances, ordered the work stopped. In 1485, the Duc de Savoie, who had obtained the book, commissioned Jean Colombe to finish it. Colombe was also a superb artist and the Duc de Berry would have been quite content with the way he finished one of the richest records of a rich age.

January

In the first of the series of the Book of Hours miniatures, the duke sits down on a bright January day to a meal in the castle hall. The duke, clad in a blue gown and fur hat, chats with his red-robed priest while a court chamberlain, holding his staff of office, invites a queue of courtiers to approach and receive New Year's gifts. Some strapping young knights of the court walk around the table sampling the fare of roast game and fowl, and two puppies roam the table at will, gobbling from the dishes. On the wall in back is a huge tapestry depicting historic battle scenes.

February

On a bitter cold midwinter day a red-capped peasant and his womenfolk warm themselves at the open hearth while another (*right*), blowing on chilled fingers, hastens back to the hut through the farmyard. In the forest nearby a young man hews wood for the farmhouse fire and along a road behind him a fagot-laden donkey is prodded toward the village. Inscribed in Latin on the tympanum above is the Julian calendar for February, the month of Aquarius the Water Bearer and Pisces the Fish. Across the sky rides Phoebus, the sun god, his chariot drawn by winged horses.

March

In the first days of spring the duke's peasants are out plowing the fields with their yoke of oxen and trimming the grapevines in the walled vineyard. This is the land around the Château de Lusignan, one of the Duc de Berry's favorite residences. The castle is famous as the setting for an old French fairy tale about a bewitched noblewoman named Mélusine who every Saturday became a serpent from her waist down. When her husband, Raymondin, discovered her plight, Mélusine was turned into a dragon (*upper right*) and spent the rest of her days haunting the castle towers.

April

In the meadows of the Château de Dourdan, court maidens kneel in their flowing robes to pick spring wild flowers. At left, the noble in the red cap and the young lady with the long golden hair plight their troth by exchanging rings in the presence of witnesses. In the garden at right, fruit trees, bound and trimmed, are bursting into bloom. Two fishermen haul their net in the small lake in front of the fortress. Inside these high walls the Duc de Berry kept some of the choicest samples of the goldsmith's art as well as many of the illuminated volumes from his great medieval library.

May

The festival of the first of May and the full flowering of spring were celebrated by the Duc de Berry's gallant company—as they were in other courts of medieval France—by the wearing of "gay green" dresses and garlands of leaves. Here beneath the towers of Riom a cavalcade rides through the woods behind a troupe of merry trumpeters. The occasion is graced by the presence of a prince of the royal blood, dressed in the king's colors—black, white, red. The dogs in the foreground seem to be the same puppies that dined on the duke's table in the January miniature.

June

From the Hôtel de Nesles, his residence on the left bank of the Seine in Paris, the Duc de Berry could look down in the month of June on this gentle agrarian scene just west of the Ile de la Cité. Beyond the peasants, cutting and gathering in hay, and across the river rises the royal palace occupied by King Charles VI before he moved to the Louvre. To the left, within the palace grounds, are the twin orange towers of the Conciergerie which is still intact and where in 1793 Marie Antoinette was imprisoned. At right are the high cross and the ornate Gothic spires of the Sainte-Chapelle.

July

In the rich land around the Château de Poitiers, which was built in the shape of a triangle where the Clain and the Boivre rivers meet, the duke's farmers are shearing sheep and reaping the July wheat with its scattering of wild poppies. Built in the twelfth century, Poitiers was remodeled for the duke by a famous medieval castle architect named Guy de Dammartin. After the Duc de Berry's death, King Charles VII moved to Poitiers. The château served as this fainthearted French king's court until Joan of Arc prevailed on him to engage the English at the siege of Orléans.

August

Introduced into Europe by the Saracens, falconry became one of the Christian gentry's favorite diversions. Here, not far from Paris, a party rides out to the hunt near the duke's Château d'Étampes. Leading the hunt is the falconer, who carries a decoy at his waist and two hunting hawks on his wrist. His dogs are trained to point the game before the falcons are released. The first gentleman, with the lady riding behind him, is sending his falcon after a pheasant or a hare. In the fields around the château, peasants, harvesting the wheat, take time out for cooling dips in the small stream.

September

This miniature of grape harvesting at the Château de Saumur is the work of two artists. Pol de Limbourg had not completed his work on the September and November pages of the calendar when the Duc de Berry died and the project was halted. For this page, de Limbourg had sketched the whole scene and painted in the castle. When work on the book was resumed sixty-nine years later at the order of the Duc de Savoie, Jean Colombe took up where de Limbourg had left off, painting in the peasants gathering the grapes in the vineyards, which still produce the wines of Saumur.

October

From his Paris residence, looking in another direction over the Seine, the duke had a magnificent view of the old Louvre. On this sunny October afternoon, citizens of Paris promenade along the riverbank in front of the palace just as they do today. In the duke's flat meadows on the left bank of the river men are harrowing the fields and sowing grain for the early spring crops. Birds cluster in the furrows and to keep them out of a section already sown with grain, the peasants have placed a network of strings hung with flapping white rags and a scarecrow decked out as an archer.

November

This realistic scene, which might have taken place on any of the duke's estates in western France, is entirely the work of Jean Colombe. He does full justice to the stocky French peasants and the vibrant colors of late autumn. Here a swineherd hurls his heavy stick into the branches of oak trees to bring down a shower of acorns for his hogs. The long-snouted swine which resemble their remote ancestor, the wild pig, have to forage for themselves in the forest. Fattened on the fall harvest of nuts, they will be slaughtered and salted down for the duke's staple winter fare.

December

On a frosty morning in the forest of Vincennes near Paris, a wild boar is brought to bay by the duke's huntsmen. One of the ravenous pack of hunting hounds has to be pulled off by the ears to keep him from tearing his prey apart before the boar is given the *coup de grâce* with spears. Over the tawny winter woods rise the tall keep and the seven square towers of the castle of Vincennes where the Duc de Berry was born. This succulent boar, which had roamed wild in the duke's woods, ended its days in the month of Christmas served up almost whole on the duke's banquet table.

RENAISSANCE MAN

One family, the Medici, catches like a jewel in its many facets the full glory of the Renaissance. A wool carder by trade and an affable, democratic man by nature, the great Cosimo de' Medici became the benevolent despot of Florence in 1419. His grandson, Lorenzo the Magnificent, was the patron of Leonardo, Pico and Michelangelo, and a fine poet in his own right. By the time of Cosimo I, whose splendor is witnessed in this bronze bust by Benvenuto Cellini, the Medici had made a dozen popes and had seized power in half of Italy.

III

RENAISSANCE MAN

IN the fourteenth century the intellectual and spiritual climate of Europe was changing. The Middle Ages were not yet dead but dying, and a new era was struggling into life. This was the Renaissance, which began in Italy and swept north across the Continent.

Italy in the preceding century had been like the corner of a garden where the sun strikes warmest. While other Europeans were still at work on the problem, Italians had completed the development of a language. By trading east and west, Italians had accumulated fortunes which they were ready to spend, if someone could show them how. The rulers of their city-states, despotic and warring though they were, at least offered periods of calm and stability. The whole peninsula was ready to burst into flower at the breath of a warm wind.

This breath the Italians found in the classics. For many centuries, in their own libraries and in others all around the Mediterranean, the works of Homer, Plato and Aristotle, of Horace, Cicero and Ovid had lain forgotten. For centuries statues, urns and tombs of incredible beauty had lain buried. Then suddenly, prompted by three great heralds of the Renaissance, the poets Dante and Petrarch and the prose writer Boccaccio, Italians began to rediscover them. A great wave of delight swept over the land, as fragment by fragment, the cultures of Greece and Rome again emerged. Scholars and merchants, priests and courtiers, princes and soldiers began to dig and collect, to read and translate. So enraptured were Italians by antiquity that they turned savagely on the nearer past and coined the scornful term "Dark Ages." To the soaring architecture of that period they gave the word "gothic," meaning "barbarous." At each new classical discovery they applauded, wept and worshiped. Even much later, when the famous Laocoön group was excavated, it was drawn through the streets on a triumphal car. Cannons boomed and church bells pealed while onlookers pelted the statue with flowers.

FIRED by the classics, Italians orgiastically began to re-examine and explore two vast fields: man, and the world. They looked at their own bodies and found them not shameful and corrupt but beautiful, alive, warm and lovely. The mind of man was not a storage space for superstition and the lore of doom. The world was not a gloomy antechamber, nor man a diseased wretch waiting guiltily until death admitted him to the room beyond. Italians looked about them, and their cry of exultation was epitomized by the greatest of Renaissance poets, Shakespeare, in words that might have been uttered at the creation: "This goodly frame, the earth . . . this most excellent canopy, the air, look you, this brave o'erhanging firmament, this majestical roof fretted with golden fire. . . . What a piece of work is a man! How noble in reason! how infinite in faculty! in form, in moving, how express and admirable! in action how like an angel! in apprehension how like a god!"

All over the Italian peninsula a wonderful coruscation of life erupted and shimmered in the sun. It was semipagan, it

One man, Leonardo da Vinci, shown in this self-portrait in chalk, embodied in his vast nature almost the whole civilization of the Renaissance. Not only a great artist, he was the first engineer of his day and one of the most daring scientific experimenters of all time.

was violent, it was lustful and reckless, but beautiful and fascinating beyond words. On one day, the whole of Rome was in a paroxysm of delight over the perfectly preserved body of a Roman girl, dead a thousand years, found in a tomb. On the next, a newly unearthed book of Cicero sent scholars into ecstasy. Strange animals and fabulous foodstuffs came from overseas; witches were discovered in Parma; Venice, called by a contemporary observer "the greatest eunuch factory in Europe," fulfilled a profitable contract with the Turks; the Medici developed a wonderful new strain of falcons; some hopeless fool defended the idea that the world was not flat. Self-expression became the consuming desire and the glory of men. The age of the individual had arrived.

IN the streets, a spangle of passing colors showed in the bright daylight. There might be a pageant or a procession or a troop of gaily dressed cavalry with flapping pennons. Every day there was the bravo with his long hose tight on his swelling calf, sword on thigh and short cloak swinging; the artisan in his apron trudging under a load; the courtesan with her bleached yellow hair curled and stiffened; the master craftsman or merchant in a long cloak; the cardinal in scarlet, the visiting ambassador in ermine, the lady in brocade with a gold band on her hair. In Florence for a time, so brave was the insistence of the ostentatious individual, no man would dress like another.

Into this age in the year 1405, to the family of a lesser noble, was born Aeneas Sylvius Piccolomini, the eldest of eighteen children and named, as countless of his contemporaries were named, after a classical hero. Although he was not to become one of the greatest men of his times, Aeneas's life and thoughts were to reflect those times so accurately that he would be known, five centuries after his death, as "a mirror of the Renaissance." Pinturicchio's paintings of Piccolomini's career, shown in the four following pages, reflect the rich pageant of the ambitious Renaissance man's life.

At eighteen, having studied with a village priest, Aeneas went to Siena and enrolled in its university. He went without supper three times a week to save money to buy manuscripts. He labored over Latin texts, learned to speak in imitation of Cicero, to write in imitation of Boccaccio. But since education was merely a part of what the Renaissance demanded of its ideal *l'uòmo universále*, the universal man, Aeneas also learned how to sing and dance in Siena's famous festivals and what to say when he lay beside the fountains with those he called "pleasant ladies."

In 1425 the famous monk Bernardino da Siena so moved Italians by his attacks on the decay of the times that they tossed all articles of vanity, wigs as well as jewelry, into a great fire. Aeneas himself was tormented by the conflict that repeatedly disquieted Renaissance man, the conflict between earthly and spiritual values. Under Bernardino's influence he decided to turn monk, but his friends dissuaded him.

As a young man, Aeneas surveyed the fields in which he might become successful—in the Renaissance, talent could open almost any door—and chose the Church. He became secretary to a bishop and in 1432, at twenty-seven, went to the Council of Basel.

Something like representative government had developed in such councils, where churchmen from all over Europe met to conduct Church affairs. On this occasion the reigning Pope in Rome, Eugenius IV, feared the delegates were assuming too much power and ordered the council dissolved. Instead, the churchmen after devious intrigue elected their own Pope, Felix V, and forced Eugenius into temporary exile. This conspiracy did not shock or even surprise Aeneas—conspiracy was then so common that two Italians could scarcely meet without engaging in it. And exile for Eugenius, although unpleasant, was really a minor matter inasmuch as he might well have been poisoned to death. As it was, Aeneas, who throve on intrigue, was involved in a plot to kidnap him, which fortunately did not succeed.

After the Council of Basel, Aeneas prospered. He changed his masters as rapidly as he could do so to his profit, finally becoming secretary to Pope Felix himself. He began to write poetry and prose, including a witty, immoral play. When the rulers of Europe refused to recognize Felix, Aeneas, too, brushed him off and went to Austria to join the retinue of Emperor Frederick III. Frederick, recognizing a brilliant man when he saw one, pronounced Aeneas poet laureate of the Holy Roman Empire and crowned him with a laurel wreath. However, Aeneas's talent for diplomacy was more useful to Frederick than his pen. He accomplished several delicate missions for the emperor, including one which arranged a marriage between Frederick and Eleanora of Portugal, and another which took him back to Rome, where he made his peace with the annoyed Eugenius, now the acknowledged Pope. This done, he began to shuttle back and forth between Rome and Vienna, milking both masters with great skill.

Aeneas Piccolomini was a humanist—a man whose intellectual life was dominated by the newly revived classics, but who had countless other interests as well, and who struggled with hectic violence to live as many lives as possible. In his fortieth year he was a scholar, an orator, a novelist, poet, playwright and politician. He was also a ladies' man, if not an outright rake, as he accused himself of being in his brutally self-critical autobiography. But these accomplishments were not enough. Harried, perhaps tortured, by the same drives that made Lorenzo de' Medici become statesman, financier, poet, musician, patron, Hellenist and playboy, and that led the incomparable Leonardo da Vinci to paint the *Mona Lisa* and *The Last Supper* and meanwhile to be a military engineer, scientist and aeronautical experimenter, Aeneas in middle age embarked on another effort. He had always been close to the Church as a secretary and adviser to ranking officers, but he had never been within it. Accordingly in 1446 he took orders as a subdeacon, "forsaking Venus" as he wrote, although not because he was particularly conscience-stricken. The Church offered many advantages to a talented man—even the papacy was not unthinkable, and on this goal Aeneas set his eyes. Within twelve years he reached it. The achievement is remarkable, almost fantastic, but it becomes credible in the light of the times in which Aeneas moved.

FIFTEENTH century Italy lived under one short creed, propounded by the Florentine architect Alberti: "Men can do all things if they will." Alberti meant first to affirm the soaring belief of the Renaissance in the potency of man.

As a bishop's secretary in 1432, Aeneas Sylvius Piccolomini, age 27, traveled from Siena to Basel, Switzerland. Here (*foreground*) he rides a white stallion, preceded by the red-robed Bishop of Fermo. The entourage, which includes broad-hatted prelates, a page with greyhound and the bishop's grooms, has just reached the walled and fortressed town of Talamone to embark for Genoa on the galleys seen in the harbor. The rainbow and clouds symbolize the storm which almost wrecked their ships before they made port in Genoa.

As poet laureate, crowned by Holy Roman Emperor Frederick III, Piccolomini, now 36, kneels in the presence of a crowd of court retainers and turbaned Orientals. In the background, on the steps of the loggia, two soldiers play cards. Above them, on the balcony, an angry citizen busily beats his wife, three women admire a bouquet of flowers and another woman shakes a cloth from a window. Above them all, in the sky a purposeful hawk, a bird which often appears in Renaissance paintings, pounces upon a flying duck.

As Bishop of Siena, Piccolomini at 46 arranges the marriage of Emperor Frederick III to Eleonora, the 16-year-old daughter of the King of Portugal. Piccolomini is clothed in his magnificent episcopal vestments and a peaked bishop's miter. Standing to the right of the man wearing the cross is Piccolomini's nephew Andrea, whose brother, later Pope Pius III, had Bernardino Pinturicchio paint these frescoes celebrating his predecessor's illustrious memory. In the background is the town of Siena, with its cathedral.

As Pope Pius II, Piccolomini, now 56 and head of the Church for three years, sits on a throne in a chapel while canonizing Catherine of Siena, whose body is shown on a bier at his feet. Surrounding him is a group of cardinals and other clerics holding tapers and reading from the Bible. In the lower half of the fresco are prelates, friars and monks who attended the canonization. Among them (*at left, wearing a blue cape*) is a figure which is thought to be the young painter Raphael, who was a good friend of the artist Pinturicchio.

But by "all things" he meant precisely that—the beautiful and divine, the monstrous and grotesque.

The reigning families of the Renaissance, the despots who governed the city-states, were constantly resorting to atrocity to settle their rivalries. There was a king of Naples who took great pleasure in embalming his enemies and keeping them in a trophy room, handsomely dressed. Borgias, Medici, Carraras, Visconti and Sforzas waded through blood to make themselves masters of some patch of territory no bigger than an American county. In Foligno a tyrant named Corrado captured three hundred members of a rival family, the Rasaglia, cut them into pieces of portable size and loaded them on asses which were paraded through the city for the instruction of the people. In Bologna the Marescotti declared war on the Canetoli and hunted them down in the streets for three days, keeping tally by nailing the steaming hearts of their enemies to a palace door.

In finance, the procedures were less bloody but not less cruel. The bankers of Florence organized the finances for the Crusades and the Hundred Years' War and lent money to almost every court in Europe. (The sign of the Medici, red balls on a field of gold, has been only slightly altered to become the symbol of pawnbrokers throughout the world.) But when they lent money, Florentines charged usury of staggering size. "Twenty-five per cent is nothing at all," said a contemporary maxim, "fifty per cent will pass the time away, and a hundred per cent is interesting." When bankers advanced funds to Edward III of England, a poor risk, they exacted interest of 260 per cent and demanded as security the reverend person of the archbishop of Canterbury. It is a monstrous and also ridiculously funny fact that the archbishop was duly packed off to the Continent and held as collateral.

The golden city of the Medici was set about with towers ten and twelve stories high built for the bankers and businessmen—known as *delle torre*, "towered men." The sun, striking these towers, falling upon the palaces and cathedrals and multicolored pageants, illuminated the time and place with the rare beauty that saturated the Renaissance. While some men screamed and haggled, other men sang. Raphael, da Vinci, Titian and Correggio mixed their paints, undisturbed by the fact that nearby some Borgia mixed his poisons. Donatello and Michelangelo wrought their sculpture, Alberti designed his gardens, untouched by the unbelievable corruption around them.

Learning was no longer the province of monks and theologians; the *magnifico* had leisure for reading as well as for falconry and adultery; and there were restless minds for whom pious reading and medieval romances had grown tedious. The popes long ago had assembled a library of Latin classics and some Greek, and in the "humanist" movement that now began the popes' secretaries were tireless. The copying and collation of newly discovered manuscripts became an industry for hundreds of scribes. A fantastic fervor possessed men of letters. Lorenzo de' Medici's favorite scholar, Poliziano, not only wrote imitatively in Latin and Greek but thought creatively in those languages.

The passion of the Italian humanists to make classical Latin and Greek literature their own became a European passion. The humanist Erasmus of Rotterdam took a Latin first name, Desiderius (the one desired). Into the council chambers of Europe circulated a candid manual of statecraft, *The Prince*, by a retired Florentine diplomat, Niccolò Machiavelli. The princes of Europe, including Henry VIII of England, profited all too well by it.

At this time, a revolutionary invention for duplicating books was put into operation and enormously hastened the diffusion of ideas. If the printing press had been invented two centuries before, Europe would have been filled with copies of the *Romance of the Rose*, the works of St. Thomas, the *Divine Comedy*, the *Song of Roland*. Two centuries later and the craze for Latin and Greek classics would have spent itself; works of all periods would have been printed together. But Gutenberg's press at Mainz, and the first presses in Italy at Subiaco and Venice, were set up in the second half of the fifteenth century, at the height of the humanist revival. As a result, Christendom had all at once to re-absorb the civilization of Greece and Rome.

"The Renaissance," wrote Symonds, "was so dazzling in its brilliance, so confusing in its rapid changes, that moral distinctions were obliterated in a blaze of splendor, an outburst of new life, a carnival of liberated energies." How men chose to use their energies was their own affair—they could do all things, and the atmosphere of a carnival was congenial to sudden greatness or infamy.

IN 1447, only a year after entering the Church, Aeneas Piccolomini became bishop of Trieste, then bishop of his beloved Siena. A year later, still serving both the Pope and Frederick, he was cardinal and prince of the empire, posts he used skillfully, if without scruple, to amass a fortune. In 1458, upon the death of Calixtus III, Aeneas was in a position to strike for the papacy. The favored candidate was the archbishop of Rouen. But Aeneas had behind him a lifetime of experience in such matters, and before the archbishop could marshal his supporters Aeneas was Pope. He chose the name Pius II, remembering Virgil's description, "pious Aeneas."

His election was acclaimed by the swarms of humanists, liberals and libertines with whom he had long associated. But when they flocked to Rome to share in the patronage and favor he seemed certain to dispense, they found him greatly changed. Pius II was a sober Pope, jealous of the dignity of his office, a man who had risen through corruption to become incorrupt. He was deeply moved by the fall of Constantinople to the Turks in 1453, and ceaselessly preached a crusade against them, spending little time in patronizing the arts or awarding sinecures to his friends. For ten years he tried vainly to unite Europe in an effort against the East, and when at last he succeeded it was time for him to die. He left Rome for Venice, intending to set sail from there with an army, but en route he was attacked by a fever which killed him on the 14th of August, 1464, at the age of fifty-eight.

Aeneas, the mirror, reflected both good and evil. He was an individual in an age of individuals, talented, unscrupulous, sometimes immoral, but at the last, noble. All facets of life interested him and he wrote about everything from *The Miseries of Courtiers* to *The Nature and Care of Horses*. He had within him the sense of the wonder and power of man, the sense of spring, lovely and cruel, that was the Renaissance.

The Encounter

The Slaying

The Lady Whose Cruel Heart Was Torn Out for Love

THE favorite author of the Italian Renaissance was Giovanni Boccaccio (1313–1375), whose stories of love and violence were eagerly read and unabashedly imitated. The *Decameron*, which is Boccaccio's most famous work, is a collection of one hundred tales, supposedly told by a group of ten young men and women who fled Florence during an epidemic of the Black Death. Safe in a villa near Fiesole, they whiled the days away telling stories. One of these stories inspired an artist of the school of Botticelli to paint the scenes above. This is the story:

IN Ravenna, that most ancient city of Romagna, there were of old many nobles and gentlemen, among whom was a young man named Nastagio degli Onesti, who became exceedingly rich on the death of his father and an uncle. As happens to young men without a wife, he fell in love with a daughter of Messer Paolo Traversaro, a girl of far more noble birth than he, whom he hoped to win by his actions. But however fair and praiseworthy they were, they not only failed to please her but actually seemed to displease her, so cruelly, harshly and unfriendly did the girl behave. Perhaps this was on account of her rare beauty, perhaps because her lofty and disdainful nobility of birth made her despise him and everything that he liked.

This was so hard for Nastagio to bear that for very grief he often desired to slay himself. But, dreading to do this, he very often determined to leave her or, if he could, to hate her as she hated him. But all this was in vain, for it seemed that the less hope he had, the more his love grew.

AS the young man continued to love and to spend money recklessly, his friends and relatives felt that he was wasting both himself and his possessions. So they often advised and begged him to leave Ravenna, and to go and live somewhere else for a time, to diminish his love and his expense. Nastagio several times made mock of this advice; but unable to say "No" to their repeated solicitations, he agreed to do it. He made great preparations, as if he were going to France or Spain or some other far-off land, mounted his horse, and left Ravenna accompanied by many of his friends. He went to a place about three miles from Ravenna, called Chiassi; and having set up tents and pavilions there, told his friends he meant to stay there and that they should return to Ravenna. There Nastagio led the most extravagant life, inviting different parties of people to dine or sup, as he had been accustomed to do.

Now, in very fine weather about the beginning of May, he began to think of his cruel lady, and ordered his attendants to leave him alone so that he could dream of her at his ease; and in his reverie his footsteps led him into the pine woods. The fifth hour of the day was already spent, and he was a good half mile inside the woods, forgetful of food and everything else, when suddenly he thought he heard a loud lamentation and the wild shrieks of a woman. Breaking off his sweet reverie, he raised his head to see what it was, and to his surprise found himself in the pine forest. But, in addition, as he looked in front of him he saw coming toward him a very beautiful girl, naked, with disordered hair, and all scratched by the thorns and twigs of the brambles and bushes in the wood. She was weeping and calling for mercy. Beside her he saw two very large, fierce mastiffs, savagely pursuing her, and frequently snapping cruelly at her; and behind her on a black horse was a dark knight, with grief and anger in his face, with a sword in his hand, who often threatened her with death in dreadful and insulting terms.

This aroused astonishment and terror in his soul, and finally compassion for the unfortunate lady, from which was born the desire to set her free from such agony and such a death, if he could. But, finding himself unarmed, he ran to tear off a tree bough in place of a cudgel, and began to advance toward the dogs and the knight. But the knight saw him, and called to him from a distance:

"Nastagio, don't meddle here, let me and these dogs do what this wicked woman has deserved."

AS he spoke the dogs seized the girl by the thighs, bringing her to the ground, and the knight dismounted from his horse. Nastagio went up to him, and said:

"I do not know who you are, though you seem to know me; but I tell you it is baseness in an armed knight to want to kill a naked woman, and to have set dogs at her, as if she were a wild beast. I shall certainly defend her as far as I can."

Then said the knight:

"Nastagio, I am of the same country as yourself, and you were still a little child when I, whose name was Messer Guido degli Anastagi, was more deeply in love with this woman than you now are with your Traversaro. Owing to her cruelty and pride, my misfortune caused me in despair to kill myself with the sword you see in my hand, and I am damned to eternal punishment. Not long afterward, she, who had rejoiced exceedingly at my death, died also, and died unrepentant, believing that she had not sinned but done well; but for the sin of her cruelty and of her rejoicing at my torments, she too was and is damned to the punishments of hell. When she descended into hell, the punishment imposed upon us was that she should fly from me and that I, who once loved her so much,

The Banquet

The Wedding

should pursue her as a mortal enemy, not as a beloved woman. As often as I catch her I kill her with the very sword with which I slew myself, and split her open, and drag out (as you will soon see) that hard cold heart, wherein love and pity could never enter, together with her entrails, and give them to these dogs to eat.

"After no long space of time, in accordance with the justice and the will of God, she rises up again as if she had not been dead, and once more begins her anguished flight, and I and the dogs pursue her. Every Friday at this hour I catch up with her here and slaughter her as you will see. And do not think that we rest on other days. I catch her in other places where she thought or wrought cruelly against me. Having changed from a lover to an enemy, as you see, I am condemned in this way to pursue her for as many years as the months she was cruel to me. Now let me execute divine justice, and strive not to oppose what you cannot prevent."

Nastagio was terrified by these words, and there was scarcely a hair of his body which did not stand on end. He drew back and gazed at the miserable girl, awaiting fearfully what the knight would do. When the knight had done speaking, he rushed like a mad dog at the girl with his sword in his hand, while she, held on her knees by the mastiffs, shrieked for mercy. But he thrust his sword with all his strength through the middle of her breast until it stood out behind her back. When the girl received this thrust, she fell forward still weeping and shrieking. The knight took a dagger in his hand, slit her open, took out her heart and everything near it, and threw them to the mastiffs who hungrily devoured them at once.

But before long the girl suddenly rose to her feet as if nothing had happened, and began to run toward the sea, with the dogs continually snapping at her. The knight took his sword, remounted his horse and followed; and in a short time they were so far away that Nastagio lost sight of them. After seeing these things, Nastagio hesitated a long time between pity and fear; but after some time it occurred to him that it might be useful to him, since it happened every Friday. So, having marked the place, he returned to his servants, and in due course sent for many of his relatives and friends, to whom he said:

"You have long urged me to refrain from loving my fair enemy and to cease my expense. I am ready to do so, if you will do me one favor—which is that next Friday you will come and dine with me, and bring Messer Paolo Traversaro, his wife, his daughter, all their women relatives, and any other women you like. Why I want this you will see later."

They thought this a very small thing to do. So they returned to Ravenna, and invited those whom Nastagio wanted. And although it was hard to get the girl whom Nastagio loved, still she went along with the rest. Nastagio made preparations for a magnificent feast, and had the tables set among the pines near the place where he had seen the massacre of the cruel lady. He placed the men and women at table in such a manner that the girl he loved was exactly opposite the place where this would happen.

The last course had arrived when they all began to hear the despairing shrieks of the pursued lady. Everyone was astonished and asked what it was. Nobody knew. They stood up to look, and saw the agonized girl and the dogs and the knight. And in a very short time they all arrived in front of them. Great was the uproar against knight and dogs, and many started forward to help the girl. But the knight, speaking to them as he had spoken to Nastagio, not only made them draw back, but filled them with astonishment and terror. He did what he had done before; and all the women, many of whom were relatives of the suffering girl and of the knight, and remembered his love and death, wept as wretchedly as if it had been done to themselves.

When the massacre was over, and the lady and the knight had gone, those who had seen it fell into different sorts of discourse. But the most frightened was the cruel lady beloved by Nastagio, who had distinctly seen and heard everything, and knew that these things came nearer to her than to anyone else, for she remembered the cruelty with which she had always treated Nastagio. So that in her mind's eye she already seemed to be flying from his rage and to feel the mastiffs at her sides.

Such fear was born in her from this that, to avoid its happening to her, she could scarcely wait for that evening to change her hate into love and to send a trusted maid-servant secretly to Nastagio, begging him to go to see her, because she was ready to do anything he pleased. Nastagio replied that this was a happiness to him but that he desired his pleasure with honor, which was to take her as his wife, if she would agree. The girl knew that she herself had been the only obstacle to this hitherto, and replied that she was willing. So making herself the messenger, she told her father and mother that she was willing to marry Nastagio, which greatly delighted them. Next Sunday Nastagio married her and made a wedding feast, and lived happily with her for a long time.

Nor was this the only good which resulted from this terrifying apparition, for all the ladies of Ravenna took fear, and from that time on became far more compliant to the pleasures of the men than they had ever been before.

In Elegant Villas The Rich Went Rustic

"ROUND about Florence," says a fourteenth century chronicle, "lie many villas in a transparent atmosphere, amid cheerful scenery, and with a splendid view; there is little fog and no injurious winds; all is good, and the water pure and healthy. Of the numerous buildings many are like palaces, many like castles costly and beautiful to behold." Italy was full of such pleasant country places during the Renaissance. Some of the more splendid ones were designed and adorned by great artists.

To decorate their magnificent villa on the mainland north of Venice, the Barbaro family hired Paolo Veronese, one of the great Venetian masters. Working with his brother, the artist filled his murals with the glowing figures of classical gods. Then, in an astonishing burst of realism, he painted on the walls his own friends and patrons, looking like flesh-and-blood people caught peering through half-open doors or gazing down from ornate balconies. These masterpieces of *trompe l'oeil* (eye-fooling) art appear on the three following pages.

Life in the country houses attained a refinement of naturalness that had not been known in Europe since the elegant rustications of the ancient Romans. Shaded from the sun in the cool bosk of a grove, breathing air refreshed by the plashing of a fountain, well-educated men and women sipped cool wines, laughed softly and spoke low in the musical Tuscan tongue. They spoke of Platonic love, the plots of popes, two ways to train a falcon and three to cut a peach, the glories of their art, the briefness of their lives. And at night, in the fragrant gardens, by the glimmer of many lanterns, they saw a masque or heard a poet read and, to the sensuous irking of flutes, made courtly love.

It was the fashion of wealthy Italians in the Renaissance to adorn their villas with architectural fantasies. This fifteenth century drawing shows the neoclassical fane of a villa garden, in which two Italian aristocrats, personified as Paris and Helen of Troy, languish lovingly.

"Whoever does not go to the office," said a Renaissance proverb, "is a thief." Since wealthy Italians were as assiduous in business as they were in pleasure, much of the year was spent in town. A man of quality lived in his easeful *casa*, or town house, and enjoyed a leisurely round of dances and dinner parties. Such a party, crowded with guests, is shown in this panel by an unknown Florentine artist.

The eye is masterfully cheated in the main hall of the Villa Maser. Only the marble rack (*lower right*) and the molding around and above the door have three dimensions. Columns, niches, musicians—even the child in the doorway—are flat as the wall they are painted on.

The grand vaulted ceiling of the villa's Olympus Room is enriched with Veronese frescoes of Greco-Roman deities. At the summit, Immortality is enshrined in light, and around her (*left to right*) sit

Mercury, Diana and Saturn. Sledge-wielding Vulcan fills the panel at left, and fruit-bearing Cybele the one at right. The balcony, along with the villa's mistress and the other figures on it, is an illusion.

The Isola Bella's Theatre d'Eau is a sculpture gallery alfresco. It stands at the summit of the verdant isle, which was once a barren rock. All the soil for the gardens was brought from forty miles away.

The Fine Art of Landscape

THE Italians have a word that the rest of Europe has borrowed —alfresco. For in Italy, more than in any other country of Europe, life has been lived in the fresh air. In summer, when every blind is shut against the scorching sun, the Italian house is an airless hotbox; in winter, when the moisture drips from the thick stone walls, it is rather like a furnished tomb. Yet at all Italian seasons it is pleasant to be in the open air. Upon this premise, in the Renaissance, a fine art of landscape was developed. The father of this art was the architect, musician, classicist and scholar Leon Battista Alberti, one of the first "universal men" of the Renaissance. Its masterpieces are the outdoor parlors of the great villa gardens of north and central Italy.

Alberti prescribed the geometric gravity of the gardener's art—the rigid pattern of hedge, the severe colonnade of cypress, the strict rectangle of the formal pool. In the exquisite parterres and terraces of the finest gardens the regularity is relaxed with an unexpected niche, a sudden little temple, a wanton accent of evergreen against the sky—or, as at the peerless Villa d'Este, with a pretty interpolation of fountains. All these ideas attained their last extravagance on the Isola Bella in the middle of Lake Maggiore on Italy's northern border. There, by an effort that persisted from 1500 to 1690, the counts of Borromeo converted an island into a wondrous tiered garden for the pleasure of their ladies, who had complained that in the family castle on the lake shore the gaiety of their revels was impaired by the shouts and groans of the prisoners in the dungeons beneath.

Like some water demon startled in his sleep, this fearful sculptured form arises from a pond at the Villa d'Este near Rome to gulp the waters down his gaping maw and spew them in a gush from his nose.

← The most elaborate of the Villa d'Este's six hundred fountains is the Water Organ, so called because the fountain played a hydraulic organ in the pavilion above it.

Four Men Taught the Renaissance

Pico: How to Think

THERE were four men who, through their writings and examples, stood out as teachers of the Renaissance. Giovanni Pico della Mirandola (1463–94), one of the great humanists, taught the Renaissance new ways to think. Youngest son of the prince of Mirandola, who claimed descent from the Roman emperor Constantine, Pico entered the University of Bologna at fourteen, tired of it after two years and spent the next seven years wandering among the schools of Italy and France. There he acquired the classical learning and the inquiring mind which were characteristic of humanism. He collected a great library of the ancient authors and learned, in addition to Greek and Latin, Hebrew, Arabic and Chaldee.

Inclined to mysticism, Pico became absorbed in the occult cabala writings, in which he hoped he would be able to find final proofs of the divinity of Christ. Out of these studies he developed strange views on theology which he set down in nine hundred questions and answers. These were condemned by Pope Innocent VIII and the next Pope, Alexander VI, had to issue a special brief to establish Pico's orthodoxy. After this brush with the Church, Pico dedicated his life to one of the Renaissance's major concerns —reconciling the teachings of Christianity with the philosophy of Plato. He settled in Florence and became a luminary in the brilliant circle of Lorenzo de' Medici, where Plato was the staple of conversation.

Unlike many humanists Pico had a deep respect for learning other than that of classical antiquity; unlike many scholars of the Renaissance he did not fall into the pit of pedantry; and unlike many of his half-pagan, often amoral associates he was a devout and moral Christian. The cast of Pico's mind, at once modest and magnificent, is revealed in his oration on the dignity of man: ". . . man is a little world, in which we may discern a body mingled of earthly elements, and ethereal breath, and the vegetable life of plants, and the senses of the lower animals, and reason and the intelligence of angels, and a likeness to God."

Machiavelli: How to Govern

NICCOLÒ MACHIAVELLI (1469–1527), who taught the Renaissance how to govern, wrote *The Prince*, a manual for rulers which has had a distinguished readership both among Renaissance and modern politicians. Machiavelli learned politics by firsthand observation as a civil servant in Florence and later as ambassador to Cesare Borgia in Rome. Cesare's combination of political audacity, prudence, cruelty, fraud, firmness and flexibility charmed Machiavelli, who saw in Rome's ruler the potential unifier of Italy.

But though he was an astute student of politics, Machiavelli was a clumsy practitioner. For trying to switch allegiances in Florence he was arrested, racked, imprisoned in a dungeon and finally sent to live on his farm. By day he wore work clothes and tended his land. At night he put on his best suit and sat down at his desk to write his masterwork, *The Prince*, whose hero was an idealized Cesare Borgia.

The book was not printed until after Machiavelli's death but the manuscript was widely read, having great influence and making the author many enemies. It brought a new realism to political thinking. The Middle Ages had assumed an ideal in the organization of states and the conduct of statesmen. Machiavelli, more practical, assumed that man is a political animal and will behave like one. He founded the science of politics in the modern sense. His prince is a self-made dictator through whom Machiavelli hoped a republican state might be achieved. In Machiavelli's politics necessity could overrule ethics, but he was realistic rather than deliberately unscrupulous, practical rather than cynical. "A prince," he wrote, ". . . must imitate both the fox and the lion, for the lion cannot protect himself from traps, and the fox cannot defend himself from wolves. One must therefore be a fox to recognize traps, and a lion to frighten wolves. Those who wish to be only lions do not understand this. . . . Injuries should be done all at once, so that, being felt less, they offend less; benefits should be given little by little, so that the flavor of them may last longer."

Castiglione: How to Live

WHILE Machiavelli was writing *The Prince*, a different kind of Renaissance man was writing a very different kind of book. Baldassare Castiglione (1478–1529) was the prototype of the modern gentleman, and his famous book, *The Courtier*, is the greatest of all guides on etiquette. Published by the Aldine Press in Venice, it was for its time a best seller. An English translation was published as early as 1561.

Castiglione, who held the title of count, was born on his small family estate near Mantua. He received a thorough Renaissance education, the equivalent of a first-rate private school education nowadays. He had an aptitude for almost everything, real proficiency in nothing. His ambition and natural vocation was to make himself welcome in his world. As a cultured and witty diplomat and statesman, he became a bright star at the court of Lodovico Sforza, the able despot of Milan. Later Castiglione attached himself to the duke of Urbino.

The court of Urbino was one of the most tranquil in Italy. Conversation was a high art there and *The Courtier* is told in a series of conversations held in the drawing room of the duchess. The talk was always urbane, never too studied and the figure of the gentleman who emerges from these talks is the ideal that has come down almost unchanged from the Renaissance. If Machiavelli's prince was a specialist in the art of realistic politics, Castiglione's courtier was a specialist in the art of elegant living. But while Castiglione preached a life which was graceful and pleasurable, he still recognized the responsibilities of the aristocracy. Said one of the speakers in *The Courtier:* "The purpose, then, of the perfect courtier, I submit, is this: that he should win, by the qualities these gentlemen have bestowed on him, the favor and confidence of his master so completely that he may and always will tell him the truth, in whatever concerns him, without fear of his displeasure. Hence I should say that music, games, pleasure-making and the other graces of the courtier are the flower of his calling, but its fruit is to induce and aid the prince to govern well."

Savonarola: How to Die

GIROLAMO SAVONAROLA (1452–1498), the man who tried to teach the Renaissance how to die, was in his religious fervor a throwback to the Middle Ages. In his assertion of the religious rights of the individual and his defiance of the authority of the Pope, he was a forerunner of the Protestant Reformation. As a young Dominican friar, Savonarola was so ascetic that his superiors had to force him to modify his religious austerities. Sent to the Florence of Lorenzo the Magnificent, Savonarola preached apocalyptic sermons against the city's worldliness and the corruption of its churches. Thousands crowded to hear his fiery descriptions of the hell which awaited those who died without having repented. He became the focus for political opposition to the Medici and, after Lorenzo's death, the leader of the bloodless revolution which drove them out.

Theocratic ruler of a revived Florentine republic, Savonarola reformed the tax laws and the judiciary and tried to transform pleasure-loving Florence into the city of God. For a while he succeeded. Carnival fripperies and books judged to be indecent were publicly burned. The city's children were organized to carry out Savonarola's reforms and to report their parents' lapses. Husbands and wives left each other to enter monasteries and convents and in the city both sexes dressed with puritan plainness. The artist Botticelli, who had delighted in painting pagan goddesses, was so affected by Savonarola's example that he burned all his nude studies.

As Savonarola's sermons against the corrupt Church became more and more violent, a cardinal's hat was dangled before him as a bribe. He retorted: "No hat will I have but that of a martyr reddened with my own blood." Reluctantly the Borgia Pope, Alexander VI, excommunicated him. Savonarola urged the monarchs of Europe to depose the Pope. But by this time Florence had had enough. There was a great revulsion against the autocratic preacher. A mob seized Savonarola. He was tortured, tried for heresy, hanged and his body burned in the public square.

Michelangelo's *Moses*, carved for the tomb of Pope Julius II in Rome, is said by many critics to be the finest sculpture of the age.

Half Italy, Half Eternity

A RENAISSANCE historian records that a friend of Raphael, when first he looked upon the master's *St. Cecilia*, was so overcome by its faultless beauty that he died. This supreme compliment came fittingly at the close of the supreme epoch in the history of the visual arts. The epoch began in Florence, two hundred years before Raphael, on the day when a schoolboy named Giovanni Cimabue cut classes to watch some Byzantine painters redecorate a chapel. Cimabue learned their trade and softened the stiff divinities of the Byzantine hagiolatry to a more human texture. His pupil Giotto set the figures free from their charmed stance and let them wander through scenes that are half Italy and half eternity.

From these noble beginnings the arts of fresco and sculpture went forward, under the patient patronage of the brilliant Medici dukes, with the slow majesty of organic growth. Never since the golden age of Athens had the artist enjoyed such consideration or his works such esteem. Lorenzo Ghiberti, the finest of the early Florentine sculptors, was permitted to toil for twenty-seven years upon a single bronze door for the Baptistry at Florence (*opposite page*). For a hundred years the Florentine craftsmen perfected their disciplines under the stern admonition of Byzantine and classical examples. Then came Masaccio (whose name means Dirty Tom), an unkempt, shambling genius who bellowed his theory that art should not copy art, but life. Others followed Masaccio and the way leads steeply upward through Leonardo, who produced masterpieces so readily that painting often lost interest for him, to Michelangelo. In him the three great arts of the Renaissance—painting, sculpture and architecture—found their summit and summation. After him there was little left for the age to say.

"They are so fine," said Michelangelo of Ghiberti's doors, "they would grace the Gates of Paradise." The Second Door (*above*) is wrought with Old Testament scenes. The panels, reading in pairs from the top down, show the creation and fall of man; Cain and Abel; Noah; Abraham; Jacob and Esau; Joseph; Moses on Mount Sinai; Joshua at Jericho; David and Goliath; Solomon and the Queen of Sheba.

The First of the Masters

IN the person of Giotto two ages join without seam; in his work they are welded in a blaze of religious passion as intense as any ever expressed in paint. Like his friend Dante, Giotto di Bondone (1276–1337) was one of the last great men of the Middle Ages and one of the first of the Renaissance. In his pictures the dead tableaux of medieval iconography seem to be caught at the instant of melting into warm, breathing life. With Giotto, the attention of European painting shifts subtly from the wealth and movement of drapery to the human form within it and to the soul within the form. Giotto's advance in style was as great as his expansion in spirit. He was the first European painter to develop a coherent perspective, and the first to grasp the importance of a strong composition. The frescoes for the Arena Chapel at Padua, two of which are seen on these pages, are among Giotto's grandest conceptions. At left, in the *Adoration of the Magi*, divinity is sheltered in a simple shed. The faces of the Holy Family are among the most gravely beautiful that Giotto ever painted. Above, in his depiction of *The Massacre of the Innocents*, Giotto shows that he could give body to the bestially profane as well as to the serenely sacred.

Much Renaissance painting was high entertainment as well as great art. In that broadly secular spirit, with perhaps more regard for his commission than for the facts, Benozzo Gozzoli decorated the famous Medici Chapel. In this panel he depicts the journey of one of the kings to see the Christ Child. The procession is decked in full medieval caparison. Gozzoli's patrons, the Medici, take all the principal parts in it. The king is Lorenzo de Medici, later to be called "The Magnificent." Behind him (*left to right*) in the front row ride Piero, Giuliano, Lorenzo and Cosimo, his illustrious relatives. The artist rides between two bearded men, wearing a cap with the words *opus Benotii* (the work of Benozzo). In the background lies a Palestine that never was in any age, a landscape spotted with Italian castles and topiary trees, hawks in pounce and deer in flight —and all very warm for December.

The strain of calm, harmonious humanism runs broadly through the mature Renaissance and very deeply in the art of Piero della Francesca. The picture above is one of Piero's frescoes of the old medieval story of the True Cross. It shows the queen of Sheba, accompanied by her handmaidens, kneeling in adoration of a balk of timber. This wood is of the tree that sprouted in the mouth of Adam from a seed put there by the Archangel Michael. The queen divined that "the Saviour of all the world should be hanged thereon . . . by whom the realm of the Jews shall be defaced and cease. . . . Solomon, for this cause, made it be taken and dolven deep in the ground."

To Renaissance man the riots of the blood were as important as the ardors of the spirit. Sensuality is especially evident in the work of Sandro Botticelli, the Florentine, where it inspired poetically painted reveries of mythic languishment. The head of the goddess Flora (*above*) from Botticelli's painting of a pagan rite of spring, *Primavera*, is perhaps the finest portrait ever made of sensual ravishment, an incarnation of depraved May. Botticelli was the most insistently personal artist of the Renaissance. While other painters were developing the grand manner of the high Renaissance, Botticelli created his own style of intense and delicate melancholy.

The golden sheaves of artistic genius, ripening for three centuries in sunny Italy, were gathered at last into one man: Michelangelo Buonarroti. The supreme expression of his world-vision, the mightiest artistic accomplishment of the Renaissance, was achieved in Michelangelo's frescoes of the Sistine Chapel of the Vatican. Four and a half years the fierce Florentine labored, his neck wrenched back, to cover the 10,000 square feet of ceiling with 343 colossal figures depicting the creation, the fall of man and the Flood. The

fresco shown above is Michelangelo's conception of two episodes from the Fall—the taking of the forbidden fruit and the expulsion. In 1512 Pope Julius II, impatient to show the finished ceiling to the public, threatened in the course of a violent dispute to throw Michelangelo off his scaffold. "That you shall not do!" cried the artist, and quit without putting the final touches to his masterpiece. Twenty-four years later, at the request of another Pope, he filled the end wall with his awesome vision of the *Last Judgment*.

Crafts became arts at the touch of men like Benvenuto Cellini, the goldsmith and sculptor. He made this dainty golden salt and pepper cellar, only 10¼ inches across, for Francis I of France. The salt boat is guarded by Neptune, god of the sea; the pepper bin is shaped like an arch of triumph and has for its custodian Tellus, goddess of earth. Cellini, according to his famous and flamboyant autobiography, was a craftsman in love as well as in gold and an intriguer at several courts, who more than once had to flee from his mistakes.

THE GLORY OF VENICE

The power and elegance of Venice were personified in the doge, elected minister of the aristocratic merchants who for more than six hundred years controlled the great city-state. The life of a doge was spent in the trammels of a ritual as elaborate as any king's. Within these limits Leonardo Loredano, a member of the first family of Venice, was one of the wisest doges. Around 1505, he sat for a portrait by one of the finest Venetian painters, Giovanni Bellini. In his man, the painter caught the magnificent practicality of Renaissance Venice.

IV

THE GLORY OF VENICE

In their palace by the Grand Canal the rulers of Venice met to debate an offer of murder. For a consideration the archbishop of Trebizond had volunteered to poison Marsiglio da Carrara, the ruler of Padua. The minutes of this fourteenth century meeting survive, for the Republic of Venice, the first modern state and the most stable and efficient government in Europe between the fall of Rome and the rise of Britain, left almost intact the most massive and detailed secret files in history.

"Inasmuch," say the official minutes, "as the said archbishop offers to poison Marsiglio da Carrara by means of Francesco Pierlamberti of Lucca, and wishes to travel in person with the said Francesco that he may assure himself of the actual execution of the deed; but for this purpose he requires a poison, which he charges himself to have made by a capable poison master if the money be supplied him; and further inasmuch as the said archbishop . . . says he has spent 180 ducats of his own money: Be it resolved, that for making the poison, for necessary expenses, and for buying a horse for the said archbishop—for his own is dead—the sum of 50 ducats be given to the archbishop and his companion, Francesco Pierlamberti. Ayes 10; noes 5; doubtful 1."

The thrift with which 130 ducats were thus shaved off the archbishop's bill is typical of the business instinct which for centuries made the Republic of Venice the greatest mercantile power on earth. The swift acceptance of the offer is typical of her statecraft, for Venice had mastered the practice of power politics centuries before Niccolò Machiavelli preached it in *The Prince.* This mastery enabled her cluster of swampy islets to stand off the overwhelming strength of the mainland powers of Europe and Asia and to dominate for nearly eight hundred years the commerce of Asia and the Mediterranean.

Twentieth century readers to whom the weapons of Renaissance politics are unfamiliar may be shocked to learn that for more than five hundred years Venice employed an official poisoner; that at various times Venice attempted to poison the Holy Roman emperor, the king of Hungary, two despots of Milan, the sultan of Turkey, Charles VIII of France, Pope Pius IV and the czar of Russia. They may be further surprised to know that Venice invented bacterial warfare. In 1649 she sent a physician with a flask containing powdered buboes to spread bubonic plague among the Turkish army in Crete. "*Venenossissima ac resurgens vipera,*" a French ambassador once called her—"a very venomous and indestructible viper."

In part this passion for poison as an instrument of policy was a custom of the times (insanity from poisoning was so common that the Renaissance had a name for it—*erberia*). In part it was due to the republic's peculiar position—a cluster of sea islands at the head of the Adriatic, through the ages threatened by Franks, Lombards, the papacy, Milan, Genoa (Venice's great naval rival), France, Spain, Hungary, the Byzantine Empire and the furious lunges of the Ottoman Turks. In part it was a heritage of that gorgeous East for

---

Once did She hold the gorgeous east in fee;
And was the safeguard of the west: the worth
Of Venice did not fall below her birth,
Venice, the eldest Child of Liberty.
She was a maiden City, bright and free;
No guile seduced, no force could violate;
And, when she took unto herself a Mate,
She must espouse the everlasting Sea.
And what if she had seen those glories fade,
Those titles vanish, and that strength decay;
Yet shall some tribute of regret be paid
When her long life hath reached its final day:
Men are we, and must grieve when even the Shade
Of that which once was great, is passed away.

WILLIAM WORDSWORTH
On the Extinction of the Venetian Republic (1802)

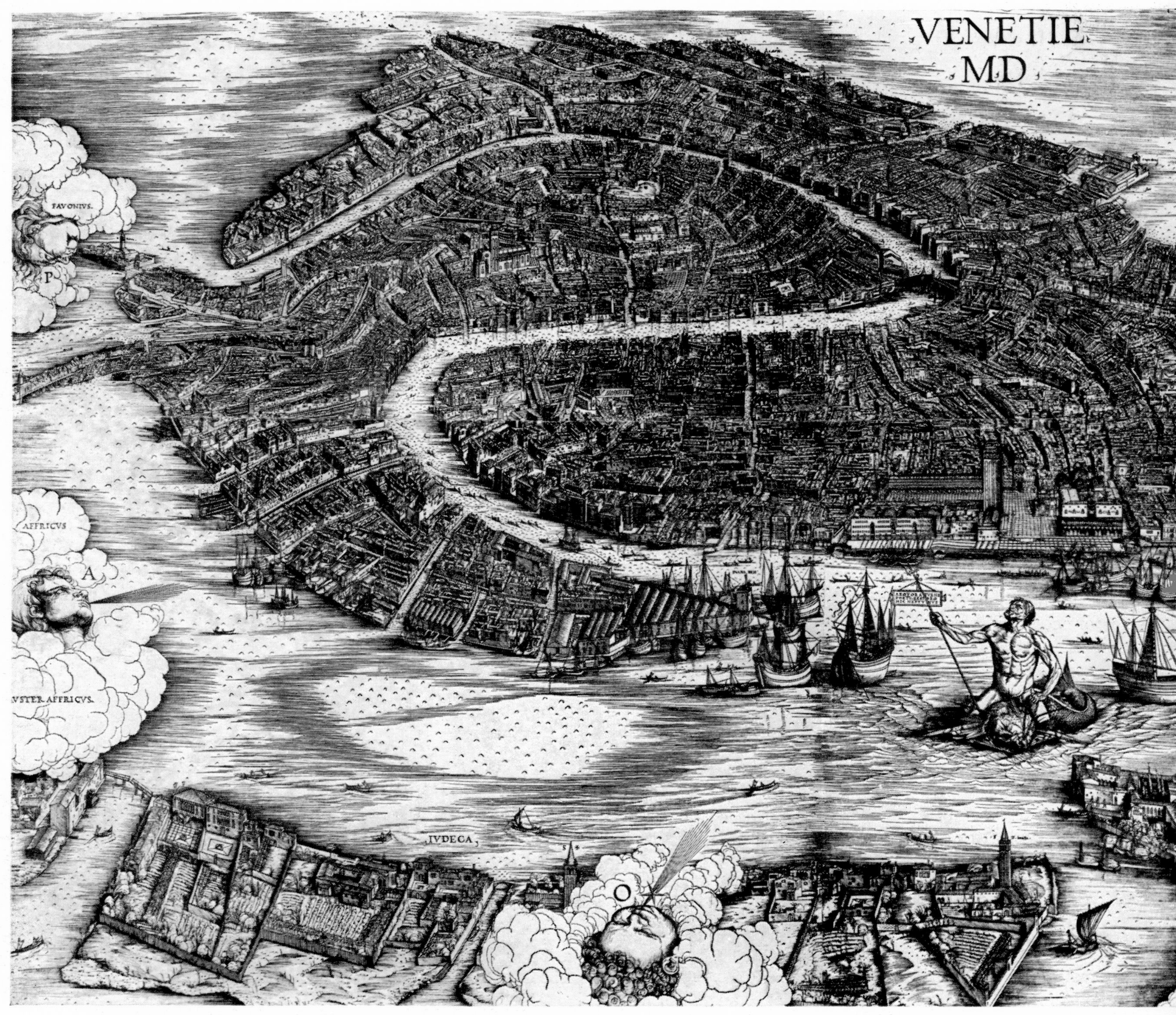

whose commerce and culture Venice, during the centuries of her greatness, was the golden gate to Europe.

For Venice was almost as much an Eastern as a Western city. The aura of Asia was over her as the fragrance of spice was said to envelop the Spice Islands, spreading far out to sea. It gleamed in the brilliant tesselation of her piazzas and the Byzantine mosaics of her church walls. It glowed in gold and jewels from St. Mark's, ornate like a Byzantine crown, in which the unmatable styles of Gothic and Byzantine meet and, as in a baffling marriage, blend.

Eastern violence and despotism were implicit in her government, a closed oligarchy of patrician merchants run by the Council of Ten, whose motto was "*Secretezza et iterum secretezza*" (Secrecy, and then more secrecy). The council's life-and-death decisions were usually without appeal and beyond review. Its nocturnal police were the sinister *signori di notte* (lords of the night). Its agents, the dread *soirri*, made arrests by muffling their victims' heads in their cloaks before whisking them off. The Orient was incarnate, too, in the doges, the dukes of the Venetian Republic, whose dignity was imperial but who more and more tended to be resplendent figureheads of the state's pageantry.

In the fifteenth and sixteenth centuries the long-latent esthetic genius of Venice ignited from the Renaissance an Oriental sunburst of color and an Oriental voluptuousness, fleshy and fluent. These, combined with a vigor born of seafaring and a sense of space and motion born of wind and waves, whirled Venetian painting to heights rarely attained in the history of art.

THE sumptuousness of the forms which was so much a part of the glory of Venice had flowered from a few mud banks. Venice was born in the agonies of Rome's death. (She died, thirteen centuries later, the oldest republic on earth, at

the hands of the French Revolution and Napoleon in the birth pangs of modern Europe.) Her founders were displaced persons, Roman fugitives from the Huns. About the year 450 they fled, in the shipwreck of their world, to the marshy Venetian islands. There they joined the handful of original settlers, simple fishermen, saltmakers and perhaps a few patricians who hoped to ride out the collapse of civilization near what, in quieter times, had been their seaside villas. On clear days the refugees could see across the lagoon the source from which the land of their refuge had come—the blue line of the Alps. The mud banks had been washed into the sea by rivers coming down from these mountains through north Italy's plain.

The key to Venice's greatness was her destitution. Everything had to be brought to the islands—vegetables, fruit, grain, cloth, wood (and later stone) for building. While most of Europe shattered into a thousand quarreling feudal castles, concerned chiefly with fighting and farming, Venice

Venice is shown here in a map made in 1500. Through the city, like the letter *S* written backward, twists the Grand Canal, the city's main street. Midway along it is the famous Rialto Bridge, where goldsmiths and jewelers displayed their wares. Near the center of the map, directly behind the sea-god Neptune, is the Doges' Palace and, on its left, the Piazza San Marco. At the right is the rectangular water basin of the Arsenal, shipbuilding center for the Venetian fleet, which is anchored in the map's foreground. Near the top is the island of Murano, where Venetian glassblowers developed their art and continue it today.

looked seaward and lived by the only means she had—trade. Unlike the mass of medieval men, the Venetians were never tied to the soil. Venice knew no serfs and her people, despite the paternalistic despotism of their government, felt the freedom of seafarers who can never be regimented because they are always on the move. They kept for a thousand years the independence of mind of those who mix with men of other nations and creeds. They kept, in form at least, the government of a republic. Other Italian city-states came under the power of individual despots and fell, after the Renaissance, in the rising surge of European nationalism. But Venice kept the flexibility of a government in which many of the people retained the right, if not the real power, to govern themselves.

At first the Venetians traded with the mainland in light, shallow boats which with the addition of the slender beak and sternpost, graceful as the curve of lifting waves, would one day become gondolas. But the open sea was the buoyant highway. Beyond its tossing horizon lay the rich bazaars of Antioch and Alexandria and the golden domes of Constantinople, opulent capital of the Byzantine Empire, of which Venice at first was a nominal dependency. In time her galleys, powered by wind or banks of rowing slaves and grouped in convoys for protection, drove down the Dalmatian coast, went into the mouth of the Nile, and passed through the Bosphorus.

She has been called "a joint stock company for the exploitation of the East." For five hundred years Venice lived for little else. Trade was the pulse of policy and trade tempered for Venice the crusading enthusiasms of medieval Europe. Moslems and Christians alike were her customers. Trade made Venice prefer peace to war, which was itself but a reflex of trade and which she waged fiercely when she had to. Trade defined her foreign policy, which consisted in supporting her weakest neighbor until he became strong enough to threaten her, at which moment she abandoned him.

Discovery was a thrust of trade, which drove her merchants to some of the most famous explorations in history. It drove the three most famous of merchants—Marco Polo and his father and uncle—to open up to the incredulous Middle Ages the wonders of India and Kublai Khan's China.

VENICE's empire came to her not, like Britain's, in what has been called "moments of absent-mindedness," but as a calculated commercial risk. She acquired Istria for wood for her ships. She acquired Dalmatia to control the coastal pirates. She acquired Morea, Crete and Aegean islands in the shipwreck of Byzantium, which she helped the crusaders to conquer in order to reinforce her monopoly of Eastern trade. To secure her food supply she eventually acquired possessions on the Italian mainland, extending from Lake Como on the west to the mouth of the Po on her south.

All these territorial treasures, widely separated by the sea, were threaded together by her shuttling ships, which she standardized (for Venice knew about standardization long before Henry Ford) so that her trading galleys could be quickly

The Remarkable Travels of the Polo Family

1. The travels of the Venetian, Marco Polo, aroused new European interest in the East. On their first trip Marco's father, Nicolo, and his uncle, Maffeo, journeyed as far as Bokhara (without Marco).

2. For three weary years the brothers were detained at Bokhara. At last, freed by an accident of war, they were invited by an emissary to Kublai Khan to accompany him on his journey to Cathay.

5. They stopped in Rome to see the Pope, who gave them letters and presents for the Great Khan and two theologians for the conversion of Cathay. The priests became frightened in Armenia and ran away.

6. When at last they reached the Great Khan's capital, the Polos were joyfully received. Marco (not shown here), an able and energetic young man, became one of the emperor's trusted ministers.

converted to ships of war. Her galleys were built in the Arsenal, the dynamo of Venetian sea power. Dante, seeing in a vision the lake of burning pitch in Hell, could think of only one comparison: "*Quale nell' Arzana de' Veneziani bolle l'inverno la tenace pece*" . . .

As in the Arsenal at Venice,
In winter they boil the sticky pitch . . .

During the Renaissance, in the fourteenth and fifteenth centuries, the Arsenal was the biggest industrial plant in the world. It manufactured everything from nails to cannon, turning out complete ships on its assembly line. "As one enters the gate," wrote a Spanish visitor in 1436, "there is a great street on either hand with the sea in the middle, and on one side are windows opening out of the houses of the Arsenal, and the same on the other side. And out came a galley towed by a boat, and from the windows they handed out to them, from one the cordage, from another the bread, from another the arms, and from another the ballistas and mortars, and so from all sides everything that was required. And when the galley had reached the end of the street, all the men required were on board, together with the complement of oars, and she was fully equipped from end to end. In this manner there came out ten galleys fully armed, between the hours of three and nine." In 1570, during the war with the Turks, the Arsenal turned out a hundred fully outfitted galleys in a hundred days. Four years later, when King Henry III of France was visiting, he was shown a galley which had only the keel and ribs in position. Then he sat down to a two hour feast. When he got up, the galley, now completely constructed, equipped, armed and manned, was launched in his presence.

If this efficient dynamo hummed with the shipbuilding that floated Venetian power, the city itself hummed with the life that depended on the ships. The Rialto, the main bridge over the Grand Canal, was the hub of commercial Venice. The surrounding wharves, streets and piazzas teemed with the most cosmopolitan population in the world—Turks, Byzantine Greeks, Cretans, French, Spanish, English, Russians, Germans, even a delegation of Japanese. The docks were piled high with Venetian export goods—salt and salt fish, wooden utensils, wrought iron, damask and cloth of gold for which the city was famous, woolen goods, gold and silver filigree work and the wonderful Venetian glass from the nearby little island of Murano, the most beautiful glass that Europe has ever produced.

THE galleys, moored in the heart of the city, unloaded the spoils of Europe, Asia and Africa—silks, satins, cotton goods, furs, spices and sandalwood from as far away as Timor, and marble looted from the temples of Greece or Syria for the churches of Venice.

This surf of wealth, dramatically transacted and dryly noted in the voluminous merchandising and banking records of the city, poured in upon the *banchine* (landing stages) and

3. The journey took a year. Once arrived, however, the Polos were handsomely entertained. The Great Khan questioned them closely about Europe and sent them back home with letters to the Pope.

4. After a journey of four years, and a round trip of fifteen, the two brothers arrived in Venice. Nicolo found his wife had died, leaving him a son. With young Marco in tow, the brothers again started east.

7. Marco Polo accompanied the Great Khan on gorgeous hunting expeditions, riding on great elephants, and undertook important missions of state for which he was rewarded with immense wealth.

8. But at last the Venetians became homesick and besought the emperor to let them be off. Reluctantly, he consented. In 1295 they finally reached Italy, where Marco wrote the story of their travels.

The wedding of the doge and the sea was celebrated every year in the greatest of Venetian festivals. The doge was borne to the rites in his barge of forty-two oars, while the citizens rowed after him.

Water sports were a natural diversion among the seagirt Venetians. Even the gay ladies, once a year, would roll up their sleeves, take the oar of a gondola and race each other down the Grand Canal.

piazzas of Renaissance Venice, and flooded the lives of its citizens with unparalleled prosperity. It was visible in the Venetian manner—the characteristic air of authority, luxury and indolent well-being. It was visible in the city's gorgeous trappings, like the walls of St. Mark's which were veneered with marble columns stripped from Greek temples and sliced to reveal the grain of the stone. It was visible in St. Mark's *Pala d'oro*—the gold retable which had taken Byzantine and Venetian craftsmen three hundred and fifty years to complete and whose enamels showing the life of Jesus and the saints were set with more than two thousand emeralds, pearls and rubies. It was visible in the horses of St. Mark's, brought to Venice after the crusaders' sack of Byzantium. It was visible in the painted fronts of the merchants' buildings like the Fondaco de' Tedeschi and the Fondaco de' Turchi or in the Palazzo dei Contarini, called the Cà d'Oro because of the splendor of its gilt façade. It was visible, above all, in the magnificent panoply of the official festivities.

One of these festivities occurred whenever a new doge was installed. On that occasion the craft guilds, each in a different costume, marched past the doge, two by two, in ostentatious parade. The furriers were dressed in ermine. The clothes of the ten master sailors were decorated with vermilion stars. The master weavers of gold cloth were dressed in cloth of gold and garlands of pearls and the master glassmakers in fur-trimmed scarlet. The goldsmiths wore garlands and necklaces of gold and silver and precious stones. The clothmakers carried trumpets, cups of silver and jars of wine, and the combmakers and lantern makers carried lanterns filled with live birds.

But the most impressive festival of the Venetian year was the wedding of the doge and the sea, *La Sposalizio*, held on Ascension Day—originally to commemorate the sailing of Doge Pietro Orseolo II to his victory over the Dalmatians in the year 1000. The doge would appear on his official barge, the *Bucentaur*, rowed by young merchant princes. Thousands of gondolas and other craft would follow in his wake to the Lido, the sandy spit at the edge of the Venetian lagoon. The bishop of Castello rowed out to meet the doge and offered him peeled chestnuts, red wine and a bunch of red roses in a silver vase. After prayers the bishop blessed a gold ring. The doge then rose from his seat, threw the ring into the Adriatic and cried, "*Desponsamus te, mare, in signum veri perpetuique dominii serenissimae Republicae Venetae*" (We wed thee, sea, in sign of the true and perpetual domination of the most serene Venetian Republic). After Mass the doge held a great reception and official feast. The Piazza San Marco became the scene of a great fair, where the reveling went on uninterruptedly for eight days.

FROM all over Europe men came to see and be impressed by the famous city whose merchants, in power and luxury, were the peers of Europe's monarchs. Dante, in the long inferno of his exile from Florence, wandered beside Venice's canals. Petrarch, humanist and sonneteer, sometimes called "the first modern man," visited Venice and in grateful memory bequeathed her his incomparable collection of ancient manuscripts and books, for which Venice built the world's first public library. Benvenuto Cellini was her guest. Pietro

Aretino, "the scourge of princes" and prototype of today's columnist, penned from Venice the wittily scandalous personal attacks from which the great men of the Renaissance paid him to desist. In Venice he was safe from the daggers of outraged victims and the rack of the Inquisition, since Venice never permitted the Church a free hand on her soil. Manuel Chrysoloras and the other Eastern scholars who taught Italy to read Homer in the original entered the West through the water gate of Venice.

Few of them lingered long, for Venice was not, like Florence, a conflagration of the mind. But they brought to the splendid, worldly, commercial city of the sea the cultural upheaval which we call the Renaissance. To its intellectual ferments Venice added little. But there is a genius of place, and Venice was caught by a visual music of the sea and air. The water sucked at the mooring posts, lapping the stone stairs of the docks. Over the city, air quivered like liquid glass and blazed with lights reverberated by the sea or softened into mist which deposited salt crystals on the tinted façades of the *palazzi*. Sometimes the sky was tumultuous with such storms as ships sustain on the open sea. Sometimes, in immense contrasting silence, the clouds sailed, like fleets, out to the Adriatic. Color saturated Venice from the sky and water. And while the city went about her daily, worldly tasks of buying and selling, it entered, like the beauty born of murmuring sound, into her stony face as each *palazzo*, bridge and ship rode above its shadow in the still canals. This dreamy presence beside the waters shimmered into incomparable life in the art of seven painters: Gentile and Giovanni Bellini, Giorgione, Titian, Carpaccio, Tintoretto and Veronese.

THERE is an art of irreducible simplicities: noble in the light of man's hope, tragic in the consciousness of man's fate. This is the art of Giotto and Michelangelo. But there is another art—an art of the grace of opulence, of the fully ripened character, of the full-blown flesh, of the bursting fruit, of life without the implications of fate. Of this art, adult and autumnal, the Venetians were the masters. It was still, by and large, a religious art. But those indolent Madonnas are the women of Venice. Those cherubs, playing their musical instruments, are the urchins who swarmed the quays.

This supreme art was a sunset. By the seventeenth century the conquest of Byzantium by the Turks had shut off Venetian trade with the East. With the opening of the new routes to Asia and the New World, Venice lived more and more on small change and past greatness. She did not go down at once. Anchored on her islands, she swung with the currents of history in which she no longer played a decisive role. For two more centuries she listed, settling as a doomed ship settles until, when Napoleon arrived and Wordsworth wrote his obituary sonnet (*page 103*), she sank.

"Men are we," Wordsworth wrote—the only living creatures that conserve in memory the cultures that have made us what we are. The shade of Venice's greatness has long since merged with history's deeper shadows. The panoply, the lavish life, the teeming trade, lie with her galleys fathoms deep in time. But the memory of the Sea-born City haunts us still, like the luminous streak left by an oar at night or Dante's *tremolo del mar*—the tremulous play of light and waves at sea.

The happiest day of the week was payday at the Arsenal, the Venetian navy yard. The Arsenal employed 16,000 men, whose wages were a major factor in the city's economy. The pay wicket is at left.

The good-natured rivalry between sections of town was conducted with a Latin vehemence. On holidays the sectional mobs would rush together on the bridges, and throw each other in the water.

Venice produced little sculpture, but notable among that is Verrocchio's bronze of the famous captain, Bartolomeo Colleoni.

A Feast for the Eyes

"HORAS *non numero nisi serenas*," reads the legend on a sun dial in Venice. "I count only the sunny hours." The sentence might run for a sole caption to the brief, glorious volume of Venetian art. Where the Florentine Renaissance turned its thoughts inward to the spirit, the Venetian lifted its face to the soft brown of the Adriatic, to the blue of the Italian sky, and to the fierce white of the Julian Alps—and so spread a feast for the eyes of a richness that no other painting provides. The great Venetians did not have the human roundness of much other great Renaissance art; but they had a degree of human heat that Western art had not experienced since the Greeks.

Oddly enough, Venice was slow to hatch its great painters. The native Venetian arts were glassblowing and ornate leathercraft, and these were brought to a perfection envied all over Europe. All at once, with the introduction of oil painting from Flanders in the middle of the fifteenth century, a whole brood of painters sprang up. For this warm new medium Venetians gladly abandoned the cool art of fresco.

First of the city's great painters were the Bellinis, Jacopo and his two sons, Gentile and Giovanni. From the school of Giovanni Bellini came first the gorgeous Giorgione and then the magnificent Titian, the chief glory of Venetian painting who lived for ninety-nine years and painted for more than seventy. Even in decline, the Venetian school could still shake wonders from its failing brush—the works of Tintoretto and Veronese. One glowing century of genius, and then the fever of creation died slowly into the long Adriatic evening.

In this gorgeous piece of painted melodrama, Tintoretto tells the favorite folk tale of the Venetians: how, in 828, some stop-at-nothing patriots of the island-city snatched the body of St. Mark, the patron saint of Venice, from its tomb in Alexandria, Egypt. In the legend, the soul of St. Mark comes in a tempest to drive the Alexandrians to shelter and give the daring Venetians a free run for their ships.

Titian painted *Sacred and Profane Love* around 1512. The title, which became attached to it later, is the expression of a theme that fascinated Renaissance minds: the conflict between earthly, sensual love (the dressed figure) and pure, celestial love (the nude).

Pastoral Symphony was completed around 1510 by Giorgione, one of the first Venetians to perfect landscape art. In this bucolic scene he reflects the longing of the sea-girt Venetians for the green inland hills. The seated men are a courtier with his lute and a peasant.

In *Mars and Venus*, a full-blown Venetian version of the Greek myth, Veronese painted the gods being tied together by Cupid with a pink ribbon. The painting catered to Renaissance love of classical stories and of beautiful, sensual scenes which bore no moral.

Procession on the Great Piazza

VENICE was a perfect setting for pageantry. Its Piazza San Marco (*above*) was like a stage whose church and palaces formed a spectacular backdrop for the almost daily parades of priests and merchant princes, nobles and festive ladies. The pageant pictured here, called the *Corpus Christi Procession*, was painted in 1496 by Gentile Bellini, half brother of Giovanni Bellini, who painted the portrait of the doge which appears on page 102.

The square, whose looks have changed little in the four and a half centuries since this procession took place, was dominated by the many-domed church of St. Mark which, like Venice itself, was an oddly harmonious mixture of Western and Byzantine influences. While St. Mark's was being built, Venetian merchants vied with one another to bring back from their voyages treasures to adorn the new edifice. Marble was shipped from Constantinople, columns from Egypt, capitals from Greece, porphyry knights from the Levant. The four horses over the central arch were cast in bronze in the time of the Roman emperor Nero. Both the inside and outside of the church were embellished with mosaics which told stories

from the Bible and glittered like sunlight on water. Next to the church, at right, is a corner of the doge's palace, its walls set in a diamond-shaped pattern of marble. Next to the palace is the base of the great campanile, or bell tower. At the far left is the library, its roof a clutter of chimney pots.

The procession itself, the city's most solemn religious festival, was painted for the local Great School of St. John the Evangelist. The school had in its possession a relic of the Holy Cross that had repeatedly worked miracles. This relic was paraded inside its gold reliquary (*center*) once every year. Leading the procession is a band of choristers, followed by candle bearers and some other Church officers. The doge and his honored guests watch from the palace and library. Directly behind the canopy (*in center foreground*) kneels a citizen from Brescia named Jacopo de Salis. Jacopo is praying that his injured son, not shown here, may be healed by the power of the relic. In the center of the piazza people quite accustomed to goings-on at St. Mark's stroll about casually, gossiping about new ships and traders, gaping at the wealthy merchants and their retinues.

Renaissance Crossroads

AMONG his many works Vittore Carpaccio painted few that were literal scenes of Venice. But, however fanciful or foreign his subject, the setting and the citizens, the travelers, envoys, sailors, ships and seacoasts were almost always those of his own city. In *The English Prince Takes Leave of His Father* (*above*) he shows a bustling seaport with a flotilla of Venetian ships, one keeled over and being repaired by black galley slaves. His *The English Ambassadors Before King Mauro* (*right*) is Venetian in all but name.

The interest in ambassadors was thoroughly Venetian. Set at the world's crossroads and dependent on foreign trade, Venice was the first state to set up a regular diplomatic service in the modern style, staffed by experienced career men. Its ambassadors at foreign courts were among the best informed men of their time; their reports, which exist today among the city's archives, constitute a history of the great European cities from Moscow to Madrid. On their missions ambassadors took horses, carriages, coachmen, servants and even musicians to advertise Venice's wealth.

In the fourteenth and fifteenth centuries Venetians were the busiest travelers in Europe, and their fleet was the largest in the world. It was owned by the state and rented vessel by vessel to the city's merchants. The design of each ship and the duties of its crew were prescribed by law and each ship was required to carry an orchestra. "Venice exults," sang the poet Petrarch, "the august city, the sole shelter in our days of liberty, justice, and peace . . . a city rich in gold but more rich in fame, potent in strength but more in virtue, founded upon solid marble, but upon yet more solid foundations of concord and harmony—and, even more than by the sea which girds her, by the prudent wisdom of her sons defended and made secure."

The panels at left and below were done by Carpaccio to commemorate the story of St. Ursula, a fourth century princess of Brittany who, according to legendary account, was slaughtered by Huns along with eleven thousand other virgins. Here, in a fifteenth century Venetian setting, Ursula's betrothed bids farewell to his father (*left*) and bride's parents (*right*).

Three of the nine paintings Carpaccio did in his Ursula series are concerned with the work of ambassadors, figures of importance to Venice. Below, Ursula's father, the king of Brittany, receives the British ambassadors. Portrayed under the archway at left are several members of Venice's famous Loredano family. At right, Ursula converses with her father.

Veronese's *Battle of Lepanto* celebrates the sea engagement which Venice and her allies fought with the Turks in 1571. Above the battle the city's patron saints intercede with the Virgin on behalf of the Venetian fleet, while black shadows of anathema fall on the heathen. Venice won a famous victory, but the effort weakened her and in a few years the Turkish fleet regained control of the Mediterranean.

THE AGE
OF
EXPLORATION

The wide new worlds the explorers found were quickly mapped. This sixteenth century Spanish chart plots the coasts of Africa in accurate detail. Landmarks are noted around the edge, such as "Magdalena River," "Gulf of St. Thomas," "low land," "palms" and "mountains." But the Dark Continent's interior is still peopled with legends. Near the center, bearing a cross, stands the mythical Christian king, Prester John, whose supposedly fabulous realm was one of the goals that lured explorers into their voyages.

V

THE AGE OF EXPLORATION

FOUR centuries after Columbus had reached the New World, a Minnesota farmer grubbed up a stump on his farm and found a flat stone embedded in the roots. On the stone was an inscription in Scandinavian runes. For nine years the stone served as a step to the farmer's granary. Then it was translated. The runes read:

"8 Goths and 22 Norwegians on [an] exploration-journey from Vinland through the West. We had camp . . . one day's journey north from this stone. We were [out] and fished one day. After we came home [we] found ten [of our] men red with blood and dead. AV[e] M[aria] save [us] from evil."

A shorter inscription on the edge of the stone bore the date: 1362.

What did this inscription mean? What had happened in the night of history? What shrieks had died away, in thinning circles of unheard horror, into the continental quiet? Who were those "8 Goths and 22 Norwegians," and what were they doing in the middle of Minnesota more than a century before the discovery of America?

The Kensington Stone, as it is called, may or may not be a peculiarly inscrutable hoax; scholars cannot make up their minds. But there have been undeniably authentic discoveries in the same general region—medieval Norse battle-axes, a spearhead, a fire steel, a Viking's hatchet and, in Ontario, a Viking's grave and moldering arms.

In 1492, Christopher Columbus, by dramatizing the ordeal whereby he burst into an unknown hemisphere, dramatized the fact that a new age—the Age of Exploration—had begun. But all through the Middle Ages parts of northern Europe had been dimly aware of land far out in the western Atlantic. There were the multiple legends of St. Brendan, the Irish monk who had crossed the open sea in a currach of stitched hides and found a distant land in the west—St. Brendan's Isle—which mariners still looked for during the explorations. Even in the ancient world Iceland was known by the name of ultima Thule, which meant the end of the earth, for Pytheas of Massilia (Marseilles), a contemporary of Alexander the Great, had supposedly made a voyage there. But ages which believed in hippogriffs and unicorns laughed at reports of seas of floating ice, winters when there was no daylight and summers when there was no night.

WHEN the Norse sea rovers reached Iceland around 860 they found that others besides Pytheas had been there. On the shore they discovered crosses, bells and books in Irish characters. By 982, Eric the Red had reached Greenland from Norway and by 986 had colonized it. By the year 1000, Eric's son Leif was blown upon the North American coast, probably Nova Scotia or Massachusetts. He had no trouble finding his way home. Because of the abundant wild grapes, Leif called the new land Vinland. More than one attempt was made by Greenlanders to set up posts around Cape Cod and Martha's Vineyard. But the savages attacked in overwhelming numbers. In one battle the Norsemen were routed until

Henry the Navigator, prince of Portugal, was scholar and scientist for the explorations. His group of experts at Sagres, on Cape St. Vincent, made accurate astronomical observations, collected geographical data and drew reliable maps and charts for seamen's use.

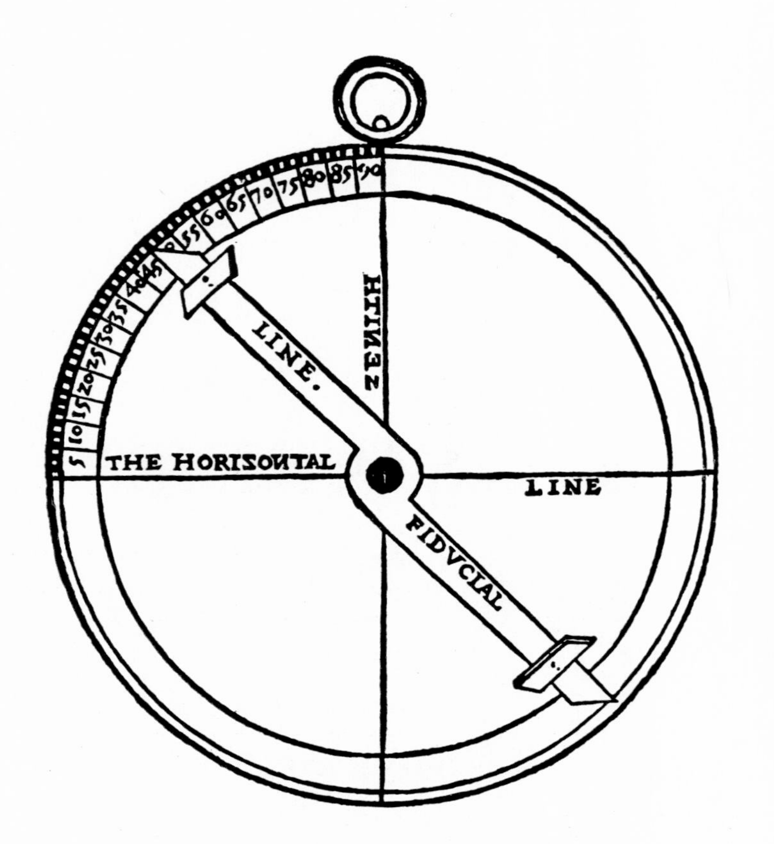

Improved navigational instruments were necessary for long voyages out of sight of land. The astrolabe *(above)*, invented by the Greeks and taken over by Portuguese from Arab seamen, measured the height of the sun and gave an approximation of the observer's latitude as well as the time of day. The man below demonstrates its use on land, sighting on a tower of known elevation for comparison. On shipboard, the navigator used a mast for this purpose.

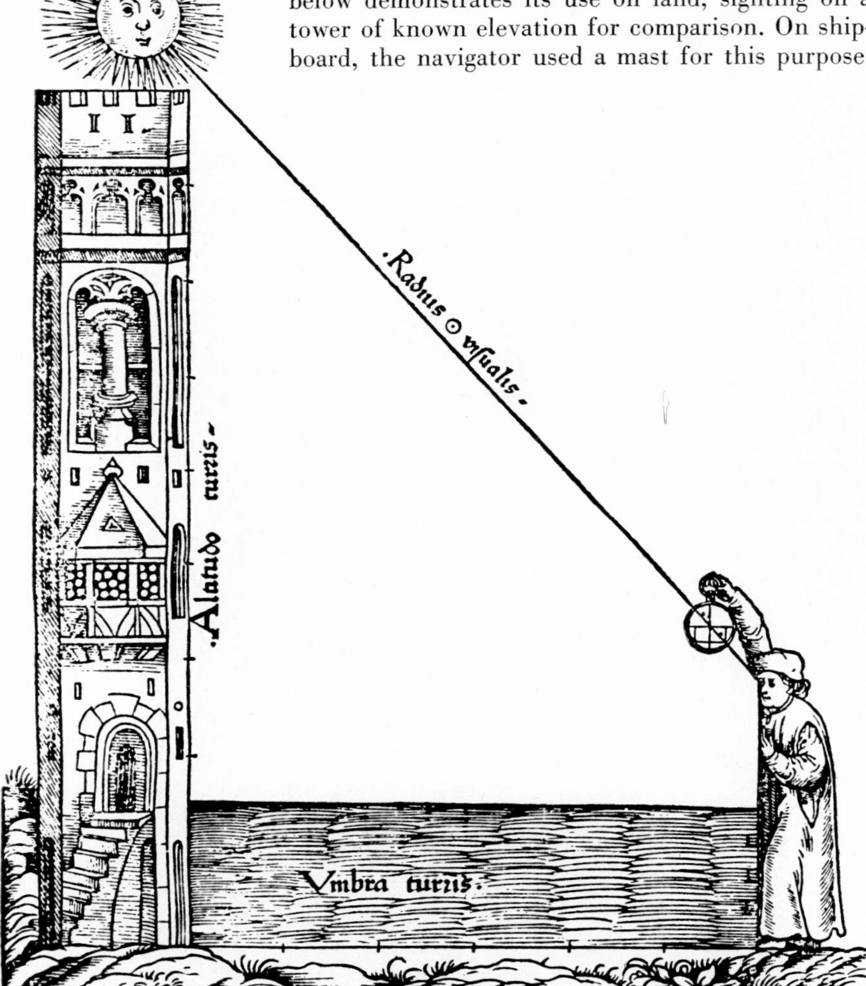

Eric the Red's daughter exposed her breast and whetted a sword against it. This gesture so shocked the native New Englanders that they fled.

Greenlanders were so familiar with the American coast that they had divided it into three regions—Helluland, the wastes of Labrador; Markland, probably Newfoundland, where Greenlanders went for masts and timbers; and Vinland. And medieval Europe was well aware of Greenland. For decades the bishopric of Greenland was part of the archbishopric of Hamburg. Three popes wrote of their concern for this Christian outpost. Greenland paid regular tithes and Greenland's products were in brisk demand in Europe's markets—especially walrus rawhide for leather thongs and white falcons for one of the Middle Ages' favorite sports. Through Greenland, Europe had intercourse with the New World. But the Norsemen left only a few records. Men and ships shuttled to and fro as in a kind of fog. Now and then the fog parts for a tantalizing moment to record briefly, as in 1121, "Bishop Eric Gnupsson . . . went from Greenland in search of Vinland."

But the Greenland traffic was not medieval Europe's only reminder that there was "something" beyond the green sea of darkness, the Atlantic. Sometimes off the shores of Europe and the Atlantic islands sailors found sticks carved with an intricate, savage art unknown to Europe. Sometimes the bodies of strange men floated up. These were not the bodies of Moors or Negroes with whom the late Middle Ages were familiar. They had broad faces and possibly were Indians who had been carried eastward by the Atlantic currents.

Thus medieval Europe strained toward America as a sail strains from a mast. But the wind that must fill it was fitful and lacked consistent force. That force was supplied by the Renaissance.

The Age of Exploration was the energy of the Renaissance hurling itself into the conquest of space to reveal the modern world. The qualities wanted for discovery were the qualities which the Renaissance nourished and which challenge calls forth in men—alertness, audacity, endurance, vigor. With the explorations, European men gathered their strength and by a brilliant stroke of intellect and daring enlarged for their own profit a world grown too small.

The drive was toward the riches of the East. Its spices and precious stones, its silks and velvets, its gold and silver brocades were in steady demand. But a cargo of the grosser and bulkier European manufactures could not bring back many of these rarer Eastern goods. Cash, therefore, was needed to buy Eastern wares. Hence there was a drain on European bullion and in turn a second motive for discovery: the land of El Dorado with its gold-paved streets and diamond pebbles lay westward in the mists, waiting to be found.

The age of discovery was made possible by certain technical developments in naval architecture and navigation: the construction of more seaworthy ships, the improvement of the card compass, the quadrant (for reckoning latitude) and the portolano, navigators' maps of considerable exactitude.

The age was also made possible by the fact that Europe for the first time was developing a complex commercial economy. With the general revival of European trade there began to emerge the devices of capitalism—partnerships, credit, interest—which permitted easier transactions and provided capital for new ventures. With this capital at their disposal, the rulers of the rising national states—France, Spain, Portugal and England—could finance the search for all-water routes to the East by which they could avoid the territory of the Mohammedan Turks and the heavy tolls on trade which the Turks exacted. The Church encouraged the search out of aversion to the Mohammedans and eagerness to find new spiritual fields to conquer.

And, as much as anything, the age was made possible by the vision of two men, Henry the Navigator, a prince of Portugal, and Christopher Columbus, the wool carder of Genoa.

Henry was the organizer of victory. His mother was a daughter of John of Gaunt, the English kingmaker. His cousin was Henry V of England. Prince Henry established himself at Sagres. On this rocky point he built a palace, a chapel (for he was an intensely religious man), an observatory, and housing for the cartographers, mathematicians and navigators who soon surrounded him. At Lagos nearby he constructed docks and shipyards. A systematic study of charts and navigators' records was begun. Soon Sagres had assembled the best geographical and nautical library in the world. Nautical instruments were developed. At Lagos the caravel, the best sailing ship of its time, was constructed.

Henry was obsessed with opening a sea route to the Guinea coast of Africa and by a desire to find Prester John, the mythical Christian ruler whose fabulously wealthy kingdom the Middle Ages located first in Asia, then in Africa. When Henry began his work no Portuguese navigator had been farther south than Cape Bojador. It took twelve years for a Portuguese ship to pass it. Criticism of Henry's projects as dangerous and profitless was intense. For while few navigators believed the world was flat, many believed that in the tropics "the sun poured down sheets of liquid flame," the ocean boiled and the searing heat turned white men black. But Henry's men passed Bojador and came back safely. Later expeditions brought back gold dust and slaves, and criticism died away. Companies were formed to exploit the new wealth.

Prince Henry took success with the same "virtuous obstinacy" as failure. He sold slaves to finance his expeditions but he insisted that the captives be baptized. By the time Henry died (1460) his captains had sailed south more than fifteen hundred miles and west past the Azores, more than a third of the way across the Atlantic. In 1486 Bartolomeu Dias made the decisive voyage. His three ships pushed on toward the end of Africa. For thirteen days, while the men's teeth chattered with fear and the sudden cold, the little ships were driven south before a storm. Then Dias turned north and found land to larboard. He had rounded the Cape of Good Hope.

Wrote Luiz de Camoëns of his countrymen's exploits in *The Lusiad*, the epic of Portuguese discovery: "*E se mais mundo houvera, là chegará*" (And if there had been more of the world, they would have got there).

If Prince Henry prepared, Columbus personified the Age of Exploration. His story is one of the world's great legends, and the instinct of the world has been quite right to reject the censures of his detractors and to read the meaning

The cross-staff, with which the man above takes a sight on the sun, was used, like the astrolabe, to give latitude. (There was no instrument to give longitude, which had to be figured by dead reckoning.) Below is a Portuguese table of declination of the sun, an essential in calculating latitude by use of the cross-staff. A calendar of saints' days is listed at the left.

KL Março tem dias .xxxi. ha lũa .xxx. ho dia .xij. hõs no .xij.

		Di: Domes	Lugar. sol Pisces	Declinaçã: sol Graã	Minu.
d	Adrian martyr ⁊ simplici	1	20	3	59
e	Donado martyr ⁊ basilci	2	21	3	35
f	Martinino martyr pēça	3	11	3	11
g	Lucio papa ⁊ martyre	4	23	2	48
A	Sam focas martyre.	5	24	2	24
b	Victor ⁊ victorino marti	6	25	2	0
c	Thome d agno confessor	7	26	1	36
d	Appollonio martyre.	8	72	1	12
e	Os qrēta martyres.	9	28	0	48
f	Alexandre ⁊ gaio martyr	10	29	0	24
g	Quarenta mil martyres	11	1 ♈	0	0
A	Sam gregorio papa ⁊ co	12	2	0	24
b	Sam leadre bispo bispo	13	3	0	48
c	Leeo papa ⁊ martyrr ⁊ do	14	4	1	12
d	longinus martyr.	15	5	1	36
e	Gertrudis virgem ⁊ mart	16	6	2	0
f	Patricio bispo ⁊ confesso	17	6	2	24
g	Anselino bispo ⁊ doutor	18	7	2	48
A	Joseph d nossa senhora	19	8	3	11
b	Gutbberto confessor	20	9	3	35
c	Beento abade fundador	21	10	3	59
d	Paulo bispo ⁊ confessor	22	11	4	22
e	Pigmete preste ⁊ martyr	23	12	4	46
f	Theodoro psbi Dia d jejũ	24	13	5	9
g	Anũciaçã de nossa senhora	25	14	5	33
A	Sam castorio martyre	26	15	5	56
b	Joani yrmitam confessor	27	16	6	19
c	Marcello papa ⁊ grondan	28	17	6	43
d	Quirino martyr eustalio ⁊	29	18	7	6
e	Sam segundo martyre·	30	19	7	29
f	Felice pappa ⁊ babina vi	31	20	7	5[illegible]

of the age between the legend's lines. Most meaning lay in the character of a man possessed of practically nothing but a great idea, which he put across against tremendous odds. The drama was heightened by the fact that the idea was right in theory and wrong in practice and that Columbus' failure was vastly more successful than his dream of success.

The idea, of course, was the paradox that the East could be reached most quickly by sailing west, that India, China and Japan lay not too far beyond the frightening silences and the terrifying rages of what Portuguese and Spaniards called the "Ocean Sea." The failure, due to a simple miscalculation of the earth's circumference, meant the providential disclosure of the land mass of the Americas.

One of Prince Henry's navigators had been a Portuguese nobleman named Bartolomeu Perestrello. Columbus married Perestrello's daughter and spent considerable time studying his father-in-law's maps and cosmographical works. He also struck up a correspondence with the Florentine astronomer and cosmographer Toscanelli. Some time before, Toscanelli had been asked by the king of Portugal if there was a shorter route to the Indies than around Africa. In 1474 Columbus asked the same question and Toscanelli gave a direct answer. "Sail westward," he said, and sent a navigator's chart along with his reply. Fourteen years later Columbus carried both Toscanelli's idea and his chart when he set out from Palos in the *Santa Maria.*

The rest of the Columbian epic is familiar, evocative and satisfying. He tried to get backing from the king of Portugal and was turned down, paid court to Queen Isabella and King Ferdinand of Spain and had set out in despair to offer his services to the king of France when a royal messenger overtook him. He stood out for some rather stiff terms and managed to get most of them. Columbus was to be admiral of all the seas and lands he might discover. He was to be viceroy of his discoveries. He was to have ten per cent of all profits from the new lands.

ON August 3, 1492, Columbus' small fleet of three vessels set sail from the harbor of Palos. The *Niña* and the *Pinta* were smaller than many a Viking craft. The *Santa Maria* was larger. On board were ninety men, including an interpreter who spoke Hebrew and Arabic and might prove useful with the Grand Khan. The seventy-day voyage was exceptionally smooth. On the night of October 11, Columbus saw a light. He summoned Pedro Gutiérrez, butler of the king's dais, who also saw it. They called Rodrigo Sánchez, whom the sovereigns had sent along as their personal controller. At first, as is the nature of such men, he did not see the light. But at last it was officially seen. "It appeared like a candle that went up and down, and Don Cristobál did not doubt that it was the true light, and that it was on land; and so it proved, as it came from people passing with lights from one hut to another."

The sovereigns had promised 10,000 *maravedis* to the man who first sighted land. At two o'clock in the morning Rodrigo de Triana, a sailor, cried, "Land! Land!" from the *Pinta*. But the reward was given to Columbus for reasons reported by the Spanish historian Herrera: "He [Columbus] saw the light in the midst of darkness, signifying the spiritual light which was introduced amongst those barbarous people. . . ." In his disappointment Rodrigo de Triana became a Mohammedan.

The Spaniards went ashore on an island in the Bahamas which the Indians called Guanahaní. While the natives stood watching in awe, Columbus unfurled the banners of Spain and renamed the island San Salvador. Falling on their knees, he and his men uttered their "immense thanksgiving to Almighty God."

THIS was the moment toward which the vision had unknowingly tended. The rest was tumultuous anticlimax. Columbus was to enjoy a great triumph in Spain—soon chilled by the suspicion that his new lands were not Asia. He was to search with trifling results for gold and discover tobacco. He was to make three more voyages, discover the mainland of South America, see Central America and make his crew sign a statement that Cuba was a part of Asia, for he would not relinquish his vision of the greater reality. "*Il mondo e poco*" (The world is small), he insisted, arguing to the bitter end against his glory and the facts of longitude.

But the great moment had been on Guanahaní when he had turned a hemisphere from the darkness of oblivion to human knowledge and hope as, in the subtropical light, the old concept of the world became a thing of the past and the actual world was revealed.

In the Age of Exploration Europe moved its power out across the oceans. Portugal outflanked the religious barriers of Arab, Turk and Moor by pioneering the sea route to India and the East. Five years after Columbus made his first voyage, Vasco da Gama, following the route taken by Bartolomeu Dias, swept around the Cape of Good Hope and up to Zanzibar, then across the Indian Ocean to Calicut on the coast of India.

The wealth of India flowed back to Europe. But except for a savage commercial, military and religious energy, the Renaissance gave little to the East. It was too greedy, too intolerant and too busy exploiting.

Soon the Portuguese commander Alfonso de Albuquerque had swept the Arabs from the eastern seas and established a Portuguese empire which controlled the Red Sea and the Indonesian trade. With the addition of Macao in China, this empire lasted until Dutch power rose in the seventeenth century to appropriate it.

One more momentous voyage was made by a Portuguese (serving under the Spanish flag). In 1520, Fernando Magellan penetrated the strait that now bears his name. He and the crews of his three ships were the first white men to burst into the ocean which he called Pacific—though a Spaniard, Vasco Núñez de Balboa, had already seen it from a peak in Darien and claimed it for the Spanish crown.

Antonio Pigafetta, one of the ships' company, has left a description of the first Pacific voyage. "We were three months and twenty days without getting any kind of fresh food. We ate biscuit, which was no longer biscuit but powder of biscuits swarming with worms, for they had eaten the food. Rats were sold for half a ducat apiece. . . ." At last the one surviving ship limped back to Spain—without Magellan, for he had been

For centuries sailing ships had got along with a single square sail which made it easy to run before the wind but very difficult to tack into it. To cross the vast ocean reaches the explorers' ships had to be more seaworthy and able to sail into the wind. This sixteenth century warship carried the rigging which was the model for Western sail arrangements for six centuries. To the single, square-rigged mainmast have been added a square-rigged foremast and a mizzenmast astern with a fore-and-aft sail for greater maneuverability.

Columbus' landing was described by him in a letter published in 1493 with these illustrations. The artist envisioned a land studded with castles, homes and steeples (*below*). But what impressed Europeans most was the fact that the natives (*above*) went around naked.

killed in the Philippines in a fight with natives. The globe had been circumnavigated.

Spain's opportunity had been great, for she dealt with vast colonizable tracts of the earth. The only aboriginal cultures that the Spaniards encountered, the splendid Inca and Aztec empires, they looted and obliterated. The conquistador Hernando Cortes with a handful of followers captured the capital of Montezuma and enslaved the Aztec nation. Francisco Pizarro, an illiterate who could not sign his own name, performed the same exploit on a greater scale in Peru, capturing the Inca king, extorting a ransom worth more than $15,000,000, then killing him.

As Spain expended its energies on conquest and get-rich-quick plunder, new nations took to discovery. England had early sent out John Cabot, like Columbus a Genoese, who had become a naturalized Venetian. On two voyages he sighted the coast of North America at Labrador. Like Columbus he thought that it was Asia. France hired Giovanni da Verrazano, a Florentine, and presently a galaxy of French explorers—Cartier, Champlain, La Salle, Père Marquette—staked out claims to Canada, the Great Lakes country and the Mississippi valley. The Dutch explored the Hudson River country.

IT was soon pretty well understood that the New World was a continental land mass, and a frantic search began for a passage to Asia around or through the Americas. For the two continents had acquired a name. Amerigo Vespucci, a Florentine, sailing first under the Spanish, then under the Portuguese flags, had explored the coast of South America. Through a map-making fumble, he had given his name to both continents.

From Peru and Mexico, the great treasure galleons still ferried to Europe the Inca and Aztec wealth and the gold and silver dug by those enslaved nations from the mines that had been theirs. In Spain and Portugal the wealth did very little good. The influx of bullion and the sudden increase in currency brought a weakening inflation. Neither Spain nor Portugal kept the wealth because they could not put it to work. It flowed quickly north to France, the Netherlands and England, which had what was lacking in the south: energy, efficient labor and an emerging middle class which could and did use the wealth to build up their burgeoning capitalism.

Most important for the world as a whole, the explorations made Europe the base of world empire. Through the following three centuries the European nations, in bitter rivalry and war, fastened their dominion on the resources and markets of the globe. Colonies became the support of countries that got them early and kept them. (They also became the envy of those, like Germany, that came too late.) In idle moments historians sometimes speculate on how things would have been if another dynamic culture like the Arabic, stirred by another crusading religion like the Mohammedan, had beaten Christian Europe to the great work of exploration and colonization. Fatefully, it was Western man whose culture and institutions were projected, sometimes with explosive force, into every corner of the globe. Four centuries after Columbus there was no living civilization which had not been deeply penetrated, if not totally revolutionized, by the ways of Western man.

Vasco da Gama of Portugal was the first to find what most of the other explorers were looking for: a sea route from Europe to the rich Orient. In 1497 he rounded the perilous Cape of Good Hope and started up the east coast. On his loop around Africa, da Gama met many savage tribesmen, some of whom he subdued with cannon and crossbow, others with gifts of tinkling bells. Reaching Ethiopia, da Gama went east across the Indian Ocean and landed at the Indian port of Calicut. There he offered his cargo of washtubs, cotton cloth and casks of oil in trade for spices and jewels. The local merchants were not impressed with the dicker, and da Gama went home with precious little to show for his 28,000-mile trip. A second voyage (1502–03) was a greater commercial success, and the wealth of the eastern trade began to flow westward. This portrait shows da Gama after the king had rewarded him by making him viceroy of India.

Portraits of New Worlds

THE map was a thriving form of art in the Age of Exploration. Geographical facts were few and artistic fancy free. Cartographers of the sixteenth century had to rely as much on the bibble-babble of returning seamen as on the sober entries in ships' logs. On their charts they depicted both. Improbable sea monsters wreathe among uncertain latitudes; impossible land mammals sport upon uncertain topography. Nevertheless, some of the map-makers made surprisingly shrewd guesses at the facts and thoroughly charming interpretations of the fancies. Their work was accurate to advise the mariner, gaudy to please the general eye and sometimes beautified to attract the connoisseur. Some of the handsomest maps, painted in France during 1547 by an unknown cartographer, are reproduced on these pages. They have a French touch of curious detail and homely wit that lightens the grave beauty of the cartography. In the illustration of the landing of Jacques Cartier (*below*), simple, shabby Indians gaze in wonder at the gaudy and obviously loud Europeans, while even the mild bears seem to hold conference on the matter. A fat and comfortable priest stands in the foreground of the party, and several ladies are generously provided to the expedition. (Possibly the priest was there; the ladies, so far as history records, definitely were not.) Like most cartographers of his day, the Frenchman tastefully strewed the open sea spaces of his chart with the large, geometric rose whose petals tell the points of the compass. He also suited the lay of the land to the shape of the parchment. In all these maps, north is at the bottom. To give the two Americas a more familiar look, turn the book upside down.

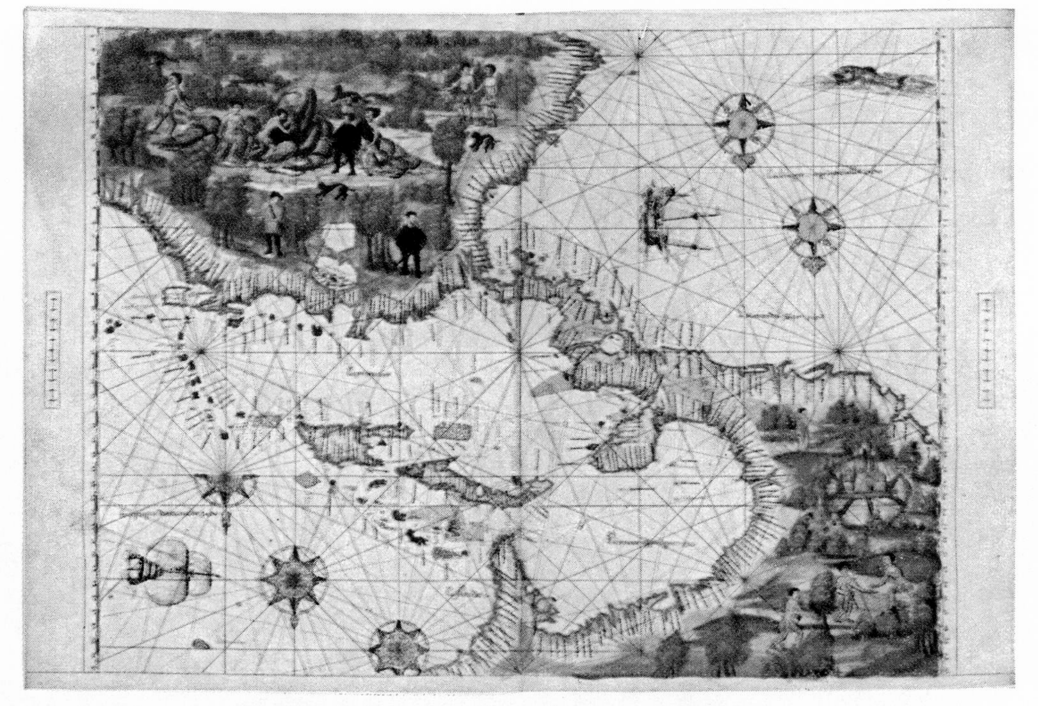

The Caribbean cradle of Spanish exploration is shown upside down, but with fair accuracy except for a European citadel in Mexico.

Cartier's landing in Labrador, in 1534, is celebrated in this map. The French explorer, wearing a short cloak, stands surrounded by the members of his crew. The river that flows behind them is the St. Lawrence.

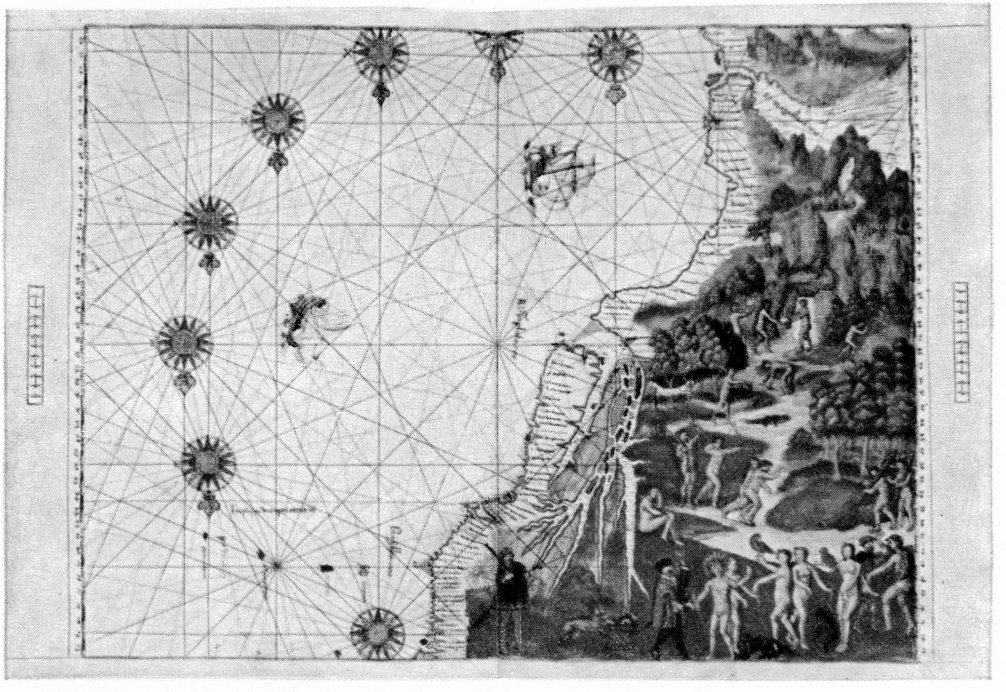

The Argentine coast is less closely drawn, except in the exuberant details of the La Plata estuary which Sebastian Cabot had explored.

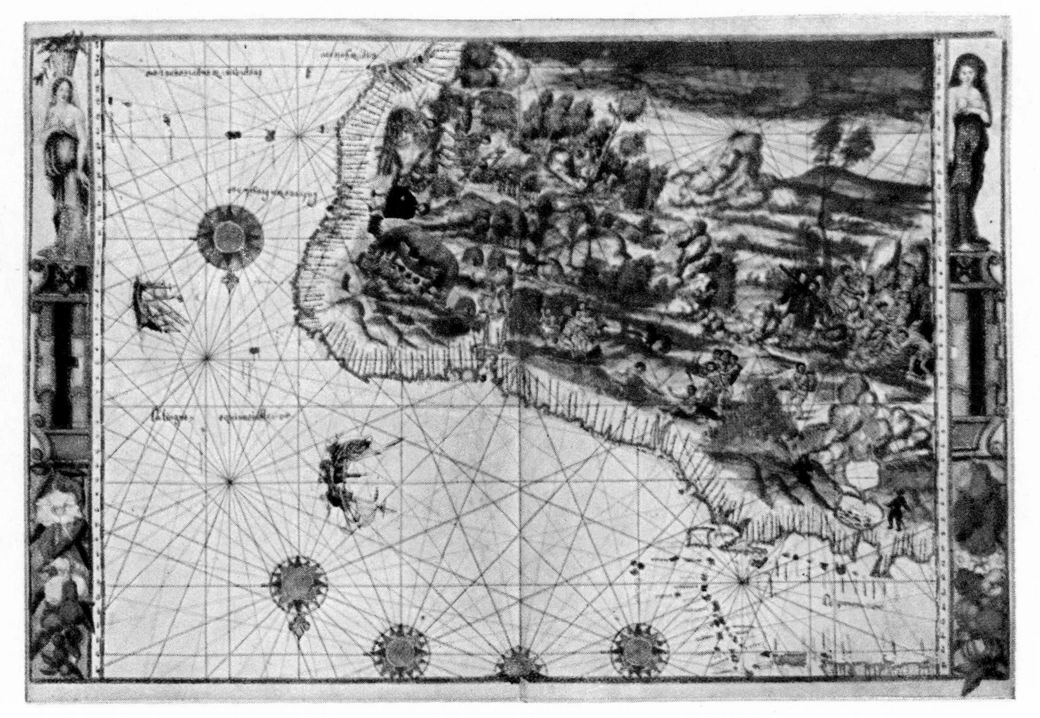

The nose of Brazil was a well-known feature, but only the mouth of the Amazon (*center*) was explored. At right, slaves dig for gold.

The Giraffe Parade, a Flemish tapestry made around 1525, was based on tales of returning travelers. In this reception for Portuguese traders in India native children ride polka-dotted giraffes led by bearded grooms. Wide-eyed Europeans found other wonders on their eastern voyages: featherless birds that "bray like asses," precious stones so common that slaves wore them as shoe cleats.

Potatoes and Utopias

LIKE a sea wind, news of the new worlds swept across Europe, sharpening men's appetites and minds. Every returning galleon brought a cargo of new materials and new flavors and new ideas. From Arabia came coffee which was to stimulate brilliant conversation in the coffeehouses of England. From other lands came tea, cocoa, tobacco, quinine, vanilla, sarsaparilla, lima beans, yams, tapioca, peanuts, corn, squash, tomatoes, potatoes (which are roots, wrote one of Magellan's men, "nearly like chestnuts in taste"). From Mexico came a large, handsome bird which the English called turkey, under the misapprehension that it came originally from Turkey, and which the French called *dindon*, under the misapprehension that it came from India. There was another less welcome import: syphilis. Though historians still argue the matter, this disease—which existed in America but probably not in Europe before 1492—was most likely first brought to Europe by Columbus' men and the Indians who came back with them. Picked up by Spanish mercenaries employed by the French in a war with Naples, the disease spread with awful speed.

While most Europeans were entranced or alarmed by the many tangible results of the explorations, philosophers saw in the broadened horizons a fresh chance for men to create a better way of life. Inspired by Amerigo Vespucci's account of his voyages, Sir Thomas More wrote *Utopia*, in which he envisioned an idealistic society, free of war and want, that might be set up in an unspoiled new world.

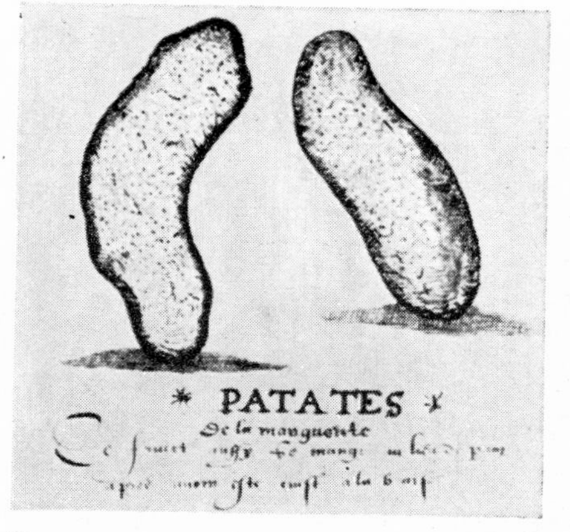

Potatoes were years becoming a staple food in Europe. At first they were cooked in wine or used as preserves.

Coffee came from Arabia, where the natives drank from big cups. Mocha, a coffee port, provided a popular name.

Cocoa beans from Mexico and Central America, mixed with sugar and vanilla (another discovery), made chocolate.

Utopia, the product of Sir Thomas More's hopeful imagination, was a mythical island off the coast of South America where wealth was divided equally and everyone lived in happy cooperation.

Tea came from China. It was brought into Europe by the Dutch and was then taken up eagerly by the English.

Giant crabs, pictured by de Bry, attack a shipwrecked crew off India. While the crew builds a boat from the wreckage, guards fend off the huge pincers. The crabs were supposedly big enough to slay men.

A penguin massacre by Dutch sailors takes place off the Straits of Magellan while the ship waits. The birds were edible and tame. Enough were killed, de Bry reported, to fill twenty-eight ships.

A market held by natives of Cartagena in South America abounds in fruit, fish, pepper, grain, gems and golden neckpieces. The garments worn by the natives were made of overlapping feathers.

A test of immortality is made in Puerto Rico. To disprove the myth that white men could not die, the natives held one under water until he drowned, examined the corpse (*left*), then took it to their chief.

Chinese locomotion, especially for women of high station, often consisted of sedan chairs hung with silken curtains. Chinese also used wagons fitted with sails which wafted them over flat terrain.

Peru's "Silver Mountain," then the world's richest silver mine, is pictured in cross section. Miners carry ore on their backs as they scramble up the rope ladder. The topmost man carries a candle.

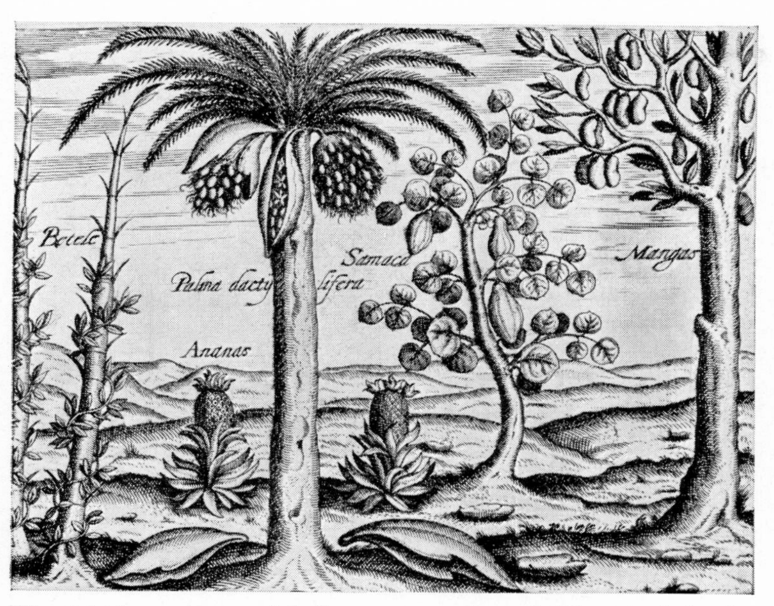

The fabulous plants of India were catalogued. They include the betel vine, whose leaves are chewed; the pineapple, "the best fruit in smell and taste"; the date palm; the "samaca" and the mango.

The Faraway Places

WITH no cameras to record the explorations, people who stayed at home during the age of discovery had to rely on artists to show them what the new lands were like. By far the busiest artist in this field was Theodore de Bry, of Frankfurt, Germany. De Bry, assisted by his sons, assembled a series of accounts of travels, illustrated them either out of his own imagination or from sketches made by voyagers, and published them in a series of fifty-seven books, grandly entitled *The Amazing but True Explanations of the Life & Manners of the Wilds in the East and West Indies.*

His illustrations, some of which are shown on these pages, are hardly remarkable for accuracy, but they conveyed to Europeans the excitement and fascination of faraway places. They incited many romantic stay-at-homes to invest their money in treasure hunts and wildcat voyages and, like recruiting posters, they beckoned young men down to the sea and lured them on to fabled lands where "fountains spout gold" and "all fruits are delicious to eat."

On the island of Ormuz, the temperature went so high that homes were built with holes in the roof and husbands and wives slept in caskets of water. Natives were also plagued by worms on their legs.

Tree dwellers in South America astonished Spain's explorers, who likened them to magpies. The treed natives fight with stones, water and arrows, but the attackers have the advantage of a sharp ax.

Beasts found in India include the elephant, whose tusks were sold mainly to the Portuguese, the crocodile, rhinoceros, tortoise and armadillo. In de Bry's imagination elephants were frightfully fat.

Javanese dancers, in separate rows of men and women, awed explorers by their sinuous movements. The musical instrument, something like a marimba, was made of sugar-cane stalks topped with metal.

A flying fish was drawn by John White. The Indians, said an observer, "hang and dry the fish . . . and they cut out fat to use instead of butter and sauce."

The American Indians

FOR half a century after the voyage of John Cabot in 1497, North America was a continent in waiting. The Spaniards sent desultory expeditions northward in search of gold—Narváez into Florida, de Soto across the Mississippi, Coronado through the southwest—but none was found and they soon lost interest. The French thought of North America chiefly as a base from which they might launch an attack on the Spanish dominions to the south. Not until 1540 did Jacques Cartier strike into Canada; still another seven decades passed before de Champlain established the fur trade there; and the prodigious explorations of La Salle, Joliet and Père Marquette came still later.

The British were even less interested in the colossal orphan. Indeed, they seemed positively in a fury at the mass of land that blocked the northwest passage to India. But as captain after luckless captain turned back from the search, Britain's public men began to consider the worth of the continent in hand. In 1585 the first British colony in North America was established at Roanoke Island, off the coast of what is now North Carolina. It failed, though not disastrously; but a second colony, sent out in 1587, disappeared in the wilderness without a trace. Yet errors of the colonists were shrewdly analyzed in the reports of agents, and later settlers were thereby enabled to avoid many of them. Most observant of all the reporters were Thomas Hariot, who wrote a long treatise on life in Virginia, and John White, who brought back a sheaf of water colors (some of which are reproduced on these pages) that gave to his countrymen their best description of the New World.

According to Hariot, the "tortoises, both of the land and sea varieties," were observed to be "more than a yard in breadth . . . good to eat, as are their eggs."

After a victory or an escape, said Hariot, the Indians "light a great fire. . . . Men and women sit around it, each of them holding a rattle made of a gourd." These they "shake as they sing and make merry."

A chief, when he died, was flayed and the flesh was scraped off his bones. Rewrapped in the dried skin, the bones were laid ceremoniously beside those of previous chieftains in the royal mausoleum.

This water color by John White gave Europeans a look at the Indians of Virginia and "the manner of their fishing." The braves in the background are trying their luck with spears tipped with needle-sharp fish tails. The Indians in the dugout "cannow" are cooking the catch. The picket fence at left is a simple fish-trap. Hammerhead sharks do not make the work any pleasanter.

The Defeat of The Armada

FOR nine historic days in July, 1588, the supreme powers of the Old World, Spain and England, fought a great sea battle for possession of the New. Among other things, Spain had been angered and alarmed by the cheeky buccaneering of Hawkins, Drake and Frobisher, who yearly took in prize a third of Spain's rich gold fleet on its way home from the Americas. The Invincible Armada of some fifty great galleons and eighty auxiliary vessels set sail to sweep the seas of Britain's scavenging sea dogs. The battle began in the English Channel, off Plymouth (*see maps at right*). For three days the fleets feinted at each other. At last the Spaniards made anchorage in the Calais roads. Next night, in the action depicted above, the British loosed fire ships into the Spanish formation. The Armada dispersed to the four winds in complete disorder. The British pursued, but most of the galleons made their escape under cover of a squall. In the end, however, less than half of the Spanish navy reached its home port. Britannia ruled the waves and over them, in the colonial centuries to come, would transport free men and free institutions to build the free societies of North America.

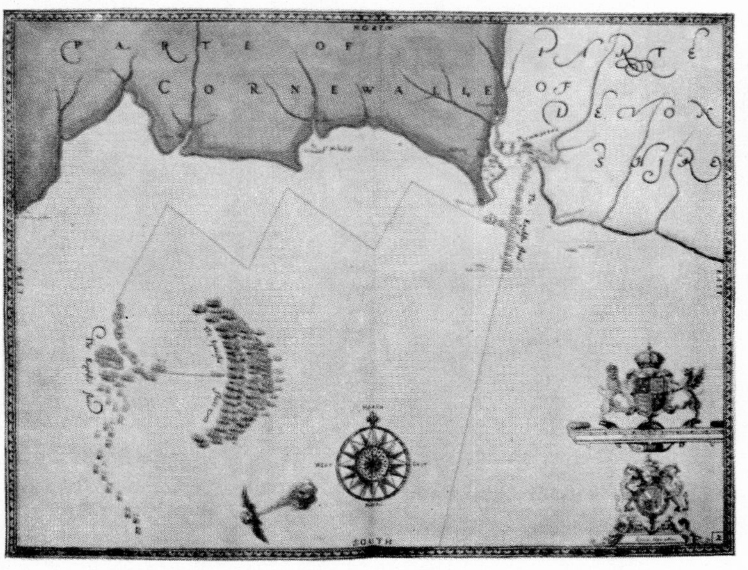

As the main English fleet gathers at the rear of the crescent-shaped Armada, reinforcements scurry out of Plymouth to join the fight.

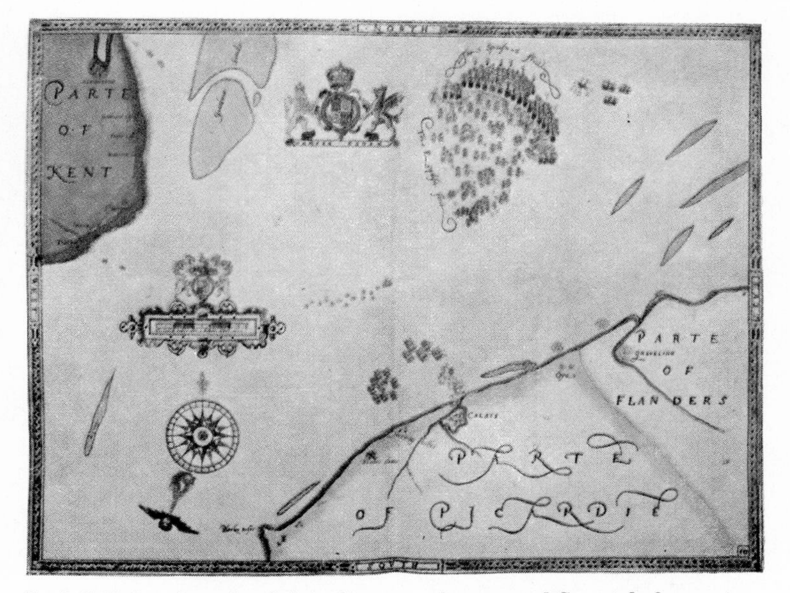

In full flight after the Calais disaster, the massed Spanish formation is chased out to sea by the agile tactics of the free-sailing British.

POTEST NEC

The Age of Elizabeth

SHE hath neither gown, nor kirtle, nor petticoat," wailed the good governess of the poor little Princess Elizabeth, Henry VIII's neglected child, "nor no manner of linen, nor forsmocks, nor kerchiefs, nor rails, nor body stitchets, nor handkerchiefs, nor sleeves, nor mufflers, nor biggens." The same, by a fair metaphor, might be said of the poor little kingdom the princess inherited in 1558 in her twenty-sixth year. Yet when the great queen died at seventy, her island kingdom was reckoned the most powerful in Europe, and overseas it had laid the groundwork for a magnificent colonial empire.

The main single credit for the rise of England belongs to Elizabeth herself. She was a plain woman with a bad complexion, red hair and a considerable vocabulary of profanities with which she augmented her powers of persuasion. Her courtiers flattered her that she had the head of a man (by which they really meant that they could not trick her) and the heart of a woman (by which they actually implied that she was vain). Between shrewdness and vanity the able woman steered for forty-five years a course that kept England at peace by keeping her enemies at war. Elizabeth's main queenly merit was her ability to use (and refuse) a bee swarm of brilliant men. With Leicester and Burghley she mended the rents in the nation's economy and composed, at least for a time, the violent faction between Catholics and Protestants. With Drake and Hawkins she pirated the wealth of Spain. With such accomplished gallants as Raleigh, Hatton and Essex she amused her private hours in a sofa dalliance that, as would appear, exhausted in epigram what she declined to spend in bed. By 1604, when a treaty of peace announced to the watchful chancelleries of Europe that Spain had been surpassed by her rival of the north, the old queen was dead. Yet of her lifelong "marriage to her kingdom" a thriving new England had been born.

Sir Walter Raleigh was an Elizabethan beau ideal—consummate courtier, skillful poet, bold seaman, sponsor of Britain's first colonies, the introducer of tobacco and potatoes, favorite of the queen.

In 1603, Elizabeth died and England, weary of a war that had been essentially won but could not be effectively concluded, patched up a treaty with Spain. Its signing was one of the first important acts of James I, the new king. In this painting the Spanish and Austrian negotiators are seated at left of the table, the English at right; the British secretary of state, Robert Cecil, is in right foreground.

← Elizabeth, in this contemporary painting, is dressed to the last extravagance of Renaissance court costume and stands regally on a map of the country she made great.

The busy Thames River at London Bridge is shown in this engraving made by Nicholas Visscher in 1616, the year of Shakespeare's death. The bridge itself, which travelers acclaimed as the marvel of the kingdom, was lined with shops and dwellings "so as a man . . . would judge himself to be in the street." Above the gate tower at the near end of the bridge the heads of traitors are exhibited on pikes.

The paragons of the age were a brother and a sister. Sir Philip Sidney was a poet of genius, a soldier of daring, a man of natural nobility; when he died in battle at 32, all England mourned. His sister Mary, countess of Pembroke, was the most charming and learned of Elizabethan women. Her son was the patron of Shakespeare. Her death provoked a scarcely known poet, William Browne, to write a famous epitaph:

Underneath this sable hearse
Lies the subject of all verse:
Sidney's sister, Pembroke's mother;
Death! ere thou hast slain another
Fair and learn'd, and good as she,
Time shall throw a dart at thee.

Tobacco, "a tawney weed" brought from America, added its fumes to the English air, as this comedy's frontispiece attests.

Adventure in the English Air

OVER Elizabethan England, stirred by the late-arriving Renaissance, the age of discovery blew a bright blue wind of adventure. Proud of their country, pleased with themselves and their accomplishments, Englishmen took a zest in merely living that made their little island fairly bounce upon its silver sea. The country squire sat upon his acres, the cobbler on his bench, as proudly as the queen upon her throne—and both professed to know as much of politics as she, and a little more of the classics. In the van of all the excitement were the English merchants, who headily set out to conquer the world in the name of commerce. What profit they could not take by cunning they seized by force. And in the English yeoman the merchants had a proper tool of imperialism. These yeomen, wrote Shakespeare, "do sympathize with the mastiffs in robustious and rough coming on, leaving their wits with their wives: and then give them great meals of beef and iron and steel, they will eat like wolves and fight like devils." Among the wolves and devils, through the crush of trade and scholarship, a little band of poets pushed their way—Spenser, Sidney, Marlowe, Jonson, Shakespeare, Drayton, Webster. This single generation of Englishmen would create of its life and times the greatest body of literature since the Greek.

The spirit of the discoverers inspired the philosophers. Sir Francis Bacon developed the modern concept of experimental science and had it depicted on this frontispiece as a voyage into an unknown sea.

One outlandish British import was the Indian princess, Pocahontas, who wed a planter, became a stylish London lady.

Adventure reached its apogee in the accounts of shipwreck on far-off islands. Captain John Smith's telling of such a tale, here illustrated, may have given Shakespeare the idea for his comedy, *The Tempest.*

The Mask that Montezuma Sent

The trophies of discovery were borne back to Europe, among them the strange, grinning mask of Quetzalcoatl, the white god and messiah of the Aztecs whose advent Aztec prophecies had long foretold. When the chieftain, Montezuma, heard that six hundred white men had landed on the coast of Mexico, he told his people, "Our lord Quetzalcoatl has arrived," and promptly dispatched an embassy bearing gifts for the white god, including this mask. The man who received them was no messiah, but an unsuccessful law student and ruthless adventurer named Hernando Cortes, the Spanish conquistador. Cortes gladly assumed the identity of the god and marched toward the Aztec capital. Willingly he accepted the chieftain's hospitality—then seized, ransomed, but did not release him. Later the Aztecs drove the invaders from the city; but Cortes destroyed their armies and gave to Spain an empire several times its own size.

THE PROTESTANT REFORMATION

The fearful drama of the Reformation was enacted on the bodies of men as well as in their souls. The denouement was apt to be the burning of a Protestant heretic in such a scene as this: ". . . the cruell handling of William Gardiner, an English merchant . . . in Portugall." The text that accompanies the woodcut relates that, when Gardiner's feet had been consumed by flames, "the tormentors asked hym whether he did not yet repent hym." He replied, "The truth remayneth alwayes one and lyke unto it selfe," and so expired.

VI

THE PROTESTANT REFORMATION

ON October 31, 1517, an Augustinian monk named Martin Luther nailed to the door of the church at Wittenberg ninety-five theses attacking the Church of Rome. The Protestant Reformation had begun and the titanic assertion that all men should be free to worship God according to their own consciences plunged Christendom into its greatest spiritual crisis.

The Protestant Reformation was, to begin with, wholly the work of Roman Catholics. For in the early sixteenth century all European Christians, with insignificent exceptions, were Catholics. From Poland to Portugal and from England to Sicily, the same sacraments and services in Latin, the same hierarchy of priests and bishops, the same holidays and the same symbols united some sixty million souls.

There had been repeated attempts before Luther to change the doctrines and practices of the Church. In the intellectual ferment of the thirteenth century the Albigensian heresy had won many converts in France. In fourteenth century England the followers of the Oxford scholar John Wycliffe demanded Church reform, the translation of the Bible into the vernacular and the simplification of the service. In the next century, the fifteenth, a related movement, led by John Huss, swept over Bohemia. All these heresies were violently stamped out by the combined powers of Church and state.

But the underlying causes of unrest were not rooted out. There was among all classes, including the noble and the learned, a feeling that the Church had lost sight of its true mission. It had become wealthy, worldly and top-heavy. During most of the fourteenth century the simultaneous existence of two popes, fighting each other's claims, publicized to all Europe the parlous state of its oldest and most venerable institution.

THE resistance of the Church to needed reforms was not alone responsible for the final break. After the miserable outcome of the Hundred Years' War between England and France (1337–1453) those two countries found themselves poorer in cash and needing capital for reconstruction. They resented the paying of Church tithes to their bishops and the steady drain of Church funds to Rome, as well as the demands of the many monks begging for charity. It seemed to the laity that the monks grew fat while they themselves grew lean. Kings and nobles looked with envy on the steady accumulation by the Church of lands and other property.

The moral, political and financial corruption of the Church was a source of shame and grief to all devout fifteenth century Catholics. It was wholly and solely the intention of most of the dissident Catholics to reform those abuses. Only in the course of that reform did it become clear that the real issue was much deeper and more divisive. On one side, the conservative Catholics felt that true worship was impossible without the mediation of priesthood, sacraments, ritual, between the soul of man and God. On the other, the Protestants maintained that, in worshiping, a man's soul must find itself face

No sooner had the Protestant sects made good their break from the Catholic Church than they began to quarrel with each other. Calvin called Luther a "minister of Satan." Luther, in this cartoon, tweaks Calvin's beard in reply. The Pope holds his ears against the fracas.

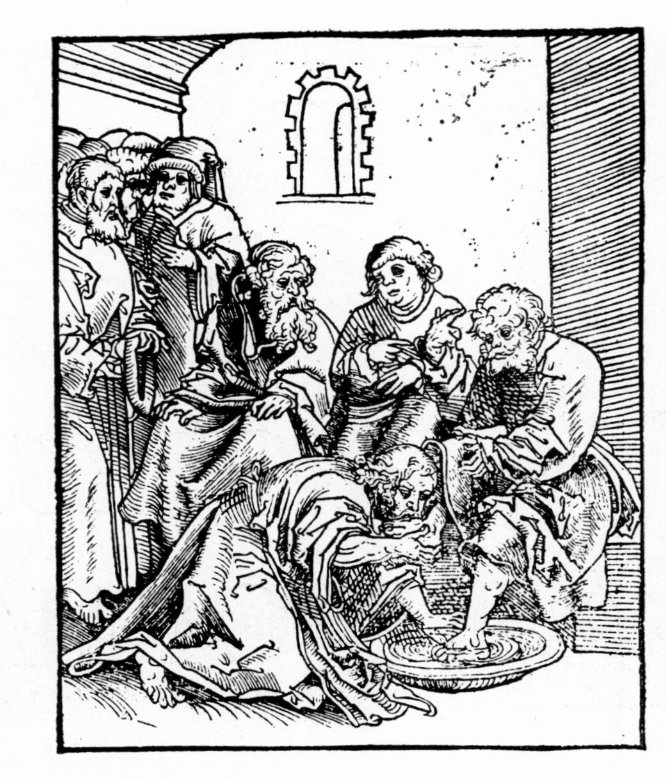

Anti-Catholic feeling found bitter expression in a series of woodcuts done by the Lutheran artist Lucas Cranach. They contrast the Pope with Christ. In the first of this pair, Christ kisses the feet of a disciple as He washes them. In the second, the Pope offers his foot to be kissed by subservient kings and nobles.

to face with God. This difference cut across the body of faith and only a forcible suture could heal it. The Roman Catholic Church attempted that suture and, in a struggle of unparalleled ferocity lasting some hundred and fifty years, it failed.

THE Age of the Reformation knew massacres that resembled battles—like that of St. Bartholomew's Day in 1572 when French Catholics murdered some eight thousand Protestants at the signal of the tocsin that still clangs shudderingly down the centuries. It knew persecutions that in duration, brutality and numbers of victims were serial massacres. It knew wars, civil wars and rebellions. It saw the revolt of the Dutch Protestants against King Philip II, the war between Protestant England and Catholic Spain, civil wars in Scotland, France, Switzerland and later in England, where the drama was heightened by the execution of a king (Charles I). In Germany, civil war turned into the Thirty Years' War and became general when most of Europe joined in. And above the rush of armies and the crash of cannon were heard the groans of martyrs and the awesome invective of bigots.

It has been observed that in the name of religion the Reformation caused more death and destruction than the Huns. For when men are resolved to test in agony the three insights that constitute their highest manhood—love of truth, love of freedom and that love of God from which alone the other two derive their meaning—horror is an inevitable reflex of humanity in strife. Nor does this horror impair at all that prayer in which the whole aspiration of the age was condensed, in which both sides of the great struggle might have united and to which John Milton, the Reformation's greatest poet, gave voice:

> . . . What in me is dark
> Illumine, what is low raise and support;
> That, to the highth of this great argument,
> I may assert Eternal Providence,
> And justify the ways of God to men.

A curious ecclesiastical deal, cynical even for that age, touched off the great charge. Prince Albert of Brandenburg, who was already archbishop of Magdeburg and of Halberstadt, had in 1514 secured the archbishopric of Mainz. But canon law forbade one man to hold three bishoprics. So the great sixteenth century banking house of Fugger lent Albert the money for the bribe which he would pay Pope Leo X to confirm him in his three offices. Representatives of both parties met formally and discussed the bribe. The Pope's deputies asked for 12,000 ducats—a thousand for each of the Twelve Apostles. Albert's men said 7,000 ducats—a thousand for each of the seven deadly sins. A compromise was reached on 10,000 ducats.

To make sure that the obligation would be met, Pope Leo X had granted to Albert the privilege of selling indulgences. In Catholic doctrine there is only one way a sinner can be saved from eternal damnation—by confession and contrition. But though he is saved from hell he is still liable to punishment for a period in purgatory. An indulgence is a promise by the Pope to remit this punishment in purgatory for a confessed sinner who has demonstrated his repentance by good works and real sacrifice (which might be a donation of money to the Church). With little regard for the spirit of this doctrine, the papal agents in Germany glossed over the fine points of theology and went about selling indulgences for prices adjusted to the sinner's means and the grossness of his sin. Half the proceeds of the sale of such indulgences would go to Albert to repay the Fuggers. The other half would go to the Pope, who needed the money to rebuild St. Peter's Church in Rome.

As pious Catholics, many Germans found this particular sale of indulgence shocking and injurious. The Catholic Church owned more than a third of all the land in the Germanies and both princes and peasants resented the drain of wealth toward Rome.

MARTIN LUTHER knew nothing about the deal between the Pope and the archbishop. He knew only that the indulgences were being sold by high-pressure methods, and that an agent of the Fugger banking house was on hand to keep accounts. Luther, moreover, believed that indulgences were

In this pair of woodcuts, Cranach draws a contrast between Christ's attitude toward money and that of the Pope. The first shows Christ driving the money-changers from the Temple and the second shows the Pope taking money from the sale of indulgences (remission of punishment for sins in purgatory).

theologically and morally wrong. In the theses which he tacked to the church door, he said: "The Pope is not able to remit guilt except by declaring it forgiven by God. . . .

"It is certain that avarice is fostered by the money clinking in the chest, but to answer the prayers of the Church is in the power of God alone."

Luther's was by no means the only protesting voice in Europe. Erasmus, the greatest of the humanist Biblical scholars, had made its corruptions the target of his witty and elegant learning. In France, another humanist, Lefèvre d'Etaples, was developing that strain of criticism which, amplified and clarified by John Calvin, would later bring the Reformation to a new pitch of power. In Zurich, Ulrich Zwingli was likewise preaching reform.

But it was Luther's voice that caught the listening ear of Europe. Thousands who read his theses or heard them read, heard, too, in the words of the unknown monk the tone of a strong man who is acting in the light of his convictions and what he conceives to be the will of God.

The response to his defiance staggered Luther. It also puzzled Pope Leo X. This son of Lorenzo the Magnificent, the greatest of the great Medici family, had been tonsured at the age of seven. At thirteen he became a cardinal. An astute intelligence imbued with the neoclassic spirit of the Renaissance and occupied with the vast political designs of the Church, Leo X found it difficult to realize the danger to the Church in the theological dispute in Saxony. Not until 1520 did he take any decisive measure against Luther. Then he issued the bull *Exsurge Domine* (Having gone forth from God . . .) which declared Luther's opposition to the sale of indulgences heretical and called upon him to recant within sixty days or be excommunicated.

Luther decided upon a dramatic action. Building a great bonfire outside Wittenberg, he publicly burned the whole canon law, signifying that he was no longer bound by it. Then he dropped into the flames the papal bull. That same year, in three powerful pamphlets, Luther formulated his position. He attacked the authority of the papacy and, in tune with the mounting spirit of nationalism that marked the age, called upon the restive German nobility to free itself from the alien tyranny of papal power. He denied the fundamental claims of the Church: that only the Pope may interpret the Bible authoritatively; that the priesthood is superior to the laity. These positions he denied in the name of the doctrine of the priesthood of all believers—the doctrine that every Christian is before God his own priest.

Finally he examined the Catholic sacraments. He found full justification only for communion and baptism, and partial justification for penance. Confirmation, marriage, holy orders and extreme unction might be customs worthy of the Church's blessing, but he denied that they were sacraments, and he thereby reduced the importance of the clergy who held the monopoly of administering them as indispensable rites.

Luther's central belief amounted to this: that salvation is possible not by good works, as the Catholics maintained, but by faith in Christ, and faith alone.

THERE was to be one more great historic scene. In 1521, Charles V, who had been recently elected Holy Roman emperor, convoked an imperial diet at Worms. One of the items on the agenda was "to take notice of the books and descriptions made by Friar Martin Luther against the Court of Rome." On the appointed day, Luther was kept standing outside the door for two hours. Then he was summoned in.

At one end of the crowded, sweltering hall stood the peasant's son, freshly tonsured and wearing his black Augustinian robes. At the other sat the most powerful monarch in Europe.

For the better part of two days Luther and the papal legates fenced theologically in Latin. At last he spoke simply and briefly: "Since Your Majesty and your Lordships ask for a plain answer, I will give you one without either horns or teeth. Unless I am convinced by Scripture or by right reason—for I trust neither popes nor councils, since they have often erred and contradicted themselves—unless I am thus convinced, I am bound by the texts of the Bible, my conscience is captive to the Word of God. I neither can nor will recant anything, since it is neither safe nor right to act against conscience. God help me. Amen."

The emperor rose abruptly and left the hall. Luther slipped out of the city. On the road to Wittenberg he was seized by soldiers. They were the elector of Saxony's men. The elector had long been Luther's friend. He had Luther conducted secretly to the Wartburg, a castle where he could hide until the danger of assassination should have passed.

In the Wartburg Luther undertook another imperative task—the translation of the Bible into ordinary German. Before the Reformation the doctrines of the Catholic Church were the sole authority for what a Christian might believe. Not the Church but the Bible, Luther contended, was the sole authority for faith. Nor could any Christian who read the Bible reverently fail to understand God's word.

But in the sixteenth century comparatively few Christians had read the Bible. It had been the first book printed when the new art was invented (about 1450) and at the time of the Reformation there were more Bibles in Europe than ever before. But these were in Latin. Wycliffe, the fourteenth century English reformer, had translated Holy Scriptures in part, but the Church still banned the reading of such unauthorized vernacular translations. Luther's powerful version was the first great work in modern German.

In earlier ages, the Lutheran outbreak might have been quickly suppressed. But now, in the sixteenth century, the political interests of the German princes, somewhat nationalist in cast, led a number of them to rally around Luther and so resist the too-powerful Emperor Charles V. A meeting of the princes at Spires declared in effect that the princes were free to regulate religion in their own territories. When later this decision was repealed by the Catholics, the Lutheran princes protested to the emperor, and it is from this protest that the new religion got its name of Protestant.

The liberating force of Luther's doctrines led to a social catastrophe. Excited by the atmosphere of revolt, the German peasants took fire and in the course of a savage uprising committed frightful atrocities. Luther, shocked by the peasant excesses and seeing his lifework threatened by the rebels' use of his doctrines, urged the authorities to drown the insurrection in blood. This decision helped to identify Lutheranism with civil authority, and it fixed its political forms. Luther's revolt was to rank as a first step, bold but limited, under princely guidance and protection. All of the Scandinavian countries accepted the new church, but there the Lutheran advance halted.

MEANWHILE, the task of spreading Protestantism had passed to another man, John Calvin. Through Calvin and his Reformed Church, Protestantism ceased to be a merely national or even Germanic movement. Inspired by his vision, expressed in lawyerlike logic and infused with invincible purpose, Protestantism would henceforth leap frontiers and convert whole nations.

Calvin, born in France in 1509, turned from the study of theology to law, returned to theology and, when only twenty-six, produced his great work, *The Institutes of the Christian Religion.* This most rational of all Protestant theologies could meet on equal terms the highly developed theology of the Roman Catholic Church. The core of Calvin's system was his faith that God is infinite and perfect—infinitely good and infinitely glorious. Man, by Adam's original sin, is wholly wicked. Yet man must "aspire to the goodness which he lacks, to the liberty of which he is deprived." God commands men to fulfill the law only to make them realize that they can do nothing without Him. God merely desires men to recognize their weakness so that they will rely on Him in all things.

Moreover, man is predestined. From eternity God has foreordained every good or evil act that every man will commit. From eternity he has predestined all who are to be righteous and all who are to be sinners. The righteous are God's elect. Since there is no way of knowing who is elect and who is not, the Christian must use this life in doing what he can for God's great glory. This somber doctrine released into the daily secular life of men an ascetic energy hitherto known only to monastic life at its highest. Worldly life became an opportunity to demonstrate the vehemence of faith.

At Geneva, a free Protestant city, Calvin sought to establish a city of God on earth. His first efforts to introduce the Calvinist scheme of the good life there were a failure. The unregenerate Genevans resented his efforts to ban dancing, cardplaying, drinking, sports and gay clothes. Calvin was ordered to leave the city. But he had touched the Genevese mind and was invited back in 1541. He refused to return until he was granted power to carry out his reforms. Accepted as leader, he was for some twenty years the religious and moral ruler of Geneva. He organized the ruling church by his ecclesiastical ordinances which laid down his whole program of life, government and thought, so that the entire city might become a church. He made Geneva a haven for Protestant refugees from other lands, so that the city became a citadel for defense of the faith and a center of propaganda for its dissemination. He did not hesitate to torture or burn men at the stake to fulfill his purpose.

From Geneva spread the men and ideas that strengthened the Dutch in their long struggle to achieve a republic free from Spain. John Knox found a haven there and went forth to harangue Mary, Queen of Scots. When Calvin died in 1564, he left Protestantism strong and expanding.

BUT a new force—the Catholic Counter Reformation—had already gathered strength and would henceforth successfully oppose the Protestant advance. No part of Western Christendom had remained wholly untouched by Lutheran or Calvinist teachings. Yet throughout Europe there was a solid core of Catholic piety which might abhor abuses in the Church but abhorred even more the thought of leaving it. Upon this piety the Church based its Counter Reformation, the great effort to purge itself of abuses and regain the souls that it had lost.

For this purpose Pope Paul III, upon the suggestion of Emperor Charles V, called a Church council at Trent. Beginning its sessions in 1545, the Council of Trent ended them, after several adjournments, eighteen years later. It opposed any compromise with Protestantism, strengthened and defined the authority of the pope and set up and carried out thoroughgoing reforms within the Church.

The correcting of abuses began at once. Bribery, luxurious

living, neglect of vows, nepotism, the traffic in offices, the sale of justice in the papal courts—all were quickly swept away. Prelates were ordered to reside at their benefices. Great banquets and hunting parties were abolished. Immorality was sternly repressed. Seminaries were opened for the proper education of priests. A new uniformity in faith and ritual was imposed.

Two great engines of authority implemented the Counter Reformation—the Inquisition and the Society of Jesus. The Inquisition was the Church's spiritual police. It had been established by St. Dominic in the thirteenth century for the purpose of detecting heretics and bringing them to justice. It had succeeded in exterminating the Albigensian heresy and had done its best to wipe out the larger reforming sect of the Waldenses. It had reached the peak of its activity in fifteenth century Spain under the cruel Inquisitor General, Torquemada. No such rigor was shown by the Inquisition in Italy during the Counter Reformation despite the increased activity of the Holy Office. But still, to achieve a doctrinal conformity, some people had to be burned, and a colony of four thousand Waldenses was killed or sold into slavery.

WHILE the Inquisition policed the regenerated Church, the Society of Jesus infused into it a new moral and intellectual vigor. The founder of the order, one of the world's great leaders of men, was Iñigo López de Recalde, now better known as St. Ignatius de Loyola. Born in the castle of Loyola in Spain's Basque country the year before Columbus discovered the New World, Loyola was thirty when the French invaded Spain. In that war he was wounded in the leg and left lame for life. During his convalescence, he asked for books of chivalric romance to read but, since none were available, was given instead the lives of the saints. Taking fire from these he decided to renounce the world and devote himself to defending the Catholic faith.

At a Dominican monastery in Catalonia, Loyola disciplined himself cruelly. He lived on bread and water, knelt for seven hours in prayer, scourged himself three hours daily and scarcely slept at all. Sometimes he was plagued by visions. Despair engulfed him. He was tempted to suicide. During the sickness that followed he became convinced that his extreme asceticism had been wrong. Angels appeared to him, showing him the road to salvation, and the saint decided to dedicate his body as well as his soul to God. For Loyola was, above all, a man of action.

He began preaching and soon gathered a group of disciples. These activities brought him to the notice of the Inquisition, which imprisoned him. Loyola cleared himself of heresy, but the Holy Office sentenced him to study theology for four years. In time he again gathered disciples who took oaths of poverty and chastity. He determined to form a holy order, called the Company of Jesus, a spiritual militia to be headed by a general with unlimited, lifelong command over the order.

LOYOLA became the first general and during the remaining sixteen years of his life directed the order's multitudinous activities. The purpose of his mission was to strengthen the Church by penetrating European society, influencing the men of all ranks who controlled it, directing education, gaining

After the Diet of Worms, where Luther proclaimed his freedom of conscience, he retired for his own safety to the Wartburg and there translated the Bible into German. Above is the title page of the original edition of Luther's Bible—a work as fundamental to German as the King James Bible is to English. Below, a contemporary cartoon shows the Pope superintending the burning of Luther's tracts.

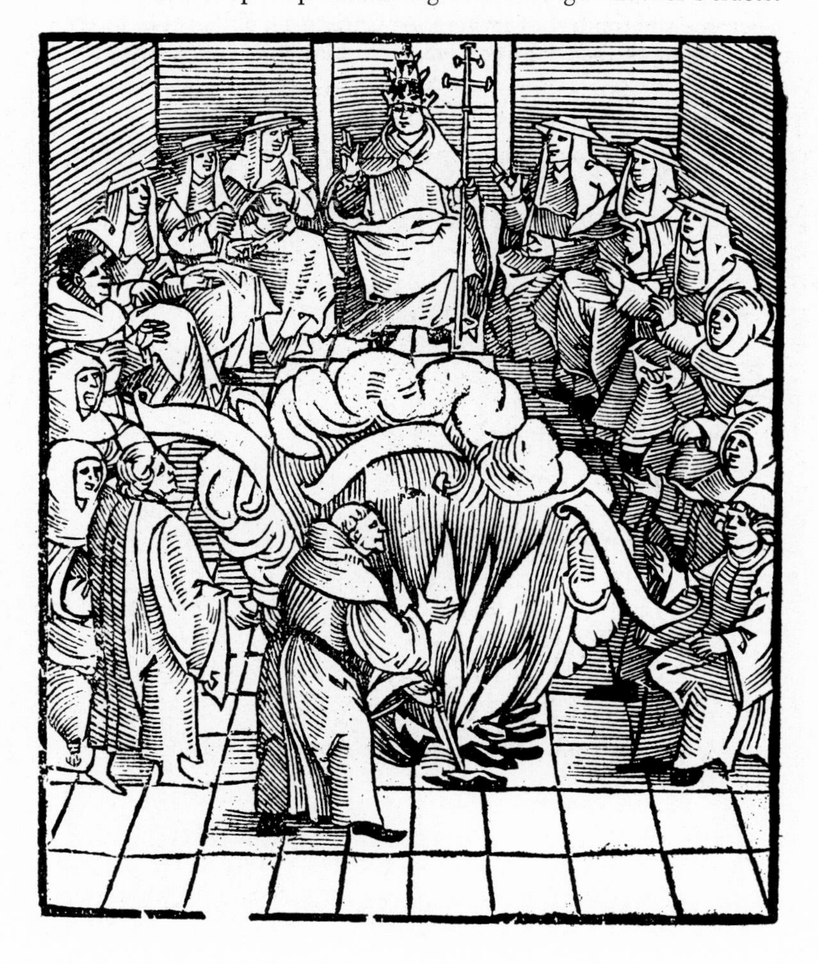

Luther's ninety-five theses are inscribed in bronze on the doors of the church at Wittenberg where he posted them in 1517. Also preserved (*below*) is his hideaway in the Wartburg, the castle where, under the protection of Frederick the Wise, elector of Saxony, he translated the Bible. In this room he is said to have thrown an inkpot at the devil, who had come to tempt him from his work.

Luther was the towering human figure of the Reformation. His violent anger was sometimes discharged in unprintable invective, as his fierce devotion was discharged in his great hymn, *Ein' feste Burg ist unser Gott* (A mighty fortress is our God). In middle age he married a nun—an act which profoundly shocked Catholics—and became the fondest of fathers. At Christmas, children in many lands still sing the songs he composed for his sons, among them the tender little carol, "Away in a manger, no crib for a bed . . ."

control of the confessional and preaching the faith in ways which would appeal to the imagination of the time.

To this end he forbade asceticism (it is better, he wrote, to strengthen the stomach and other faculties than to impair the body and enfeeble the intellect by fasting). He gave attention to the social arts by which the Jesuits could ingratiate themselves with people of influence. He preferred recruits "less marked by pure goodness than by firmness of character and ability in conduct of affairs, since men who are not apt for public business do not suit the requirements of the company." In dealing with the world the Jesuits should act like "good fishers of souls, passing over many things in silence as though these had not been observed, until the time came when the will was gained, and the character could be directed as they thought best."

Cheerful and intelligent worldliness was the Jesuit's public face. His personal life belonged to his order. He owned nothing. He was sent where the general ordered. He could be expelled and ruined in a moment. A network of intelligence agents reported to the general, who was himself subject to the surveillance of five agents of the order appointed for that purpose. In a generation, the Jesuits had spread their organization over most of Europe. Kings, ruling groups, strategically placed persons and even whole governments (like that of Portugal) were in their hands. Poland was reconquered to the Catholics and soon Jesuit missionaries were at work on four continents. And though their success and power made them dreaded even by Catholics, there was no question that their martial morals and subtle influence had rejuvenated the Church in its time of need and mightily helped to check the Protestant Reformation in its triumph.

MEN born early in the sixteenth century found themselves at its close living in a world visibly changed and still changing. The tenor and the pace of life had altered. The most permanent feature of Western civilization was henceforth to be change itself. In the boyhood of such men, the Catholic Church had been the sole spiritual power in Europe; its overthrow was inconceivable. In their old age, the Catholic Church had lost many of the western and northern nations and was reduced to a competing power even in France. In their boyhood, the temporal power of the Church, of which the Holy Roman Empire was one expression, had extended from Gibraltar to Poland. In their old age, the idea of nationalism had taken root in the double institution of monarchy and nation. Men no longer thought of themselves as members of medieval communities, more or less local, but as Englishmen, Frenchmen, Dutchmen, Spaniards.

The spirit of freedom which found its religious expression in Protestantism found its secular expression in commerce. Commerce was the high adventure of the age, calling forth in a supreme degree the qualities that the new faith and the wars of faith developed—individual initiative, enterprise, vigor.

Nor did the energy of the new spirit stop with the sixteenth century or the continent of Europe. It leaped the Atlantic Ocean and cleared a continental forest, and found a dwelling place where the new dignity of the individual, safeguarded by his new freedom of faith could, under God, build a citadel, an arsenal and an altar.

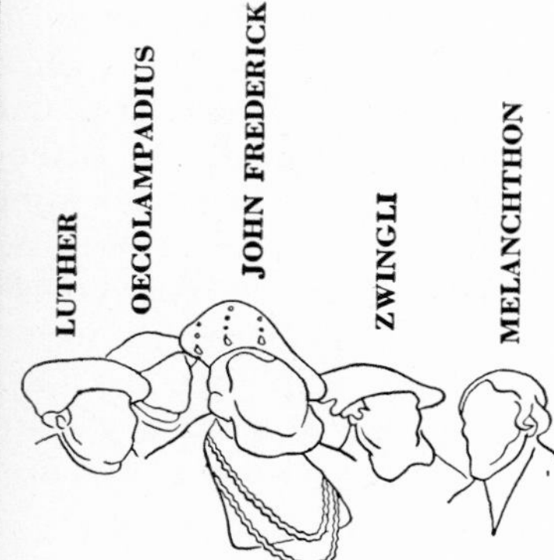

Martin Luther and his friends were painted about 1530 by Lucas Cranach, the elder, who probably pieced the picture together from portraits done in his busy workshop. From left to right are Martin Luther; John Oecolampadius; John Frederick the Magnanimous, elector of Saxony; Huldreich Zwingli, the Swiss reformer, and Philipp Melanchthon, Luther's associate. Later Oecolampadius and Zwingli got into bitter theological disputes with Luther. The magnanimous John Frederick occupies the central position in this painting because he and his family were Luther's protectors. His uncle, the elector Frederick III, sheltered Luther in his castle from the Catholics after he refused to recant any of his heretical propositions.

Attacks on the Church were made in the guise of allegories by Reformation artists. The painting above, an allegory on conditions in the Low Countries done by a Flemish artist around 1550, shows Catholics marching toward ruin. In the center is a wagon of hay which symbolizes the false delights of earth. About it both clergy and laymen are fighting for hay. Following the wagon (*left*) are a worldly pope and a mounted emperor. Atop the wagon are nude figures, probably representing sin.

The Fishers for Souls, done in 1614 by Adriaen Pietersz van de Venne, depicts Catholics and Protestants competing for converts in the Netherlands. Following Christ's words, "I will make you fishers of men," rival religious leaders pull people from a river. Anti-Catholic James I of England and Prince Maurice of Holland stand on the left bank. At right are Catholic Archduke Albert of Austria and his wife, Isabella. The rainbow symbolizes a time of peace between long religious wars.

The cruelty of Catholic Spain was set down in another allegorical picture copied by Pieter Bruegel, the younger, from his famous father's painting. It is entitled *The Massacre of the Innocents* and ostensibly shows Herod's soldiers slaying the babies of Bethlehem. But the backgrounds and costumes are those of Bruegel's own day. His object was to compare the evil of Herod with that of Spain, whose troops often came sweeping through Dutch villages slaughtering the Protestants.

Mary Stuart, Queen of Scots, never met a man—save one—who remained impervious to her royal charms, and her beauty fired even the unknown painter of this portrait. Mary had four husbands and many lovers; in the end a woman, England's Virgin Queen, contrived her ruin. "Passion alone," a poet wrote, "could shake the double fortress of her impregnable heart and ever-active brain."

From the pulpit of the Cathedral of St. Andrews in Fife, John Knox preached his crusade against Mary, Queen of Scots. His listeners compared him to "five hundred trumpets blustering in our ears."

The Queen and the Preacher

OF all the characters, great and small, who swept through the bloody drama of the Reformation, none were more oddly paired than Mary, Queen of Scots and John Knox. Mary, the daughter of a Scottish king, had gone to France at the age of five to become the child bride of Francis II and had acquired all the graces of the French court. She was a devout but tolerant Catholic. Knox, the son of a Scottish farmer, had been a French prisoner and galley slave, had studied with Calvin and had braved persecution in four countries for preaching the new Protestantism. He brought to Scotland a Presbyterian creed modeled on that of Calvin's church and an eloquence fired by hatred of the Catholics. He was short, with bulging brows and long black beard. Mary was tall, slender and possessed of such warmth and beauty that historians still find it difficult to judge her impartially. Both Mary and Knox had high intelligence, high courage and a high, hot hate for each other.

By 1560, pushed by Knox, who was the most influential preacher in the land, Scotland had suppressed Catholicism and adopted Protestantism as its official religion. So when Knox heard that Mary, after her husband's death, was sailing home to occupy Scotland's throne, he feared that once again his country would be ruled by the Church or "the synagogue of Satan," as he called it. Mary was quite willing to let Protestantism flourish in Scotland. But, she said, "I will defend the Kirk of Rome for I think it is the true Kirk of God." Then Knox called Mary a Jezebel and the Church of Rome ". . . a harlot . . . polluted with all kind of Spiritual fornication. . . ." In open argument Knox could always outtalk the queen and reduce Her Majesty to unmajestic tears.

When Knox first glared at Mary under his heavy brows he was already middle-aged and his adventures, except for marrying a girl of seventeen, were nearly over. But Mary's tragedy was just beginning. Finding a husband for the widowed queen of nineteen became a chief concern for all her counselors, including England's Protestant Queen Elizabeth, who was anxious that Mary make an alliance with England instead of some rival power. A distant cousin, vain and handsome Henry Stuart, Lord Darnley, was found acceptable to all parties and Mary wed him in 1565. Eager for power and jealous of Mary's influential secretary, David Rizzio, Darnley became the focus of a plot against his own wife and Rizzio. When Rizzio was murdered, Mary vowed revenge and when Darnley was killed in a gunpowder explosion, suspicion fell at once on the queen and her Protestant lover, the earl of Bothwell. Three months later, she married Bothwell.

HOUNDED now by Protestants and Catholics alike, the queen's miseries increased. Knox intensified his campaign of vituperation against her. Refusing to trade the life of Bothwell for her throne, she finally abdicated in favor of her son James VI and spent the last nineteen years of her life as a virtual prisoner of her old enemy, Elizabeth. Knox died, but he seemed to have called down heaven's curse on Mary. A queen without a country, Mary plotted to help Spain invade England and dreamed of replacing Elizabeth on the throne. Elizabeth discovered the plot and brought Mary to one of history's most famous trials.

Although Mary pleaded her cause with superb eloquence—the exact degree of her guilt has never been settled—she was sentenced to death in 1587. With majestic tranquility she mounted the scaffold. After she had kneeled on a cushion and bowed on the block, the fumbling axman had to strike three times before he severed the head. As he grabbed it by the hair to show the onlookers, he found he was holding only the wig, and Mary's head rolled grotesquely to the floor. With it the Reformation in England lost a great enemy and John Knox, now fourteen years dead, won the final victory.

Art, to John Calvin, was a saucy bawd—to be eyed with suspicion. Calvin therefore seldom had his portrait painted. These classroom doodles by an irreverent pupil are among the few likenesses extant.

Calvin and the New Piety

THE Protestant Reformation was the greatest religious revival Europe had experienced since St. Paul came out of Asia crying the Messiah. Piety became a lifelong adventure, earnestness the mien of delight. Holiness was snatched out of the mouths of saints to become the daily bread of millions of ordinary men. For a brief, beatific instant of history it seemed as if the society of men might truly become a "society of saints."

John Calvin thought so. At the age of twenty-six, Calvin had written his *Institutes of the Christian Religion*, the great theological summary of Protestantism, and had quickly been acclaimed as the Luther of France. "*Decretum Dei aeternum horribile*" (God's everlasting law is frightful), the *Institutes* declared, and on this iron idea Calvin built his church. His theology prepared men to face the total animosity of the universe; and the theocracy he founded at Geneva provided them with a stern rehearsal of their fate. His city was first divided into quarters. For each quarter a body of elders was appointed, with right of entry and full search not only to a man's house but also to his conscience. To assist the elders in their inquisitions, an army of spies was set loose in the community. Their presence became so commonplace that the posted regulations of the inns contained this item: "Nobody shall be allowed to sit up after nine o'clock at night except spies." The law of Calvin was no less severe than his God's. The arrangement of a woman's hair was prescribed and the displacement of a wanton curl might be punished by the husbandly lash. Capital punishment was decreed for such crimes as adultery, blasphemy, heresy and witchcraft.

Toward the end of his life, racked with disease, Calvin pursued a senseless reign of terror in Geneva. Nevertheless, Geneva continued to be the mecca of Protestantism, the Holy City to which many of the dissenting sects turned for a common inspiration. The spirit of John Calvin proved greater than the man and the sternly beautiful doctrine of Calvinism survived the heartless practice he made of it.

In England the Pilgrims, a group of separatists from the Established Church, were among the most pious of the dissenters. Seeking freedom of worship, one band of Pilgrims left England and settled at Plymouth, Massachusetts. In this painting by Johann Schwartze the Pilgrims are shown at their first public prayer. Elder Brewster is leading the service and Miles Standish stands in the foreground.

England was the first nation to make Protestantism its state religion. The Church of England, established by Henry VIII, was fortified by Elizabeth and James I, who authorized the famous translation of the Bible that bears his name. King James is shown here at an Anglican service, held in 1620 in the court of old St. Paul's to raise money for the "speedy reparation" of the cathedral.

This engraving by Charles van Mallery depicts two scenes in the history of the Society of Jesus. At left, Pope Paul III confirms the society; at right, St. Ignatius de Loyola receives its laws from God.

The Council of Trent, shown at work in a contemporary engraving, affirmed the theology while revising some of the practices of Catholicism. The council met at three long sessions between 1545 and 1563.

Martino Martini, an early Jesuit missionary in China, is shown here, dressed as a mandarin, on his way to pay a visit to the emperor. Father Martini was the first European to make a map of China.

The Counter Reformation

As the tumult of Protestantism raged outside the Church, the cries of loyal critics arose within. The result of this double assault was the Catholic Counter Reformation, a movement as deep and broad and enduring as the Protestant Reformation itself. The Catholic reformation began at the center of the Church, the Vatican. A succession of great popes first put their *Curia* in order, then proceeded, by means of the sessions of the Council of Trent, to extend the reform through the college of cardinals to the episcopates and finally into the ranks of the priesthood. In this task, and in conducting the ideological war against the Protestant sects, the Church brought into play the most efficient body of Christian soldiers ever organized—the young and vigorous Society of Jesus.

The order of Jesuits had been established a few years before, in 1540, by St. Ignatius de Loyola, a Spanish devotee of the faith who had once been a soldier. His society was organized in military cadres on the principle of absolute obedience. A Jesuit swore to obey his superior officers "like a corpse which can be turned this way or that, or a rod that follows every impulse, or a ball of wax that might be molded in any form." The Church now hurled this praetorian guard of the faith into the battle for men's minds. In Italy, by their inspired preaching, the Jesuits brought on a tremendous religious revival among the common people. In Germany they drove a deep wedge into the mass of Lutheran converts.

Not only Europe but the world was divided into Jesuit provinces. At the death of Loyola, sixteen years after the society was founded, Jesuit missionaries were already at work along the Amazon and the Congo and in the wilds of Abyssinia. Francis Xavier, the greatest of the early Jesuit missionaries, voyaged from Ceylon to Cochin China to the Moluccas and north to Japan, preaching everywhere and baptizing tens of thousands. In the soul-searching of its own reformation, the Catholic Church had found a new depth of meaning in its beliefs and a fresh release of its evangelical power.

In North America the Jesuit missionaries suffered hardship and death in bringing the gospel to the Indians. Here the martyrs St. Jean de Brébeuf and St. Gabriel Lalement are tortured by Iroquois.

Francesco Gichè deliniavit Sculpsit

An Auto-da-Fé

At the height of the Catholic inquisition in Italy, a burning of heretics was run off with all the fanfare of a carnival. This eighteenth century engraving by Francesco Giche depicts an auto-da-fé (act of faith) held in Palermo, Sicily, for Sister Geltruda and Brother Romualdo. Both the woman, a Beguine (a religious who could own property), and the man, a friar, were accused of "Quietism and Molinism," with some "Illuminism and Impeccability" thrown in. The convicted pair—wearing the heretics' tall caps—burn in the center of the stockade. A slab of stone prevents them from seeing each other and so finding company in their misery. Sister Geltruda, says the chronicler, met her end in silence, but Brother Romualdo perished "with much weeping and exclamation." Nearby, the masked judges menace the victims with crosses; the privileged get a close view of the proceedings; lesser heretics huddle beside the tumbrils that brought them and await their own punishments. In a great ring around the whole proceedings stand the loges of the wealthy spectators who appreciatively watch the performance. In the space between, the wine merchants have set up shop (*center foreground*), carriages and bravoes parade, money-changers with scales pursue their business (*right foreground*) and all the world makes holiday.

Henry VIII

Charles V

Francis I

The Birth of the Nations

IN the autumn of 1555 the last of the great Holy Roman emperors stumbled off the throne and into a monastery. Charles V had planned wisely and fought well to keep together, on the foundation of a universal Church, the international character of his empire. Yet all through Charles's reign a mysterious force had operated to pull the old order apart.

This force, which emerged from the curious interrelationships of the Renaissance and the Reformation, was nationalism. Its influence was felt all over Europe at once. In Spain, a bulwark of the Holy Roman Empire, nationalism was nourished by the sudden showers of gold from the Americas. In the Netherlands, religion and nationalism collaborated to foment Protestant rebellion against Catholic Spain, and a bloody war for independence absorbed the first energies of the new nation. In France, the patriot's new zeal was for years expended in the aggrandizing schemes of Francis I.

In England, however, nationalism found a cunning exploiter in Henry VIII. Henry's private desires fortunately conjoined with England's public interest. The break with Rome gave Henry Anne Boleyn; it gave England a national church. His ruthless suppression of the barons allowed Henry to express his taste for power; it allowed England to escape an ominous civil war and to consolidate under a central authority. But the Continent—and particularly Germany—was ravaged by a war that raged without stop for a hundred years. Only in 1648, by the Treaty of Westphalia, was the violence of the Reformation concluded in a balance of power among the states.

In 1520, the new potencies of France and England met for treaty-making upon the Field of the Cloth of Gold near Calais. Henry VIII, eager to outvie Francis I, threw up a palace covering twelve thousand square yards. However, nothing was accomplished in a month of banquets but the death of twenty-two hundred sheep.

The Treaty of Westphalia ended the Age of the Reformation. For the liberated Dutch, Adriaen van Nieulandt painted their Prince Frederick Henry doffing his sword, while his son receives an olive branch from the Angel of Peace. A figure symbolic of the united provinces sits at center with a lion (for fortitude) by her shoulder. →

The merchant George Gisze was one of the Protestant traders of northern Europe who came to dominate the Continent's business. A north German, he represented the Hanseatic houses in England where, in 1532, Hans Holbein painted this famous portrait. Gisze, who dressed far more elegantly than did his later bourgeois brethren in the Netherlands, sits in his office surrounded by business accessories—money box, scales for weighing gold, metal ball containing twine and, for decoration, a beautiful vase of pure Venetian glass.

The Rise of Bourgeois Man

BEHIND the huge historic events of the Reformation, certain subtle changes were transforming the basic fabric of society, bringing into being amid the smoke and fury of religious and dynastic struggles a remarkable new species of man. Bourgeois man, product and progenitor of the middle class, turned out to be the heir of all the former ages. His golden hour was the seventeenth century, his cradle the Netherlands.

In that time and place bourgeois man, crossing the abyss that had for so long divided aristocrat and peasant, ruled and owned not only a nation but a world empire. Possessed of neither a hereditary aristocracy nor a strong clerical authority, Holland was the first modern state to be governed in its entirety by businessmen. They owned its wealth, controlled its politics and dominated its philosophy. From 1600 to 1690 the prosperous Dutch were the wonder and envy of debt-ridden Europe. Travelers marveled at the miracle that had bequeathed to a fog-covered, land-poor morass of "united bogs" the commercial and financial supremacy of the Western world.

With the curiosity of a modern anthropologist, Sir William Temple, English ambassador to The Hague in 1668, analyzed the strange race which had wrought this miracle. "The merchants and tradesmen," he wrote, "are of mighty industry. Never any country traded so much and consumed so little. They buy infinitely, but 'tis to sell again. They are the great masters of Indian spices and Persian silks, but wear plain woolen and feed upon their own fish and roots. They sell the finest of their own cloth to France and buy coarse out of England for their own wear. They send abroad the best of their own butter and buy the cheapest out of Ireland for their own use. They furnish infinite luxury which they never practice, and traffic in pleasures which they never taste."

"Their common riches," Temple observed shrewdly, "lie in every man's spending less than he has coming in." Not only was their frugality and asceticism a strong bar to idle self-indulgence, but "the general intention every man has upon his business" appeared to leave them no time even for the enjoyment of love. "All appetites and passions seem to run lower and cooler here than in other countries, avarice excepted," Temple explained. "Their tempers are not airy enough for joy, nor warm enough for love. This is talked of sometimes among the younger men, but as a thing they have heard of, rather than felt. I have known some that impersonated lovers well enough, but none that I ever thought were at heart in love." As for drinking, he added, "the merchants and traders never do it in the morning nor till they come from the Exchange." In the evenings, they would sometimes partake of wine and brandy, "as the only reward they enjoy of all their pains, and as that alone which makes them rich and happy in their voluntary poverty who would otherwise seem poor and wretched in their real wealth."

To an English aristocrat in the lush age of the English Restoration, the frugality and sobriety of the Dutch seemed no

The Amsterdam Exchange was the financial pulse of Europe. On the open floor bulls and bears met in daily battle, state loans were floated and shares of corporations were busily traded. Any respectable businessman could walk into the Exchange and start trading.

The busiest harbor in the world during the seventeenth century was Amsterdam's, which stretched along the Y, an arm of the Zuider Zee. The port was protected with a stockaded row of pilings to prevent unfriendly ships from entering. Amsterdam prospered not only from respectable traffic which crowded its harbor but also from the loot brought in by the *Watergeuzen*, the pirates of the North Sea.

In the harbor of Batavia, half a world away from Amsterdam, a chief agent of the Dutch East India Company stands with his wife and a native boy. The Dutch built the port of Batavia for their ships, then used the ships to carry Asiatic trade between Asiatic ports. With the freight-carrying fees, they could buy Eastern goods and ship them to the Netherlands without having to draw out scarce bullion.

less extraordinary than the freak of fate which made them the masters of European economy. Their country had, as Daniel Defoe observed, "neither corn, hemp, tar, timber, lead, iron, arms, ammunition, woolen manufacture, or fish of their own growth." The entrance to the port of Amsterdam, through treacherous shoals and tidal flats, offered as many perils as a voyage to Spain. Yet Amsterdam was undisputed mistress of the world's trade. The Bank of Amsterdam dictated world currency values. The Amsterdam Exchange was the world's chief trading mart. The Dutch economic empire stretched from Java to the Hudson River. The Dutch businessman, minus blue blood or cultural tradition, fired by no great patriotic allegiance or religious or intellectual dogma, had somehow become the peer of the greatest monarchs of Europe. How did it happen that bourgeois man, this uninspired parvenu, could dare to appropriate the earth and claim the seventeenth century as his own?

THE rise of bourgeois man coincided with the rise of capitalism. By 1500, trade between Europe and Asia had brought great wealth to the free cities of Italy. With their fleets and warehouses, they handled Europe's imports—silks, spices and Oriental handicrafts, and its exports—rough woolen cloth, minerals, and fair-skinned Christian girls and eunuchs for the harems of the Ottoman Empire. The merchants of Venice and the bankers of Florence were the first businessmen to enjoy the new wealth of Europe.

Yet, despite their head start in history, the Italian cities were not the true incubators of the middle class. Year by year their riches trickled over the Alpine passes to the north and west. The mineral wealth of the Tyrol and the Baltic trade brought early prosperity to the northern cities. In Lübeck, Augsburg and other German towns the features of bourgeois civilization began to evolve: building regulations, paved streets, lighting, fire departments. Frankfurt maintained a municipal doctor and Nuremberg, a street cleaner. While the landed aristocrats lived among their livestock in dank stone castles, the city burghers dwelt cozily in bright, painted houses with glass windows, private libraries and running water in the kitchen and conducted their affairs from handsome offices with thick carpets and paneled walls. A fifteenth century British visitor observed that the middle class of Nuremberg lived better than the king of Scotland.

Augsburg was a town of millionaires. Out of its population of eighteen thousand in the year 1540, some 278 citizens commanded fortunes totaling more than 10,000,000 gulden ($200,000,000 in 1951 purchasing power). The giant of these, the first great self-made millionaire of western Europe and perhaps the most influential business tycoon of all time, was Jacob Fugger the Rich. The wars of the late fifteenth century had produced a mining boom not unlike that of nineteenth century America. Towns grew overnight; miners' unions fought to keep an eight-hour day and went on strike. (A miners' strike in 1496 was settled by arbitration with an agreement to behead ten of the union leaders and three company officials.) By canny trading Fugger bought up enormous mineral holdings until he held virtual control of Tyrolean silver and Hungarian copper. He exploited them along modern capitalistic lines, introducing water-driven machinery to increase production and keeping control of transportation and marketing. He invested his profits in textiles, lands, castles and quicksilver mines. His banking business was given the right to mint currency. His worldwide newsletter service was the Associated Press of sixteenth

The East India House in Amsterdam was the headquarters of the world's first great corporation. It was office, warehouse and arsenal for the fleet. Its cellars were fragrant with bales of spices, its halls enlivened with the armor of countries where company ships called. In an abattoir at back, herds of cattle were slaughtered and the meat salted for use by the fleet.

century Europe. Between 1500 and 1527, Fugger's fortune increased from 200,000 gulden ($4,000,000) to 2,000,000; on his death in 1546 it was estimated at 4,000,000 gulden. He advanced the funds with which Charles V bought his election as Holy Roman emperor, in what was subsequently termed the biggest business deal of the century. When the debt was slow in being repaid Fugger wrote his emperor a dunning letter such as no bourgeois had ever dared address to his monarch. "It is evident and clear as day," he wrote, "that Your Majesty could not have secured the Roman Crown without me, and I can show documents to prove it. . . . Accordingly I humbly request Your Majesty . . . to command that my outstanding sum of money together with the interest for the same be returned and paid out to me without any further delay." Dictator of the finances of half of Europe, intimate of kings, Jacob the Rich still never succeeded in climbing out of the middle class. The patricians of Augsburg blackballed him from their clubs, excluded him from their gatherings and snubbed him to the day of his death.

IN the end it was the Netherlands that ushered the middle class into its inheritance. Even before the great discoveries, Baltic and Venetian trade routes had crossed in the Low Countries. With the opening of the Atlantic ship lanes, Antwerp became the chief port and queen city of Christendom. Each week two thousand freight wagons and ten thousand peasant carts rumbled through its gates with the wares and produce of a continent. Four hundred ships often rode in on a single tide, disgorging on its quays wool from England, tallow from Norway, pitch from Sweden, grain from France, silks and spices from the East, gold from the Americas and the silvery haul of the North Sea fisheries. In Antwerp, insurance first became big business—life insurance as well as cargo and ship insurance. The Antwerp Bourse, founded in 1531, was the world's original stock exchange.

Antwerp's decline began with the great crash of 1557, which was precipitated by the bankruptcy of Spain. Drained by wars, paralyzed by a feudal economy, Philip II finally revealed to a horrified world the desperate state of Spain's exchequer: 11,000,000 ducats in debts and expenses against only 1,330,000 in assets. Although German and Italian bankers bled themselves white in an effort to stave off universal disaster, Spain's bankruptcy was soon followed by that of Portugal, France and the Spanish Netherlands (Belgium). The collapse of the Antwerp Bourse wiped out investments of over 20,000,000 ducats. Even the House of Fugger was irreparably shaken, and in 1650 it, too, went under.

Out of the great debacle a new kind of businessman arose amid the salt marshes of the northern Netherlands. The growth of this empire was not in the tradition of the conquistadors, for the Dutch shied away from bloody battles over empty wilderness. They left the exploitation of the forests to the Spanish and French and concentrated instead on trade. Neither manufacturers nor producers, they made themselves the universal "waggoners of the waves." The Dutch, wrote Daniel Defoe, "are the Carryers of the World, the middle Persons in Trade. . . . They buy to sell again, take in to send out." Their merchant marine numbered sixteen thousand ships out of an estimated total of twenty thousand for all Europe. The fast, low frigates developed by the East India Company for double duty in trade and battle were unbeatable in both. So swift and skillful were Dutch builders that their services were sought by all the maritime states of Europe. The king of Spain commissioned them to build an entire war fleet, equipped to the last cannon ball, and on delivery sent it to attack Holland.

The syndics of merchant guilds were the boards of directors of the day. These are the syndics of the cloth-makers guild grouped for a portrait by Rembrandt. Formed by merchants to regulate trade practices, the guilds helped establish the position of the middle class. But their regulations got in the way of bourgeois man's enterprise and the power of the guilds waned.

The Dutch East Indies Company was a kind of private admiralty. Most of the company ships carried letters of marque authorizing them to hijack treasure on the open seas. The line between trade and piracy was imperceptible in the operations of the company whose dividends averaged eighteen per cent for 198 years. Dutch operatives took the trade of Japan, Borneo and Java from the Portuguese, planted outposts in Australia, harried Spaniards in the Mediterranean, Venetians in the Adriatic and Swedes in the Baltic, swept rival traffic from the Rhine, seized the absolute monopoly of the Russian fur trade and, after buying Manhattan Island for $24, cut it up into lots and made a killing in real estate. "Are they with force unable to invade?" asked a British pamphleteer. "No matter: they'll undo the world by trade."

The Amsterdam Exchange succeeded the Antwerp Bourse as the trading pulse of Europe and it was there that all the techniques of Wall Street fully evolved. The first bears began operating about 1608 and were known as "counterminers" or "misanthropes." The bulls were called "lovers." The Dutch operators, a British observer wrote in bewilderment, "invent new ways of trade—great quantities of brandy being disposed of every year, which are never intended to be delivered." By mid-century Amsterdam was the seat of operations for the exchequers of Europe and the Amsterdam Bank had acquired a reputation as the safest financial haven on earth.

The Dutch bourgeois did not have to operate behind the panoply of crown and scepter; he not only ran the state, he *was* the state. The wealthiest families of each city controlled politics, and the wealthiest city, Amsterdam, ran Holland. In each generation a "*kring*," or clique, of dominant families monopolized key jobs in government, the church, the militia and the schools. The greatest business dynasty of the seventeenth century was the Bicker family who, by a domestic arrangement, coolly divided the world's trade among themselves. Andries Bicker, burgomaster of Amsterdam, chose the Russian fur monopoly; one of his brothers, the rest of the Baltic; another brother, south Europe and the eastern Mediterranean; and the youngest, Cornelis, all the Americas. Besides running Amsterdam, Andries was manager of the East India Company. Cornelis managed the West India Company—and so successfully that in 1628, following the capture of the Spanish silver fleet, it declared a fifty per cent dividend. The third brother, Jan, operated one of Holland's great shipyards. Andries's son-in-law commanded the municipal garrison.

TO foreigners, the Dutch business oligarchy was puzzling and not altogether attractive. The philosopher Descartes, who lived in Holland from 1629 to 1640, complained that "every man thinks only of himself and his business interests, and whoever has nothing to do with business and trade . . . is completely disregarded." Sir William Temple, summing up his observations, stated flatly: "Out of such a nation can come neither good conversation nor great statesmanship."

These somewhat bilious views stemmed in part from the fact that business and trade had not become quite respectable in Christian Europe. For a thousand years the basis of the Church's social ethics had been St. Paul's words, "Having food and raiment let us be therewith content. . . . For the love of money is the root of all evil." To desire more than "a sufficient livelihood" was avarice, a deadly sin. "The man who buys in order that he may sell dearer," Aquinas wrote, "is justly condemned, since regarded in itself it serves the lust of gain."

The Protestant Reformation had opened the floodgates of business enterprise. A keynote of Calvinism, particularly as it was expanded and developed by the Puritans in the

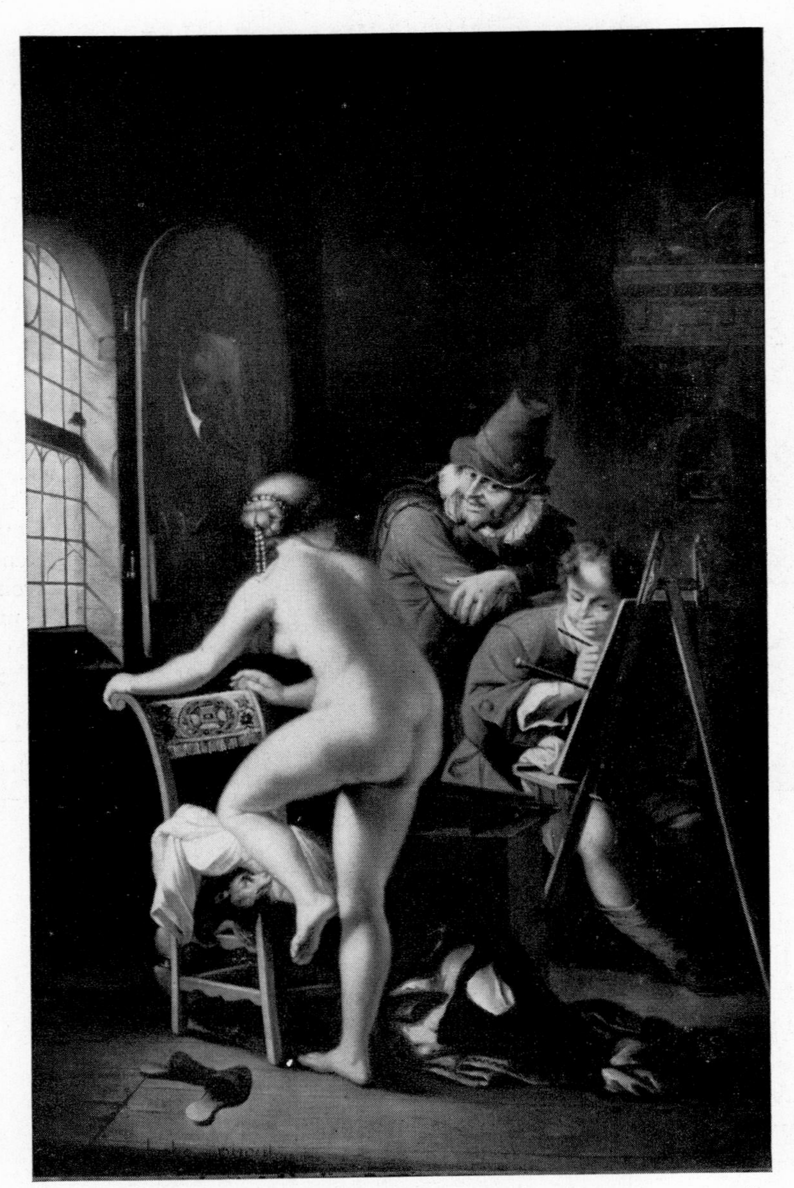

Bourgeois prosperity was shared by Dutch painters who generally had a good market for their work. Artists found it useful and profitable to become specialists—one in canal views, another in portraits, or household scenes or nudes. Above, Arnold Houbraken shows a painter's studio, featuring the Dutch idea of an attractive nude; below, Joos van Craesbeeck shows a determinedly convivial group.

century following Calvin's death, was the concept of dedication to one's calling. "The Great Governour of the world hath appointed to every man his proper post and province." Whatever a man's calling might be, it was his Christian duty to pursue it to his fullest abilities. In his own shop the tradesman could "most confidently expect the presence and blessing of God." Thus pursuit of economic gain, which was once regarded as a dangerous frailty if not a sin, became an ethical duty to be undertaken for the glory of God. Poverty was not a virtue. Indeed, it was the Christian's moral obligation to choose a gainful occupation and "drive it as far as it will go." In this bracing philosophical climate the Dutch middle class came to flower.

Although Puritanism colored the economic ethics of Holland, it never became the obsessive force it did in England, where it touched off a civil war, or in New England, where it produced a theocracy. The Dutch bourgeois were too stubbornly practical, too levelheaded to be dominated by any abstract mystique, and they were essentially tolerant in religion, persecuting neither Catholics nor Jews. Holland was the haven for refugees from all the religious wars of Europe.

ALL in all, the Protestant Dutch businessman was considerably more full-blooded than the dour and pious Roundheads across the Channel. He tended, for one thing, to indulge his children—or rather, as the scandalized French saw it, to spoil them—by refraining from corporal punishment at home and enjoining it in schools. His adolescent daughters were inclined to be saucy. His wife, often well-heeled in her own right, seemed independent and self-assured. The Dutch bourgeois treated even his household servants with amiability. There was something fundamentally homely and perhaps ludicrous about the sight of him scuffing around the house in carpet slippers, tending his tulips and puffing on his extravagantly long-stemmed clay pipe.

His house also reflected his individualistic spirit. When the Dutch patroon made his fortune he did not, like the Florentine merchant princes, erect a palace or, like the German millionaires, a dark, cluttered townhouse. He reared a comfortable dwelling with high, wide windows through which the sun could stream. His house was often surrounded by impeccable groves of precisely planted trees and inside it was spotless. The uncarpeted floors were of gleaming tile, daily scoured and sanded. Neat and functional, the Dutch home emphasized comfort rather than esthetic indulgence. Yet, a contemporary historian observed, "the plainest and most modest burgher had a house full of pictures, and there was nothing unusual about finding from one to two hundred paintings in a modest home."

The sun began to set on the Dutch business empire following the Anglo-Dutch wars of 1652–1674 which were wars for commerce, ignited by jealous merchants of both countries. By the end of the century the hub of commerce was shifting westward as it had before, this time to the island across the Channel. But the Dutch had shaped the mold for the proud, self-governing bourgeois—the middle class whose members would in time dominate the free nations of the West and be hailed by a nineteenth century statesman as the "natural representatives" of the human race on earth.

In this detail of Jan Vermeer's study, *A Woman Weighing Gold*, a girl looks on her gold and jewels with loving solicitude. The velvet of her jacket was a famous Low Countries product. The fur probably came from a trading post in Russia, the gold from colonial markets.

The Lowlands: A Man-made Pattern

THE Dutch? "A little people of merchants," sniffed the historian Hippolyte Taine, "lost on a pile of mud." Yet beauty grew in the mud, and the merchants were men who could appreciate it. In this *View of Haarlem*, Jacob van Ruisdael painted the kind of beauty Dutchmen liked to see in their landscape—the useful loveliness of tidy towns and fertile farms, peaceful spires and graceful windmills. The fields of the lowlands spread away as far as eye can see in a gentle diagram of sweet prosperity. The sturdy dikes enclose the fields and the straight canals divide them with the prim rigor of lines on a graph paper.

No other landscape in Europe is so intimate or seems so much the work of human hands—as indeed it is. The work began a thousand years ago, when the Dutch found their country slipping away beneath their feet. The Rhine and the Scheldt and the careless waves were washing it out to sea. Nothing daunted, the sturdy Dutchmen threw up dikes to push back the incursive ocean and dug canals to carry off the floods. With windmill pumps they drained the marshland. In the seventeenth century alone they added two hundred thousand arable acres to the land and developed on them an agriculture as thrifty as any on the Continent. A system of crop rotation was perfected, and the cultivation of fruit trees and flowers was conducted with an unprecedented success. The growing of the tulip, a flower imported from Turkey, became a great industry—and a greater craze. A speculation in bulbs began that raised their value to more than their weight in gold. One bulb sold for 3,000 florins, and then was traded for a carriage and pair of horses. Another was exchanged for twelve acres of good land. In 1609, a bulb sold for 13,000 florins. In 1638 the market collapsed and thousands were ruined. Yet it is significant of the Dutch that they should have been betrayed into a financial panic in part by their love of beauty as well as by their love of gold.

Solid, stolid and careful, a burgher and his wife pose for Rembrandt van Rijn: she, quilled and goffered to the nines; he, the model *mijnheer* in his glossy black velvets and stark white ruff. Her plumpness was considered an attractive attribute by the well-fed Dutch.

A Game of Skittles, painted by Pieter de Hooch, takes place in an ordered garden. Skittles (bowling), skating, cards, backgammon and a primitive variety of golf were favorite pastimes. The Dutch liked their houses stately and plain, their clothes rich and elegant.

In *The Linen Closet* by de Hooch, a young woman learns housewifely duties by helping her mother store linen in a handsomely carved closet. The Hollanders were among the first to make common use of underclothes and bedding. The child is playing with a golf club.

The practical burghers of Holland had little use for music. An air that was sung was a breeze blown by—what did a man have to show for it? But a painting of a piece of music, that was another thing—a man could hang it on his wall. This glowing piece of visual music, *The Concert*, was painted by Gerard Ter Borch, who loved to display rich fabrics and fine woods, all enhanced by a warm Dutch light.

The Gallant Offering is by Jan Steen, who in the seventeenth century ran a public tavern in the Dutch city of Leiden and knew well the rowdy scenes he loved to paint. In a good-natured parody of flowery courtship, a young roisterer prances through the door, bearing two onions and a salt herring which he grandly presents to a buxom *vrouw*. At portraiture of the common gesture, the Dutch were unsurpassed.

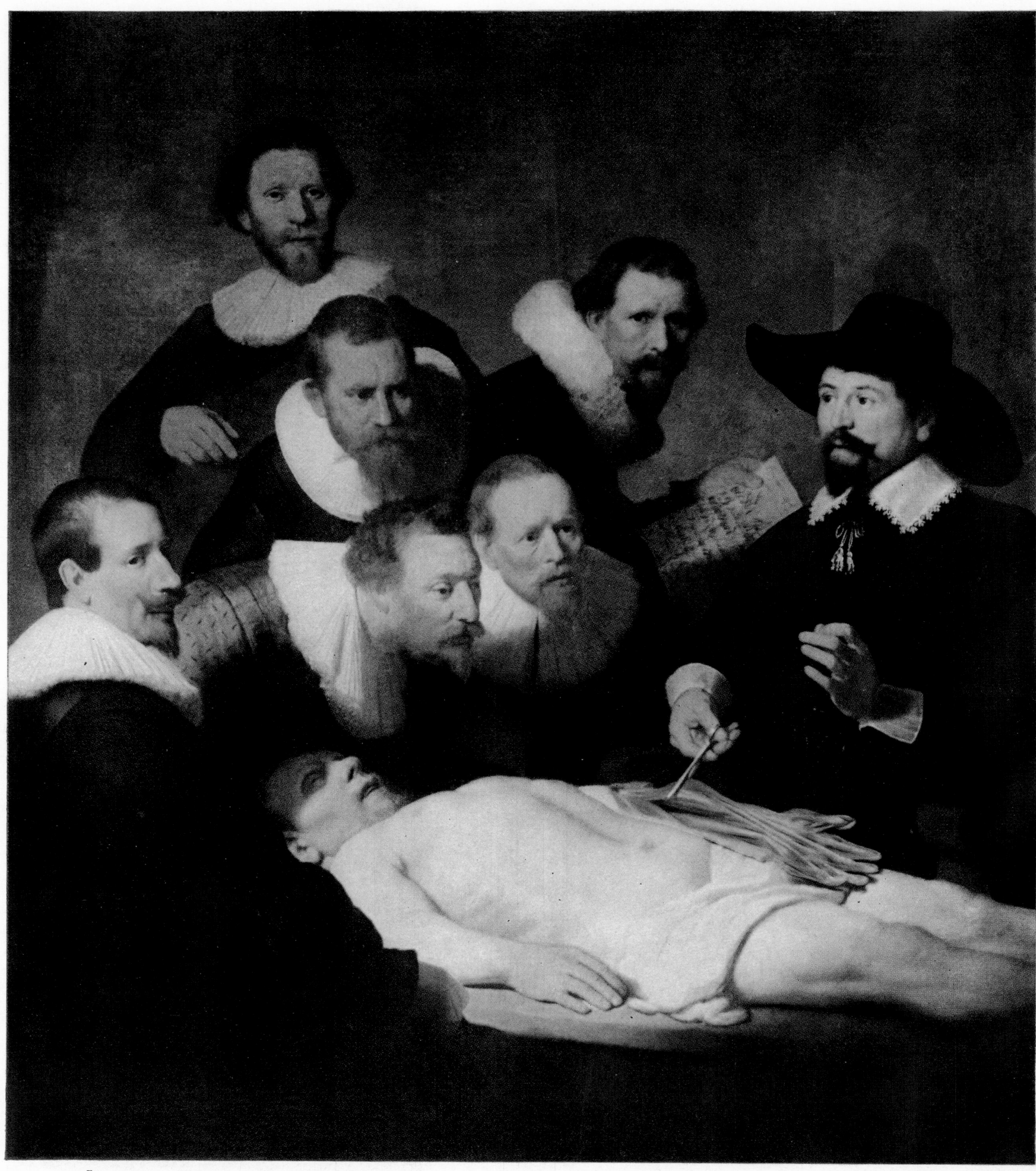

In painting *The Anatomical Lecture of Professor Nicolaes Tulp*, Rembrandt was not performing a mere exercise in the macabre, but illustrating a strong tendency in the spirit of his time—the discipline of natural curiosity to scientific method. The new interest in anatomical knowledge aroused the medical men of Europe to a passion of dissection and helped found the modern science of healing. At times the demand for corpses outran the supply and a ghoulish profession of "resurrectionists" grew rich robbing the cemeteries.

The Dawn of Modern Science

"SINCE a babe was born in a manger," the philosopher Alfred North Whitehead once observed, "it may be doubted whether so great a thing has happened with so little stir." For the dawn of science came quietly, hardly noticed in the thunders of the Reformation and the Thirty Years' War. Yet during the astonishing age of genius that began in 1543 with Copernicus' revelation of the earth's movement around the sun and culminated with the publication of Newton's *Principia* in 1687, man's whole picture of the world about him was forever altered. In the most dazzling outburst of the scientific intellect in history, the misconceptions of two thousand years dissolved and new concepts arose which would ultimately produce the Industrial Revolution and the machine age of modern times.

Throughout the entire Christian era, science had lain dormant and men had viewed nature through a veil of erroneous ideas inherited from the ancient Greeks and scrupulously cultivated by the medieval Scholastics. Paradoxically, the Greeks were by no means always wrong. Many of them came unbelievably close to the truth. In the fifth century B.C., Anaximander and Empedocles foreshadowed Darwin by suggesting that all life originated in the slime of primordial seas and evolved by means of natural selection and survival of the fittest. Leucippus, Democritus and Epicurus developed an atomic theory of matter. Heraclides held that the earth was a sphere and rotated on its axis once daily. Aristarchus of Samos not only realized that the earth revolved around the sun, but first appreciated the relative size and distance of the sun and moon and the immense remoteness of the fixed stars. Eratosthenes of Alexandria computed the circumference of the earth to within two hundred and twenty-five miles. Yet owing to the exigencies of history it was not these inspired perceptions which survived, but rather the misapprehensions of Aristotle, whose reputation so far transcended those of all the other ancients that for two thousand years his utterance on any subject was accepted as final. Aristotle held that the mysteries of nature could be unraveled by abstract deduction from "self-evident" principles. To such a question as "why is sea water salty?" he would have answered, "Because it is the nature of sea water to be salty." Aristotle was the favorite philosopher of the medieval Church, and as late as 1750 no student could graduate from Oxford who questioned even one of his precepts.

THE key to the brilliant explosion of scientific accomplishment that produced the age of genius was a profound change in methods of thought, characterized by an eagerness to observe and to experiment, and above all to determine how things happen, rather than why things happen. The scientist's calling, as Sir Francis Bacon first defined it in his enormously influential work, *The Advancement of Learning*, in 1604, is "to put nature on the rack and compel her to bear witness." Where the Aristotelians sought by pure contemplation to arrive at some vast over-all view of nature, the

Dutch physicist Christian Huygens improved the refracting telescope of the early seventeenth century which, to correct chromatic aberration, had been getting impractically long and more cumbersome. Huygens eliminated the tube, placed the outer lens on a pole.

The world's first modern observatory was built by the astronomer Tycho Brahe on an island off Denmark in the late sixteenth century. Equipped with underground shops, a printing press, a library and every type of instrument save the telescope (which was not invented until 1608), it set new standards of accuracy. This picture shows the domes of its underground observatories and some instruments.

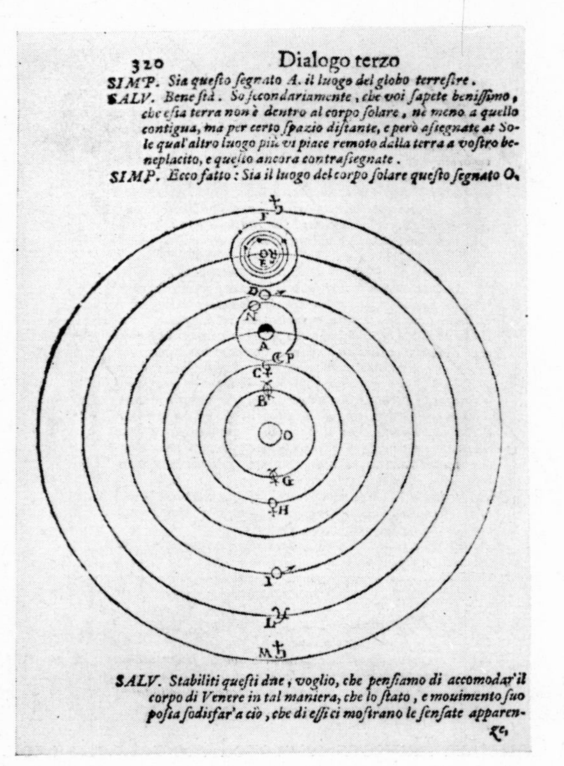

320 Dialogo terzo

SIMP. Sia questo segnato A. il luogo del globo terrestre.

SALV. Bene stà. So secondariamente, che voi sapete benissimo, che essa terra non è dentro al corpo solare, nè meno a quello contigua, ma per certo spazio distante, e però assegnate al Sole qual'altro luogo più vi piace remoto dalla terra a vostro beneplacito, e questo ancora contrassegnate.

SIMP. Ecco fatto: Sia il luogo del corpo solare questo segnato O.

SALV. Stabiliti questi due, voglio, che pensiamo di accomodar'il corpo di Venere in tal maniera, che lo stato, e movimento suo possa sodisfar'a ciò, che di essi ci mostrano le sensate apparenze.

Galileo's drawing of the solar system shows the sun and the orbits of six planets. The earth is shown with its one moon; Jupiter, with four.

Galileo's telescope, which he built himself, reduced distances to one-thirtieth, revealed starry wonders.

Galileo noted the positions of Jupiter's satellites from January 14–25, 1611, on the back of a letter addressed to him in Florence (Firenze).

triumphs of Galileo, Newton and their heirs grew out of their passionate interest in facts and details, their willingness to measure things (rather than merely classify them), to verify their observations by controlled quantitative experiment and to state their findings in precise mathematical terms. "Now if a man will begin with certainties," said Bacon, "he shall end in doubts; but if he will be content to begin in doubts he shall end in certainties."

When the great age of science dawned, the accepted picture of the universe was still that of the Alexandrian, Claudius Ptolemy (who died about 168 A.D.). Ptolemy's blueprint of the solar system had enabled astronomers for fifteen hundred years to predict the planetary movements with remarkable accuracy. Its only flaw lay in the fact that its premises were wrong, for Ptolemy placed the earth at the hub of the universe and had the sun and other planets revolving around it.

In 1512, a highly educated and versatile Pole, Nicolaus Copernicus, began the arduous years of computation that ultimately led him to his great conclusion that the earth is a "wanderer," while "the sun, as if sitting on a royal throne, governs the family of stars which move round it." Handicapped by poor eyesight, erratic instruments, a morass of conflicting observations and above all by his delusion that the planets travel in the perfect circles ordained by Aristotle, Copernicus took twenty years to bring his mathematical theory into agreement with existing observations. When he had completed his work, *De Revolutionibus*, he suppressed it for another decade. Contrary to popular opinion, the Church did not at first get very concerned about *De Revolutionibus* and it was not until 1616 that it landed on the Roman Catholic "Index" of forbidden books. But Luther attacked it violently and a number of distinguished laymen publicly disbelieved it —among them Shakespeare, Montaigne, Bacon and Pascal.

MEANWHILE two other great astronomers contributed materially to the validation of Copernicus' ideas. The first was the Dane, Tycho Brahe, who, on an island off Elsinore, constructed an elaborate and sumptuously equipped observatory. Tycho was the most meticulous observer the world had known. He not only constructed better instruments than had ever been employed but, what was far more important, he evolved the modern scientific method of taking many observations and averaging out the errors.

The paradox of Tycho's career was that his painstaking readings were applied by his youthful assistant, Johannes Kepler, to improve the Copernican theory which Tycho had attacked as contrary to physics and to Scripture. Try as he would, Kepler could not at first make Tycho's observations fit any known theory. But after Tycho's death he took the daring step necessary to bring fact and theory together. That step was to postulate that the planets revolved not in Aristotle's ideal circles but in elliptical paths. As soon as Kepler made this inspired assumption everything fell into place. In two books, written between 1609 and 1619, Kepler defined the laws of planetary motion with such accuracy that no error was discovered for two hundred years.

At about the time that Kepler published his planetary laws, astronomy received a tremendous impetus from the invention of the telescope by a Dutch optician named Hans

Tycho Brahe, the Danish astronomer, was a fiery, truculent man who lost part of his nose in a duel. An ingenious craftsman, he made himself a new nose of gold and silver and wore it until his death.

Galileo was a professor of mathematics at the University of Padua from 1591 to 1610. His lectures were so popular that a special hall, seating more than two thousand, had to be obtained for his public.

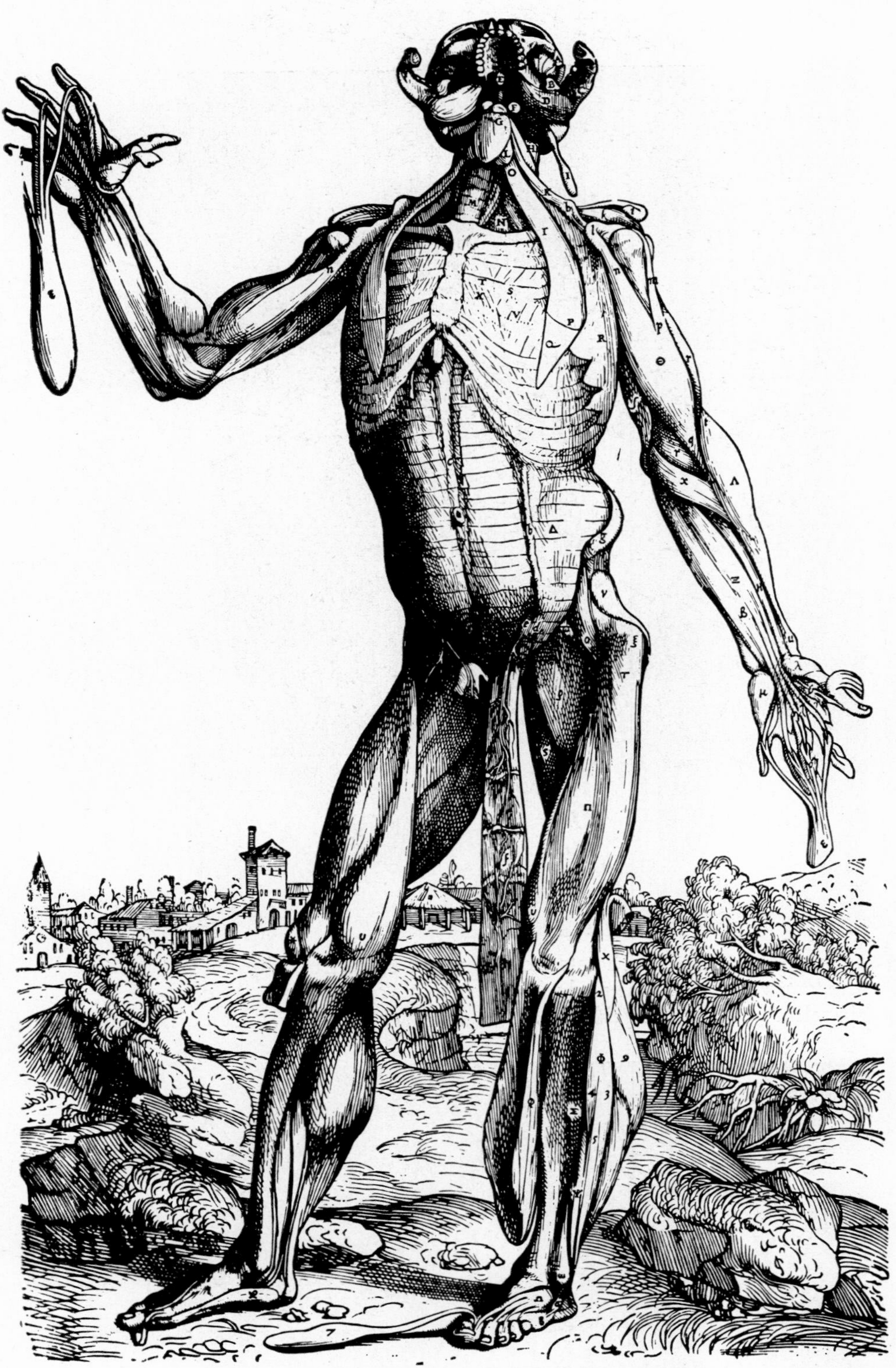

Modern anatomy began in 1543 with the publication of Vesalius' *Fabrica*, which first accurately described the human body. This woodcut shows a cadaver with jawbone split and muscles cut away.

Lippershey. Word of this new invention reached Professor Galileo Galilei in Italy, and with no further information than that such an instrument could be made, he set to work grinding lenses and in the interval of a few days constructed a practical telescope. In the next two years Galileo discovered most of the major features of the heavens. He discerned the mountains and craters of the moon, the phases of Venus, the moons of Jupiter, and sunspots. The passage of the sunspots across the solar disk told him that the sun rotated on an axis and enabled him to calculate its period of rotation. The movements of Jupiter's satellites showed him a solar system in miniature. And the phases of Venus proved to him that the beautiful "evening star" shone by solar light and revolved not around the earth but the sun. By these three observations alone Galileo delivered a death blow to the Ptolemaic system and confirmed Copernicus' theory beyond scientific doubt.

Perhaps the greatest experimentalist in history, Galileo discovered many of the phenomena from which Newton later on was to deduce his most fundamental laws of mechanics. Galileo's most famous experiments were with falling bodies. By dropping cannon balls and musket balls simultaneously from the Leaning Tower of Pisa he established two principles of supreme importance: one, that the speed of a falling body increases uniformly during its descent (the law of uniform acceleration); and secondly, that, excluding the factor of air resistance, objects fall at the same rate of speed regardless of their size or weight. In another experiment he observed, by rolling balls along a horizontal plane, that the balls tended to keep rolling in a straight line until they were checked by friction and air resistance—thus inspiring Newton's law of inertia. Galileo's studies ranged the entire contemporary field of physics. He invented the thermometer and correctly explained the principles of sound, discovered the law of the pendulum and made sketches for a pendulum clock which was subsequently made (with improvements) by the Dutch physicist Huygens, in 1657.

Galileo's astronomical findings, sustaining Copernicus' theory, landed him before the Inquisition for heresy in 1613. On this first encounter he escaped with a reprimand but, in 1632, his integrity as a scientist overcame his caution and he published the trenchant *Dialogue On the Two Chief World Systems* in which the Ptolemaic cause came out a miserable

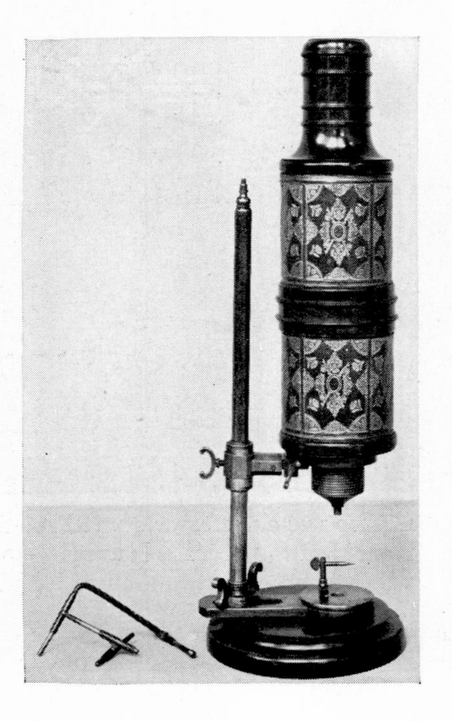

Through this handsome microscope the English scientist Robert Hooke made many discoveries, chief among them the cellular structure of matter. The first microscope was constructed in 1590 by the Dutch optician Zacharias Jansen.

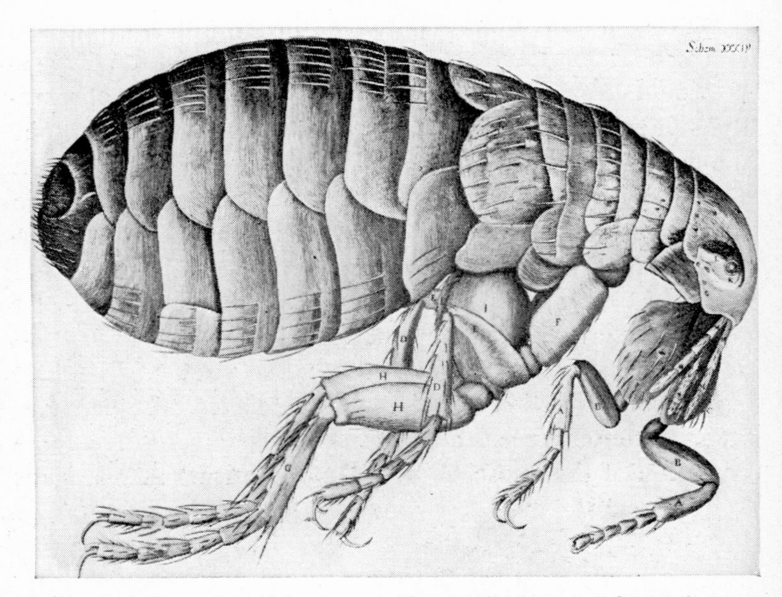

The invisible world came to view as Hooke and other microscopists revealed the details of tiny animals, like the flea above. The great Dutch observer Leeuwenhoek first spotted bacteria and protozoa.

second best. His book was banned and Galileo was held in custody for three months. At his trial he was found guilty and sentenced to recant all Copernican doctrines and do penance for three years. This time he obeyed and the remainder of his life was spent in less controversial fields. He died in 1642—the year of Newton's birth.

In other fields of science the rate of progress was scarcely less spectacular. A Dutch physician named Vesalius did for anatomy what Copernicus did for astronomy, by practicing dissection and describing his findings in a monumental treatise on the human body. At the University of Padua, chief cradle of sixteenth century medical research, two professors, Eustachius and Falloppius, advanced the study of physiology and gave their names to parts of the body. The greatest single medical advance of the age was made by Sir William Harvey, personal physician to Queen Elizabeth, who in 1628 discovered the circulatory route of the blood from the heart through arteries, veins and lungs. Chemistry came into being as a science with the work of the seventeenth century Englishman Robert Boyle, who first defined elements, mixtures and compounds, thus pointing the way to all the subsequent developments in quantitative chemical research.

But the major theme of the age of genius was physics. Within the space of a few decades following the death of Galileo the whole theoretical foundation of modern technology took shape. It was not until the mathematical tools were at hand that physics could evolve, for the basis of modern science is measurement. The sixteenth century saw the great blossoming of mathematical discovery with the development of decimals, logarithms, cubic equations and the modern system of algebraic notation. Pascal evolved the theory of probability, which provided the basis of modern statistics. And Descartes blazed the trail for Newton by combining algebra and geometry into the immensely useful synthesis of analytical geometry, whose most familiar feature is the graph of horizontal and vertical coordinates.

The greatest mathematician of all happened also to be history's greatest scientist. No other man possessed in such rich measure Sir Isaac Newton's triple endowment of mathematical genius, experimental skill and philosophic insight. "Nature was an open book whose letters he could read without effort," Einstein once remarked of him. Yet the paradox

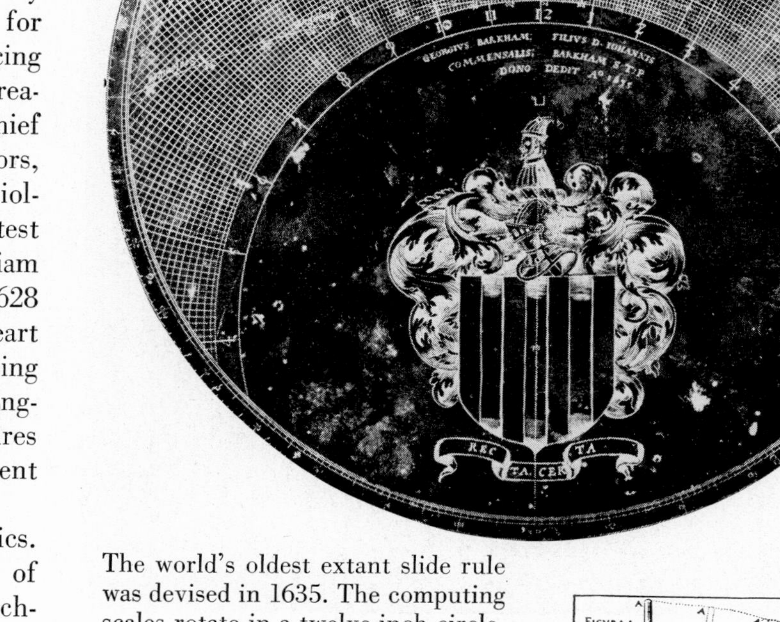

The world's oldest extant slide rule was devised in 1635. The computing scales rotate in a twelve-inch circle.

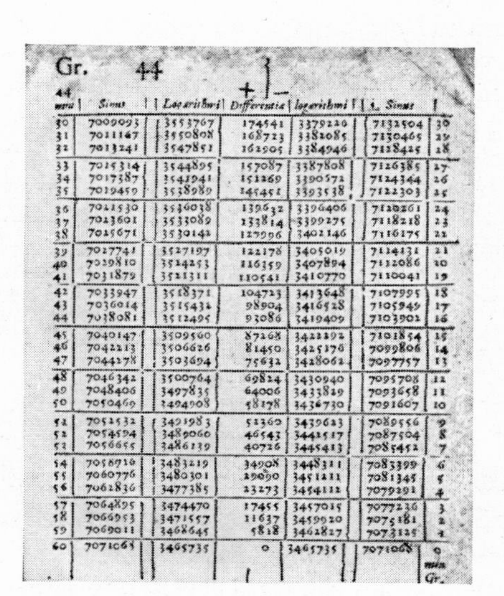

Gr. 44

44 min	Sinus	Logarithmi	+ Differentia −	logarithmi	Sinus	
30	7009093	3553767	174541	3379226	7132504	30
31	7011167	3550808	168723	3382085	7130465	29
32	7013241	3547851	162905	3384946	7128425	28
33	7015314	3544895	157087	3387808	7126385	27
34	7017387	3541941	151269	3390572	7124344	26
35	7019459	3538989	145451	3393538	7122303	25
36	7021530	3536038	139632	3396406	7120261	24
37	7023601	3533089	133814	3399275	7118218	23
38	7025671	3530142	127996	3402146	7116175	22
39	7027741	3527197	122178	3405019	7114131	21
40	7029810	3524253	116359	3407894	7112086	20
41	7031879	3521311	110541	3410770	7110041	19
42	7033947	3518371	104723	3413648	7107995	18
43	7036014	3515432	98904	3416528	7105949	17
44	7038081	3512495	93086	3419409	7103902	16
45	7040147	3509560	87268	3422292	7101854	15
46	7042213	3506626	81450	3425176	7099806	14
47	7044278	3503694	75632	3428062	7097757	13
48	7046342	3500764	69824	3430940	7095708	12
49	7048406	3497835	64006	3433829	7093658	11
50	7050469	3494908	58178	3436730	7091607	10
51	7052532	3491983	52360	3439623	7089556	9
52	7054594	3489060	46543	3442517	7087504	8
53	7056655	3486139	40726	3445413	7085452	7
54	7058716	3483219	34908	3448311	7083399	6
55	7060776	3480301	29090	3451211	7081345	5
56	7062836	3477385	23273	3454112	7079291	4
57	7064895	3474470	17455	3457015	7077236	3
58	7066953	3471557	11637	3459920	7075181	2
59	7069011	3468645	5818	3462827	7073125	1
60	7071068	3465735	0	3465735	7071068	0
						min Gr.

The first logarithmic table, an exponential system of computation, was put out by a Scot, Napier, in 1614.

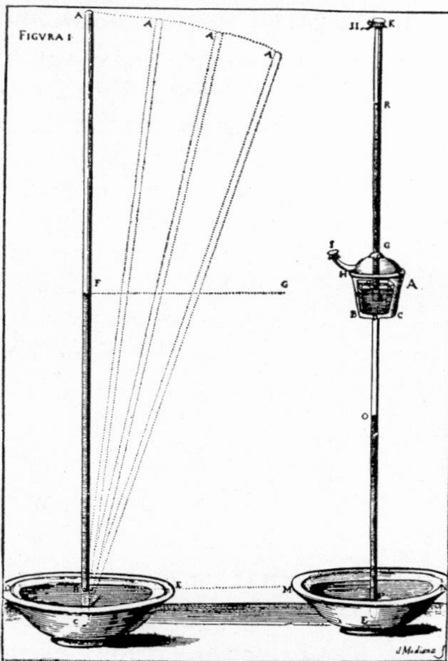

Evangelista Torricelli invented the barometer in 1643 after experimenting with tubes inverted in mercury.

The force of air pressure was demonstrated by Otto von Guericke, inventor of the air pump, in 1654. Galileo had tried to create a vacuum and failed. But with his pump Guericke withdrew the air from two bronze hemispheres and proved in a famous experiment at Ratisbon that teams of horses could not separate them. When air was admitted through a stopcock the hemispheres came apart.

A momentous event in medical history was the publication in 1628 of Harvey's epochal treatise on the circulation of the blood. Until then medicine had been retarded by erroneous views about the function of the heart and blood vessels, chief among them being that the blood moved in a tidelike manner, backward and forward, that the arteries carried air as well as blood, and that the heart manufactured "spirits" necessary for the body. As lecturer at the Royal College of Physicians, Harvey performed experiments which led him to an almost perfect picture of the circulatory route of the blood through the vascular system and of the structure and physiology of the heart.

of Newton's life was that until the day he was laid to rest in Westminster Abbey, he alone in the scientific world never felt he had accomplished anything truly important. Repeatedly through his career Newton suppressed his discoveries, lost or casually discarded crucial calculations and complained pettishly of being badgered when the Royal Society asked him to submit a paper. He purposely armored his masterwork, the *Philosophiae Naturalis Principia Mathematica*, which has often been called the greatest scientific work ever produced by the human intellect, in abstruse and glacial Latin rhetoric and studded it with forbidding mathematical notations, in order, as he explained later, "to avoid being baited by little smatterers in mathematics." Again and again he made it clear that physics and mathematics bored him. In his later years he devoted his great intellectual energies almost exclusively to theological studies and analysis of the prophetic books of the Bible.

NEWTON was a student at Cambridge when, one day, a diagram in a book on astrology led him to consult Euclid, and Euclid in turn led him to Descartes' work on analytical geometry. By the age of twenty-two his mathematical talents had fully matured. In 1664 Cambridge was closed by the plague and Newton returned to his home for two years. There, in enforced solitude and seclusion, he hit on three of his most inspired ideas. Between 1665 and 1667, while still in his early twenties, Newton evolved the law of gravitation, invented differential calculus and discovered the spectral composition of light. There is good evidence for the familiar story that the law of gravitation came to him as he sat one day in his orchard and watched an apple fall from a tree. Other scientists had suspected a relationship between the planetary movements and the fall of objects to the earth's surface, but it was Newton who first synthesized and expanded the known facts, which had been developed experimentally by Galileo, Kepler and others, into mathematical law—the famous Law of Universal Gravitation which states that "Every particle of matter in the universe attracts every other particle with a force varying inversely as the square of the distance between them and directly proportional to the product of their masses."

But Newton did not pursue the subject. He returned to Cambridge when the plague was over and two years later was appointed Lucasian professor of mathematics. For nearly two decades thereafter Newton taught classes and conducted his private research in fields other than physics. Meanwhile some other scientists, notably Robert Hooke and the astronomer Edmund Halley, had begun to suspect that the elliptical orbits of the planets postulated by Kepler might be shaped by an attractive force from the sun which varied inversely as the square of the distance—though Newton had never made public his gravitational theory. But their mathematical resources were inadequate to cope with the problem, which indeed entailed mathematics of the highest order. One day in August, 1684, Halley visited Newton at Cambridge and asked him point-blank if he knew what type of curve would be described by a planet influenced by gravity in the inverse square ratio. "Newton immediately answered 'an ellipse,'" Newton's nephew reported afterward. "Struck with joy and amazement, Halley asked him how he knew it. 'Why,' replied he, 'I have calculated it'; and being asked for the calculation he could not find it, but promised to send it to him."

KEEPING his promise, Newton repeated the calculation and in so doing refired his own interest in the subject, evolving enough new material for a series of lectures. Then, as though fed by some inner, involuntary fire, his inspiration continued to blaze, and he began to expand his ideas into a comprehensive treatise on terrestrial and celestial mechanics. "By now," wrote Newton's biographer, J. W. N. Sullivan, "he was . . . completely in the grip of his mathematical genius. . . ." He seldom left his room, seldom saw anyone, never took recreation and slept only four or five hours a night. Once in a while he would walk briefly in the garden outside his quarters, but after a turn or two he would halt, and, according to his secretary, "run up the stairs like another Archimedes, with a 'Eureka!', fall to write on his desk standing without giving himself the leisure to draw a chair to sit down on."

The *Principia* was presented in part to the Royal Society in April, 1686, and published *in toto* the following year. It was at once recognized as a work of monumental stature. Newton divided the *Principia* into three books and a hundred and ninety-two propositions. In the first two books he dealt with terrestrial mechanics, defining the concepts "mass," "force," and "momentum," and setting forth his famous three laws of motion:

1. Every body continues in its state of rest or of uniform motion in a straight line, except insofar as it may be compelled by impressed forces to change that state. (This is known as the law of inertia.)

2. The rate of change of momentum is proportional to the force producing the change and takes place in the direction in which the force acts. (From this second law of motion is derived the crucial equation, a basis of most modern engineering: $F = ma$—force equals mass times acceleration.)

3. To every action there is an equal and opposite reaction.

The third book of the *Principia*, opening with the stirring proclamation, "I now demonstrate the frame of the system of the world," extended his mechanical laws to the heavens and gave a complete picture of celestial mechanics. It enunciated the law of gravitation and showed how it governed all the movements of the solar system—not only those of the planets, but more intricate interrelationships and perturbations. Newton also explained in full detail how the gravitational pull of the sun and the moon caused the ocean's tides, and how the orbits of comets might take the form of huge, elongated ellipses (an observation that enabled Halley to predict the return of the comet named for him). Another section dealt with the motion of fluids and the propagation of waves, thus creating the new science of hydrodynamics.

UNSHAKEN and unquestioned for more than two centuries, Newton's great enunciation of natural law still stands today as the basis of modern technology and indeed of man's whole understanding of the visible world about him. From 1687 until the opening of new domains of knowledge by Max Planck and Einstein between 1900 and 1905, science advanced solely by the application and extension of Newtonian laws. Every development in engineering, physical theory, dynamical astronomy and indeed the whole range of applied science rested ultimately on the propositions of the *Principia*. With a single blow Newton destroyed the old, capricious, animistic world of Aristotle and the Scholastics and reared in its place an orderly, predictable universe of mathematical law.

Although Newton's underlying physical assumptions are known now to be inadequate for interpreting the extreme frontiers of human knowledge—the realm of great velocities and great temperatures, the unseen domain of the atom, the interiors of stars and the reaches of outer space—and although his concepts of mass, force, space, time and gravitation have been superseded by the deeper and more subtle generalizations of twentieth century theory, the picture of the visible world they give remains essentially the picture that Western man sees and understands today.

Not least of Newton's bequests was the change he helped bring about in man's whole approach to science. For Newton and his contemporaries removed scientific thought from the realm of speculation and brought it into the domain of facts, observation, mathematics and experiment. The priceless heritage of the age of genius was a living organism of science, an international fellowship of teachers and experimentalists.

Only son of an obscure English rural family, Isaac Newton was a solitary, absent-minded boy who liked to build mechanical toys. At the age of 26 he was appointed professor of mathematics at Cambridge where he proved a difficult and unpopular teacher. He often lectured to an empty room and spent most of his time pursuing his private researches. An aloof, humorless man, Newton never married and had no interest in literature, music, country life, food, women or social diversion. He was twice elected to Parliament and in 1696 was appointed warden of the mint. In 1703 he was elected president of the Royal Society, a position he held until his death.

Although Newton was only forty-four at the completion of the *Principia*, he never again devoted his full energies to scientific pursuits. It was as though his great effort of 1686–87 had exhausted his interest, if not his talent. When he died, on March 20, 1727, at the age of eighty-four, he was still incredibly unconvinced that his scientific work might have any lasting value. Yet he had been deeply venerated in his lifetime, and for two centuries after his death he was virtually deified. So thoroughly were his laws tested and confirmed in later years, and so consistently did they work, that the conviction grew among scientists that, given the present position and velocity of every particle of matter in the universe, the future of the universe could be predicted for all time and its whole past revealed.

NEWTON would have scoffed at this. For in his heart he felt that he had only fingered the outer fringes of reality. "I do not know what I may appear to the world," Newton remarked shortly before his death, "but to myself I seem to have been only like a boy playing on the seashore and diverting myself in now and then finding a smoother pebble or a prettier shell than ordinary, whilst the great ocean of Truth lay all undiscovered before me."

A Page of Newton's Calculations

Dec 21 A. 30 B. Jan 13 C. Mar 2 D.

ASB = 9.14.10 = 9,23611. ASD = 23.25.56 = 23,43222.
ASE = 71.45.29 = 71,7575. AB = 1610260. AD = 4061353. AE = 11721437.
SAB = 85,381945. SAD = 78,28389. SAE = 54,12125. AfB = 42.29.27
= 42,49083. AgD = comp. 80 51.56 = compl. 80,86555 = 99,13445. AhE = 173.4.51 = comp. 173,08083 =
SAa = 23.59.28 = 23,99111. fAB = 10,9373056. gAD = compl. 10,227500 = 77,72500. hAE = 7,811236.
SBb = 57.14.45 = 57,24583. ABf = 28,136112. SDd = 81.25.28 = 81,42444
ADg = 3,14055. SEe = 65.18.52 = 65,314444. AEH = 11,19319. d
AS = 10000000

sin AfB 42,49083.	9.8296006.	827.	68,6
sin ABf 28,136112.	9.6734575.	1418.	866,7
AB 1610260	4.2068798.	270.	162
Af 1124172	13.8803373		1028,7
	4.0507367		960
	4.0508327	.386.278	(72

Tang. AfB.

sin AgD 99,13445	9.9944505.	122.	67,7
sin ADg 3,14055	8.7385896.	13798.	758,9.
AD 11721437.	4.0689646.	370½.	161,9
Ag 6504127.	12.807542		920,8
	2.8131037		853.
	2.8131890.	66)	18 (27

sin AgD 99,13445. 99944505 67,7
sin ADg 314055. 87385896 758,9
AD 4061253 . 46086593 . 106. 156 815,9
13.3472439
3.3527934 747
Ag 2253550,75. 3.3528687 193)106 (575
Ag 2253555,75.

sin AhE 66,91917	9.9637359.	323.	296,2
sin AEh 11,19319	9.2879430½.	3833.	1222,7
AE 11721437.	5068 9646.	370½.	161,9
Ah 2473322	14.3569076½		1384,6
	4.3931717½		1088,4
	4.3932806.	175½.)	39 (222

1349528 = fg. 3597494 = fh. 2247966 = gh.
Temp ab = 9°1'.33.27" = 217,5575. bd = 3349747222 | 4.5250120.
Temp ad = 23.0.31.56 = 552,53222. be = 1487988,33 | 5.1725995
Temp ae = 91.1.32.45 = 1704,54583.

fi.bi + bi.dk + dk.gk = fi.gk

fi.bi	100000000	.99619003 (.1522.)	126
bi.dk	4337 5590 (200)150.	47423558. 78½	170½
dk.gk	10.7934705. 4836. 2686. 2742	100000000	133½
	15.1313037	14.7072094	
		9.5729657	1374081 (115) 13 (113
fi.gk.	10.0000000		

fi.bi	10.0000000	9.9619129
bi.el	4.3375740	5.2318517. 255. 117.
el.hl	10.3702542. 2101. 1927.	10.0000000
	14.7080209	15.1937763
fi.hl.	10.0000000	10.4857554 3060239½ (1418) 56 (395

fi.gk.hl :: 10000000. 37408113. 3060239½.
fi.figk = ik fg. fi + hl = il − fh :: 10000000. 6259188,7. 40602395.
[6259188,7. 40602395 :: fg = 1349528. N = 8754180.
:: ik. il + N − fh = ik + 5156686.0]
ik. il :: fg. N :: ik − fg. il − N.
N = 5994703.
il − N. ik − fg, 5.1725995. 4.5250120
ik − fg. il − fh :: 4.7965180. 5.6085516.
il − N. il − fh. 9.9691175 10.1335636
9.9691175
0.0000000. 0.1644461
9.8355539. 10.0000000
il − N. il − fh :: 6847844. 10000000

il − N. il − fh. (division) N − fh :: 6847844. 10000000. 3152156.
N − fh = 2397219. Ergo il − fh = 7605014, nec non
fi − gk = ik − fg = 11723746,5.
fi = 1873045,7. ik = 2521902⅔. il = 11202508. Tang AfB = 9162765
gk = 700671,05. bi = 1716227,6. dk = 4357660,2.
Tang AgD = 62192668.
dk − bi (= 2641432,44). ik (= 2521902⅔) :: bi. ai = 1638565,3.

dk − bi	4.4218341.	164½.	53⅓.
ik.	4.4017278	.172	4,6.
	0.9798937		−48
	0.9798889		
bi	4.2345078	253	70
ai	4.2144637		

ai = 1638565,3 . 265) 173 (653
:: r. ch. bai, 9.9798889.
Ang bai = 46,32613

Aa = 4635783.
s: AXa, 22,33502. 9.5798079
Aa 4635783 4.6669231
s: Aab 46,32613 8.0863152
9.8592634. 723. 443
Ax = 882313,46. 4.9456229 49⅓) 17 (3446. Sx = 1176866
9.6091430. 1704. 189.
s: Aa 23,99111 4.6954771 87½) 42 (48 ay = 3871372
ax = 4959948.

s: AXa	9.5798079
cs: AXa	9.9661318
	4.0707270
Sx.	3.6505349 97) 40 (412
Sy 4472341,2	
Xy 1088575,6	4.0368588 401) 304 (756

This page in Newton's own hand, one of thousands that went into the preparation of the *Principia*, shows his calculations to determine the orbit of Halley's comet. At the top are the dates on which the comet appeared, and at upper right a sketch of the earth's orbit around the sun (S) and the positions of the earth (A, B, D and E) on the dates when the comet (c, below the circle) had been observed. With Newton's mathematical help, Halley was able to predict that the comet would return about every seventy-five years, which it has.

THE AGE
OF
ENLIGHTENMENT

Louis XIV, king of France for seventy-two years and great-grandfather of Louis XV, set the stage for the Age of Enlightenment. He also set the pattern for the highly personal system of French government that lasted until the Revolution. No wizard at statecraft, Louis nevertheless was a model monarch at a time when France, in arts and arms, was the strongest country in Europe. This allegory shows Louis crossing the Rhine—an entirely fictitious incident, set down to symbolize his annexation of territory across that river.

VII

THE AGE OF ENLIGHTENMENT

MADEMOISELLE DE COIGNY kept a corpse in her coach. The age of reason was dawning in France—it was the eighteenth century—and there were otherwise just not enough minutes in those days of wonderful enlightenment for mademoiselle to pursue, like other dedicated bluestockings, the fascinating study of anatomy. But with the corpse handy and her scalpel as keen as M. de Voltaire's wickedly witty mind, she could, while rattling over the Paris cobbles, slice and eviscerate in daily officiation at the new faith whose deity was reason, whose ritual was science and whose high priests were the *philosophes*, the new order of literary skeptics. The outstanding ones, glittering with intellectuality, were Baron de Montesquieu, Denis Diderot, Jean Jacques Rousseau and M. de Voltaire, especially Voltaire, for he had given the Enlightenment its watchword, "*Écrasez l'infâme*" (Crush the infamous thing). The infamous thing was generally taken to mean intolerance on the part of any religious or social authority, but the censors of King Louis XV were inclined to think it meant the Church and the court. For with the knife-edge of his wit, M. de Voltaire had been anatomizing both for half a century.

In the history of the human spirit the Enlightenment was an interlude between the stake and fagots and the guillotine. It may be dated from about the beginning of the eighteenth century, when western Europe was exhausted by dynastic wars, to 1789, when the French Revolution opened the cycle of great social wars which, by the middle of the twentieth century, had again all but exhausted Europe and are still far from ended. The Enlightenment flowered under Louis XV, though it had its roots in the time of Louis XIV, who reigned from 1643 to 1715 and outlived his son and two grandsons, handing on to his great-grandson, Louis XV, a nation in which the king was absolute monarch and in which a bureaucracy ran the government by an inflexible pattern of precedent.

In the history of nations the Enlightenment—a name established in usage by the philosopher Immanuel Kant—was the age when, as the result of conflicts culminating in the Seven Years' War (in American history the 1756–63 French and Indian War), the French lost much of their great colonial empire in the east and west to the British. It was the age when Prussia under Frederick the Great was the principal power in central Europe, and Russia under Catherine the Great the principal power in eastern Europe.

In the history of economics it was the age when the production of wealth, which had been steadily increasing in Europe since the Middle Ages, reached a vast new volume. Maritime commerce was swelling with the development of the New World, the exploitation of new colonies, the trade with the East. Overland commerce was pulsing along the newly constructed canals and roads. In England a process for smelting iron with coke was invented. The flying shuttle and the spinning jenny were developed.

In art it was the age when painters reproduced the gay upper-class life of the day with a spirit that gave grace and

The Enlightenment grew more and more to prize anything that was both topical and clever. This elaborate, seagoing coiffure was very popular with aristocratic ladies after the French naval victories of 1778. Other hair styles portrayed mountains, forests and gardens.

This is the Duc de Guise dressed up as an American savage for a royal pageant and tourney (*see pp. 194–195*). The duke, who had heard that the Indians wore head feathers, overdid his part a bit.

elegance to the frivolity of court society. In social history the Enlightenment was the age when the middle class, which controlled the new sources of wealth, began to challenge the once dominant aristocracy for overt power in the state which they as bureaucrats were already administering.

The great divide of cultures is the moment when men feel within themselves a force equal to the vicissitudes of new vision. The vision of the Enlightenment was freedom—freedom from superstition, freedom from intolerance, freedom to know (for knowledge was held to be the ultimate power), freedom from the arbitrary authority of Church or state, freedom to trade or work without vestigial feudal restrictions. This vision was embodied in the American Bill of Rights (for eighteenth century America was also a part of the Enlightenment) and in the French Revolution's Rights of Man.

IN the name of this vision the Enlightenment gave a new direction to European culture. Before the Enlightenment culture had been essentially religious. Carrying farther the work of the Renaissance, the Enlightenment made culture essentially secular. Before the Enlightenment the proper study for mankind had been the will of God. The proper study for mankind, said the Enlightenment with the voice of Alexander Pope, is man. Revelation had been held to be the highest form of truth. Looking back to Descartes, the seventeenth century French philosopher who had synthesized mathematics and philosophy, and to Newton, the English mathematician whose laws of gravitation and motion had laid the foundation of modern science, the Enlightenment sought system and reason in all things. There is no truth, said the Enlightenment, which cannot stand the test of reason. Slowly and surely the Enlightenment began that process whereby philosophy, the search for truth, was supplanted by science, the search for facts. Theology, the effort to know God's will, was replaced by history, the record of man's follies.

The Enlightenment is one great source of modern culture. In a brief hundred years it revised the fundamental ideas of human destiny and purpose which Western man had clung to for more than a thousand years. The Enlightenment was the intellectual chemistry whose gradual precipitate was the modern mind—secular, practical and utilitarian.

The function of the Middle Ages had been to reconstruct human civilization from the debris of Rome. The function of the Renaissance had been to liberate the creative energies of the individual man and to reunite the culture of the ancient world with the culture that man had developed since. These movements had been organic and their central ideas were evolved, not superimposed. The Enlightenment in France was a movement of ideas, and its immediate purpose was to reform or revolutionize French life.

It was a rather discouraging prospect. For one doubt rarely assailed the otherwise skeptical French mind of that century: few doubted that French civilization had reached a perfection unmatched in human history.

In the Louvre there hangs a picture by the eighteenth century painter Olivier. Behind an open clavichord sits a little boy. Above him, high, delicately white-paneled walls rise to the cornices; ceiling-high windows of many panes let in the light, or, more probably, through them the light within holds off for a moment the crowding dark without. Above a tall mirror, portraits of two noble women gaze down from their height at a company below. It is the salon of the Prince de Conti, one of the most distinguished salons in eighteenth century France. Its presiding spirit is the prince's mistress, the Comtesse de Boufflers, who is busy with a chafing dish, for on these intimate occasions servants are excused.

The boy at the clavichord is young Wolfgang Amadeus Mozart, the most famous child prodigy of his time. The little company is quite unconscious that it is dwarfed by the noble proportions of the hall it has chosen for its setting. In stiff, knee-length, embroidered jackets, the men stand and talk or roam about; the women, like honeybees, with wide panniered skirts and tight bodices above tiny, corseted waists, sit, rove, flirt with their fans. The conversation, like an intricate, dignified dance, weaves in and out, retreats, softens, swells, as one or another joins or falls out; sometimes wit, like a grace note, flashes, sometimes laughter tinkles.

WE know the names of these figures to which even recollection can now give no more duration than a note of music—the Princesse de Beauvau, the Comtesse d'Egmont, the Maréchale de Luxembourg, the Maréchale de Mirepoix. These are among the great names of the eighteenth century salons and they pluck wistfully for a moment at the iron chord of history as the quills of a harpsichord pluck at its metal strings.

Conversation was the impalpable element that held the men and women of this society in a common bond. The eighteenth century talked itself into the immortality of memoirs and anecdotes, for conversation was an art; indeed, in France the age had none greater. It was talk of dry grace; common sense and clarity were its prerequisites. Talk was an easy modulation of *bon mots*, gallantries, clear analysis of political and moral questions, light mockery of the question of human fate —brilliant, winged, facile talk.

Sometimes the sharp thrusts were merely catty, as when her friends praised Mme. de Lutzelbourg for being, at sixty-eight, one of the most active women in France. "As active," snapped the Marquise de Polignac, "as fleas can make her." Sometimes a flash of wit like burning magnesium ribbon lit up character or problem. A talkative cardinal was describing to skeptical Mme. du Deffand the martyrdom of St. Denis, who, when his head was cut off, picked it up and carried it in his hands. What was less well known, explained the cardinal, was that the saint walked with his head under his arm all the way up to Montmartre, a distance of some two miles. "*Ah, Monseigneur*," said Mme. du Deffand gravely, "*en pareil cas, il n'y a que le premier pas qui côute*" (In a case like this, it is only the first step that is painful).

This glittering, brittle, fastidious life of the salons made eighteenth century France the motherland of European culture and made Paris the capital of the human mind. It was a woman's world. Louis XV was the legitimate king of France, but in his time the country had as many separate reigns as the king had mistresses. There was the reign of Mme. de Mailly, of Mme. de Châteauroux, of Mme. de Pompadour (whom the king's daughter, Mme. Adelaide, called "Mama Strumpet") and of Mme. du Barry.

VISITORS to Paris noted "the monstrous regiment of women." Wrote the political philosopher Montesquieu (whose own election to the Academy was the work of Mlle. de Clermont): "There is no one holding an office at court, in Paris or in the provinces, without a woman through whose hands pass all the favors and sometimes the injustices he can dispense. All these women entertain mutual relations; and form a kind of republic whose ever active members help and serve one another reciprocally; it is like a new state, within a state; and anyone at court, in Paris or in the provinces, who sees the ministers, magistrates and prelates perform their duties, unless he knows the women who govern them, is like a man who sees a machine in play quite clearly but who is ignorant of the springs that move it."

These women were terrifying in their hold on power. Mme. de Tencin was a wisp of a woman who kept Versailles in a tight mesh of her intrigue. Consider her unemotional statesmanship on the question of sending Louis XV to the Flanders front: "Between us, it is not that he is capable of commanding a company of grenadiers; but his presence will do much good. The troops will accomplish their duty better and the generals will not dare to fail in theirs so openly. . . . A king, whatever he be, is for the soldiery and the people what the ark of the covenant was for the Hebrews; his mere presence is a presage of success."

Here is the Maréchale de Mirepoix reassuring Mme. de Pompadour, who had been badly frightened by rumors that a rival was threatening to oust her from the king's confidence: "The friendship the king bears you is the same as that he bears your apartment and surroundings; you have adapted yourself to his manners and stories; he is not embarrassed, he does not fear to bore you; how can you expect him to have the courage to uproot all this in one day?"

Here is Mme. de Jully, candidly discussing her husband with his sister: "M. de Jully would be astonished indeed if someone were to tell him that he does not care for me at all. It would be a cruel trick to play on him, and me also, for he is the sort of man to be thoroughly put out if he were robbed of his hobby."

The worldliness is of a piece with the wit and explains better than definitions the only reverence eighteenth century France knew—the reverence for reason. These women were tacticians of character. Their realism was of the unclouded kind that is invulnerable to pity. Their world held for them only one terror-ennui; and only one horror-a lapse of taste. It was one of the most elegantly unreal worlds in history, a world which drained away the resources of a country and lay oppressively on an impoverished and overburdened people.

OF the four men—Montesquieu, Diderot, Voltaire and Rousseau—who chiefly meant the Enlightenment to this scintillant and foredoomed society, Montesquieu has special importance for Americans. This student of government wrote a book called *The Spirit of Laws*, which became almost a manual for the Founding Fathers of the American republic. Montesquieu had studied the English parliamentary system and he ascribed to it a sort of Newtonian equilibrium made up of checks and balances among the executive, legislative and judicial powers of government. Though his picture was idealized, it represented, Montesquieu thought, the spirit of the British constitution and it became both spirit and practice of the American Constitution of 1789.

Denis Diderot had an all-embracing influence on his country, for he had an omnibus talent. A distant precursor of Freud in his psychological tale, *Le Neveu de Rameau*, evolutionary biologist at the dawn of the age of evolution, art critic and devout philosophical materialist, he was most famous for his editorship of the *Encyclopedia*, or *Classified Dictionary of Sciences, Arts and Trades*. This vast work, to which practically all the *philosophes* contributed, was the greatest single propaganda focus of enlightenment in France. Voltaire wrote the articles on history, Rousseau, the articles on music. The physiocrats, Turgot and Quesnay, wrote on economic subjects, advocating economic enlightenment in the form of *laissez faire*—free trade and enterprise—unhampered by mercantilism which had placed the hard hand of state regulation on business.

The plan was ambitious, the success remarkable. The editors made a brave effort to keep an enlightened, critical and scientific attitude and to free themselves from the prejudices of the past. The *Encyclopedia's* articles on science insisted on the experimental method. The most advanced views on political economy were presented. The happiness of the people was declared to be the chief purpose of good government. The historical and religious articles were surreptitiously censored by the pious printer after they had left the editors' desks. But free thought and attacks on authority were slipped into casual pieces. Thus the article on Aius Locutius, a Roman

Once the site of the royal hunting lodge, Versailles grew to a community of 150,000 under Louis XIV and Louis XV, who

deity, urged freedom of speech; the article on Juno cast doubt on the Virgin.

Banded together to advance tolerance and reason, the encyclopedists nevertheless quarreled among themselves. Many of them, Diderot included, fell into bitter arguments with Voltaire because he acknowledged the existence of a creator, although Voltaire's god was not the God of Christianity but the impersonal supreme being of the deists, a god who created man and then left him to his own devices, having no interest in his actions or ultimate salvation.

The Enlightenment had no more complete or prolific son than Voltaire. He was almost involuntarily witty and organically skeptical. But what Voltaire believed, he believed fanatically. He believed in the physics of Sir Isaac Newton, the philosophy of John Locke, freedom of thought, civil rights and personal security. In his *Age of Louis XIV* and his *Essay on the Manners and Spirit of the Nations* Voltaire revolutionized the writing of history by discussing social and cultural movements instead of simply chronicling the succession of kings and wars. But his famous work, one of the few books of the Enlightenment that is still read for pleasure, is *Candide*, which savagely satirized the complacent belief,

made it their home and court. The king lived in the big palace (*center*). Noble families lived in the buildings around it.

derived from Leibnitz, that this is the best of all possible worlds. Unlike other *philosophes*, Voltaire had cut deep into a more enduring subject than doctrinaire controversy or the battle of ideas—the eternal subject of human folly.

Voltaire and Diderot had been the popularizers of the scientific and philosophic sides of the Enlightenment. Jean Jacques Rousseau was the great prophet of the democratic revolution in every field. His *Social Contract*, with its theory of the right of the sovereign people to rule, gave powerful impetus to the French Revolution. Through Rousseau, the Enlightenment leads directly to the Revolution. He was dead before it came. So was Voltaire. This was a pity, for a very minor confrontation of values during the Revolution's Terror might have tickled the old philosopher's ironic sense. Mme. de Gramont had possibly never had an idea in her unenlightened head when she was called before the Revolutionary Tribunal to stand trial for her life. Had she ever aided the aristocrats who had escaped abroad? the court asked her. Mme. de Gramont knew that if she answered yes she would be guillotined at once. For some seconds she looked at her judges in silence, then, "I was going to answer no," she said, "but life is not worth the lie."

The King Entertained With Pretentious Pageantry

SINCE one of the great purposes of the monarchy in France was to symbolize the glory of the realm, the king frequently held lavish fetes to impress the court and visiting nobility. Two of these galas are shown here. The one above is an elaborate tourney where, in the main event, men dressed as knights in armor attempt to pierce a ring while riding at a full gallop. Louis XIV, however, wanted the tourney to be as pretentious as possible, so he ordered a pageant in which the competitors were to represent the peoples of five great

The first day of a vast three-day fete at Versailles included a concert tableau, performed between an avenue of trees, extolling the beauties of the four seasons and employing animals from far-off lands.

The second day saw the erection of a huge outdoor frame as a stage for the presentation of a comedy and

nations—Romans, Persians, Turks, Indians and American savages. Each of the nations was headed by one member of the nobility, with the king himself heading the Roman section. Space for such a complicated spectacle was a problem, but it was finally held in front of the Palais des Tuileries, in the heart of Paris. In this scene part of the Roman entourage, having paraded through the city, files into an amphitheater which seated fifteen thousand spectators, among them Queen Maria Theresa's guest, the queen of England.

The engravings below show part of a three-day fete at Versailles, the king's enormous country residence. This, too, had a central theme, built around a legend of an enchanted island where brave knights, captivated by the island's charm and beauty, enjoyed wondrous pleasures with the aid of a magic ring. Though the festival itself lasted for only three days, the king invited his hundreds of guests to stay for nine. The palaceful of company passed the time at balls, banquets, riding, hunting and other country pleasures.

a ballet performance. The king's six hundred guests are gathered in tiers of specially constructed seats.

The fete on the third day is enacted before a lavish model of the Palace of Alcina (*background*) on the fabled, enchanted isle guarded by strange and fearsome water monsters. Fireworks ended the festival.

Aeronauts, Athletes, Masons, Mesmerists

Scientific experimentation was popular during the Enlightenment, particularly if it was as exciting as this balloon ascension in 1783 which was engineered by the two Montgolfiers, the Wright brothers of their day. Made of cloth, the balloon was filled with hot air rising from a straw fire. It carried in its basket a sheep, cock and duck and remained aloft eight minutes.

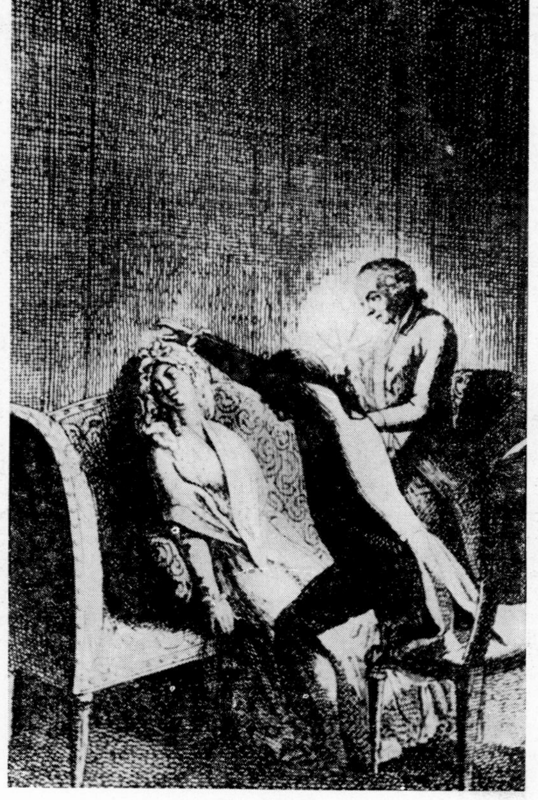

Scientific fads included hypnosis, here being practiced on a woman. The pioneer in hypnotism was Anton Mesmer, whose "mesmerism" allegedly cured many varied aches and pains.

Anticlerical feeling was fostered by the society of Freemasons. Here, in the inner sanctum of their lodge, members of the order initiate a newcomer who stands blindfolded (*left*) before a symbolic banner. Formed years earlier to promote charity, fidelity and Christianity among its members, the Freemasons during the Enlightenment became primarily a society for men without religious affiliations. It was a very important organization whose membership included such notable figures as Voltaire, Mozart and Frederick the Great.

Sex, sport and speculation were important interests. At left is a chorus girl of the day, an opera entertainer. In the center, athletes engage in the game which eventually grew into modern tennis. At right is John Law, promoter of the disastrous "Mississippi Bubble." A Scotsman of real financial genius, Law founded a national bank in France, got a monopoly to exploit the Mississippi River area, took over management of France's national revenue and, piling scheme on scheme, built an edifice which toppled in the great panic of 1720.

Mme. du Châtelet, musician, linguist, mathematician and hostess, was Voltaire's mistress. When she died, the picture in her locket was not of Voltaire or her husband, but of a third man.

Mme. du Deffand's guests included French and English notables like Montesquieu, Voltaire, David Hume and Horace Walpole. Although nearly blind, she led a salon until she died at 83.

Mme. D'Épinay conducted a brilliant Paris salon which Rousseau and Diderot frequently attended. Her spicy *Memoirs* were thought to be almost too spicy, thus had wide readership.

Lively Ladies and Enlightened Salons

THE eighteenth century salon did far more than the court to advance the Enlightenment. Here the most sparkling minds of the day discussed, in nimble and intelligent conversation, the newest and the oldest ideas. For a hostess out corralling celebrities, wit and charm were more important than mere nobility. Many wealthy ladies devoted their full time to their salons, trying hard to get important guests and to give a special character or flavor to their gatherings. Philosophers flocked to the salon of the Duchesse de Choiseul, economists to that of Mme. de Marchais. Other hostesses saved certain days for certain topics. Tuesdays at Mme. de Lambert's were reserved for aristocrats who liked to discuss morals and metaphysics, Wednesdays were for authors and artists. Some hostesses went to great lengths to demonstrate their seriousness, conducting courses in physics and chemistry in their drawing rooms.

At the salon of the Comtesse de St. Brisson in Paris, bewigged aristocrats gather to hear a small chamber orchestra. Many nobles subsidized composers to write music for such affairs, or wrote and performed music themselves. For a time, the greatest musical catch was the astounding Austrian prodigy Wolfgang Amadeus Mozart who, when only 8, gave recitals of his own compositions. Some habitués of salons thought all this entertaining was bad: it did not leave any time for talk, which was the real reason for having a salon.

Madame Jeanne Bécu du Barry, a onetime Paris courtesan said to be the illegitimate daughter of a monk, officially succeeded Mme. de Pompadour as King Louis XV's mistress in 1769, thus illustrating, among other things, the heights to which a woman of charm and wit could rise in the Age of Enlightenment. Gay and seductive, but not interested in politics, du Barry was nevertheless viewed in her time as an evil influence on the king. She played her final role not in the boudoir but on the block. In 1793 her pretty head, here painted by François Drouais, fell to the guillotine of the Revolutionary Tribunal as she vainly cried out, "Let me live one more little minute!"

The King and His Mistress

LOUIS XV of France (*opposite page*) became king at 5, wed a Polish princess at 15 and posed for this portrait by Hyacinthe Rigaud at 20. A well-intentioned but weak monarch, Louis predicted the disaster that was to come after him in his famous remark, "*Apres nous, le deluge!*" (After us, the deluge!) He was a smallpox victim at 64, and was hastily buried in quicklime for fear of an epidemic.

Mme. de Pompadour, a middle-class girl, was Louis' mistress for nearly twenty years during which she virtually ruled France. To the pompous court she brought a sprightly naturalness, an honest affection for Louis and a real talent for government. Even the queen liked her. Boucher's portrait shows a quill beside her for some of the bright and spicy correspondence the era delighted in.

Antoine Watteau, the greatest French painter of his time, did *The Halt During the Chase* in 1720 while visiting M. and Mme. de Julienne at their estate on the River Marne. He persuaded his host and hostess to pose for the couple (*center, facing front*) resting on the ground with their tired companions after a hunt. Hunting and riding were particularly popular with the nobles, grand ladies often spending the morning enjoying a leisurely canter through the Bois de Boulogne. In praise of eighteenth century women such as these, the brothers Goncourt wrote, "... From the height of a horse, a woman looks a thousandfold more willing, more alluring, more enterprising, more venturesome; the horse gives her a new magic...." While most equestriennes wore somewhat tailored habits for riding, Watteau's were painted in billowing satins, as if they had stepped out of a stately minuet.

In *A Fête at Rambouillet*, which is considered one of the most beautiful landscapes ever painted, Jean-Honoré Fragonard portrays the exquisite and elaborate beauty of French aristocratic country life.

Pastoral Picnics on a Grand Scale

IN the Enlightenment, life at court suddenly seemed too formal and stilted, so the aristocrats joined in a great back-to-the-land movement. In pursuing pastoral pleasures, however, they managed to take most of the elaborate etiquette and formalism of the court along with them. No sylvan glade was adequate for a rustic outing until an army of gardeners had made it ready, no picnic a proper one without a corps of liveried attendants.

A Fête at Rambouillet (*above*) portrays a typically earthy sojourn at a country château. Near a waterfall and woodscape, painstakingly designed to look like the Italian countryside, members of a party enjoy their simple pleasures. Some, dressed in their fanciest silks and satins, go for a ride in a boat topped with an elegant canopy and decorated with lavish scrollwork. Others sit among the beauties of nature—behind a carved stone balustrade.

Inside the château there was gossip and gallantry amidst the dancing and gaming. Lest this be thought useless, the ladies busied themselves at a valuable trade: unraveling. From the finest cloths they removed the inlaid gold and silver threads, which they then resold. One woman of the court got 600 francs for the thread she unraveled from a magnificent harp cover and never troubled her head that the cloth had just cost her lover 2,500 francs.

A host of other things occupied the aristocracy. The proper château uniform, for instance, was important. For a week end at Mme. de Pompadour's Bellevue a noble gentleman had to wear purple velvet trimmed with gold lace. It would never do to show up in the Crécy costume (green with gold buttons).

Self-expression through acting was also important, since private theatricals were the rage. Château guests spent days at rehearsals. Extemporaneous operettas and playlets were put on to celebrate birthdays or to greet arriving guests. This theatrical effusiveness spread into personal relationships: there was much kissing, much extravagant posturing and much decorous fainting by the ladies.

In *The Swing*, Fragonard captured the coquettish romanticism of the era, which liked to cover its worldliness with a false air of innocence. Fragonard, an artist of great verve and delicacy, was for a time on the court payroll and most of his paintings chronicled the frivolous activities of the aristocracy. His scenes were idealized rather than accurate but none of his patrons ever minded that.

The Toilet of Venus was painted by François Boucher, probably for Mme. de Pompadour's château at Bellevue, where she collected a whole gallery of his work. Boucher's intimate paintings of ladies in disarray enjoyed a tremendous vogue and were widely hung in boudoirs as well as salons. Here, attended by loving cherubs and her traditional doves, Venus gracefully dawdles at her dressing.

Jean Jacques Rousseau (1712–78) who led the battle against formalism and artificiality, went around in a loose flowing robe and fur headdress.

In *Emile*, Rousseau wrote a treatise on education urging that children be brought up in natural ways. Here a mother nurses her baby herself instead of using a wet nurse, while staying healthily outdoors.

The Return to Nature

JEAN JACQUES ROUSSEAU was a contradictory man who had a highly contradictory effect on his age. His belief that civilization is evil and that man is by nature good until corrupted by society entranced an era which scorned nature and prized its own artificial ways. His urging that people should cultivate the virtues of simplicity led the sophisticates of a sophisticated age to dress as shepherds and live in made-to-order rustic palaces. And Rousseau himself, the great believer in simplicity, was anything but a simple man.

The son of a shiftless French watchmaker living in Switzerland, he ran away at the age of sixteen in an early rebellion against authority: he thought he had been unjustly punished. Making his way to France, he attached himself to the household of a young widow (who became his mistress), composed an opera, wrote for Diderot's *Encyclopedia*, invented a system of musical notation and finally became a literary light. His famous *Confessions* was one of the frankest and most readable books of self-revelations ever published. His novels, *The New Heloise* and *Emile*, were philosophic tracts. France read the books mostly for their stories and sentiment but still paid some attention to their practical preachings. Rousseau insisted that vacations in the country are healthful, that tight corsets are bad for pregnant women, that mothers should nurse their own babies and that children should be allowed to behave like children, not be forced to become little adults.

No solitary, rustic, clear-thinking philosopher, Rousseau was a man who often let his emotions rule his mind. In his confused and troubled life he had three mistresses and five illegitimate children. He suffered from hypochondria and delusions of persecution and his bitter attacks on the mannered society of his day were made partially because he was so socially inept that he felt like a lout when involved in it.

Whatever his motivations, Rousseau envisioned the noblest of principles for government and society and his famous political work, *The Social Contract*, eventually became a handbook for the men of the French Revolution. Though Rousseau had been dead a dozen years, they used *The Social Contract's* thoughts and language in their efforts to set up a government that recognized the moral and legal equality of all men, the sovereignty of the people and the supreme authority of the general will. Rousseau's faith in democratic government has influenced every free government in the world.

Spurred by Rousseau's teachings, Marie Antoinette had this rustic mill built near Versailles. Here she and her ladies-in-waiting came to dress as shepherdesses and milkmaids and lead the "simple life."

Voltaire (1694–1778) was a lean, long-beaked, bright-eyed man who hated exercise, loved feminine company.

Skeptical Philosopher

THE most famous writer and jack-of-all-social-trades during the Enlightenment was François Marie Arouet who, after being jailed for his writings, changed his name to Voltaire. He wrote enough plays, polemics, histories, verses and romances to fill seventy volumes. Today his best-known work is the cynical adventure story, *Candide*, an attack on the pious philosophy that everything was for the best.

For much of his long life, Voltaire was in trouble. He was sent to the Bastille for publishing libelous lampoons, was beaten up by the bullies of a duke he insulted, had his satirical attacks on the Church and government burned and several times went into exile. A courageous fighter for justice, he endangered his own position by defending the family of a Protestant named Calas who had been executed for a crime he did not commit. A man of wide intellectual range, Voltaire was also enormously vain and would viciously attack anyone who threatened his position. A philosopher, he was also a shrewd investor who made a fortune out of financial speculations.

In 1750 Voltaire was invited to live at the court of his long-time admirer, Frederick the Great. There he spent three years, arguing and bickering with the monarch whose poetry he compared to dirty linen. He did not dare return to Paris until 1778, when the city greeted him as a triumphant hero. Worn out by the acclaim, Voltaire died at the age of eighty-three.

Frederick the Great of Prussia (1712–86), Voltaire's patron, liked to write poems in French and play the flute.

The story of *Candide* by Voltaire lampoons an eighteenth century idea that the world is a reasonable and well-ordered place. Its foolishly optimistic hero, Candide, dwells with a baron who, when he finds the boy dallying with his daughter, kicks him out.

In the Bulgarian army Candide sees the horrors of war. Though dreading the sight of wantonly raped and murdered women and children, he still maintains that there is no effect without a cause. Everything is necessarily linked up and arranged for the best.

More bloodshed is described to Candide by an old crone he meets in his travels. She tells how she was captured in her youth by pirates and then fought over by other pirates and Moors (*above*). But even with horror piling on horror, Candide remains optimistic.

In South America, Candide spies two girls who are being bitten by monkeys. When he gallantly shoots the beasts, the girls bemoan the loss of their pets. Finally Candide gains the wisdom to view the world as it really is and settles down to cultivate his own garden.

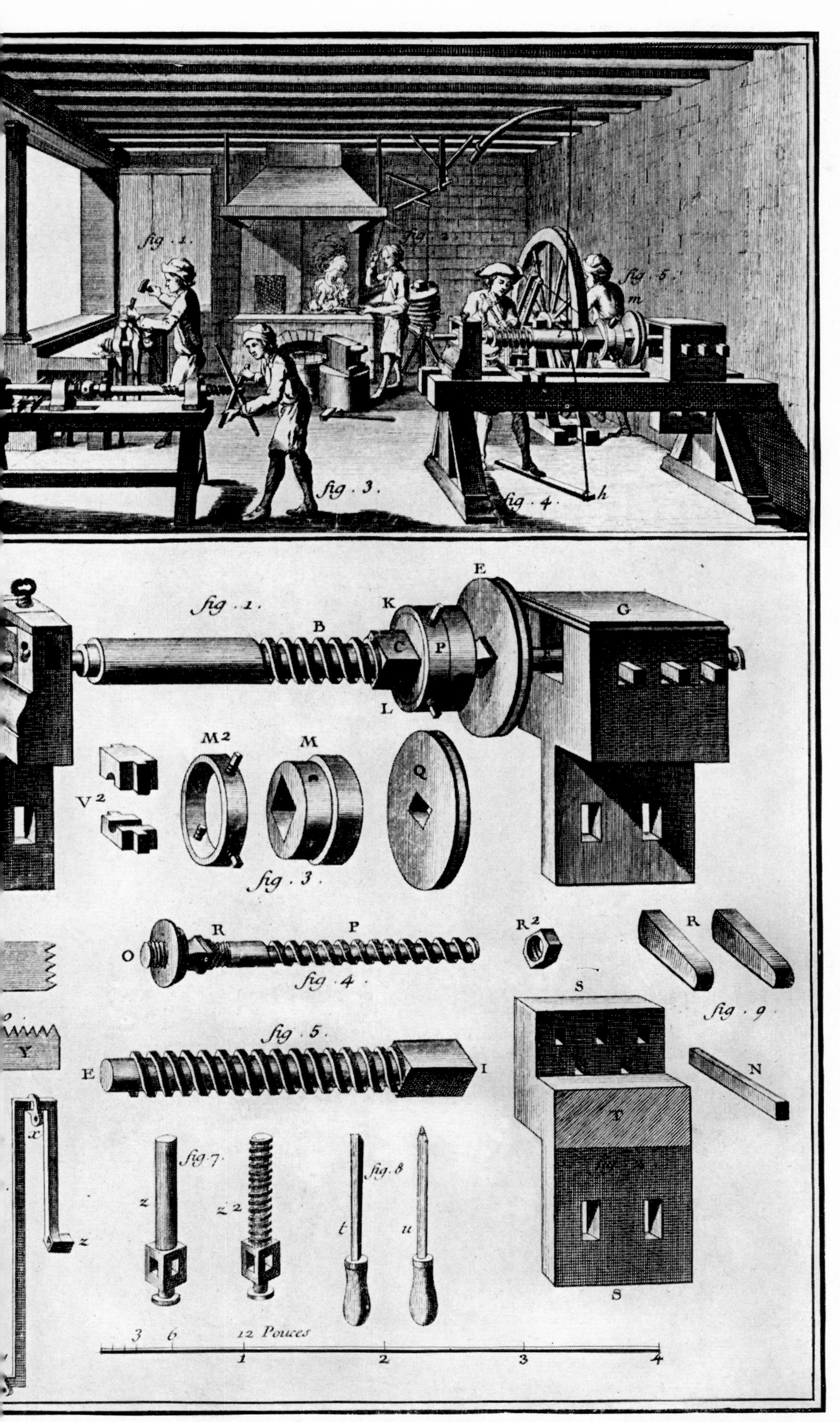

Sketches from the *Encyclopedia* show how fully the articles were illustrated. The top scene is of men at work in a factory where large press screws are threaded. The drawing includes a forge, an anvil and an early foot-operated lathe for cutting threads into wood. The lower sketch contains a breakdown of this lathe, showing details of the manufacturing method. Some threaded screws which are the end-product of the shop are at bottom. The letters and figures are keyed to descriptions in the French text of the *Encyclopedia*.

Denis Diderot (1713–84), an earnest man, always worked hard and sometimes cut loose in wild declamations.

Serious Encyclopedist

THE thirst for knowledge which animated the enlightened eighteenth century was satisfied to an impressive degree by Diderot's *Encyclopedia or Classified Dictionary of Sciences, Arts and Trades*, a work of enormous social and political significance. Denis Diderot aimed to collect in one many-volumed work all the period's new but largely inaccessible knowledge. Churchmen, fearing the encyclopedist's spirit of speculation, constantly harassed the editor and his colleagues, who included the best writers in France. For twenty years Diderot worked at the *Encyclopedia*, often hiding out with the text.

He spent his days at workshops and his nights setting down what he had learned. By thus disclosing and spreading trade secrets, he helped bring to an end the guilds' restraints on industry.

Short of funds and still in trouble with the authorities, Diderot was about to sell his library in order to provide a dowry for his daughter when Catherine the Great, empress of Russia, heard of his difficulties. An admirer of the Enlightenment's intellectuals, she bought Diderot's books, then not only allowed him to keep them but also paid him an annual salary as librarian-custodian. In 1773, Diderot spent several months at Catherine's court in St. Petersburg, arguing impudently with her, forgetting to call her "Your Majesty" and sometimes, in the heat of a philosophic discussion, even slapping the royal knee.

Empress Catherine the Great of Russia (1729–96), Diderot's patron, took liberalism more as fad than as fact.

The Need to be Well Wigged

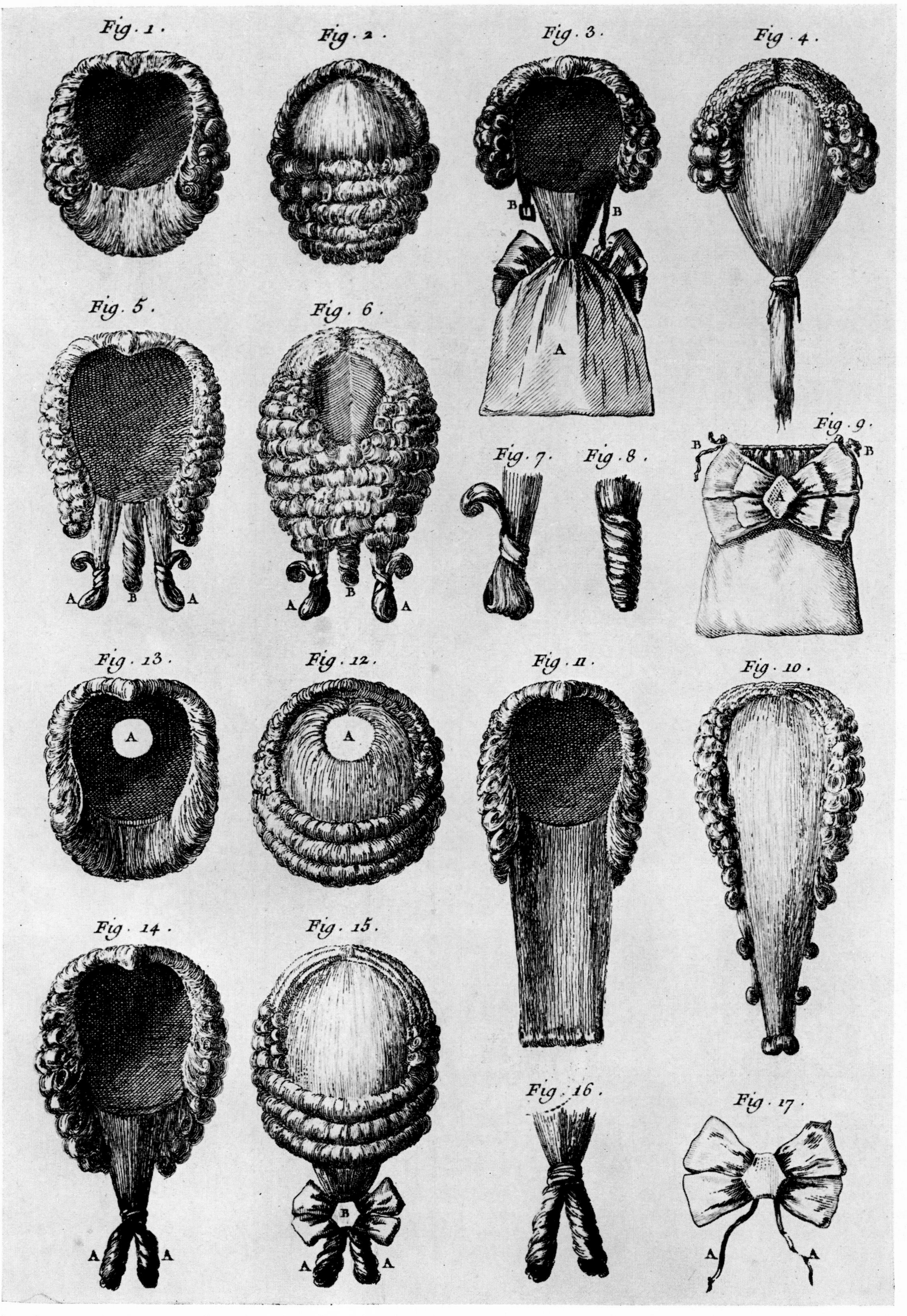

In a day when even manservants and coachmen powdered their hair, wigs were a matter of such importance to noblemen that Diderot included pages of wig illustrations in his *Encyclopedia*. Noble children wore wigs and sons, like their fathers, carried tricornered hats tucked under their arms because fashion required a hat and it was hard to wear one over a wig. Some wigs were occupational, like the abbé's wig (*Fig. 12*), but most were matters of taste, like the bag wig (*Fig. 3*), the knotted wig (*Fig. 6*) and the newly growing wig (*Fig. 10*).

EIGHTEENTH CENTURY ENGLAND

The century which grew rich with trade and empire proudly showed off its wealth in magnificent, well-ordered country estates where the great men of the realm lived, played, hunted and ran the affairs of state. Chatsworth (*above*) is the seat of the dukes of Devonshire.

Through this arch, in the days of the eighteenth century dukes, flowed a waterfall which cascaded down the steps and was then led underground to be fed into the fountains (one, the Emperor, threw a 267-foot jet) which played in the finest formal gardens in England.

VIII

EIGHTEENTH CENTURY ENGLAND

RICH, young William Beckford put down the book he had been reading, a tome on the new deist religion, and scribbled gaily in the margin, "Hurrah! no hell." To Beckford, who typified the more fortunate Englishman of the eighteenth century, the news removed the one dark cloud, the one discordant element, from his universe. Everything else—everything in this world—was very harmonious and solid and handsome and very much of a piece. Nor is it difficult for us to see what he meant; for though Beckford's England has been dead for a century and a half, it stares out at us a dozen times a day—in the architecture of houses, the furniture of rooms, the prints on people's walls, the plates on their dinner tables. It is the chief glory of many museums, the first prize at many fancy-dress balls; a single grandee of the period, Lord Chesterfield, has conferred his name on a code of manners, a style of sofa and a brand of cigarettes.

Eighteenth century England is still scattered all about us because, to an extent equaled by few other eras, it signifies a way of life. Even before we think of it as the century when England became Great Britain, or when Great Britain lost the thirteen colonies, or launched the Industrial Revolution, or achieved parliamentary government—even before eighteenth century England suggests any of these momentous facts, it evokes a scene, it suggests an age when men strove to be reasonable, and when life was leisurely and things had elegance. It was the last stop before the modern world was reached; the last time that a hundred years did not alter the picture of civilized life almost beyond recognition. In its prevailing mode eighteenth century England had about it an ordered sense of movement, something between a march and a minuet; it had equally about it an atmosphere of light—the reign of superstition was almost ending and that of smoke had not yet begun.

It was less an era of growth than of superb consolidation. The previous era had seethed with violence; the coming one would boil with activity. England, betweentimes, grew rich as she grew restrained, and embossed common sense with style. The seventeenth century had been sanguinary and bigoted and intense. For his insistence on the divine right of kings, Charles I in 1649 went magnificently to the block; while to be rid of divine right England had to submit to the dictatorship of Cromwell and his Puritans. The Stuarts came back to the throne with Charles II in 1660. But in 1688, Protestant England forced his stubborn, papist brother, James II, to go. At his going something like the seventeenth century went also; for spiritually eighteenth century England begins with 1688, as it concludes with 1789. The year 1688 brought James's Protestant son-in-law and daughter, William and Mary, over from Holland to be king and queen of England. But it did more. Thanks in great part to its principal interpreter, the rational philosopher John Locke, it spread the doctrines of individual liberty and religious tolerance and produced a spirit of militant common sense.

It would be hard to say whether this new spirit chiefly set

The century which made a fetish of elegance also made a point of laughing at it. No headdress ever grew quite this long and no sedan chair was equipped with a hinged top. But the caricature came close enough to truth to sting and strayed far enough from fact to amuse.

The earl of Chesterfield (1694–1773), successful statesman, intemperate gambler and paragon of politeness, wrote a still famous series of letters to his son, explaining in witty and precise detail how a perfect gentleman should behave.

The duchess of Marlborough (1660–1744), the wife of England's great general, was a bold, hot-tempered, able, politically ambitious woman who dominated mild Queen Anne, snubbed her and, finally going too far, fell from royal favor.

William Blackstone (1723–80), an undistinguished judge, wrote the famous *Commentaries* which in England was considered a good text and in America became an oracle, reverently consulted by struggling lawyers and jurors.

up fences or pulled them down. While it put an end to abuses that had hemmed man in, it suddenly set limits to his vision of the world. But the fences that did come down were of much the greater significance, because they had actually been like walls. The Englishman, during the century, was to become a great deal more the slave of convention but a great deal less the victim of authority. He was to be free, at any rate, to enslave himself. Where through history he had always been harangued about his duties, Locke reminded him of his rights. Hand in hand with the age of reason go the rights of man, goes the great watchword of the century, liberty-freedom "not to be subject to the inconstant, uncertain, unknown, arbitrary will of another man. . . ." The rights of man, to be sure, were in great part property rights; it was not an age when the poor were offered much chance or much charity.

But while the walls of arbitrary authority were coming down and those of religious intolerance were being breached, neat hedges and palings were everywhere going up. For hundreds of years life in England and Europe had been splendidly but dangerously dramatic; there had been no end of violence, of exaltation, of conspiracy, of bloodshed. Now men were sick of drama, and they rebounded to the idea of life as civilized comedy. But civilized comedy cannot be played without rules; without, in fact, quite strict ones. So, at this particular turn of time, the policy arose not of driving the devil out but of fencing him in; not of thirsting after omniscience but of resting happy in reason; and of shrugging the shoulder in preference to unsheathing the sword. The eighteenth century gentleman thus set up, in the common interest, a great many thou-shalt-nots. Thus it was commanded: Thou shalt not talk about thyself lest thou bore thy neighbor; or it was enjoined: Thou shalt not become overzealous, lest thou disturb the peace. No word was a greater slur than the word "enthusiasm." This atmosphere made social life very harmonious; the drawback was that it raised etiquette a good deal higher than ethics.

CERTAINLY in its search for harmony eighteenth century England constantly resorted to compromise; but compromise was a quality it admired. Experience showed that two men with strongly opposed ideas of the truth would certainly shout, and might very well shoot, at each other; whereas two men trying to find a common area of agreement seldom raised their voices and usually achieved their ends. The age of reason was willing to give up some of the grandeur in life to get rid of some of the muddle; eighteenth century people saw no more point to squandering energy than money.

Their guide, their god, was common sense; which, when joined to natural British pluck, they felt would solve any difficulty—even Robinson Crusoe's on an island. They were not wrong; the combination gave England tremendous security and power. No doubt it cost something; it led to a certain stifling of the imagination, a certain withering of the emotions, a certain contraction of the soul. What saved the age from aridness and unbearable Philistinism was that quality which gives it a retrospective glamor, a lingering bouquet—its enormous sense of style.

For, though common sense was its god, it worshiped it with elaborate ceremony. It cared terribly—in a moral view it cared far too much—about appearances; velvet gloves concealed not only mailed fists but itching palms. Yet much else, beyond prudence and hypocrisy, contrived to give the life of eighteenth century England an air. It was, for one thing, very much the age of the aristocrat; it was, for another, not

James Cook (1728–79), last of the great explorers, claimed the Australian continent for England and rediscovered Hawaii. By use of malt and sauerkraut, he conquered scurvy and kept his crew healthy on a thousand-day voyage.

Lady Mary Montagu (1689–1762), brightest lady intellectual of her day, was a vivid, untidy woman who wrote brilliant letters, hated bores and fools and brought native costumes and smallpox inoculations to England from Turkey.

Edward Gibbon (1737–94) was in Rome in 1764 musing amid the ancient ruins when the idea for his history struck him. Twenty-three years later he finished the last of the seven volumes of *The Decline and Fall of the Roman Empire.*

the age of the machine. The aristocrat brought distinguished manners into everyday life. An aristocrat spent all his leisure hours acquiring style and *ton;* and his leisure hours, to steal a phrase of Heine's, often amounted to twenty-four a day. His education was in many respects a disgrace; he might attend Oxford or Cambridge for years without setting foot in a lecture room or even meeting his tutor. But he did learn there how to cut a figure in the world; no one could saunter more charmingly or philander with more grace.

BUT at its best the sense of style went well beyond this, went far, indeed, toward fulfilling a high aristocratic ideal. Probably the aristocratic ideal came closest to being personally achieved in Lord Chesterfield, who is most famous for the letters of advice he wrote to his son but whose greatest feat, as one critic said, was to "create himself." For what Chesterfield did, in setting down his rules for a gentleman's behavior, went a good deal beyond nature and a little outside it. Such was the noble earl's view of distinction that he forbade many harmless amusements; a gentleman, for example, must on no account ever laugh out loud. The objection to this is that it is so harmonious it has ceased to be human; and the gentleman, in the end, is less a man than a work of art.

And style in eighteenth century England was not just a matter of stance and stride, of paying a compliment or wearing a coat. It was something men commanded in the stress of business, in the teeth of adversity. They snubbed with style: "The honorable gentleman," retorted one M.P. to another, "would seem to be indebted to his memory for his jests and to his imagination for his facts." They died, nay, went to the scaffold, with style: Lord Balmerino, condemned for supporting Stuart claims to the throne, "lay down; but being told he was on the wrong side, vaulted round and immediately gave the sign by tossing up his arm, as if he were giving the signal for battle."

As it was perhaps the most lustrous period of the aristocrat, in a sense it was the last. The eighteenth century aristocrat owned everything, it might be said, except the future. For quite as much as he set the fashion and the pace, he made the laws and held the offices and scooped up the money and owned the land. Because the patrician had outstanding style, it is easy to forget that he often had uncommon ability. Lord Chesterfield was indeed a great gentleman, but he was also an admirable lord lieutenant of Ireland and a secretary of state.

The great eighteenth century aristocrats had their very serious faults, but it would not be easy to find a comparable body of men with more varied talents. The best of them were really spectacular performers, endowed with a fantastic energy that they monstrously abused; they were like sets of human fireworks, crackling and glittering and illuminating the heavens and suddenly blazing forth again after they were supposed extinct. It was not so much that they went round the clock without even pausing for sleep, but rather how much and how many kinds of things they could pack into their day. On no condition would they, to begin with, forego their normal pleasures, their dalliance and their drinking and their gambling; but, having emptied a sensational number of bottles, they were quite likely to issue forth and electrify Parliament; also, in the same day, to help design a grotto, compose an epigram, translate an ode, amuse a great lady, assist an author, exercise a horse, perpetrate a hoax, administer a province and read for an hour in Mr. Pope.

The aristocratic ideal was far more a dream than it was

In rowdy Billingsgate Market, beside the docks of London, loud-mouthed and abusive fishwives hawked their wares, got into brawls and sought out the newly paid sailors as they came off their ships.

In the pillory at Charing Cross, minor offenders against the law were held up to public ridicule with heads and hands locked in a frame. Many were pelted with garbage, a few stoned to death by mobs.

The Royal, a cockpit on Tufton Street, was the scene of wild enthusiasm and heavy betting. Paupers and peers alike were cockfight fans, some even following the favorite "teams" of cocks to fights.

ever a reality, just as the age of reason far better expresses the desire to be rational than the ability. This is not to minimize either thing. The very dream and the very desire are in themselves large achievements. But it must also be confessed that the age which made a god of decorum all too frequently made a beast of itself, and that the century which stood dedicated to reason produced some of the most unbalanced of all human beings.

ANY chronicle of England during those years is also, in part, a chronicle of excesses, a chronicle of extremes. The rich were very rich: "A man," conceded one of their tribe, "can jog along on 40,000 pounds a year"—at a time when an income of 40,000 pounds was like a million dollars today. The poor were very poor: an industrious laborer earned 9 shillings —what today would be around $14—a week. The grand were very grand: the "proud duke" of Somerset had the roads cleared of bystanders when he traveled; and his second wife happening one day to tap him playfully with her fan, "Madam," said the duke sternly, "my first wife was a Percy and she never dared take such a liberty."

Nor was there ever such immoderacy. Scholars fought duels over a Greek accent; a relative of Lord Byron's killed a man over a matter of pheasants. Everywhere men drank prodigiously: so far from remarkable was it to toss off three bottles of wine at a sitting, it was hardly respectable not to. The brave fellows tossed off six. The Methuen Treaty of 1703 which spelled the domination of Portugal by England spelled equally the domination of England by port. "Claret," pontificated Dr. Johnson, "is for boys." And while the comfortable classes got gouty—from port, they thought—the poor went to pieces from gin. During the first half of the century gin drinking reached ghastly proportions; inside fifteen years the consumption of spirits doubled, and the author of *Tom Jones* wrote that a hundred thousand Londoners lived on gin alone. In vain did parsons denounce "Gin, cursed Fiend, with Fury fraught" in favor of "Beer, happy Produce of our Isle." While their wives and children starved, a multitude of wretches grew vicious, turned criminal, went mad.

It was a brutal and audacious age of crime, with pickpockets in every crowd and highwaymen along every road, a stealthy and menacing age, a bloody and murdering one. Even so, the punishments were incredibly harsh and grew harsher as the century went on. There came to be one hundred and sixty offenses punishable by death—among them, chopping down a tree in a garden or being seen for a month with gypsies. So many men were condemned that on "hanging days" at Tyburn there was not time or room to hang them all.

Low and high life alike were exceedingly profligate, in particular early in the century when hardly a man in public life was not stained with scandal. When the glittering Viscount Bolingbroke became secretary of state in 1710, the madam of a bawdy house crowed, "Five thousand a year, my girls—and all for us!" Ladies often had little better reputations than their lords; the paternity of men like Horace Walpole is to this day a subject of doubt. "Nobody's son," sniffed Chesterfield of a certain marriage, "has married Everybody's daughter."

But the worst excess of all in eighteenth century England was the gambling; never have men played for higher stakes or stranger ones. The great clubs—whether Whig or Tory, Brooks's or White's—were essentially gambling houses where time and again an ancestral estate hung on a throw of the dice. From Brooks's a member once retired in disgust because he had won only 12,000 pounds in two months. The gambling debts of the celebrated and reckless duchess of Devonshire totaled more than a million pounds. Nor was it only money people gambled with. One man gambled away, with her consent, his wife; another gambled his child; still another, his freedom; while two others gambled their lives—the winner to string up the loser.

For all its high manners it was an age of quarrels. There was a kind of chain-squabbling in vogue: Steele quarreled with Addison, Addison with Pope, Pope with Lady Mary Montagu, Lady Mary with half her friends. Again, the age of reason seemed very often like an age of madness. Bedlam (St. Mary of Bethlehem's hospital) was so much one of the sights of London that tea was served there—while the rage to visit it might be thought a touch eccentric in itself. Beginning with Dean Swift, a whole procession of the century's poets—Smart, Collins, Cowper—went mad; perhaps to go mad was the only polite thing to do, since His Majesty, George III, often went very mad indeed.

AGAIN, as the century wore on, England's era of enlightenment craved the creepy spells of the Middle Ages; built "Gothic" piles and abbeys; wrote Gothic romances where, in a dank world of vaults and midnight, everything clanked and shrieked and groaned. But even more than it wanted to shudder, a too-long-repressed England wanted to weep. And weep it did—and in time all Europe after it—when a milksop printer of genius, Samuel Richardson, wrote his novels *Pamela* and *Clarissa*. As *Clarissa* came out in installments and Clarissa's virtue became ever more gravely endangered, all England pleaded that the poor girl should not be ravished; but Richardson was relentless and presently all England wept buckets of tears.

Assaulted by human feelings, reason was next to be shaken by faith. The deism of Locke and Bolingbroke, and later the outright skepticism of Gibbon and Hume, prevailed in high society and the intellectual world right through the century. But midway through it the rest of England, which a lazy church had rendered apathetic, began to hearken to the blazing call of John Wesley and George Whitefield who, denied pulpits, preached in the open fields and converted thousands and then tens of thousands to Methodism.

For almost fifty years, from the day Queen Anne quitted the throne in 1714 to the day George III ascended it, the Whig lords, the squires and great merchants ran England. They were so powerful that they really constituted the government and the opposition both. In Queen Anne's reign the great duke of Marlborough's victories at arms raised England, after a century of struggle, to the most commanding position in Europe. Then, after peace had been signed, the Whig prime minister, Robert Walpole, put England on her feet by stabilizing her political life and by giving her—actually by compelling upon her—a long interval of peace. A whole generation of peace had reaped for England a rich harvest of plenty. Trade grew, commerce multiplied, the middle

The Bank of England, which was founded privately, had a harried, speculation-ridden beginning. But by mid-century it was entrusted with administering the national debt and became more respectable.

Brooks's was founded as a gambling club by twenty-seven lords and noblemen. It had strict social and gaming rules. Joining any other club was frowned on and betting in the dining room was forbidden.

Lloyd's, once a dock-area coffeehouse, became the great insurance combine. The subscription room (*above*) had booths for talking business, a big clock and an anemometer, and a ships' newsboard.

class gained steadily in wealth, self-confidence and power. Under Walpole, England kept shop with wonderful success; and so became, for good and all, a nation of shopkeepers.

Walpole left office in 1742 and there followed fifteen years of bungling administration until Pitt made his majestic entrance as secretary of state in 1757. Walpole was not merely the antithesis of Pitt; he was also the very necessary antecedent. He had to make England prosper through peace before Pitt could make her powerful through war. The two men, so alike in their masterfulness, so utterly different in their methods—the one all rudder, the other all sail—offer in the eighteenth century that mixture of the hardheaded and the heroic which has been, in almost every century, the key to England's success. But where Walpole worked grubbily behind the scenes, Pitt performed, with the utmost éclat, on a brilliantly lighted stage. Joining Frederick the Great against half of Europe in the Seven Years' War, Pitt devised a global strategy to match England's vast ambitions, and made the year 1759—the year of Quebec and Minden and Guadeloupe and Quiberon Bay—one of England's most triumphant.

But in 1760 a new king, George III, came to the throne with a most decided conviction that it *was* a throne. The handsome young man did not need to believe in the divine right of kings; sufficient, to his mind, were their purely human opportunities. He did not need to challenge the belief that Parliament ruled the country; he, in his turn, would simply rule Parliament—by bullying it where he could, by bribing it where he must. He quickly rid himself of Pitt and, after much dabbling in ministers, found the mouthpiece he wanted in Lord North, a more decent man and more competent minister than most Americans are given to believe at school, but one who could never get George's permission to resign and could never muster the courage to resign without it.

George was in a fair way to achieve his ambition of running the country. It took the American Revolution to foil him.

The real cause of the Revolution was economic and stemmed out of Britain's mercantilist policy, out of a nation of shopkeepers condemning her colonies to be a "nation of customers." The colonists could only buy from—or by way of—Britain, while Britain did not have to buy from them, and no other country was permitted to. Hence they were more and more becoming a nation of smugglers; and now that England owned Canada and there was no longer any danger of a French invasion, their strongest tie with the mother country fell away. George III or no George III, the colonies would sooner or later have had to be given considerably more rope; but had George and his ministers not bullied and bungled, had there been no Stamp Act or uproars over "taxation without representation," the colonies might have been appeased with something like dominion status. As it was, the slaps at their pride stung them as much as the drain on their purses.

George's pigheaded methods made all Britain's enlightened statesmen regard the rebels less as enemies than as allies: to a Pitt or to an Edmund Burke, who delivered the famous speech on conciliation with the colonies, the Americans were defending the British constitution against the British, while another M.P., Charles James Fox, could characterize a British victory over Washington as "the bad news from Long Island." Lord North's attempt in 1778 to offer the American

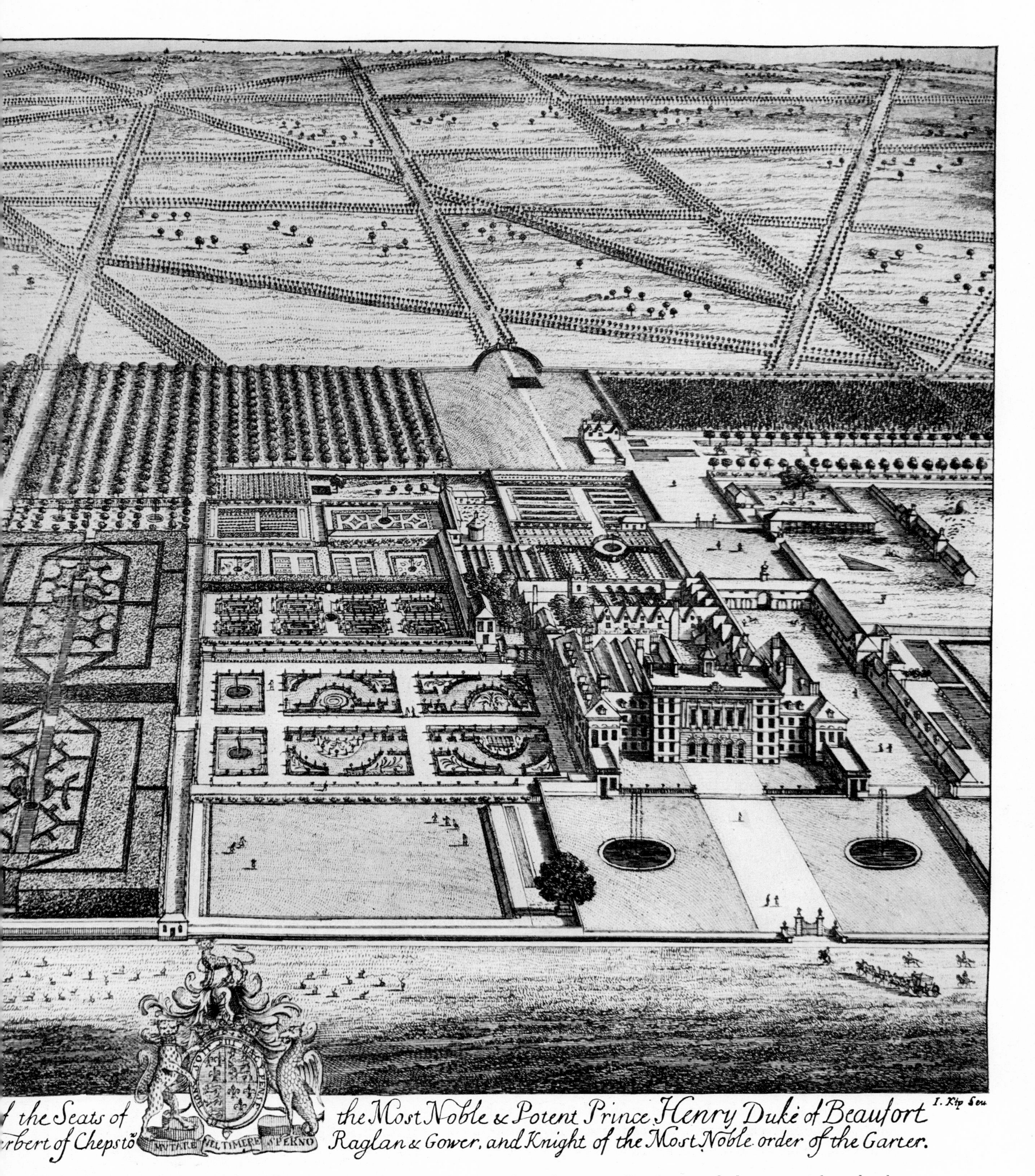

Badminton, ancestral home of the dukes of Beaufort, was a magnificent fifteen-thousand-acre estate almost ten miles in circumference. A cluster of formal gardens and mazes lay along one side of the house and broad avenues of beeches stretched out toward the parks where herds of red and fallow deer roamed. The estate gave its name to the game of badminton, imported from India and first played there.

colonies a kind of dominion status came too late; by then they were committed to independence and, by then, with France and later Holland and Spain all at war with her, England was clearly doomed to "the most damaging and humiliating defeat" in her history. But the loss of the colonies possibly saved England from something worse; for had George won the war he would have become so highhanded that the English might have had to rebel against him themselves. It was a great try, this last grab of a British monarch for extensive power; it was also a decisive one, for as a result no subsequent British monarch was to have any power at all. When, after the colonies were lost, the younger Pitt finally drew the royal claws, monarchy in England became little more than a synonym for pageantry.

In America, out of the struggle with George III there was born a union of independent states that unhesitatingly accepted, for the most part, eighteenth century Britain's principles of government. The colonial assemblies had been much like miniature British parliaments and as time went on had arrogated to themselves more and more legislative powers. Out of their experience in these assemblies the Americans developed strong notions and beliefs which, after two tries, they wrote into the Constitution and its first ten amendments. Thus the executive was ruled out of the legislature for fear he might try to rule over it; control of finance, in the United States as in Britain, was vested in the lower house; in the U.S., as in Britain, judges were made independent of legislature and executive alike; and such cherished civil rights as habeas corpus and trial by jury were jealously retained. On the other hand, the Founding Fathers of the American republic rejected such deep-rooted English principles as the monarchy and the established church.

IN spirit the new U.S. political system clearly trumpeted Locke, whose writings had been widely reprinted in newspapers before and during the American Revolution. But in actual structure the U.S. system followed the concepts of the French political philosopher, Montesquieu, who in his turn had drunk of British political philosophy. In his celebrated book, *The Spirit of the Laws*, Montesquieu simplified somewhat and idealized the British constitution. Because of Montesquieu's theories, the U.S. president is not a member of Congress (as England's prime minister is of Parliament) and he is elected independently of it.

On the heels of the American Revolution came two other momentous ones—the French Revolution and the Industrial Revolution. The whole tune, and still more the whole orchestration, of life was to be immensely altered. England in the century ahead would worship very different gods—steam and iron, respectability and reform. In the New World, the frontier and its raucous demands for democracy would change the ordered patterns of life which the seaboard colonies had copied from England. But in both the mother country and her rebellious American offspring, the value that the eighteenth century had put upon individualism and the rights of individuals would still remain. It would imbue all the life and thought of the new century which was to make Britain the greatest empire the world had ever seen and was to prepare the United States of America for the power that was later to come.

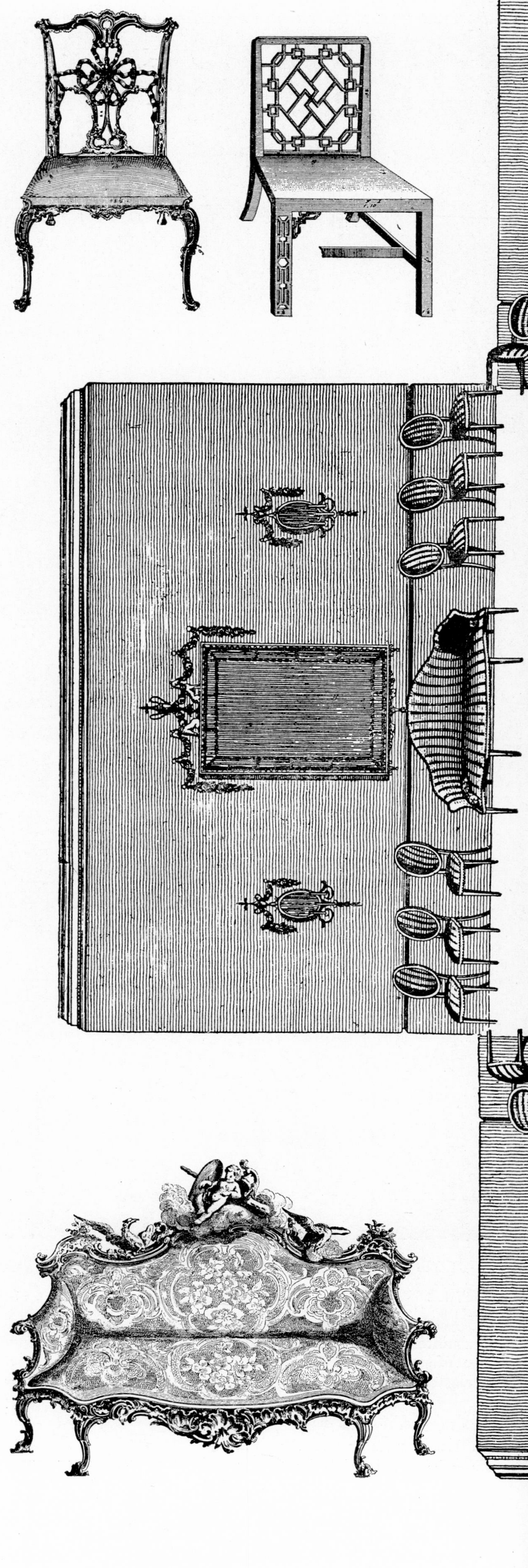

Great Furniture Makers

IT was a fine time for furniture makers—and there were fine ones on the job. England's gay and discerning society afforded ideal patronage for them: it was eager for new styles; it wanted the best of workmanship and taste; it had plenty of money to pay for what it wanted. It had as guide and consultant the most famous of all English interior decorators, the architect Robert Adam. And as its craftsmen it had skilled joiners and carvers whose work was delicate, imaginative and superbly proportioned.

Chippendale, though unheralded in his time, was the first of the great designers. His special gift lay in giving various styles a common ground of taste, proportion and comfort, as demonstrated in such differing pieces as a carved ribbon-back chair and a Chinese-motif chair (*top left*) and an ornate sofa (*bottom left*). Hepplewhite refined and lightened Chippendale's work. He cut down ornamentation, reduced seat widths from twenty-two inches to twenty and, by better design and construction, achieved fragility without sacrificing strength. He drew up the four-walled sketch for a proper drawing room which surrounds this text. Sheraton, the designer who closed this golden era, had no shop of his own, merely publishing his ideas for furniture design. He combined simple straight lines with graceful curves to produce furniture of rare beauty, as in his chairs (*top right*) and his simple, balanced sideboard (*bottom right*).

Fashion in the arts turned for a while to the silhouette, whose mannered charm delighted the era. This group portrait is titled *The Sitwell and Warneford Families.*

Fashion in entertainment veered to opera which, then as now, gave *grande dames* a chance to show off while listening to the singers, largely brought in from Italy.

The height of fashion in great ladies was→ portrayed by Thomas Gainsborough, in an art that displayed the orderly elegance the century prized. Opposite is his *The Honorable Mrs. Graham.* The extreme beauty of the lady so fired Gainsborough that he painted her on four occasions, once as a servant girl carrying a broom.

On the Mall, a promenade three-quarters of a mile long, every Londoner of fashion strolled casually with his lady, hoping to be seen.

Life in Town

FOR the people of quality London was the capital of the world. A tenth of England lived there. In the great city the rarest goods were to be bought and the most fascinating sights to be seen —the lions in the Tower, the waxworks on Fleet Street, the artificial cascade at Vauxhall, the theater at Covent Garden, the maniacs in Bedlam. But the main thing was not so much to see as to be seen. Perfumed ladies and powdered fops paraded themselves before the people in every public place, from the Mall (*above*) to Ranelagh Gardens (*below*), sipping tea, chatting and strolling round and round, as one observer said, "like asses in an olive mill."

The city itself was a boisterous, bawdy, deafening place. In its narrow streets numberless signboards creaked and clanked over the shopwindows, carriages clattered over the cobbles and hawkers shoved heavy barrows through the crowds. On the river, below London Bridge, stevedores and sailors cursed and bellowed as they unloaded the incessant cargoes—silks from India, furs from Canada, sugar from the Barbados: the sumptuous recompense of empire.

The Rotunda in Ranelagh Gardens, a pleasure palace 555 feet in circumference, was heated in winter by a huge central fireplace.

The Thames ran softly through the town, as Canaletto showed in this picture he painted on the terrace of the Duke of Richmond's house in Whitehall. In the foreground the duke's guests take the air. And over London, on the farther shore, rises the dome of St. Paul's.

Life in the country

THE long wet winter cooped Londoners in the city and kept the country squire and farmer bogged down or snowed in. So as soon as good weather came, the Englishman rushed outdoors to kick up his heels like a heifer. On the shady village greens, squires and even noblemen mixed with commoner folk for games of cricket and mugs of beer. For the great national flat races at Newmarket (*right*) the sporting bloods came a-riding from London, from Colchester, from Olney and Norwich, some in gracious chaises, some in creaky traps. The horses they bet on were among the world's best, descendants of the imported Turkish and Arab stallions which began the Thoroughbred line. Queen Anne herself was an ardent racing fan and sometimes dipped into the national treasury to donate a fat purse.

Neither the dowdy Anne, who ruled England until 1714, nor fat German George I, who succeeded her, cared much for the nice disciplines of court life. Society revolved around country estates where the nobility and gentry talked politics, farmed, watched over the tenantry, rode to hounds, drank copiously and ate and ate and ate.

The great race meeting at Warren Hill, Newmarket, was painted by John Wootton. This part of the canvas shows the king, who has just arrived in a chaise and will sit in the private grandstand for royalty.

The Wedgwood family, noted makers of pottery and chinaware, posed for artist George Stubbs in a little grove near Etruria Hall, their country estate in Staffordshire. Josiah Wedgwood and his wife, Sarah, sit among their seven children. At Josiah's elbow, in modest advertisement, stands a piece of Wedgwood's famous Black Basalt ware. Paintings like this were called "conversation pieces."

The sun never set on the afternoon cup of tea. In the prosperous eighteenth century the British consolidated their customs and carried them intact to the ends of the earth. In this scene by John Zoffany, the finest painter of conversation pieces, a colonial family, the Auriols, is pictured having a collation under a jack fruit tree in India precisely as they might have taken it under an English oak.

The Quest for Culture Went On at Home and Abroad

TOWARD the end of the century a traveler with a statistical turn of mind told Gibbon, the famous historian, that forty thousand Englishmen—masters and servants—were living or touring on the Continent. By far the greatest part of this army was made up of prosperous businessmen engaged in a colossal culture binge, trying to fill their heads as they had filled their wallets. On the Continent they could drop in at the great galleries, mix with the nobility, be addressed by every innkeeper as "milord" and be cheerfully fleeced by almost every art dealer.

With the complacency of successful bargain hunters, the merchants lugged their culture cargo home by chaise and wherry. Statues, paintings, *bibelots*—the indiscriminate harvest of foreign fields was poured hudder-pudder into their town and country houses. By this process England soon accumulated the grandest heap of beautified rubbish since the Roman businessmen began to cram their villas with inferior Greek antiques. Sometimes there were true masters among the false. Dean Swift claimed to have picked up a genuine Titian for £2 5s. But as a broad business proposition the art trade was one in which England took a rooking. A hundred years would pass before the spurious treasures could be unloaded on the cultural innocents of a greater middle class that arose across the sea.

While the sons of the culture-hungry merchants were off with their tutors on the "grand tour" of the Continent, the daughters stayed home, where some of them went to ridiculous finishing schools to learn to flutter like a lady and perhaps catch a nobleman's younger son. But the nation's real center of wit and learning was the coffeehouse (*below*). Early in the century scores of them sprang up all over London to serve the popular new drink imported from Arabia. The coffeehouses became the regular hangouts of men like Swift and Addison, Burke and Johnson, Fox and Bolingbroke. In them, any Englishman who could find a seat at the table and a thought in his head could take part in the best conversations of his day.

To the coffeehouse the wits came to eat and drink, to hear and to be heard. Art, politics, theology, food, war—all were paid brilliant lip service by sharp tongues of the time. Ladies were not invited.

Englishmen abroad all stopped at the Uffizi Gallery in Florence, where John Zoffany painted this picture of old masters and new rich. In the group at left, Earl Cowper, Sir John Dick and the earls of Plymouth and Dartmouth surround Zoffany, who is holding a Raphael *Madonna* for inspection. At right the Honorable Felton Hervey and Sir Horace Mann discuss Titian's *Reclining Venus*.

Samuel Johnson, shown in the tinges of his usual melancholy in this portrait by Sir Joshua Reynolds, was one of the century's literary leaders and the subject of its best biography, Boswell's *The Life of Samuel Johnson*. Enormous, half-blind and violently irritable, Johnson was a literary dictator, a firm Tory and an ardent classicist. His cultural influence was so important that he became a national institution, supported by an awed monarch on a government subsidy. Johnson was a formidable conversational bully. He used to crush opponents with remarks like one he made at a violin recital: "Difficult do you call it, sir? I wish it were impossible."

Johnson and Boswell (*above*) return from a night on the town. Dr. Johnson is muttering, "I smell you in the dark." Waking with a hangover the next morning (*right*), Boswell opens a prayer book and reads: "And be not drunk with wine wherein there is excess." He notes: "Some would have taken this as a divine interposition."

The Writers' Circle

THE writer was coming into his own. Books were selling well: Gibbon's *Decline and Fall* went rapidly into three editions, Richardson's *Pamela* into four editions in six months. Though they were not yet paid royalties, writers did not have to sell their manuscripts outright to publishers. They could work in collaboration with booksellers or they could go directly to the public and sell "subscriptions" before their works were completed. Under this system, buyers paid half the purchase money in advance, the other half when the book was delivered. Writers still depended on patrons, but most were now in a position to agree openly with Johnson's comment to Lord Chesterfield: "Is not a Patron, my Lord, one who looks with unconcern on a man struggling for life in the water, and, when he has reached ground, encumbers him with help?"

Johnson sat as a schoolmaster over most of the rising literary and artistic figures of the day. About once a week, at the Turk's Head tavern, he headed earnest, witty, argumentative discussions that lasted from supper until after midnight. Johnson's circle included not only literary figures like Goldsmith the poet, Gibbon the historian and Sheridan the playwright, but also the painter Sir Joshua Reynolds, the politician Edmund Burke and the actor David Garrick. And, of course, James Boswell, Johnson's faithful biographer and a literary genius in his own right. Any judgment Johnson handed down was meant for the ages—and Boswell recorded it as such. Johnson indulged in and invoked a direct and earthy kind of verbal conflict, as when he said to the economist and moralist Adam Smith, "You lie," and Smith replied, "You are a son of a bitch."

David Garrick, whom Johnson described as "the first man in the world for sprightly conversation," was also the finest actor of the period. He did realistic characterizations and ignored the rigid posing called for by theatrical precedent. (A sample rule: in portraying astonishment, the left leg is drawn back.) In thirty years as manager of the Drury Lane Theatre, he helped revive Shakespeare and also modernized stage lighting. At right he plays the part of Richard III.

Laurence Sterne made a semifictional character of himself in *A Sentimental Journey*. In real life, he made himself a pest by soliciting subscriptions for his books in London's Ranelagh Gardens (*above*).

The adventures of Daniel Defoe's Robinson Crusoe, published in 1719, were summed up in this map showing the shipwrecked hero, his man Friday, his parrot, his encounter with savages, his rescue.

Some Very Famous People

OUT of the pages of the century's books paraded a stream of fabulous figures who were—and still are—as real and familiar as any who actually lived. The age produced Gulliver, Robinson Crusoe, Oliver Goldsmith's benign vicar of Wakefield and his loutish Tony Lumpkin; Laurence Sterne's Tristram Shandy with his blowhard Uncle Toby, who dreamed of stirring battles and hated to kill a fly; and Sheridan's Mrs. Malaprop, who spoke of "allegories on the bank of the Nile" (she meant alligators).

Not only enduring literary characters but an enduring literary form came out of the century—the novel, which was given its modern shape by Samuel Richardson. Richardson, a London printer, set out to compose a guide on letter writing "for country readers." To keep up interest, he invented a character named Pamela, who supposedly wrote the letters and recounted her adventures—how she was wooed by a rake, how she spurned his immoral advances and how, by her charm and virtue, she won him to proper marriage. Full of dull moralizing, *Pamela* was also full of shrewd character delineation. The English loved it and cried for more. Richardson gave it to them with a vengeance in a seven-volume work, *Clarissa*, whose heroine's virtue had a grimmer reward than Pamela's.

The increase in writing—and in reading by the middle class—hastened a revolution in the quantity and quality of literary output. Besides the novel, the era created the modern essay, produced the first good journalistic writing and social commentary, and witnessed a running interchange of informative and still entertaining letters.

In Henry Fielding's *Tom Jones*, Squire Western rages at hearing of his daughter's love for Tom. A foundling, Tom has many adventures, not all creditable, before he attains success and Miss Western.

Clarissa was Samuel Richardson's widely popular tear-jerker about a genteel girl who died of shame after being kidnaped and seduced by her lover.

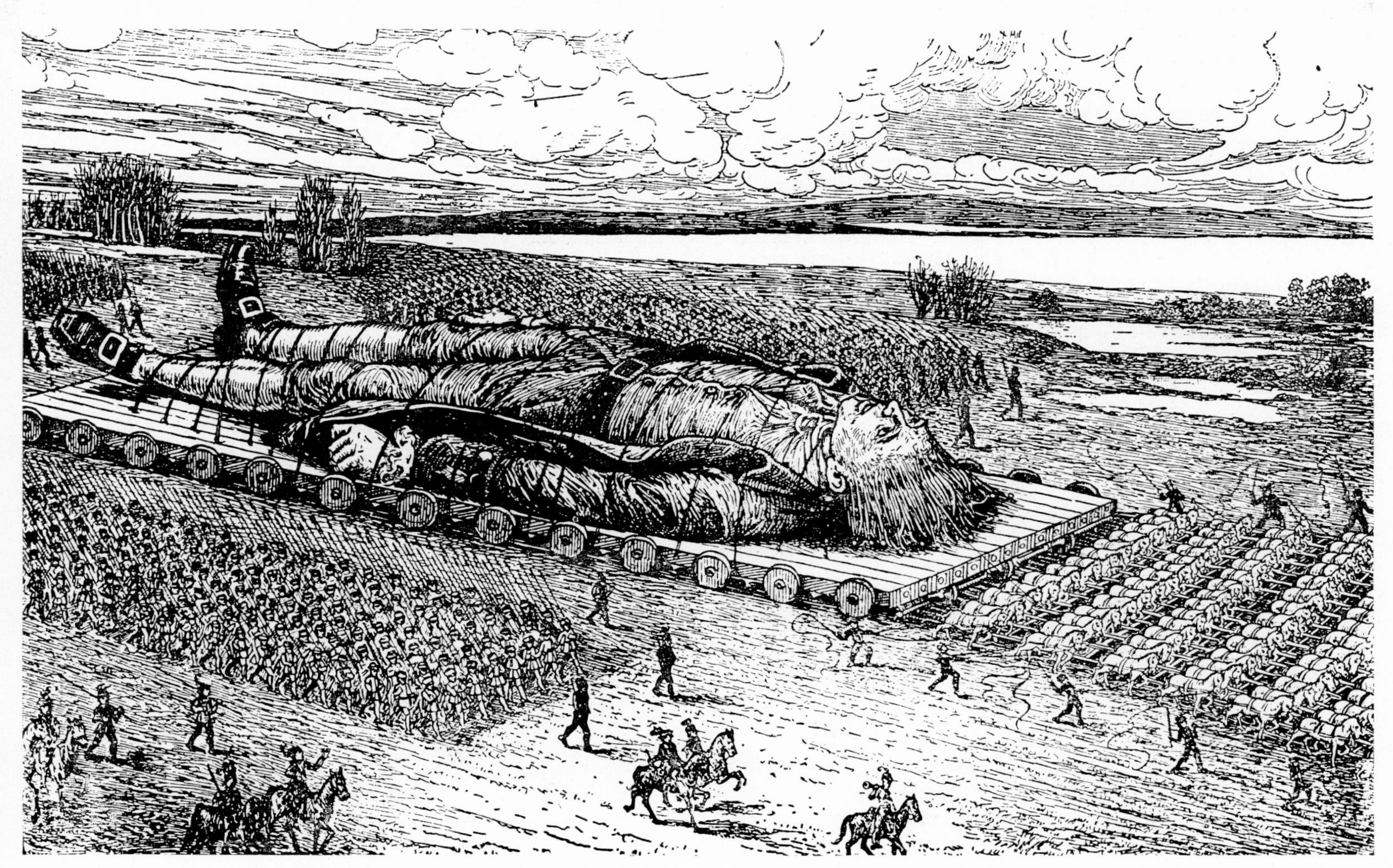

Gulliver's Travels, Jonathan Swift's satire, was read more as entertainment than as a ruthlessly bitter commentary on the English political scene. Shipwrecked on the island of Lilliput, Gulliver was captured by inhabitants only six inches tall who were always waging petty wars. He was tied up by his captors and, he said, "Fifteen hundred of the emperor's largest horses were employed to draw me."

George Whitefield, Wesley's spellbinding colleague, preached in all weathers and all seasons and crossed the Atlantic thirteen times to do his work. Because of his cross-eyes he was called "Dr. Squint."

John Wesley, founder of Methodism, traveled two hundred and fifty thousand miles and in his lifetime gave more than forty thousand sermons. "I look upon all the world as my parish," he wrote.

Wesley and Methodism

JOHN WESLEY was an earnest man in a land of religious indifference. One day in 1738, when he was a young priest given to Spartan piety, he experienced a great revelation. "I felt my heart strangely warmed," he said. His friend, George Whitefield, had the same experience. And soon thousands of others in England also felt their hearts warmed as Wesley and Whitefield, in one of the most remarkable spectacles in Christendom, went out into the streets and fields to preach a new kind of religion.

The faith they preached, later known as Methodism for Wesley's insistence on a methodical manner of worship, was imbued with a democratic approach to salvation. Christ, they said, would save not only the predestined elect but all men who chose to live righteously. The pious pair took themselves to prisons and slums, withstood hooting and violence, and won their converts among the lower classes, hitherto spurned by more respectable churches. Banned

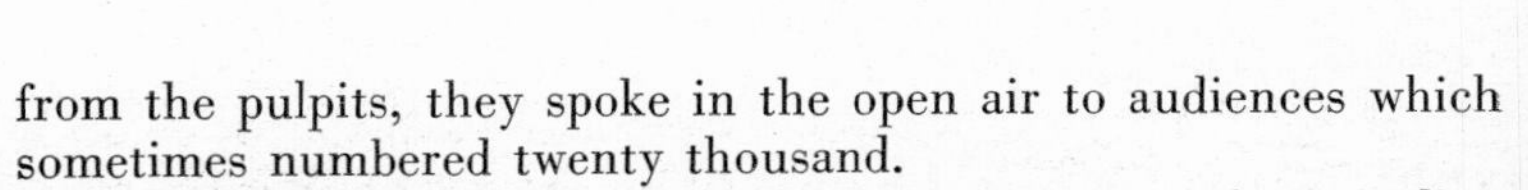

from the pulpits, they spoke in the open air to audiences which sometimes numbered twenty thousand.

Whitefield was the more dramatic orator. A man of astounding vocal powers, he could, said the great actor David Garrick, pronounce "Mesopotamia" in a way that would reduce an audience to tears. The skeptical Lord Chesterfield became so overwrought while listening to Whitefield describe a blind man approaching a precipice that he screamed out, "Good God! He's gone!"

Whitefield signed them up, but Wesley kept them marching. He was the man who could plan and give orders. He could speak while ". . . my heart was filled with love, my eyes with tears and my mouth with arguments"—and, thus speaking, could force his followers into a strait-laced life, empty of worldly pleasures. At sixty-eight, looking back on his life and the church of 170,000 members he had founded, John Wesley declared: "I am still a wonder to myself."

En route to America in 1735 to convert the Indians, Wesley sailed with hymn-singing Moravians. He was impressed by their strict ways and calm faith during storms which terrified other passengers.

At his street meetings Wesley was jeered, beaten, stoned, dragged along highways and a dozen times was almost killed. But those who came to scoff often stayed to surrender to pious persuadings.

The Methodists remembered the Bible's promise of the New Jerusalem. Here Wesley (*center*) and Whitefield (*right*) urge sinners off the broad way which leads to hell, and on to paths of righteousness which lead into the heavenly city where angels walk and the tree of life grows. The tree bears blessed fruit and among its leaves are written the steps man goes through before he gains resurrection.

Robert Walpole, England's first prime minister, was a sturdy, country-squirish, John Bull kind of man. The fifth of nineteen children, he changed from the church to politics at 22 when his two older brothers died. Had he stayed in religion, he later said, "I should have been archbishop of Canterbury," a not unreasonable estimate of his drive. Walpole headed the government for twenty-one consecutive years, longer than anyone else. His son, Horace, was a famous literary figure, an art collector and a letter writer.

The Rise of Parliamentary Government

ON the great winding staircase of English political development, the eighteenth century is a kind of spacious landing. On the stairs themselves there is all the rushing and stumbling, the panting for breath, of life moving upward. On the landing, resplendent figures move and posture with fine deliberation and decorum. The landing of the eighteenth century signifies at once a break with the past and a bridge to the future.

No longer an age of kings, not yet an age of the people, this was the great age of patrician Parliaments. It was England's —if not all history's—most glittering age of oratory, ushered in by the elder Pitt, set grandly echoing by Pitt the younger, by Sheridan and Fox and Burke. Their voices rolled forth —solemnly at midnight, still eloquently at dawn—for the relief of Ireland or the renovation of India. To such a torrent of applause did Sheridan conclude one five-and-a-half-hour speech, that his opponent Pitt could stave off a defeat in the voting only by moving for immediate adjournment.

What the eighteenth century did in England—and for the world—was to evolve the whole technique of modern parliamentary government. The century connects the revolution of 1688 (which by dethroning a king decreed that Parliament ruled the country) with the Reform Bill of 1832 (which by extending the ballot decreed that Parliament represented the people). While it did not produce popular government itself, the century produced the machinery for popular government. It gave form to what the nineteenth century would give force.

ALL during the five centuries from Magna Charta to 1688, the English constitution had been concerned rather with making the king, the Lords and the Commons equal partners than with making the Commons supreme. Edward I, in 1275, had set up a parliament with a house of commoners as well as peers; but the Commons was then only a king's way of feeling the nation's pulse, not yet the nation's way of showing its hand.

Since the crown, from Magna Charta on, was implicitly denied the power to tax, the Commons very early acquired control of the purse strings, and in a famous phrase settled its order of business: "Grievances precede supply"; that is to say, a king must satisfy the complaints of his subjects or risk running out of funds. Yet, having established this power, the Commons then let it lapse, giving the kings, through too liberal grants, a financial independence which made it unnecessary for them to ask the Commons for money.

The great Tudors, Henry VIII and Elizabeth, always were shrewd enough to preserve the fiction that they derived their power from Parliament; their Stuart successors made the mistake of claiming their power from God. Parliament would not swallow the doctrine of the divine right of kings. Balked of levying taxes, Charles I coolly annexed ship money; unable to do away with the courts, he resorted to the Star Chamber. Unwarned by his beheaded father's fate, James II not only

At Whitehall, Walpole presides over his cabinet where, for a score of years, he was usually the only member from the House of Commons. Before this, the cabinet had met with the king. Now it met with Walpole, followed his lead and accepted his party discipline.

A Perspective View of Westminster Hall, with both Houses of Parliament.
aſsembled on the Tryal of SIMON LORD LOVAT.

Both houses of Parliament assembled in all their dignity in 1747 for the treason trial of Lord Simon Lovat, accused of conspiring against the king on behalf of the Stuart pretender. Found guilty, Lord Lovat was sent to the block—the last man ever beheaded in England. The numbers and letters on this drawing refer to: 1. The King's Chair. 2. Prince of Wales's Seat. 3. Duke of Cumberland's Seat. 4. A Chair for the Lord High Steward. 5. Lord High Steward (moved nearer the Bar for convenient hearing). 6. The two Archbishops of Canterbury and York. 7. Bishops. 8. Great Officers of State, Dukes and Marquises (on front seat). 9. The Barons (behind the Dukes). 10. Earls and Viscounts. 11. Barons. 12. Master of the Rolls. 13. The Head Master in Chancery. 14. The Judges (on the inside of Woolpacks), Masters in Chancery (on the outside). 15. The Sergeant at Mace. 16. Lord High Steward's Purse bearer. 17. Clerks of the House of Lords. 18. Four Mace Bearers and two Heralds (in front) and Peers' Sons (behind). 19. Four Mace Bearers and Lord High Steward's Gentlemen. A. The Speaker of the House of Commons. B. Members of the House of Commons (side seats). C. Other Members (front seats). D. Managers for the House of Commons. E. Soliciters & Clerks. F. Lord Lovat at the Bar with the Lieutenant of the Tower on his right hand and the Gentleman Jailer with the Ax on his left. G. The Witness giving Evidence. H. The Prisoner's Council. I. Writer taking the Trial. K. The King's Box. L. The Prince of Wales's Box. M. Box for the Duke of Cumberland and, behind, benches for the Lord High Steward's Family and the Lord Chief Justice. N. The Princess Amelia's Box. O. Foreign Ambassadors. P. Peeresses & Daughters. Q. Peers' Tickets. R. The Duke of Ancaster's Gallery. S. Gallery for Board of Works & Vice Chamberlain. T. The Earl of Orford's Gallery.

flagrantly outraged Protestant feeling in his zeal to set up popery but utterly disregarded English law. In the revolution of 1688 he lost his throne; and Parliament, under the new bill of rights, asserted its power to regulate the succession. In his coronation oath, the new monarch, William III, vowed to govern "according to the statutes in Parliament agreed upon."

The great victory for parliamentary government was won; but while 1688 decided that Parliament should rule, it by no means decided how. Constitutionally the monarch was still very powerful. He could—as both William and Anne did—veto new acts of Parliament; he could choose all the ministers, preside over them and dismiss them at will. What unfortunately the monarch could not do, for some years after 1714, was speak English. Hence George I, Anne's successor, gave up attending cabinet meetings or communicating with ministers and betook himself from the center of policy making, when indeed he didn't take himself "home" to Hannover. And England's having a German on the throne happened to coincide with her having a genius in the House of Commons.

ROBERT WALPOLE was the first great manager of the House of Commons. This burly Norfolk squire who established the long parliamentary week end so that he could indulge his love of fox hunting, this cynical manipulator who always talked smut at his dinner table because he insisted it was the one form of conversation that everybody could enjoy, this supremely efficient Whig statesman who managed to hold the reins of power for more than twenty ticklish years, is by no means eighteenth century England's best-known figure; but he is conceivably its cardinal one. Walpole has not come down the years enhaloed, for his methods have sadly tarnished his achievements. Utter realist and complete cynic, he accepted the maxim that one must govern either by corruption or by force and unblinkingly chose corruption. He never made the one remark he is universally famous for—"Every man has his price"—but he would scarcely have jibed at it.

Walpole gave sinew and direction to England's public life. Under him the art of managing the Commons, rather than of winning the support of the king, became the basis for governing the country. And this new basis for governing went hand in hand with a new method of government. Walpole crystallized the idea of party government.

He was, in effect, England's first prime minister, turning what had been a cabinet council of miscellaneous advisers to the crown into the modern one-party cabinet of jointly responsible administrators. Walpole, who officially held the post of first lord of the treasury, assumed responsibility for all the ministers. When he stood up in Parliament in 1725 to explain and defend the actions of the foreign minister, he set a notable political precedent—and an alarming one to Englishmen. The office of prime minister, complained a group of lords, is "unknown to the laws of Great Britain, inconsistent with the constitution and destructive of liberty." "An odious title," somebody called it.

But though he abjured the title of prime minister, Walpole persistently and shrewdly sought the power. Coming to office as man of the hour during the South Sea Bubble panic, he

For his attacks on George III, John Wilkes was illegally expelled from Parliament. Crying "Wilkes and Liberty," voters re-elected him four times. But the king's influence kept Wilkes from his seat.

George had trouble with his ministers, and odd coalitions resulted. This cartoon ridicules a coalition of Fox (*center*) and Burke (*right*), bitter opponents of the king, with Lord North, the king's man.

managed over the years to have his chief rivals dismissed one by one from their ministerial posts. As head of the Treasury, he controlled the largest share of patronage and he used this advantage unscrupulously to enforce coherence of party policy. His cabinet ministers had to be of one mind on major issues and, in theory at least, had to be of the same mind as a majority of the members of Parliament. Walpole himself carried the theory of ministerial responsibility to its logical conclusion by resigning in 1742 because he disagreed with Parliament on declaring war. It was an act which many Englishmen applauded as a matter of practice, since they were glad at last to be rid of Walpole, but deplored as a principle, since the ministers were supposed to serve at the king's pleasure, not Parliament's.

Until Walpole came to office, it had been the king's custom to give the principal ministries to peers or to elevate to the peerage any commoner who had been given high office. This left the burden of defending the government in the Commons to men of lesser ability or prestige. Walpole, in one of his most significant actions, chose to spend his twenty-one years in office in the Commons, which not only increased his own effectiveness but clinched the ascendancy of the Commons.

When he finally quit office and entered the House of Lords as earl of Orford, Walpole encountered his old political opponent, Pulteney, who had just been made earl of Bath. "You and I, my lord," quipped the new Lord Orford, "are now two as insignificant men as any in England." Pulteney himself had dubbed the upper chamber a "hospital of invalids" and its august deliberations ran to whether a sickly peer might usurp a seat near the fire. Until the middle of the nineteenth century the House of Lords continued to act as a check on the Commons but it tended more and more to lose its real power and to acquire special functions, such as adjudicating divorce suits or treason trials.

Under the party system, the prime minister replaced the monarch as the country's chief executive but he by no means rendered the king a cipher. Legally the king still possessed and, until custom congealed against him, still could freely exercise great power. George I could at any time have dismissed Walpole as his minister and it was widely though wrongly supposed that George II would. Very much later George III bounced an entire ministry. And George III's whole bid for power involved acting on the letter—which was not quite a dead letter—of the law.

IN a corrupt age George III controlled Parliament by controlling a sufficient number of easygoing M.P.'s. Barring a few lawyers and the like, the House of Commons consisted of the families and friends of the great landowners and East India nabobs. Most of the members were so highly—and closely—connected that they turned the House of Commons into a kind of club. They cracked jokes, they cracked nuts, they lolled, they dozed, they coughed down bores and bunglers, they gaily insulted and libeled one another. "If Lord Shelburne is not . . . a Borgia," they would rap out, "it must not be ascribed to anything but his understanding." For the most part, they were utter worldlings: even their oratory was largely a form of magnificent theater which with luck might fetch the country vote.

But the real weakness of the House of Commons was not that its members were drawn from the upper classes. It was that they were not elected by the people. Never was there

The corruption of the period's politics was satirized by William Hogarth in a series of engravings on an election. In *Canvassing for Votes*, the candidate's agent offers trinkets to women who can influence the men, and a voter is beset by emissaries of both parties.

The Polling shows the vote gotten out. At right, a man puts the stump of his hand on the Bible, causing officials to argue whether swearing with the left

such unproportional representation. A single great family might control a dozen seats while whole cities, such as Manchester, had none at all. Sixteen thousand voters in Yorkshire returned two members; so did one gentleman in Cornwall. What with pocket boroughs and rotten boroughs, the landowners and the nabobs—and the crown itself—amassed huge voting strength. Furthermore, there were actually seats for sale, seats that took advertisements luring buyers with the incentive of "no tinkers' wives to kiss, no impossible promises to make . . . with this elegant contingency in his pocket, the honours of the State await his plucking." In most cases constituents were as few as they were docile. John Wilkes, who himself entered Parliament with a bought seat, once showed that the votes of 5,723 persons throughout the country could produce a majority in the Commons.

As seats could be bought, so could sitters. Even members who were not to be reached through bribes might be controlled through threats. Under George III, there were sinecures and perquisites to lose as well as gain. Constantly digging into his deep-lined purse, shamelessly drawing on his technical powers, George III "managed" Parliament with an adroitness that Walpole might have admired and a venality that even Walpole might have winced at. Nor were votes cast at the polls necessarily cleaner than votes cast in Parliament: for example, inviting a voter to "breakfast" became the merest synonym for offering him 24 pounds.

Yet usage and events implacably stripped kingship of just those legal powers that George as king misused. In the nineteenth century Queen Victoria might insist again and again that she would "never consent" to this or that hateful measure of Mr. Gladstone's; but she knew, quite as well as Gladstone, that she would have to. The American Revolution had put the monarch out of the firm, though the people were not yet in. Only after the 1770's could they even get in for a look—Lords and Commons used to lock their doors at will. Once some great ladies protested such a lock-out with fishwifish screaming and banging, then pretended by a half hour's complete silence to have gone away, only, when the doors were unlocked, to burst in and shriek worse than ever. Parliament even more strongly resented having its debates reported in the press; one lord expressed the utmost horror that members should be "held responsible without doors for anything they might say within."

EVENTUALLY, through a long process of evolution in which the Reform Bill of 1832 is the historic landmark, parliamentary government would come to mean popular government as well. Defeated in the Commons, an administration would be able to appeal directly to the people. Thus, governments would stand or fall, not through how many votes they mustered in Parliament but through how many seats they commanded at the polls. Out of this was to emerge an age of political democracy, of an ever widened electorate, of vigorous political reforms. Out of it would emerge a Parliament in which His Majesty's Loyal Opposition was an official part of the government, with its leader paid an official salary, its attacks on those in power an official part of the agenda. If the eighteenth century Parliament brought none of these things to pass, it made all of these things possible, before it merged—with almost too obligingly symbolic a gesture—into history. Just two years after the great Reform Bill became law, the Houses of Parliament, where Walpole and Chatham and Pitt had exercised their sway, burned to the ground.

hand is legal. An idiot (*center*) is conjoled by two sides. Behind is a dying voter, carried to the polls. At left, Britannia's coach breaks down from this rottenness.

Traditionally, successful candidates were carried in chairs through the streets. In *Chairing the Members*, a victor is jounced unheeded past indifferent servants, screaming pigs, a street fight, a monkey on a bear and a barrel of beer being brought out to the populace.

A Rogues' Gallery of Royalty

The parsimony of George III and Queen Charlotte is the butt of a cartoon by James Gillray. Among the scathing details: the meal is scant—eggs and greens; there are flowers but no coals in the grate.

The prince of Wales, later George IV, is shown returning from a night of gambling at Brooks's, falling-down drunk on the arms of two lackeys and wearing the hat of another member, Charles Fox.

The presentation of the German princess, Caroline, bride of the prince of Wales, causes unseemly avarice in Their Majesties, who have caught sight of the large dowry she carries in her apron.

"GEORGE," his mother taxed him, "be a king!" Alas for England, George III was every inch a king—and a yard more of the royal purple than his countrymen had bargained for. He was the last English king to dispute Parliament's power, the last to rule in fact as well as in name. The first decision of George's troubled reign was to edge the indispensable Pitt out of office in the midst of his vast and intricate wars with France; such purblind policies, generally pursued through the next twenty years, almost demolished the work of the previous three hundred.

George's subjects were appropriately grateful for these favors. In the privilege of pub and Parliament they reviled his public actions; in the safety of pseudonymity they ridiculed his private life. Cartoons and broadsides jeered at his pinchbeck penny-wisdom, sneered at his moral priggery, apostrophized the scarce beauties of his dear German wife or examined the scarce brains of his beloved children. These insults were added to a grave psychological debility in the man. At first his attacks seemed to take the form of mere melancholy. Later he began to suffer paroxysms of an almost demonic energy. He would leap into the saddle and literally ride a horse to death beneath him. He ran a footrace with a horse. He went into talking jags. Soon he began to have thrashing attacks of madness. The last nine years of his life were spent in lunacy, while a regency ruled in his stead. "After all," a great lady in London wrote when he died in 1820, "it only means that there is one less poor, mad king in the world."

At the height of his headstrong power George III posed with the royal family for a John Zoffany portrait. This was in 1771 when Queen Charlotte had borne six of her fifteen children. At this period the family was a happy one but after public and private misfortunes came they were described by one courtier as "the most unhappy family in the kingdom . . . the princesses so much so as to go into fits."

The glorious death of Wolfe in the full tide of victory on the Plains of Abraham stirred the British as few other events of their long war with France. In this painting by the American, Benjamin West, Wolfe is shown dying in his officers' arms, while the battle rages.

In this contemporary drawing of Plassey field, the British forces stand at left before a wood. Their cannon fire into the face of the famous elephant charge. The elephants retreat in terror, making havoc in the masses of the enemy, who are about to cut and run.

The Lion and the Lily Fight for a World Empire

ONE day in March, 1738, the respected members of the British House of Commons gravely inspected a pickled human ear. Whereupon, in an indignant vote of acclamation, they declared war upon Spain. This petty "War of Jenkins' Ear," provoked by a Spanish coast guard who incontinently disfigured the captain of a British blockade-runner, was the last snort of the British lion for its old, outfought colonial competitor. A new and greater rival had appeared. Imperial France had raised her lily banner of conquest from Bengal to the Canadas and dared the British Empire to a fight for life. The dare was taken. In the skirmishes of a hundred years and a total war of seven, Britain gained an undisputed empire of land and sea grander than any since Rome's.

The crucial campaigns were fought not in Europe but in the outlands of Asia and America. In India one Robert Clive, a humble clerk in the colonial service, took command of the scantling British forces and wielded them with such resource that the French went staggering from defeat to defeat. In 1757 at Plassey, in one of the decisive battles of world history, Clive routed a native army of fifty thousand men with a posse of thirty-two hundred men. The French had lost, and the British gained, the richest fief of their empire.

In the New World the French forged a chain of forts around the British colonies along the Atlantic seaboard. From Massachusetts to Pennsylvania the Seven Years' War fumed and flared on furious peripheries, until William Pitt sent General James Wolfe with nine thousand men to take Quebec, the chief stronghold of New France.

For two months Wolfe laid siege to the fortified heights; when a discouraged subordinate warned him that the task was impossible, Wolfe delivered his famous dictum: "Impossible is a word found only in the dictionary of fools." At last, by a night ruse, he landed his main forces at the rear of the French. The French commander, the Marquis de Montcalm, launched a hasty counterattack. In a fierce engagement on the Plains of Abraham the French defenses were cracked, and the British broke through to stop the heart of French colonial power in the New World. Montcalm and Wolfe were both killed in the action. The death of Wolfe in the midst of his historic victory is depicted in the painting at left.

At the end of the Seven Years' War France had lost Canada and India; the seas were swept of her men-of-war and merchantmen. The magnificent indolence of Versailles had cost her a world empire, which passed now into the more businesslike hands of the British.

Chatham's Collapse

The greatest war minister in British history, William Pitt, the elder, first earl of Chatham, took direction of the Seven Years' War and brought Britain from disaster to victory. Ravaged by gout and neurotic delusions, Pitt nevertheless ruled himself and the Empire with unshakable will. He had "eyes that could cut a diamond" and the most deadly tongue that ever spoke in Parliament. And it spoke to the dramatic end—when, as this painting depicts, he collapsed at 69 in the midst of a passionate oration on the American question.

THE AGE OF REVOLUTIONS

This engraving shows the Place de la Révolution, Paris, on January 21, 1793. Drums roll ominously and thousands of Parisians watch. "Silence!" cries Louis XVI from the scaffold. The drums are still. "Frenchmen, I die innocent . . ." he begins. But a general shouts: "Drums!" They start again and the king is unheard. "Executioners, do your duty," says the general and Louis Capet, resisting, is tied to the plank. The guillotine's blade falls. The executioner holds up the severed head and the shout goes up: "Vive la République!"

IX

THE AGE OF REVOLUTIONS

On December 1, 1789, the National Assembly of France, busy with the reforms of the French Revolution, listened to an affecting speech by a kindly physician of fifty-one. He had long been offended by the cruelties and the inequities of the old penal code, which not only hung men by the neck, burned them at the stake, broke them on the wheel and inflicted penalties on their innocent families, but which also reserved to the nobility the privilege of a brisk death by beheading. The doctor was not especially eloquent, but his argument appealed to advocates of Liberty, Equality and Fraternity, and the Assembly unanimously voted his bill to make all penalties equal, "whatever the rank and state of the guilty person," and in the case of capital punishment to use a simple and humane machine of the doctor's own invention.

Dr. Joseph-Ignace Guillotin's machine was a device which cradled the bound, recumbent body of the condemned so that his neck was twelve feet below a suspended blade. When this blade descended, it sliced the victim's head into a basket. A humanitarian, the doctor was mortified when his contemporaries christened his machine *la guillotine.* A political moderate, he was horrified by the extravagant use to which it was put a few years later during the Terror. He was, in fact, arrested as a counter-revolutionary and almost suffered the final irony of being executed by his own device. But he survived to die peacefully under Napoleon.

Both in its kindly origin and in its dreadful triumph, the guillotine stands as a fit symbol of the Revolution. It was the product of an enlightened eighteenth century mind, anxious that even the criminal should be spared unnecessary pain. It was a machine and therefore, in that early dawn of the Industrial Revolution, a source of excitement and pride. And in the good doctor's intention it was a part of a wider scheme to abolish privilege and achieve equality—even in death.

The revolutionary Assembly which lent its sympathetic ear to Dr. Guillotin was one of the most remarkable legislative bodies in history. To begin with, it was the creature of the old regime, called into being by Louis XVI to help finance his extravagant court and unwieldy government. But at once it declared its independence of the king and seven months later, when it adopted the guillotine, it had already brought to tumultuous birth a social order which bore the marks of a modern democracy.

France was ripe for revolution. A moribund feudal system imposed class distinctions and money dues which bore very little relation to the actual structure of society. A top-heavy administrative system had piled agency upon agency through the centuries. An outworn economic system cramped the rising class of businessmen while the old hulk of feudalism allowed galling exemptions for the nobility and the clergy.

France under Louis XVI was scarcely a tyranny. The king was a rather agreeable fat man, fond of hunting and puzzled by politics. A better—or a worse—monarch, willing to use ruthlessly a mercenary army still in large part obedient to his command, might have stifled the Revolution at its start. But

Nine months after Louis' death, Marie Antoinette, who was called "the widow Capet" by the Tribunal, took the same fatal ride and was sketched by the artist David as she rode in the tumbril. Having failed in plots to overthrow the Revolution, she died bravely.

On July 14, 1789, a mob stormed the Bastille, overwhelmed a force of 130—mostly retired soldiers—and murdered the prison commandant. A few hundred attackers were killed and seven prisoners freed.

Mobs demanded to be heard, and not even the people's deputies were safe. One bitter day a group of the poor and the

Louis was well-intentioned and helpless. His queen, Marie Antoinette, was an Austrian, ignorant of French opinion, self-willed, firm at just the wrong times. The famous tale that, when told the people had no bread, she replied, "Let them eat cake," is almost certainly an invention. But it is one of those inventions that is a kind of truth, for that is what her people thought she would say.

The expense of the court at Versailles was a major drain on the state treasury. This, combined with a wheat crop failure and a series of wars, brought the French government, in 1789, to bankruptcy. Louis' ministers advised him that the only way to raise money was to summon the States-General, the ancient feudal assembly of France. This body had not met for a hundred and seventy-five years but Louis was now desperate enough to convoke it. The States-General gathered at Versailles in May, 1789.

By feudal custom this body was composed of three houses—nobles, clergy and commons—which had always met separately. Louis had been induced, in recognition of the rising middle class, to double the size of the Third Estate (commons), making it the equal of the other two estates combined. The first act of the Third Estate was to demand that the other two houses join it in a single National Assembly, which the Third Estate, supported by certain liberal nobles and clergy, would be able to dominate. The king refused, then yielded. Feeling its strength, the new Assembly vowed it would not disband until it had written a constitution for France.

The delegates did their work in the midst of amazing disorder. They legislated in open session, in a crowded hall, before galleries that applauded and hissed as if at a play. The widely assorted members included many remarkable men: Mirabeau, scapegrace nobleman and great orator, a practical politician caught up in a situation where politics were wildly impractical; Lafayette, the hero of two worlds, the splendid figure of an idealistic noble but no man for parliamentary give-and-take; Danton, Marat and Robespierre, the leaders of the radical faction, who gradually moved into control of the Assembly; and a great number of assorted nobles, priests, lawyers, teachers and actors. There were constant interruptions by deputations of admirers, critics and special pleaders for everything from county seats to universal peace. At one point a former baron named Anarcharsis Cloots, self-styled "ambassador of the human race," led before the Assembly a grateful delegation of "representatives of all mankind," including some authentic specimens but also "Australian aborigines" and "American Indians" who had had recourse to the facilities of the Parisian theatrical costumers.

THE radical leaders among the delegates knew what they wanted and they were well organized to get it. For a generation, educated Frenchmen, mostly of the middle class, had been reading and talking about the ideas of the Enlightenment. Hundreds of pamphleteers and journalists had echoed, amplified and transmitted to the many the notion of the rights of man and a possible heaven on earth. In a great variety of voluntary groups, the *sociétés de pensée* (societies for thought), salons, literary clubs, Masonic and other fraternal lodges, even in *tabagies* (smoking clubs), Frenchmen had been talking about ways of reforming society. The delegates who came from this heady background were prepared to transform their ideas into the reality of government.

The Assembly moved swiftly toward its goal of making

hungry charged in among the legislators, cut off one man's head, mounted it on a pike (*center*) and cried for bread.

Riding to his death, Berthier de Sauvigny, commissioner of Paris, is confronted by a dreadful sight as he stands in the tumbril: the head of his father-in-law, freshly severed and mounted on a pike.

Louis a constitutional monarch. But it did not move fast enough to suit the people of Paris. Rumors flew that the king was surrounding the city with troops to restore his authority. The republican fervor of Paris exploded with a wild ringing of church bells and the cry, "To the Bastille!" A mob converged on the hated fortress-prison where the great patriots of France were supposed to be languishing. On July 14, 1789—the date that France celebrates as we celebrate the Fourth of July—the jail was delivered.

The Bastille proved to contain seven prisoners—five ordinary criminals and two madmen. But at the time many felt that all the happiest portents of the Enlightenment were about to be fulfilled. The Revolution was under way in an atmosphere of hope almost impossible for us to imagine. News of the Bastille's fall was greeted with joy throughout the Western world. In monarchical Denmark, the writer Steffens later recalled how his father had come home one evening, gathered his sons about him and told them with tears of delight that the Bastille had been taken and that an era had begun in which "poverty would vanish, the lowliest would begin the struggle of life on equal terms with the mightiest, with equal arms, on equal ground." Years later the English poet Wordsworth, remembering his feelings of this exhilarating period, wrote:

> Bliss was it in that dawn to be alive,
> But to be young was very Heaven.

The countryside, too, was stirring. All through July, 1789, the peasants, moved by a rumor that "the brigands are coming," marched in wild hordes on the châteaux of the nobles, often sacked and burned them and almost always, with a sure instinct, destroyed the *terriers*, the documents that listed feudal dues and other obligations.

News of these disorders prompted the National Assembly to one of its most dramatic sessions. On the night of August 4, the Vicomte de Noailles, who had fought at Yorktown, urged the Assembly to pacify the people by giving them what they legitimately wanted—the abolition of the feudal system. In mounting excitement, deputy after deputy arose and renounced whatever "privileges" he might have. With tears of joy the Assembly ushered in the new world.

During the months that followed, the Assembly went ahead with its constitutional work. It framed a Declaration of the Rights of Man, seized all the property of the Church and put priests on the public payroll, opened the officer corps of the army to all ranks, reformed the penal code and education, and divided France into eighty-three administrative departments, relegating the medieval place names like Burgundy and Champagne to wine lists. France remained a monarchy, with a crown on the British model, decorative and symbolic of national unity, but with the real power in an elected legislature.

WITH this gradual evolution toward democracy neither the king nor the Paris mob was satisfied, and they made their displeasure felt in a series of great *journées*. There was the day when a great crowd of women from the Paris slums swarmed down the road to Versailles, crying "Bread!" then invaded the palace, and brought the intimidated royal family back to Paris, shouting, "We bring you the baker, the baker's wife and the baker's little boy." There was the king's craven attempt to flee France, only to be caught near the border and

On the Champs de Mars in Paris a revolutionary crowd burns cardboard coats-of-arms and emblems of the aristocracy. This city fire was a destruction of symbols. In the country the peasants did a more practical job of destruction, burning papers linking them to bondage, indebtedness and tax obligations.

brought back again, to the scorn of Paris. Finally, there was the mob's attack on the Tuileries palace and the king's escape to the refuge of the Assembly building. By then France was at war with Austria and Prussia, whose rulers had declared their intention of restoring the "legitimate" government of the French king, perhaps after taking a bit of France for themselves. If the plan for a constitutional monarchy ever had a chance of success, the implicit alliance between Louis and France's foreign foes killed it. The Assembly declared France a republic and presently sent Louis XVI to the guillotine.

MUCH to the surprise of its enemies, revolutionary France did not prove easy game on the battlefields of Europe. After initial defeats the French rallied and revealed to the world a new kind of war. The old wars had been fought by professional armies, with the caution of professionals. Now for the first time on a large scale in the modern world we see a citizen-army, fighting with patriotic zeal for the fatherland. In 1793 the convention passed the famous decree of the *levée en masse* which foreshadowed the war policy of the modern world:

> Young men will go to the front; married men will forge arms and transport foodstuff; women will make tents, clothes, will serve in the hospitals; children will tear rags into lint; old men will be carried to public places, there to stir up the courage of the warriors, hatred of kings, and unity in the Republic.

Meanwhile, war had done for the new French Republic what it does for all states under arms. It brought tight controls, censorship, the revocation of civil liberties. Amid tempestuous scenes in the new legislative Assembly, power shifted from the moderate *Gironde*, across the Plain (the center) to the radical Mountain, so called because its members occupied the high tiers of seats at one end of the hall. Then, in the already heated atmosphere of national struggle, it was easy for the leaders of the Mountain to establish a virtual dictatorship. In the name of "public safety" they sent to the guillotine a steadily swelling stream of victims—at first actual royalists, then their own political enemies and, at last, one another.

Thus the war was at least partly responsible for the Terror. But only in part, for war has not always brought terror. The men who held power in France in 1793–94, and who drew their power from the radical Jacobin clubs (so called because the first one met in a Jacobin monastery), were not merely trying to defend France from her external foes. They were trying to remake France in accordance with their ideal of a new and better world. They were not socialists; they did not believe in collectivization. But they did want a land of rough economic equality, with moral checks on the large accumulation of wealth. They had been convinced by the Enlightenment that men are by nature not wicked but good, and they held this view with varying degrees of religious fervor.

This new belief in the possibility of universal happiness on earth did not arise out of mere abstract political thinking. It had one major taproot in the increasing power of men over their physical environment, already clear in the late eighteenth century. Historians have given to this great change the name Industrial Revolution, though it might better be called the scientific and technological revolution. Together science and technology made for the men of the French Revolution a world which they could easily believe they could mold to their heart's desire. Could they not see progress all about them? Already a man could ride in his coach along the new good roads at rates even faster than the couriers of old Rome. Already new scientific agriculture was increasing crop yields per acre, improving livestock and introducing new products. Already, after a fashion, man could fly. In 1786, the Frenchman, Pilâtre de Rosiers, met a very modern death trying to cross the English Channel by air, in the newly invented hot-air balloon.

But Frenchmen in 1789 could see about them not only examples of material progress. They could see signs of political and moral progress—across the Channel where there was already a constitutional monarchy, better yet across the Atlantic where a free republic was demonstrating that the old environment of monarchy and privileged orders could in fact be superseded. Franklin, in his home in suburban Passy, was, for Frenchmen, nature's own nobleman—benevolent, democratic, wise.

To Robespierre, St. Just and their followers, the way to earthly paradise seemed clear. If they could only weed out the wicked and establish a Republic of Virtue all would yet be well. The guillotine, the revolutionary police, the thousands of Jacobin clubs, the network of the new bureaucracy were all centered on the task of making Frenchmen behave as they ought to behave. The Jacobins were in a sense Puritans. Under their brief rule human failings, large and small alike, were brought under the heavy hand of the state. During the Terror in Paris, under District Attorney Chaumette occurred the only serious attempt probably ever made to banish gambling and prostitution from the City of Light. "A gambler, a drunkard, a bad father," said the Jacobin Philip to his fellow Jacobins at Nancy, "cannot possibly be a republican."

In a hundred ways the Republic of Virtue broke in upon the routine of humdrum living. Republican patriots, the so-called *sans culottes* (without breeches), scorned the silken knee pants associated with the aristocracy and affected the long trousers of workingmen. Women who found humble democratic attire none too flattering took to the graceful robes of republican Rome. Bastille stones were popular as paperweights. The very calendar was revised, with twelve new months poetically named for the weather—month of mists (*Brumaire*), of flowers (*Floréal*), of heat (*Thermidor*). The rage for appropriate nomenclature perhaps reached its peak when the queen bee (*reine abeille*) became in some vocabularies the laying bee (*abeille pondeuse*). As the Terror mounted, tiny guillotines were sold as souvenirs.

ROBESPIERRE, "the Incorruptible," became at the end the sole master of the Revolution. In his frenzy to wipe out the enemies of the Republic of Virtue he introduced a law under which, for seven weeks, he would be empowered to multiply by ten the number of daily executions. Suddenly all the members of the Assembly felt their own lives in danger. Overnight they turned against Robespierre and sent him beneath the blade of his favorite instrument of righteousness.

The Terror was ended. Men could not stand the penetration of politics into every waking hour. On the eighteenth Thermidor, only nine days after Robespierre's fall, a Paris police report noted: "Prostitutes are reappearing with their customary audacity."

These and later reactions cannot dim the mighty significance of the French Revolution for Western civilization. If it did not yield the earthly paradise toward which the

To promote her campaign for Roman dress, Mme. Tallien wore a toga which left one breast bare. A woman of remarkable beauty and force, Mme. Tallien was an aristocrat who so charmed the revolutionary official sent to execute her that he married her instead.

With revolutionary fervor a new calendar was drawn up giving "natural" names to the months. Calendar artists found appropriate beauties for such new months as that of budding (*left*) and reaping (*right*). This calendar was in use for a mere twelve years.

The Revolution was immensely proud of its constitution. In this allegory Mirabeau, in the Elysian fields, hands a copy to Rousseau while Franklin puts a wreath on his head. Behind Rousseau are Montesquieu and Voltaire; at right are Demosthenes and Cicero.

Jacobins yearned, it did wipe out what was left of feudalism and opened the way to the ascendancy of those bourgeois interests that were to dominate the nineteenth century.

ALSO paving the way into the nineteenth century and the rise of the middle class was that other revolution—the Industrial Revolution—which had played its inspirational part in the French political convulsion. This revolution was born not in France but in England. It grew out of coal and iron and the use of steam. It was a product of capitalism and the handiwork of the so-called "commercial class." The factory with its machines revolutionized the whole economic and social structure of Western society no less thoroughly than the American and French revolutions changed the whole political structure. Its sponsors were confident that it, too, would result in a heaven on earth.

The great book of the Industrial Revolution, which embodied the best economic ideas of the time, was Adam Smith's *Wealth of Nations*, first published in the revolutionary year 1776. Smith, whose work antedates the real growth of power-driven machines and factories, saw that there was much more than machine technology in the Industrial Revolution. Smith's own illustration of the wonders of modern industry seems modest now—it is pin-making. He points out that if one man tried to do all the work of making a pin, from drawing out the wire and straightening it to finishing it, he could hardly make more than a pin a day. With one man doing but one thing—division of labor—one man's share would amount to thousands of pins. But he cannot eat pins. Division of labor implies a medium of exchange, transportation, a wide market, credit, middlemen—in short, a modern economy.

Yet machines and factories were the starting point of this revolution. They added greatly to output. More people had more things than ever before. Life took on an air of comfort and convenience undreamed of a century before. Railroads replaced stagecoaches, steamships replaced sailing vessels. New systems of distribution of manufactured goods were developed. More and better food was available at cheaper prices. Wealth increased and populations doubled or tripled. The whole business of business became a major preoccupation of Western man.

But there was a dark and ugly side to the Industrial Revolution which dimmed the glitter of its success and led on to counter-revolutions. The lot of the factory worker seemed to grow worse and worse as the production statistics grew better and better. He was herded into vile tenements stained black with coal smoke. His children worked beside him at the ill-lit machines for twelve and fourteen hours a day, six days a week. His whole life was degraded morally and spiritually and as his numbers and his woeful condition increased, he became the object of still another revolutionary reform.

The spectacle of the toiling masses under industrial capitalism sparked in the brain of a disgruntled German refugee in England a new design for heaven on earth. His name was Karl Marx and his formula was Marxist communism. His diagnosis of the social problem of the Industrial Revolution in its early stages focused on the factory worker, the lowly wage earner, the slave of the machine who owned nothing but his capacity for seemingly endless labor.

Robespierre, who led the Terror that killed some five thousand victims, himself rode to the guillotine in a wave of reaction. David's sketch shows Robespierre's bound jaw, fractured as he was seized.

Marx maintained that between this proletariat and their masters, the middle-class capitalists, there must inevitably be a pitiless class struggle. Successive booms and depressions he explained as the inevitable result of the fact that the industrialist does not allow the proletariat enough of its own total product, thereby accumulating more than can be sold and driving weaker capitalists into failure—and into the proletariat. The rich become richer and fewer, the poor poorer and more numerous. Eventually he predicted an uprising of the workers and a "dictatorship of the proletariat." Thereafter there would be no classes and hence no class struggle. The dictatorship would be followed by a "withering away of the state" and the "classless society"—in short, by heaven on earth.

MARXISM played its small and unsuccessful part in the European revolutions of 1848 but it remained for Lenin to put its principles into practice in Russia with the revolution of 1917. There the experiment of communism is still being worked out under circumstances which by no means suggest a utopia to Western man.

Perhaps it is mankind's destiny to advance from stage to stage of civilization in the everlasting hope that an earthly paradise is close at hand, just around the corner. In France the Enlightenment operated on the theory that the peaceful emancipation of human reason and goodness would result in the perfection of mankind. But the Enlightenment led to the Revolution and the Revolution led to the Terror. In Russia the ideals of Marx led to a revolution and that revolution to an even greater and more prolonged terror. We are reminded of Robespierre by Lenin's and Stalin's conviction that the ideal can be achieved rapidly by means of a dictatorship with extreme homicidal privileges. Looking back at the French Revolution through the bloody corridors of the Russian Revolution, the idea is bound to occur that the guillotine, symbol or instrument, may be an impossible accompaniment to Liberty, Equality, Fraternity—the Rights of Man.

Long days of hiding out from authorities in the Paris sewers afflicted Jean Paul Marat, bitter and uncompromising leader of the Revolution, with an irritating skin disease. In Paris, he often conducted his business while soaking in a covered bathtub. There Charlotte Corday, an idealistic and muddled girl, gained access to him by ruse and stabbed him to death, as recorded in David's *Death of Marat.*

In a famous Goya painting, *Executions After the Second of May*, Napoleon's troops massacre Spanish patriots after an uprising. So great was Spain's resistance that a quarter million troops could not subdue her in five savage years of sieges, torture and starvation.

The Spreading Revolution

THE spirit of democracy let loose by the French Revolution went on exploding, like a string of firecrackers, across the face of Europe for half a century. Though the Revolution was usurped by Napoleon and Napoleon in turn was brought down by the forces of the old order, the great upheaval had done its irreversible work. Feudal privilege and autocratic rule were dead in France; they would not survive the coming century anywhere west of the czars' Russia.

Yet in being exported, the Revolution underwent a change. The men who made the Revolution had conceived their ideals as universal principles, meant to break the chains of men everywhere. But when Napoleon used them as slogans to conquer Europe, he actually carried with him little equality, less fraternity and no liberty. The peoples of Europe embraced the democratic ideals the conqueror preached but they embraced also the conqueror's own principle of action—the idea of nationalism. The revolutionaries of the nineteenth century, like Mazzini and Kossuth, were patriots in whom the ideas of liberty and nationalism were fused as one.

Napoleon first met the spirit of nationalism in Spain where, with much show of "liberation," he had dethroned the Bourbon, Ferdinand, and installed his brother, Joseph, as king. The Spaniards rose in revolt and, with Britain's help, forced Napoleon into the long and costly Peninsula campaign.

Throughout Europe the slogans and success of the French Revolution encouraged people to rise against tyranny, foreign or domestic. In the ferment of the nineteenth century nationalists used freedom as a watchword in Greece against the Turks, in Hungary against Austria, in Italy to found a republic. In France itself revolt flared twice more, in 1830 and 1848, to wipe out remnants of the old order.

In *Liberty Leading the People*, Eugène Delacroix glorified the fierce spirit of revolt which swept through Europe after the French Revolution. He shows the French uprising of 1830 which replaced King Charles X with the moderate "citizen king," Louis Philippe. This was largely a revolt of the middle classes and men fought behind the barricades for three days and three nights with unaccustomed arms and still wearing their bourgeois top hats. Eighteen years later Louis Philippe was dethroned, this time with the help of the working class.

The biggest railroad at the start of the industrial age was the Liverpool and Manchester line which opened its 35 miles of double track in 1830 and soon set a record of 28 miles an hour. Here, drawn by a Stevenson locomotive, a train crosses a four-mile-wide peat bog.

A cross section of a powerful 1848 locomotive showed Englishmen how it worked. Pipes, carrying hot gases from the firebox to the smokestack, ran through water in the engine's big boiler. Heated to steam, the water drove the pistons, which turned the driving wheels.

A famous Continental factory was the Schneider ironworks at Le Creusot, France, painted around 1848. From this plant grew the great Schneider munitions company. Many people of the time were depressed to see how such factories were blemishing the landscape.

London in 1808 had a short, circular, novelty railway. Above, a ticket.

James Hargreaves' spinning jenny (1765) revolutionized textile production by spinning cotton or wool from many spindles at once.

The Industrial Revolution: The Machines Take Over

IN the last half of the eighteenth century and the first years of the nineteenth, a vast tinkering and turmoil seized the north of England. A poor weaver and carpenter named Hargreaves began fiddling with the old-fashioned spinning wheel; a barber and wigmaker named Arkwright began erecting spinning mills; a small, Scottish instrument maker named Watt began studying the pressure of steam in cylinders; and a workman and engineer named Stephenson began putting Watt's steam contraption on wheels.

There were a number of reasons why England should have been the scene of this industriousness. The country had an accumulation of booty and overseas possessions from the previous century's wars. London had risen as the world center of capital and exchange. Coal and iron were being more efficiently mined. An increase in population and the displacement of farm labor by a change in agricultural methods had made available a supply of factory labor. All these and other factors combined to make Britain ready for an expansion of trade and manufacture. The sum of the ferment was the Industrial Revolution.

The three great inventions of this period, shown at the right, were the spinning jenny, steam engine and steam railroad. The most crucial of these was James Watt's steam engine, which provided the power to move the new age. To sell his engine to skeptical farmers turned industrialists, Watt coined the term "horsepower" to measure the amount of work his engine could do.

Unlike other changes in man's mode of life, this one was so rapid and radical as to earn the title of revolution. But, unlike political revolutions, such as the cataclysm in France, which blaze up and then die away, the Industrial Revolution has gone on expanding from Watt's day to our own. Within a generation after 1815, most Englishmen were living in rising industrial towns. And productivity, which had risen slowly since the prehistoric organization of agriculture, began a spectacular climb. In less than twenty years England's iron and steel production jumped from seventy thousand to two hundred and fifty thousand tons a year. By 1830 all the main types of machine tools, capable of building other machines, were evolved. These machines and the products they turned out in ever mounting volume were shortly to overturn the world's economy.

James Watt's single-acting steam engine (1765), as sketched by himself, was the most important single agent of the revolution.

George Stephenson's "Rocket" (1829) opened the railway era by winning a contest to power the Liverpool and Manchester Railroad.

The type of factory landscape that began to appear with Britain's early industrial boom is shown in this 1832 view of the gala opening of the Glasgow & Garnkirk Railway. Early factories were set up near water for power. With steam, they clustered around the coal districts.

Richard Arkwright (1732–1792), who founded the factory system, was England's first textile magnate and prototype of the modern industrialist. He utilized water power and organized inventions, men and machines to run the first spinning mills. The peak of early mill development came when the mule (*right*) combined spinning jenny with winding frame to make fine English muslin.

With a flourish, the 1,440-ton *Great Western* departed from Bristol for New York in 1838 to inaugurate the first regular transatlantic service by a big steamship. She made the crossing in a fortnight, about half the time of sailing vessels, and her voyage foretold the end of sail.

William Crawshay (1788–1867), grandson of "Iron King" Richard Crawshay, was the most important of the Welsh coal and ironmasters. He inherited and greatly extended the Cyfarthfa Works. In 1825, at a cost of 30,000 pounds, he erected Cyfarthfa Castle (*left*), epitome of the "Great House on the Hill" from which the century's industrial masters watched their smoking works.

Bleak House of Industrialism

SMOKE lowering down from chimneypots," wrote Charles Dickens in *Bleak House*, "making a soft black drizzle, with flakes of soot in it as big as full-grown snow flakes—gone into mourning, one might imagine, for the death of the sun."

For many, the Industrial Revolution *was* the death of the sun. Agricultural workers, squeezed out of work and commons land by new enclosure acts, flocked into the growing industrial towns. Birmingham, Sheffield, Liverpool, Leeds, Manchester, Glasgow doubled and more than doubled their populations in the first quarter of the nineteenth century. Fearful overcrowding and the lack of even the most rudimentary building codes or sanitation systems bred disease, vice and one of the highest stenches in all history.

Working conditions were no better, as the lurid examples on the opposite page show. To a long list of ancient agues was added the new "factory fever," caused by long hours in the damp, sunless, ill-ventilated air of the new establishments. "Talk of serfs!" cried William Cobbett, first of the century's great reformers, ". . . did feudal times ever see any of them so debased, so absolutely slaves, as the poor creatures who, in the 'enlightened' north, are compelled to work fourteen hours a day, in a heat of eighty-four degrees, and who are liable to punishment for looking out at a window of the factory!" Such conditions bred their own antibodies, as witness the protesting voices of Cobbett, Dickens, a host of others. By the middle of the century, reform was moving to correct the evils.

The Stygian slums of industrial London are shown in Gustave Doré's engraving (*left*). London saw gigantic growth in the Industrial Revolution, rising from nine hundred thousand in 1800 to over two million by 1850.

In protest against working conditions, laborers vented their discontent on the machines. Bands of textile workers, led by a legendary figure called King Ludd (*above*), smashed knitting frames in 1811 and 1812. Hargreaves' home was broken into and his spinning jenny smashed, and one of Arkwright's factories was burned down.

Children being lowered to work in a mine shaft was one of the harrowing scenes illustrated in a reform tract, *The White Slaves of England*. Child labor in the home had been an evil part of the previous age, but the Industrial Revolution made it visible. In 1847, Parliament passed a law limiting children's work to ten hours a day.

Not only children worked in the mines but women, often stripped to the waist, drawing coal carts through narrow tunnels like beasts of burden, as shown in another reform tract. "It is worse when you are in a family way," said one miner. The outcry rose so high that Parliament passed drastic laws removing all women from the mines and prohibiting boys from going underground before the age of 10. The Factory Act of 1833 had thrown forty thousand children out of work, providing state education for them until the age of 9.

A nineteenth century rolling mill in Liverpool, making heavy armor plate for Great Britain's invincible navy, was photographed by the new daguerreotype process, which was another wonder of the age.

Isambard Kingdom Brunel, great engineer and builder of railroads, bridges and ships, stands for a picture before the anchor chains of the 18,914-ton *Great Eastern*, the biggest steamship of its time.

The Mid-Victorian Pinnacle

BY the middle of the nineteenth century, Britain's Industrial Revolution had brought her to a pinnacle of world power. She led the world in foreign trade, in miles of railroad, in coal, iron and steel production, in textiles, in shipping and in much else. Even under harsh conditions of early industrialism, population was growing at an unprecedented rate and life was steadily ameliorating.

The British workingman was better off than almost any of his European rivals. Machine production of cheap shoes was making him well-shod for the first time. Cheap textiles were clothing him better than ever before. Agricultural improvements and rising industrial wages were filling his larder higher than any comparable worker's on the Continent. Discoveries in medicine were beginning to lengthen his life span, and developments in city administration, schools and sanitation were making the industrial towns safer and more livable, a pattern for the world. An achievement of far-reaching importance for the continued growth of industrial centers, though unmentionable in polite Victorian society, was the development of modern plumbing and the water closet.

The Continent, watching the rising productivity and well-being of Britain, was not idle. Though starting late, France and Germany moved fast into industrialization. More efficient farming and the new means of transportation removed the threat of famine, still a dread part of life in the early nineteenth century, from most of Europe. In England, small family enterprises, expanding into stock companies, set the model for the great corporation. And in bringing for his own immense profit, the Industrial Revolution's fruits and methods into the lives of people in the far corners of the globe, Western man capped his insistent effort, begun by the first explorers and missionaries, to spread his ways over the whole wide world.

Raised upon a dais as upon the top of the world and surrounded by the banked faces of all the notables of Europe and the age, young Queen Victoria gave a royal blessing to the great Crystal Palace exposition in London. Under the enormous glass enclosure, built in 1851, were displayed the mechanical wonders and industrial arts by which the mighty British Empire had come to rule the century.

The Century's Four Prime Movers

Napoleon Bonaparte

"HE who influences princes is only an intriguer . . . he who moves the masses, changes the face of the earth." Napoleon Bonaparte, the man who found this key to power in the modern world, was one of the nineteenth century's prime movers. An unkempt little Corsican officer with hungry eyes and a dazzling mind, he rose from rags to the purple like some unholy Horatio Alger, knocked dynasties about like ninepins and conquered Europe twice over.

Napoleon picked the French Revolution out of a bloody Parisian gutter and extracted from it the one political idea that was strong enough to stand up against the old values which the Revolution had attempted to destroy. That idea was nationalism. Through it, Napoleon gave the common people a pride and part in their country that they had never had before. Nationalism offered the glory which France, and most of Europe, came to accept more and more in place of religious faith and individual liberty. And it was the spread of a fierce nationalism which helped defeat Napoleon's dream of a European order. Napoleon used the concept of the "nation in arms"—the modern conscript army necessary to total war—which destroyed the old idea of the small, professional, mercenary fighting force and gave the common soldier a chance to rise through the ranks.

Napoleon, a child of the age of reason, treated God as if He were one of his marshals, and regarded man merely as the last (and not very admirable) specimen in a vast evolutionary experiment. Like Julius Caesar, he considered freedom beside the point ("I do not hate freedom, though I gave it a wide berth when I met it on my way") because he felt supremely sure that he could create the people's happiness by edict. He gave most of Europe institutions founded on Roman law which, despite some great merit, were predicated on authoritarian rule and did much to keep the European mind from understanding that delicate balance of liberty and order on which Anglo-Saxon democracy rests. Significantly, the one force Napoleon always misunderstood and underestimated was Great Britain, which in the end beat him.

Karl Marx

LIKE Napoleon, Karl Marx sought to change the face of the earth by moving the masses. In the long run, he was far more successful, although his own time knew him mostly as a crank with a bad case of boils. A German lawyer's son who went to London as a political refugee in 1849, he lived with his beautiful, aristocratic wife in a squalid Soho flat, spending most of his time compiling economic data to bolster his apocalyptic prophesies.

Marx's day was the day of brassy faith in material progress, of science, of the machine which churned out undreamed-of wealth while the men who worked the machines lived for the most part in misery. Marx thundered: "The bourgeoisie . . . has left no other bond between man and man than naked self-interest. . . . All that is solid melts into air, all that is holy is profaned, and man is at last compelled to face with sober senses his real condition of life. . . ." But as a cure for materialist ills, Marx prescribed a far more terrible materialism. Marx's theory rests on four essential points: 1) man's ideals, religions, politics are only the result of material forces, i.e., his tools and machines; 2) all history is dominated by a struggle between various social classes for control of the "means of production"; 3) the capitalistic class lives by exploiting the working classes whose misery will steadily increase as capitalist production increases, which will finally result in capitalism's fall; 4) the world proletariat must forswear allegiance to the national states, seize the machines and the government in violent revolution and build its own society governed by "the dictatorship of the proletariat."

Actually, Marx's points numbers 1 and 2 are a gross oversimplification and point number 3 has been largely disproved by events. But the appeal of point number 4 ("Workers have nothing to lose but their chains. They have a world to win.") became the ideological force with which Lenin, Stalin & Co. built up history's most pitiless tyranny. Marx realized the potential power of the industrial proletariat, literally a new race of men. He offered them a faith (the world's first materialist religion), a goal, and a promise—terribly false though it was—of justice.

Queen Victoria

THE Victorian era (1837–1901) is one of history's great illusions. Victoria is usually regarded as a symbol of stability, peace and firm values. She created this impression because personally she was unshakable. But actually, few periods saw more profound changes than Victoria's sixty-four-year reign. In that time, Great Britain changed from a country predominantly agricultural and aristocratic to an industrial, middle-class state whose gentle pastures were blackened with smoke and whose cities swelled with slums. Britain became the workshop of the world, as well as its banking house. It could build more ships and make more arms than all the rest of the world put together. The flag followed trade. But while the prim-mouthed "Widow at Windsor" ruled her enchanted castle, many strange cooks were at work in the disenchanted basement, brewing the ingredients of a chaotic new age. In her time the world underwent a moral devaluation which replaced the ideal of morality with the idea of propriety.

Victoria, the queen who never grew up, lived in continuous, girlish mourning for her beloved prince consort, Albert (he died in 1861). She relied heavily on her favorite statesman, Benjamin Disraeli, twice her prime minister, a curly-haired dandy who treated her in the manner of an infinitely respectful lover and built her a new empire. Victoria disliked the apologetic liberal foreign policies of William Gladstone for she felt that Britons never, never must be slaves—or losers. During the Crimean War she once wrote, "Oh, if the Queen were a man, she would like to go and give those Russians . . . such a beating!" She felt sincerely that as a price for power, Britain must carry the white man's burden. Victorian England, as the world's most powerful nation, exhibited a genuine sense of duty toward the rest of the world and certainly governed its subject peoples more responsibly than any other imperial master. But Victoria, a brave little crusader with knitting needles, could neither foresee nor stop the forces that, within a generation of her death, would assail her empire and begin inexorably to drain Britain's strength.

Charles Darwin

THE political and economic revolutions of the nineteenth century were matched by the revolution of science. The best-known scientific revolutionary was Charles Darwin. As a young divinity student, Darwin became passionately interested in nature and took a five-year cruise to the South Pacific as a naturalist on H.M.S. *Beagle.* There he collected thousands of plant and animal specimens and, starting from these, began his huge work of explaining the mysterious variations of life on earth. In 1859, he published his *On the Origin of Species by Means of Natural Selection*, to explain man's evolution from lower forms of life. His great contribution to the evolution theory (which in itself was not new) was an explanation of just how evolution works, i.e., through "natural selection." By this Darwin meant that some creatures began differing from each other in small respects, more or less accidentally, which in some cases proved advantageous in the struggle for existence (for instance, longer legs to escape a hunter, stronger eyes to find prey). The animals thus favored survived and reproduced themselves, eventually forming a new species.

Darwin's theory was a milestone in the scientific explanation of the material world. It was, more importantly, a blockbuster on organized religion. It contradicted the story of creation in *Genesis*—and if the Bible was wrong there, it could be wrong everywhere. A conflict raged for decades between science and religion; at Dayton, Tennessee, in 1925, the Scopes trial dramatized the conflict in the crude terms of whether man was descended from apes. The issue of the literal truth of the Bible was dwarfed by the larger fact that Darwinism seemed to contradict Christian morals. "The survival of the fittest," a phrase coined by Spencer, was used to justify war, imperialism, cut-throat competition. People who fell by the economic wayside were written off as "unfit" for survival. All this sapped the moral fiber of Western man by promoting the notion that men were governed by natural forces beyond their control and responsibility—something Darwin, the great scientist, never intended or expected.

To many Europeans, blown about their continent by the various gales of war and tyranny and economic mischance, America seemed to lie on the western waters like a great life raft. In the nineteenth century they struck out boldly across the Atlantic and clambered aboard the raft by the millions. The Irish and the Germans began to crowd in during the 1840's and 1850's. This 1851 photograph shows a boatload of emigrants leaving the great port of Le Havre for the U.S. Late in the century, huge cargoes of humanity began to arrive from the south and east of Europe. Their numbers filled the growing cities and their breath blew hot the forge of industry.

THE AMERICAN IDEA

X

THE AMERICAN IDEA

IN the year 1607, Western man stepped once and for all onto a new stage of world history: North America. In that year the London Company established on the James River in Virginia a permanent colony of a hundred and five souls. So began the British dominion in the New World. The haughty Spanish in Florida, the ambitious Dutch along the Hudson, the hardy Swedes beside the Delaware, the daring French on the St. Lawrence came forward as challengers, but all were thrown back or assimilated. By 1700, the east coast of the continent was thick with English towns.

Half a century later these colonies were so well grown that they began to balk at the leading string still held by parent England. In 1775 was fired the shot heard round the world and a year later a rebellion became a revolution for independence. For six long years, from Bunker Hill to Yorktown, Englishmen fought Englishmen for the rights of Englishmen. In the end, the rights were won but the nationality was lost.

"What then," wondered a traveler from Europe, "is the American, this new man?" The "Americans" wondered too, but not for long. With quick decision they took up the name by which Europe knew them and began to give it a meaning. From this decision dates a new age in the history of Western man. Western civilization, bulging and thrusting into maturity like some prodigious protozoan, had at last reproduced itself. Henceforth the history of Western man would be a double tale—the European story of a great civilization struggling on the hook of nationalism; the American story of a vigorous, young society breaking a continent to its will.

In the late eighteenth century, while Frenchmen were bloodily demolishing the old order in Europe, the "new man" in the United States was peaceably establishing a new order there. The principles of the new order were bound into the American Constitution by a company of superb political workmen, the Founding Fathers. Fortunate in its principles, its laws and its environment, this new civilization gained rapidly by comparison with Europe—and often at the old continent's expense. In 1803, while Napoleon was building his European empire the hard way—by the sword, Jefferson was adding a third of a continent to the American nation the easy way; for $27,000,000 he bought the Louisiana territory from France. In the mid-century, while Karl Marx began to cry the doom of the middle class in Europe, the homestead acts were laying the basis of a vast new middle class of independent farmers in the U.S. And in 1865, as Bismarck raised the iron fist that would beat Europe almost to death during the next century, Abraham Lincoln laid a soothing hand upon the wounds of a democracy that had proven its principles in the test of battle.

ON the following pages, in pictures painted by the apprentice hand of the young nation's artists, may be seen some of the great forces that shaped the American branch of Western civilization. Beginning on page 283, the final article of this book discusses the meaning of the American experience.

George Washington was the greatest of a generation of great men. He personified the plain principle of common sense in which the disagreements of the Founding Fathers were reconciled. This portrait by Joseph Wright evinces the strength of a man on whom all sides could lean. Upon Washington's seeming permanence history formed as moss upon a moveless oak. The great men of his day sat sheltered in his shade. Without him they might never have come together; without them the nation might never have been made.

On the marl flats of Yorktown, Virginia, after hardly a battle, Lord Charles Cornwallis surrendered to Washington the last British army left on American soil. The Revolution was over. What Philadelphia had conceived, and war had long constrained in labor, Yorktown almost casually delivered. The defeated redcoats, here painted by Louis van Blarenberghe as they plodded in full panoply to their

internment, stated the tremendous fact in the song they marched to—*The World Turned Upside Down*. The trained armies of the first power of Europe had been whipped by a rabble in arms; the New World had made good its independence of the Old. For the first time in history a great people had determined to stake its destiny and to build its society upon a written guarantee of human rights.

The immense and hostile continent that waited, almost as if in ambush, for the young republic is well portrayed in this landscape painted in the Rockies by Alfred Miller. Never before had a continent been offered to a civilized people for the green experiment of their desires. Never had a people been faced with a challenge more awesome, nor met one more grandly. Within fifteen years of its

establishment, the republic dispatched Lewis and Clark to explore the wilderness across the Mississippi. Already the settlers were pouring west—through the Cumberland Gap into Kentucky; over the Alleghenies into Ohio; down the Ohio to the Mississippi; then westward in a mighty rush to the coast. Within fifty years the Americans had staked claim to the whole land of their inheritance.

Freedom was as much a condition of the early American environment as the air a man breathed. There were no customs to hinder, no institutions to oppress him except those he chose to bring from Europe or to create for himself. Under these conditions his government grew fairly naturally out of his beliefs—and so he enjoyed it. Election days in the new democracy were holidays, celebrations, feasts of freedom. George Caleb Bingham caught this spirit in his painting, *Verdict of the People*, now in The Boatmen's National Bank of St. Louis. The scene, a Missouri election in the 1850's, seems swept by a great clean wind of independence—a wind that blew the air of freedom around the world.

The immense vacuum of the New World sucked ideas from the Old with irrefutable power; and once inside the vacuum, the ideas expanded—with nothing to resist them and everything to invite—to monstrous proportions. The idea of the Industrial Revolution, brought in from England, underwent the most astonishing of these gigantifications. The first real U.S. factories were established by the 1840's. The Civil War laid down a broad basis of heavy industry—in mills like this blazing iron foundry painted by John Ferguson Weir. Thenceforward, the growth of American industry can be reckoned only by the statistics of explosion. In 1860, U.S. industrial production was about two-thirds of Britain's; by 1895 it was more than twice as great. The vacuum pulled again, and now millions of Europeans poured in to man the multiplying machinery of production. The new workmen so enlarged the market for commodities that the young industry only began to grow faster. In the twentieth century, with the assembly line, the Industrial Revolution itself moved on into the limitless vistas of American mass production.

On May 10, 1869, two halves of a continent were joined by a single rail. The tracks of the Central Pacific and the Union Pacific met at Promontory Point, Utah. In a simple rite, shown in this painting by Thomas Hill, the golden spike was driven by Leland Stanford, the Central Pacific's president (who stands at center with a sledge hammer). The East and the West were one America. The continent

was an organism, a colossal vertebrate hung upon a slender spine of steel. In less than fifty years every limb and quarter of the country would be connected by a skeleton of railroads, fed by a veinwork of highways, brought into a single intelligence and function by a system of telephone and telegraph. This was a new historic fact: now a land mass almost the size of Europe could perform as a unit.

Abraham Lincoln is the best-loved figure in American history. He has a double greatness. By his actions he preserved the nation and redeemed and broadened the promise of freedom. In his spirit he embraced the whole of the American idea, and in simple, inevitable phrases he bequeathed it to posterity: "I say in relation to the principle that all men are created equal, let it be as nearly reached as we can." And again: "As I would not be a slave, so I would not be a master. . . . Whatever differs from this . . . is no democracy."

The American Experience

WHEN Gibbon was finishing the third volume of his autopsy on the Roman Empire, he addressed himself to the inevitable question: is Western civilization vulnerable to the same forces of decay that destroyed Rome? Surveying the world of 1780, Gibbon thought not. Before concluding (with true eighteenth century optimism) that Europe's wealth, happiness, knowledge and perhaps even virtue would go on increasing forever, Gibbon candidly considered the worst that could happen. "If a savage conqueror should issue from the deserts of Tartary, he must repeatedly vanquish the robust peasants of Russia, the numerous armies of Germany, the gallant nobles of France, and the intrepid freemen of Britain; who, perhaps, might confederate for their common defence. Should the victorious Barbarians carry slavery and desolation as far as the Atlantic Ocean, ten thousand vessels would transport beyond their pursuit the remains of civilized society; and Europe would revive and flourish in the American world which is already filled with her colonies and institutions."

In 1949 another learned Englishman, Wyndham Lewis, returned to the same question. Were not Europe's two great twentieth century wars what Toynbee feared might be the deathblow of Western civilization? Undoubtedly, said Lewis, "Western man was past help, and now is dead." But this gave Lewis very little concern. European history had ceased to be interesting; what mattered now was not Western Man but universal man or, as Lewis called him, "cosmic man." And, luckily, the first prototypes of that unprecedented creature were already to be found in America, which Lewis discovered to be "an epitome of all societies . . . more universal than the Roman Empire . . .," destined to lead not just Europe but mankind into the first truly cosmic age of peace.

IN its beginning, so now: America all its life has been the place where Western Man, in confidence or despair, could still see salvation. It has been, next only to God, the final repository of his hope. "America, you have it better," sang Goethe. Hegel declared America to be "the land of the future where . . . the burden of the World's History shall reveal itself. . . ." The Frenchman Turgot called it "the hope of the world." The Englishman Richard Price called it "the fairest experiment ever tried in human affairs."

For their part, Americans felt the same way, only more so. The Founding Fathers all shared the joyous weight of what John Adams called "the best opportunity and the greatest trust . . . that Providence ever committed to so small a number since the transgression of the first pair." They were, they knew, the inheritors of all previous civilizations, yet also the founders of a wholly new one. They *felt* independent, not merely of George III, but of their European past. The Declaration of Independence was accordingly addressed, not to the king, but to "a candid world" and its "Supreme Judge."

All through the nineteenth century, new immigrants felt it too. Said one, Carl Schurz: "Mankind becomes young

The great dome of the Capitol, modeled on the majestic plan of St. Peter's Church in Rome and completed while the nation was still riven by civil war, rises three hundred feet above the city around it, in massive affirmation of the enduring strength of the Republic.

again . . . [in this] great colony of free humanity." Wrote another, dedicating his book, *Triumphant Democracy:*

> To the beloved Republic under whose equal laws I am made the peer of any man, although denied political equality by my native land, I dedicate this book with an intensity of gratitude and admiration which the native-born Citizen can neither feel nor understand. —ANDREW CARNEGIE

Thus America from its start was an intoxicating spiritual experience as well as a place to live. Even the immigrants who took a narrower view ("America is not a boarding house!" admonished Teddy Roosevelt) knew that they were at least improving their lot. Neither the wealth of America nor its exhilarating newness, however, explains very much. If we seek an answer to Wyndham Lewis's challenge or a real "meaning" in the American experience, we must follow three threads through it, three threads which intertwine with each other and with all that Americans have done, both at home and abroad. These three threads are (1) the *land* Americans have subdued and occupied, (2) the *ideas* Americans have lived by, and (3) the *habit* which has enabled them to remain comparative masters of that hardest of human accomplishments, self-government.

The Land

AMERICA was born with a noise at its back, the morning noises of three million square miles of virgin wilderness. These noises were at once sweet, howling, awesome and energizing. "A European, when he first arrives," wrote Jacques Crèvecoeur, the Hudson valley farmer, in the 1770's, "seems limited in his intentions as well as in his views, but he very suddenly alters his scale . . . he no sooner breathes our air than he forms new schemes and embarks in designs he never would have thought of in his own country. . . . The American is a new man, who acts upon new principles." Certainly the earth was new; and it stimulated at least two kinds of newness in man. It put him in a new frame of mind, and it put him in a new kind of society.

For the new frame of mind, he could partly thank the Protestant Reformation. That had given a new twist to the problem which had plagued Western Man since his beginning: the problem of good and evil. From the confines of long-fixed moral categories, the Reformation released Western Man into the custody of his own conscience. Calvinism had more impact on America than other creeds. Its central tenet—that man is spiritually helpless and his soul's fate predestined—relieved the believer's conscience of inner conflict, externalized his sense of evil and liberated him to war on his environment. There was plenty to do as the frontier was moved westward from the Atlantic seaboard. There were Indians to be driven back, fields to be plowed, trees to be turned into cradles, cabins, coffins. Behind the rowdy coastal settlements, beyond the rich plantations, the holy work of reclamation went on, stimulated by the endless challenge of the wilderness and by great bursts of Baptist and Methodist revivalism. The Calvinist mandate, handed down from Jonathan Edwards to the Beechers and the Carrie Nations, later turned the ax against evil's other outward and visible forms: slavery, poverty, the saloon. Our greatest novel, *Moby Dick*, identified evil with a whale to be killed. When the Spaniards left Mobile, the Americans had no sooner moved in than they stamped out yellow fever there. Says Luther Billis in *South Pacific*, "If there's one thing I like it's a project." The good fight was a physical effort, not a spiritual one. Americans in their time have killed, cheated and probably scalped more Indians than vice versa, but they have not (Jung to the contrary notwithstanding) had bad dreams about them. Such was the new frame of mind.

But the wilderness also put the American in a new kind of society. To some it seemed a sort of Eden, a place where the vices of civilization were shed away in the bosom of nature with Dryden's "noble savage." Indeed, Ben Franklin, after his first tour of Europe (where he had gone in the 1760's to lobby for a settlement in Ohio), concluded that "compared to these [European] people, every Indian is a gentleman." What interested Byron about Daniel Boone, that "active hermit" who opened up Kentucky and Missouri, was his presumed power of communion with nature. (But even to this day, it is not clear whether Daniel regarded himself as an advance agent of civilization or a refugee from it.) Many a white man found life with savages quite pleasant; the Lewis and Clark expedition had to shoot at least one would-be deserter to the Indians. The American's homesickness for a real Eden found its last serious spokesman in Thoreau, who wanted every man to be "like a wild antelope . . . part and parcel of Nature . . ." and claimed that "in Wildness is the preservation of the World." But this pantheistic mood conflicted with the Calvinist mandate of battle, a mandate fortified by Herman Melville's tremendous discovery (he had lived in a real Polynesian paradise) that nature itself contains a principle of evil. Behind its rainbow, he wrote, lurks a fearful whiteness, that "visible absence of color" which, like the Milky Way, "shadows forth the heartless voids and immensities of the universe, and thus stabs us from behind with the thought of annihilation"—white, the dreadful blankness of nature without mind, the "colorless, all-color of atheism from which we shrink."

SO the "new man" could not find Eden in the anarchic forest; but the land promised him a new society nevertheless. It promised him freedom through sweat and ownership. This was the most powerful promise of all.

"Here everyone may have land . . ." said Jefferson, who, when he was President, kept a set of garden tools near his executive desk. Not only need no one starve in America, but no freeman need depend much on another for his living. Some did for the sake of urban living, but "hirelings" were linked with "slaves" in "The Star-Spangled Banner," and there was always the alternative, open even to indentured servants, of walking west and planting a crop. The result was the overnight dissolution of the traditional European ties between master and servant, class and class. Although respectable Americans did not call themselves a "democracy" until the time of Jackson, they often boasted with Charles Pinckney that there was "more equality of rank and fortune in America than in any other country under the sun"—a condition which, Pinckney added, "is likely to continue as long as the unappropriated western lands remain unsettled."

Such self-feeding and self-driving citizens, neither rich nor poor, were clearly ideal material for self-government. "Such men," declared Jefferson, "may safely and advantageously reserve to themselves a wholesome control over their public affairs and a degree of freedom which in the hands of the *canaille* of the cities of Europe would be instantly perverted. . . ." To Jefferson, the ideal society was composed of the small, independent farmer owning his own acres ("I know of no condition happier than that of a Virginia farmer. . . ."). Hamilton and the Federalists tended to favor trade and manufacture, and after the Napoleonic Wars Jefferson conceded that these "handmaidens of agriculture" were essential to survival. But he did more than any other American both to propound the ideal of a yeoman's democracy and to make its realization possible, for he more than doubled the size of the new country by buying the Louisiana territory.

FOR a hundred years after Jefferson, the real history of the U.S. was the settlement of the land between the Appalachians and the Pacific Ocean. It was one of the greatest migrations in human history. It went in waves: the Kentucky fever, the Oregon and Texas fevers, the Gold Rush, the Kansas fever. Zebulon Pike announced in 1810 that a large part of America was hopeless desert; but by 1850 this, too, had yielded to Mormon resolution and irrigation and the longhorn steer. It all happened so fast that neither the Mexicans, who lost the empty half of their country to the infiltrators of "manifest destiny," nor the bison, which were reduced from an ocean to a curio in three human generations, quite knew what hit them. And where the settlers went, the "civilizers"—women, preachers, scribes, gamblers, speculators, tradesmen, schoolmarms and men of business—went too. The tempo was such that Kit Carson, in October, 1849, while trying to rescue a Mrs. White from some Apaches in the southwest, found near Mrs. White's still-warm corpse in the abandoned Indian camp a novel published that year in Boston called *Kit Carson, Prince of the Gold Hunters.* He was duly touched and embarrassed by the find.

Speed was accompanied by enormous waste—an American habit which dates at least from the Boston Tea Party. The land was disgracefully mined; as farmer George Washington explained to an English expert, Americans did not try to "make the most they can from the land, which is or has been cheap, but the most of the labour, which is dear. . . ." There was nothing unusual about the Ohio farmer who rebuffed a soil conservationist, "Young man, I wore out three farms before you was born." A Jeffersonian named George Henry Evans sold the idea of a nation of yeoman-farmers to Horace Greeley, who sold it to the nascent Republican Party, which passed the homestead acts ("vote yourself a farm"), which brought new waves of immigration, which raised land values in the Middle West, which enriched land speculators. Andrew Carnegie reckoned that after the Civil War more money was made by speculation in America than by production. Despite the speculators and the waste, the land stayed settled and produced so much wheat and corn that after 1875 it was the breadbasket for half of Europe. About 1910 the land-settling process was reversed, the farms sent people to the cities and U.S. farming began to become less wasteful of the land, though it still "makes the most of the labour" and is in fact the most mechanized agriculture in the world.

Jefferson once supposed it would take "many centuries" to settle the American land. He was wrong for a simple reason: he could not foresee railroads, which started hauling cars in South Carolina five years after his death. Within sixty years the entire country was crisscrossed by a hundred and fifty thousand miles of track. It was an achievement comparable to the settlement of the land, indispensable to it, and partly motivated by the same Calvinistic drive, as though distance and dispersal were evils to be conquered, too. There were other motives. When a gang led by Charles Crocker laid down ten miles of the Central Pacific in a single day (April 28, 1869), not only did they set a record never equaled before or since, but Crocker collected a $10,000 bet from General Casement of the Union Pacific, and Crocker's Chinese coolies could lord it over Casement's Irish who had been teasing them with dynamite. The Pony Express was a miracle of organization and would carry a half-ounce letter from "St. Jo" to the coast in an incredible ten days for $5; but seven years after Promontory Point, it was through. The quartermaster general of the U.S. Army discovered it was cheaper to ship soldiers by rail than march them; P. T. Barnum made the same discovery about the circus; for the same reason cowboys stopped driving steers over the old Chisholm trail. In the 1880's alone, the U.S. built sixty-five thousand miles of new railroad, a world's record still unsurpassed. On a Sunday in May during that decade (1886), after weeks of preparation, armies of men working from dawn to dark shifted every mile of railroad in the South from its five-foot gauge to the four-foot, eight-inch gauge of the northern roads (which had taken it from their British locomotives, which in turn had taken it from the roads built in England by Romans to the width of their chariot wheels). After that Sunday, Boston & Maine freight cars could be seen in New Orleans, and Louisville & Nashville cars in Seattle.

THE railroads could not have been built so fast without government help, mostly in the form of land grants. For such a policy there was ample precedent in American economic doctrine. Federal aid to industry was first proposed in Alexander Hamilton's classic *Report on the Manufactures,* which led to the protective tariff. It found a later spokesman on the Ohio frontier in Henry Clay. Clay's "American system" of internal improvements welcomed British capital but not British ideas of free trade. The railroads, however, created a domestic market so vast and various that it was really a substitute for Adam Smith's free trade world, within which Smith's magically effective formula found a new home. Where the tracks went, the smokestacks followed—moving toward new raw materials, creating new cities, moving again to be near new markets. It was Britain's Industrial Revolution all over again, but on a greater scale. Even Bessemer's invention, the blast furnace, had been accidentally anticipated by a Kentucky ironmonger named Kelly. By 1900 the superiority of many American and German manufactures forced the British to recognize a "crisis" in their own industrial supremacy. By World War I, the U.S. was indisputably the greatest industrial power, and since World War II, with six per cent of the world's population, the U.S. has been turning out half the world's manufactures.

And what, in all this time, was happening to Pinckney's "equality of fortune" and Jefferson's ideal of a yeoman's democracy? They both took a beating, especially during the "gilded age" after the Civil War. It was the era of "social Darwinism," a pseudo philosophy which permeated both the business world and the courts. Competition was held so sacred that the "robber barons" saw no sin in purchasing legislatures in its name. The duty of a corporation, the saying went, was to know the law, not the Ten Commandments. Bishop Lawrence of Massachusetts held that "Godliness is in league with riches." But during the gilded age, most Americans tolerated the new inequality. The fortunes amassed (Carnegie Steel alone is said to have made forty millionaires by 1900) evoked more admiration than envy. In labor circles the Socialist movement, which reached its peak between 1903 (when Gompers defeated it in the A.F. of L.) and 1920 (when Eugene Debs polled nearly a million votes for President from the Atlanta penitentiary), never succeeded in convincing the workingman that he was a proletarian. Inequality was tolerated because most Americans felt their opportunities were still fairly equal, or could be made so by some new law. Moreover, they made plenty of new laws. Waves of angry senators from the frontier states were always on hand to make them, their greatest achievement being the Sherman Antitrust Act, their most characteristic posture being for easier money.

BUT the conviction of equal opportunity was also kept fresh by the spread of free education and by two peculiar traits which Americans formed early in their contact with the American land and have never permitted to atrophy. These traits are mobility and teamwork.

Mobility—vertical and horizontal, physical and social—was the flame beneath the American melting pot. In 1846 a visiting pianist from Vienna, Henri Herz, noted with amazement how "doctors sometimes become building contractors, colonels are innkeepers, and the pianists, grocers." During every decade, more Americans have changed their addresses than during any previous decade. Mobility meant continued search, mixture, change; it was inherent in the railroads but it later took place in automobiles, which became the new verb in our "universal language of movement." The racial and cultural incompatibilities that had looked so hopeless at Castle Garden or Ellis Island soon got lost in the larger economic flux, which finally put the hillbilly in Detroit, the Iowan in Los Angeles, the housewife in overalls.

"These people associate as easily as they breathe," said Fredrika Bremer, a German visitor in 1853. Mutual aid, she discovered, was the "organizing principle" of our otherwise atomistic society. De Toqueville had noted the same phenomenon: "But, if an American were condemned to confine his activity to his own affairs, he would be robbed of one half of his existence." The American is a born busybody and teamwork sometimes takes the form of gang-mindedness, building up social pressures on the individualist which can be quite oppressive. The smallest common problem has always produced a spontaneous committee. The westbound wagon trains gathering at Independence automatically organized their own schedules, elected their own leaders. Even before the unions, mechanics' societies had their own nationwide job information services. The "club law" of the squatters was self-enforced against formal law, which was also anticipated whenever necessary by vigilantes on the frontier.

In 1902, the U.S. commissioner of labor, Carroll D. Wright, relied on what he called "the universal tendency to association in our nature" to venture an interesting prophecy about the factory system. It is, he said, "vastly superior as an element in civilization to the domestic system," because it contains this "associating principle," congregating people at work. After years of industrial strife, Wright's hunch is proving correct. Their native gift for teamwork enables Americans to surmount the supposed terrors of mechanization and the social problems of extreme economic interdependence. A new kind of industrial democracy is emerging.

In spite of the vastly expanded activities of government, spontaneous associations of citizens still keep the teamwork habit alive in all parts of American life. Every year some ten million Americans travel to one or more of some seventeen thousand national or state conventions, and practically all Americans belong to the country's two hundred thousand (at least) clubs, societies and organizations. Such activities are the guts of American self-government. They owe nothing to "equality of condition" or to Jefferson's yeoman-democracy, concepts which have been translated into our income tax and also survive in our passion for home-ownership (now over fifty per cent). But they stem directly from habits of mutual aid formed on the frontier. There Frederick Jackson Turner, the historian, found the true source of democracy. "The most important effect of the frontier," said Turner, "has been in the promotion of democracy here and in Europe."

Thus the land, whether as wilderness, process or property, has been a great determinant of the American experience. It was, as Turner said, our safety valve, bank account and Fountain of Youth; it molded our habits as a people. It was also a cause of great acts: the Constitutional Convention, for one, which was called partly to settle the inevitably conflicting land claims of the states; and the Civil War, for another, since the irreconcilabilities of North and South first came face to face in the settlement of the western territories. But more than that, the land's very size, variety and constant surprises made it easier for America to remain what Henry Bamford Parkes calls "a state of mind and not merely a place." It kept giving scale to the American dream, which is a dream of the liberation of all mankind. The American land is a finite platform at the edge of infinity.

Four Ideas

TURNER'S "frontier theory" is one of two chief attempts to explain rather than to narrate the American experience. The other, which has more transatlantic support, is the "germ theory": that American culture is altogether a transplant from Europe, and that its seeds can all be found in

Magna Charta, Thomas Aquinas, John Locke or some other European landmark. Even Jefferson, when asked for ideas for a Great Seal of the United States, proposed an image of Hengest and Horsa, the Saxon brothers who conquered Britain, to symbolize our adoption of "Anglo-Saxon political institutions." His proposal was rejected in favor of that Masonic-looking design to be found on every dollar bill, a pyramid under the Eye of God ("He smiled on our undertakings") and over the motto "*Novus Ordo Saeclorum*," roughly translatable into Shelley's "The world's great age begins anew."

This belief in a new and unique destiny has been one of four dominant ideas of the American experience which Ralph Gabriel has found running through all American democratic thought. The other three are that we live in a moral universe, that mankind is making steady progress, and that the freedom of the individual is the first political commandment. These four ideas, though they are not equally important, have together been at least as important as the land in the molding of America.

The idea of America's unique mission in the world has taken several forms, one of the noblest of them stemming from America's land-borne westward orientation. Columbus was on the right track, sang Whitman; America is still a "Passage to India," the last and greatest step toward the uniting in brotherhood of all races:

> . . . thou born America . . .
> For purpose vast, man's long probation fill'd,
> Thou, Rondure of the world, at last accomplish'd.

A somewhat more literal prophecy of our westward destiny as a nation was written in 1794 by the president of Yale, Timothy Dwight:

> All hail, thou western world! by heaven design'd
> The example bright, to renovate mankind.
> Soon shall thy sons across the mainland roam;
> And claim, on far Pacific shores, their home;
> Their rule, religion, manners, art convey,
> And spread their freedom to the Asian sea . . .
> O'er morn's pellucid main expand their sails,
> And the starr'd ensign court Korean gales.

But this American sense of mission was not exclusively directed westward toward Asia. From the beginning we were conscious of our revolutionary impact on Europe, an impact not only claimed by Turner but formally acknowledged by Lord Morley in England when he said, "The success of popular government across the Atlantic has been the strongest incentive to the extension of popular government here." Our mission was both westward and universal. In 1850, William H. Seward (who later bought Alaska) thus argued for California's statehood: "The Atlantic States . . . are steadily renovating the Governments and the social constitutions of Europe and Africa. The Pacific States must necessarily perform the same sublime and beneficent functions in Asia."

In 1823, during the same decade in which Henry Clay formulated his "American system," the unique and separate destiny of America was also boldly asserted in our foreign policy. President Monroe's doctrine, though based on a tacit deal between Secretary of State John Quincy Adams and Foreign Minister Canning of Britain, announced that our political system was "essentially different" from Europe's and that this whole hemisphere was no longer subject to colonization. Thanks to the doctrine and Britain's unobtrusive enforcement of it, the U.S. enjoyed over ninety years of isolation from European politics. When, in 1917, this period of innocent growth came to an end, it found us still in a missionary mood—indeed, in a mood for what Woodrow Wilson called a "just and holy" crusade. The failure of Wilson's attempt to negotiate a comparably "just and holy" peace, or to persuade America into the league that would enforce it, cost us much of our missionary zeal, at least for the reform of Europe. By the time a second chance came, in 1945, another revolution with a mission of its own had already arisen in Russia to confuse and challenge the American.

Besides undermining America's sense of mission, the revolutions of the twentieth century dealt an even blunter blow to another hopeful idea that Americans had long cherished, the idea of mankind's steady progress. Like Stalin's worse-than-medieval methods, Hitler's "New Era" made a mockery of our inherited optimism. The corpses of Buchenwald were viewed by several thousand GI's and VIP's, including Vice-President Barkley, with somewhat the same shattering effect on the American belief in human progress as the blow Herman Melville had received a century before in his Marquesan Eden. In a summer grove, a day or two after his beautiful Typees had returned victorious from a battle, Melville stumbled on a heap of fresh bones and flesh. It was the garbage of a victory feast. His friends were cannibals.

Although Melville could never again believe in nature, progress, or missionaries either, he did not abandon his belief in a fundamental law of the universe where man's role was to fight perpetually the evil in it. Whether most Americans still hold to this cornerstone belief today is perhaps arguable. So relaxed have the muscles of our belief become that the chief justice of the Supreme Court could recently declare in an official opinion that "there are no absolutes" and "all concepts are relative." But if that were the case, and if it were widely believed, the whole American experiment would be at an end because, without a foundation in moral absolutes, Americans could not long maintain their other great idea. The other idea has been the badge of their uniqueness, the motor of their spectacular material progress, and the soul of their political system. It is the political idea of the freedom of the individual.

POLITICS, both in theory and in practice, is the American's specialty, the art he is really good at. His wealth is chiefly the product of this art applied to the natural wealth of the land. His greatest manufacturing achievement was the manufacture of the Constitution; for the Constitution was made, it did not grow; and great artists of politics have kept it in repair ever since.

Behind the Constitution lay the Declaration of Independence, which had set forth the "self-evident" principle of the equal rights of all men, as natural gifts of their Creator. As Jefferson readily confessed, the concepts of the Declaration were not original with him, but were commonplaces of the Age of Enlightenment. Nevertheless its principles were *not* "self-evident," then or now. The British ridiculed them by pointing to our slaves; Jeremy Bentham, the philosophical father of Fabian socialism, called the whole natural rights idea "nonsense upon stilts." It is one of those things that you either believe or you don't. Most Americans (including earlier chief justices of the Supreme Court) have acted most of the time as though they believed it.

BUT it takes more than a declaration of faith to achieve self-government, especially a government whose central purpose is "to preserve these rights." It was at the Constitutional Convention of 1787 that the American political genius met its first great challenge. The delegates were fortunate in two respects. First, there were among them several great men—notably Adams, Hamilton and Madison—who not only believed in the Declaration but had taught themselves to know more about political philosophy than any men of their time. Second, they had in the previous twenty years experienced two unpleasant extremes of government, the tyranny of George III and the anarchy of the Articles of Confederation—"King Stork" and "King Log." This had sharpened their perception of the central problem of all government, the problem of man and society, of the one and the many, of freedom and order.

The Founding Fathers' answer to this age-old problem was an improvement over all previous attempts, and has not since been improved on elsewhere. It was a simple but shrewdly calculated application of federalism—a government with adequate but limited powers, those which were not enumerated being "reserved to the States, or to the people." This limitation was reinforced not only by Jefferson's Bill of Rights, but by checks, balances, varying tenures and a division of powers among the three branches of government. Each of the three branches had its partisans from the beginning. Jefferson distrusted the judiciary generally as "sappers and miners" of the popular will, but he aimed to give the Supreme Court a democratic bent by making it the guardian of his Bill of Rights. Hamilton distrusted Congress and rejoiced in the national symbolism of kinglike strength with which Washington, as first President, endowed the executive arm. Adams, the clearest thinker but worst politician of the group, put his faith in "a government of laws, not men," and virtually created the Court by appointing John Marshall (Jefferson's cousin) to be chief justice. But he also carelessly permitted Jefferson to organize behind his back a national coalition of unrelated dissident minorities, which became the first modern political party.

This party, which was later to be called the Democratic, enabled Jefferson and his successors to turn the presidency into the strongest branch of government. The presidency has ever since remained a unique office and symbol among the world's democracies, combining in one person the great functions of chief of state, prime minister of the government and tribune of the people.

Andrew Jackson played the tribune role so belligerently that he created a new opposition, the Whig party. From the ashes of this short-lived amalgam rose the new Republican party which dared to call itself "the party of moral ideas." Its first President, Abraham Lincoln, matched practical and ideal politics in a way that has never been surpassed. On the profound voting issues of the Civil War, he took the one position that would retain the North, unite the West and divide the South—the preservation of the union. Although he refused to make war on slavery, Lincoln helped the South maneuver itself into the hopeless position of making war for slavery. He left behind him something that had not been here before. With some truth Calhoun had argued that "the American nation did not exist." After Lincoln, it began to. Lowell called him "the first American." Lincoln spent half his time palavering with petty politicians, but the other half was used to put into great words and acts the basic American political principles.

Those principles are simple and three in number. The first, as aforesaid, is liberty, a God-given right of man. The second, its corollary (for rights are equal) and its rival (for rights conflict) is democracy: "Those who deny freedom to others deserve it not for themselves, and under a just God will not long retain it," said Lincoln. The third is constitutionalism: limited government by law, ceaselessly mediating between liberty and democracy, but never declaring the winner.

The Habit: Constitutionalism

THIS third principle, constitutionalism, is the only one of the three which cannot be readily defined and packaged for universal export. It is more like a national habit, the open secret of America's capacity for self-government which was mentioned earlier as a key thread through the whole American experience.

By "constitutionalism" is meant not the Constitution itself, but the reasons why Americans revere it. One reason is that it contains a principle of self-limiting power and thus expresses the American's bias against all formal government. By European standards this bias is almost anarchistic. The British, for instance, do not feel that they endangered their liberty when they whittled away judicial review and gave Parliament theoretically absolute power. Yet when Franklin Roosevelt undertook to tinker with the Supreme Court, a congressional committee of his own party reported savagely against him. Constitutionalism is what Jefferson was talking about when he said that "free government is founded in jealousy, and not in confidence." It is what Jimmy Durante meant when he said, "Don't put no constrictions on da people. Leave 'em ta hell alone."

Constitutionalism has been wrongly identified with many of its own lesser or transient aspects, such as States' Rights, or "government by laws, not men," or "concurrent majority," or the amendment to limit the presidency to two terms. It can be as offended by too little government as by too much. When Theodore Roosevelt was inaugurated, John Hay gave him a "savage relic"—a ring containing a lock of hair cut from the head of the murdered Lincoln. Roosevelt wore it at the ceremony: it would remind him, he said, always to "put human rights above property rights when the two conflicted." Constitutionalism is a correct judgment as to when there is such a conflict and when there is not.

There is always some degree of conflict in the area of constitutionalism, for in it are embedded two opposite views of human nature. John Adams had little confidence in the people as keepers of their own liberty. His cousin Sam, on the other hand, along with Tom Paine, Patrick Henry (who "smelt a rat" and refused to go to Philadelphia at all) and Jefferson, believed that the people as a whole were the most trustworthy judges of their own interests, especially if left alone. Adams feared for the few and Jefferson for the many, but both feared the same thing: arbitrary government. Both also agreed on one constitution as the best method of protecting liberty against it. Before they both died (on the same day —July 4, 1826) Adams and Jefferson, in an extraordinary exchange of letters based on a resolve "to explain ourselves to each other," had narrowed their personal disagreement almost to the vanishing point. But it is nevertheless a deep difference and it has arisen in our politics again and again.

Adams's viewpoint on human nature, skeptical of everything except liberty and original sin, aligns him with the European tradition. Jefferson, vaguer and more optimistic, cut a silver cord to Europe when he changed Locke's phrase —"life, liberty and property"—to one of his own—"life, liberty and the pursuit of happiness." Happiness was a strange political idea then; it is still perhaps the one abstraction of which no government could ever claim to be the main source—at least to a rational and virtuous electorate. And Jefferson was betting that, with free education and a sound economic base, most men would prove more rational and virtuous than not.

Constitutionalism is our guarantee that this great democratic experiment, this optimistic bet on human nature, will never be called off by government action. As long as constitutionalism lasts the American government may or may not do what the voters require for their public welfare, but it will *never* take charge of any citizen's private quest for happiness. Constitutionalism explains why honest men, though they have left America in disdain or disgust, have never fled it in desperation.

WHEN Charles Beard reassessed our system in 1942, he concluded that the Founders had "made it possible for the American people to have more justice, despite all the black marks on it, than any other people ever enjoyed over such an immense territory for so long a time—with splendid opportunities still ahead." If this is so, it is only because the people so governed are willing to pay the price of constitutionalism. The price is that citizens must take continuous initiative, voluntarily doing chores and making decisions which elsewhere are considered government chores and decisions. Despite the tremendous growth of government, Americans still do this. It is the citizens whose moral sense discovers injustice and takes appropriate corrective action. It was the moral sense of citizens—both businessmen and their critics—that transformed the behavior of the modern corporation and persuaded it to recognize the Ten Commandments as well as the laws. It is within the corporation and the other socially autonomous communities that the most meaningful experiments on the frontiers of social justice (e.g. Negro equality) are carried out. Constitutionalism is our substitute for a national community, or "sense of the State," and also for public morals, a term we seldom use. We seldom use it because only individuals have morals, not publics and certainly not states. Constitutionalism can last in America as long as the people have a strong moral sense. It was Thomas Jefferson's bet that they always would.

The Critics and the Challenge

IT appears, then, that this crucial secret of American self-government is closely akin to the other two threads of the American's experience, the land he lives on and the ideas he lives by. The three threads are in fact so intertwined that constitutionalism may even be an optical illusion. Certainly its apparent termination has been marked and mourned on many occasions in our history, especially by pessimists about human nature. Even that arch-connoisseur of freedom, Lord Acton, wrote an obituary to the American experiment—in 1861. And one cannot say the pessimists are never justified; there was a wolf and there still is.

Men have found all kinds of reasons for pessimism about America, from the potato bug to Prohibition. In St. Paul they used to sing:

> I found me out dis country vus a sell,
> I scall I go back to Norveg vere I can do so vell.

But the two chief reasons for disillusion have been some version of what Henry Adams called "the degradation of the democratic dogma," and the cultural inadequacies that made Matthew Arnold call America "uninteresting" and Sigmund Freud call it a "mistake."

Young Adams, fresh from our wartime embassy in London, read the names of Grant's first cabinet—all agents of the new plutocracy—and "blushed." He blushed not for his country, but for his own naïveté in having expected something better. He was reminded how his great-grandfather's high principles had been followed by Jefferson's politicking, and his grandfather's by Jackson's. He thought he saw a law: that each of the new interests which democracy keeps raising to power is more narrowly selfish than its predecessor. A dim apprehension of this "law" has induced many an American intellectual to turn in his chips. The McKinley tariff and the Spanish-American War were the last straw for Manchester liberals like William Graham Sumner and Edwin L. Godkin. Said Godkin: "I came here fifty years ago with high and fond ideals about America. They are now all shattered." To some conservatives, the income tax amendment was the turning point; to others, the popular election of senators. A good case for pessimism can always be made; unquestionably the extension of federal powers and services since the great depression has greatly altered the terms by which Americans govern themselves.

The artists, like the intellectuals, have also found America repeatedly disappointing. When William Ellery Channing called for a "national literature" in 1830, he got it almost at once in Emerson, Thoreau and Hawthorne, in Melville and Whitman, Poe and Mark Twain. But the gilded age and its compulsory optimism, and something that Whitman called a "pervading flippancy and vulgarity" in American life, soon soured the roots of honest creation, and Henry

James set a pattern of expatriation that esthetes have followed ever since. "Shine, perishing republic," sang Robinson Jeffers, as his fellow poets of the 1920's trooped off to Paris.

Walt Whitman (a great exception to his own statement) once complained that America had "morally and artistically originated nothing." It is true that American art, poetry, drama, music and philosophy have somehow failed to match the American achievement in politics and economics. Our chief candidate for esthetic achievement is in that Rome-like art of huge, beautiful, anonymous engineering: the Brooklyn Bridge, the Golden Gate Bridge, Hoover Dam, and the skyscrapers of Chicago and New York.

But does this matter? A true judgment on American culture must recognize what differentiates it so markedly from European culture—the modifying force of democracy. In the popular arts—notably movies, jazz, journalism—America has been both original and copious. Moreover, a large part of our cultural energy has gone into the democratic chore of diffusion. Never has "the best that has been thought and known in the world" been so quantitatively widespread, so available to all. There are more would-be painters enrolled in American art schools than the entire population of Florence in Leonardo's day. Our universities harbor more scholars, teachers, laboratories, projects, museums, collections, ideas and diversity of opinion than any other nation's, ever. The characteristic product of all this mass culture is what W. H. Auden calls "horizontal man," a brotherly type. It would be foolish to deny that Europe's class system has been more productive of "vertical man," the lone genius who makes intellectual history. Our democratic modification of culture may ask this price. But one price American democracy does not ask, and has not been paid, is the dead uniformity of which it is so often falsely accused. Uniformity is precisely what the American system is best armed against.

A single example should make this clear. Had the American been a conforming or sheeplike culture, the ideas of John Dewey would by now be the cultural law of the land. He is the leading spokesman of America's only original and most characteristic philosophy, pragmatism, which he has been selling for fifty years in that most strategic area, the teaching of teachers. Despite this long start toward an ideological monopoly (to which, being a philosopher and a democrat, he never aspired), Dewey in his ninety-second year recently acknowledged that the tide of American thought, once all his way, is now running against him. His very success had set up strong antibodies in the pluralistic university scene. Nor will this be the end of the matter. Our culture is being continuously ventilated by popular breezes. Democracy is a process. It does not pose for pictures. It does not pause to make a *summa* or even to give much advice.

AND so now in the hundred and seventy-fifth year of his national independence, the American finds himself in charge of more national wealth and power—industrial, scientific, financial and military power—than any nation ever had before. Yet on this peak he is facing a greater challenge than any people has ever faced. All his triumphs have led him, as mankind's triumphs have always led, to a new test which far transcends the mere arithmetic of power.

The challenge of Soviet communism is unlike any challenge America has ever in its past met and surmounted. It is like Melville's confrontation with the fact of evil in Paradise, except that the dimensions of this evil are more colossal than Americans had ever imagined. Two huge nations, each bigger than America, and ten lesser ones are enslaved, and all mankind is threatened not only with slavery but with an irrational dogma that denies all the premises of the American experience.

In the face of this challenge, Americans feel more nearly united, and more nearly alone, than ever before in their history. Even our artists and intellectuals are rediscovering America and rallying to the side of freedom. And meantime the capacity of other nations for sharing the onerous leadership of the struggle has been weakened—even Britain's—by war and the dead-end experiment of socialism.

ON his lonely pinnacle, the American can survey more history than he has seen before. During the past generation he rediscovered his personal links with Western Man and his membership in Western civilization. Somewhere in these turbulent years America's acceptance of responsibility for the fate of its parents' lands, for the mother and father of its own past, quietly placed itself beyond question. When Franklin Roosevelt in 1939 said, "Our American frontier is on the Rhine," he felt obliged to deny that he had said it. That frontier has subsequently been placed on the Elbe without objection. Instead of Gibbon's "ten thousand vessels for the rescue of civilization" a new vehicle called the Atlantic Community now carries Western Man on his long way.

And "cosmic man"—what of him? The American, his plans tragically frustrated in Asia, his motives suspect in India, his words banned in Russia, and his ideas still unfocused in Africa, does not feel much like "cosmic man" just yet. For one thing, he can still see further opportunities closer to home for the continued application of the first principles (his "permanent revolution") that have served him so astonishingly well up to now. He can still say what Whitman said just after the Civil War: "Our New World, I consider far less important for what it has done, or what it is, than for results to come."

Yet the prophecy cannot be confined either to our "New World" or to our new-old Atlantic Community. "Sole among the nationalities," Whitman continued, "these States have assumed the task to put in forms of lasting power and practicality, on areas of amplitude rivaling the operations of the physical kosmos, the moral political speculation of ages . . . the democratic republican principle."

America must still count itself a "Passage to India," a finite threshold to infinity, a stage in the development of "cosmic man." Otherwise Western Man has no future, and the barbarian inherits his earth. Such are the dimensions of the present struggle. All the civilization, the truths, the promises recited in this book are at stake. America is a part of this civilization—the critical and saving part.

On America almost alone has fallen the awful responsibility of holding open the door of history against the forces of evil until freedom is born anew all over the world.

—JOHN KNOX JESSUP

Two days after the Constitution had been adopted in convention, the *Packet and Daily Advertiser* published it and gave the new nation its first chance to read the document which was to guard its treasure of freedom. →

The Pennſylvania Packet, *and Daily Advertiſer.*

[Price Four-Pence.] WEDNESDAY, September 19, 1787. [No. 2690.]

WE, the People of the United States, in order to form a more perfect Union, eſtabliſh Juſtice, inſure domeſtic Tranquility, provide for the common Defence, promote the General Welfare, and ſecure the Bleſſings of Liberty to Ourſelves and our Poſterity, do ordain and eſtabliſh this Conſtitution for the United States of America.

ARTICLE I.

Sect. 1. ALL legiſlative powers herein granted ſhall be veſted in a Congreſs of the United States, which ſhall conſiſt of a Senate and Houſe of Repreſentatives.

Sect. 2. The Houſe of Repreſentatives ſhall be compoſed of members choſen every ſecond year by the people of the ſeveral ſtates, and the electors in each ſtate ſhall have the qualifications requiſite for electors of the moſt numerous branch of the ſtate legiſlature.

No perſon ſhall be a repreſentative who ſhall not have attained to the age of twenty-five years, and been ſeven years a citizen of the United States, and who ſhall not, when elected, be an inhabitant of that ſtate in which he ſhall be choſen.

Repreſentatives and direct taxes ſhall be apportioned among the ſeveral ſtates which may be included within this Union, according to their reſpective numbers, which ſhall be determined by adding to the whole number of free perſons, including thoſe bound to ſervice for a term of years, and excluding Indians not taxed, three-fifths of all other perſons. The actual enumeration ſhall be made within three years after the firſt meeting of the Congreſs of the United States, and within every ſubſequent term of ten years, in ſuch manner as they ſhall by law direct. The number of repreſentatives ſhall not exceed one for every thirty thouſand, but each ſtate ſhall have at leaſt one repreſentative; and until ſuch enumeration ſhall be made, the ſtate of New-Hampſhire ſhall be entitled to chuſe three, Maſſachuſetts eight, Rhode-Iſland and Providence Plantations one, Connecticut five, New-York ſix, New-Jerſey four, Pennſylvania eight, Delaware one, Maryland ſix, Virginia ten, North-Carolina five, South-Carolina five, and Georgia three.

When vacancies happen in the repreſentation from any ſtate, the Executive authority thereof ſhall iſſue writs of election to fill ſuch vacancies.

The Houſe of Repreſentatives ſhall chuſe their Speaker and other officers; and ſhall have the ſole power of impeachment.

Sect. 3. The Senate of the United States ſhall be compoſed of two ſenators from each ſtate, choſen by the legiſlature thereof, for ſix years; and each ſenator ſhall have one vote.

Immediately after they ſhall be aſſembled in conſequence of the firſt election, they ſhall be divided as equally as may be into three claſſes. The ſeats of the ſenators of the firſt claſs ſhall be vacated at the expiration of the ſecond year, of the ſecond claſs at the expiration of the fourth year, and of the third claſs at the expiration of the ſixth year, ſo that one-third may be choſen every ſecond year; and if vacancies happen by reſignation, or otherwiſe, during the receſs of the Legiſlature of any ſtate, the Executive thereof may make temporary appointments until the next meeting of the Legiſlature, which ſhall then fill ſuch vacancies.

No perſon ſhall be a ſenator who ſhall not have attained to the age of thirty years, and been nine years a citizen of the United States, and who ſhall not, when elected, be an inhabitant of that ſtate for which he ſhall be choſen.

The Vice-Preſident of the United States ſhall be Preſident of the ſenate, but ſhall have no vote, unleſs they be equally divided.

The Senate ſhall chuſe their other officers, and alſo a Preſident pro tempore, in the abſence of the Vice-Preſident, or when he ſhall exerciſe the office of Preſident of the United States.

The Senate ſhall have the ſole power to try all impeachments. When ſitting for that purpoſe, they ſhall be on oath or affirmation. When the Preſident of the United States is tried, the Chief Juſtice ſhall preſide: And no perſon ſhall be convicted without the concurrence of two-thirds of the members preſent.

Judgment in caſes of impeachment ſhall not extend further than to removal from office, and diſqualification to hold and enjoy any office of honor, truſt or profit under the United States; but the party convicted ſhall nevertheleſs be liable and ſubject to indictment, trial, judgment and puniſhment, according to law.

Sect. 4. The times, places and manner of holding elections for ſenators and repreſentatives, ſhall be preſcribed in each ſtate by the legiſlature thereof; but the Congreſs may at any time by law make or alter ſuch regulations, except as to the places of chuſing Senators.

The Congreſs ſhall aſſemble at leaſt once in every year, and ſuch meeting ſhall be on the firſt Monday in December, unleſs they ſhall by law appoint a different day.

Sect. 5. Each houſe ſhall be the judge of the elections, returns and qualifications of its own members, and a majority of each ſhall conſtitute a quorum to do buſineſs; but a ſmaller number may adjourn from day to day, and may be authoriſed to compel the attendance of abſent members, in ſuch manner, and under ſuch penalties as each houſe may provide.

Each houſe may determine the rules of its proceedings, puniſh its members for diſorderly behaviour, and, with the concurrence of two-thirds, expel a member.

Each houſe ſhall keep a journal of its proceedings, and from time to time publiſh the ſame, excepting ſuch parts as may in their judgment require ſecrecy; and the yeas and nays of the members of either houſe on any queſtion ſhall, at the deſire of one-fifth of thoſe preſent, be entered on the journal.

Neither houſe, during the ſeſſion of Congreſs, ſhall, without the conſent of the other, adjourn for more than three days, nor to any other place than that in which the two houſes ſhall be ſitting.

Sect. 6. The ſenators and repreſentatives ſhall receive a compenſation for their ſervices, to be aſcertained by law, and paid out of the treaſury of the United States. They ſhall in all caſes, except treaſon, felony and breach of the peace, be privileged from arreſt during their attendance at the ſeſſion of their reſpective houſes, and in going to and returning from the ſame; and for any ſpeech or debate in either houſe, they ſhall not be queſtioned in any other place.

No ſenator or repreſentative ſhall, during the time for which he was elected, be appointed to any civil office under the authority of the United States, which ſhall have been created, or the emoluments whereof ſhall have been encreaſed during ſuch time; and no perſon holding any office under the United States, ſhall be a member of either houſe during his continuance in office.

Sect. 7. All bills for raiſing revenue ſhall originate in the houſe of repreſentatives; but the ſenate may propoſe or concur with amendments as on other bills.

Every bill which ſhall have paſſed the houſe of repreſentatives and the ſenate, ſhall, before it become a law, be preſented to the preſident of the United States; if he approve he ſhall ſign it, but if not he ſhall return it, with his objections to that houſe in which it ſhall have originated, who ſhall enter the objections at large on their journal, and proceed to reconſider it. If after ſuch reconſideration two-thirds of that houſe ſhall agree to paſs the bill, it ſhall be ſent, together with the objections, to the other houſe, by which it ſhall likewiſe be reconſidered, and if approved by two-thirds of that houſe, it ſhall become a law. But in all ſuch caſes the votes of both houſes ſhall

LIST OF ILLUSTRATIONS

Illustrations on each page are listed from left to right and from top to bottom. An asterisk after a page number (12*) indicates that the illustration is in color. In the case of paintings and works of sculpture, the artist's name, if known, is given in large and small capitals (ARTIST'S NAME). The name of the photographer or the picture agency appears in parentheses (Photographer or Agency).

II MEDIEVAL LIFE

III RENAISSANCE MAN

IV THE GLORY OF VENICE

V THE AGE OF EXPLORATION

120 Prester John in Africa. Sebastian Cabot's Map of the World, 1544. Bibliothèque Nationale. Paris. (P. Sauvanaud)
121 Prince Henry the Navigator. Bibliothèque Nationale, Paris. (Anthony Linck)
122-123 Astrolabe. *The Arte of Navigation*, by Martin Curtis, London, 1561. Rare Book Room, New York Public Library. (Werner Wolff, Black Star)
Shooting the Sun. *Elucillatio Farricae ususque Astronelatis*, by Ionnes Stolferior, Oppenheim, 1524. Rare Book Room, New York Public Library. (Werner Wolff, Black Star)
Cross-Staff; A table of declination. *The Way of a Ship*, by Lawrence Wroth. The Southworth-Anthoensen Press, Portland, Maine, 1937.
125 Nef de Bande. *Les Estampes de Peter Bruegel; l'Ancien*, by René van Bastelaer, Bruxelles, 1908. Courtesy Charles Tudor.
126 Columbus' Landing at Insula Hyspaña; Islands of the New World. *De Insulis Nuper Inventis*, by Christopher Columbus, Basle, 1493. Rare Book Room, New York Public Library.
127* Vasco da Gama. Cabinet des Manuscrits, Bibliothèque Nationale, Paris. (Anthony Linck)
128-129* Vollard Portolan Chart. HM 29. The Huntington Library, San Marino, California. (Ralph Crane, Black Star)
130* *The Giraffe Parade*. Flemish Tapestry, c. 1525. French & Company, Inc. (Fernand Bourges)
131 Plan of Utopia. *De Optimo Reip. statu deque noua insula Utopia*, by Sir Thomas More, Basle, 1518. (The Bettmann Archive)
Plants from the New World. *Tractatus noui de potu caphé, de chinensium thé et de chocolata*, by Philippe Sylvestre Dufour, Paris, 1685. Rare Book Room, New York Public Library.
132-133 5 Scenes from *India Occidentalis*, by Theodorus De Bry. Frankfurt, 1590; 6 Scenes from *India Orientalis*, by Theodorus De Bry, Frankfurt, 1608. Rare Book Room. New York Public Library. (Werner Wolff, Black Star)
134 Drawings from *The Pictures of Sundry Things . . . in the Voyage made by Sir W. Raleigh, Knight, for the Discovery of La Virginea, in the 27th Year of the Most Happie Reigne of Our Soveraigne Lady Queene Elizabeth*, by John White. British Museum. Reproduction from The Clements Library, University of Michigan.
135* *The Manner of Their Fishing*, by John White. *Ibid.* British Museum. Reproduction from The Clements Library, University of Michigan.
136-137* The Fireship Attack on the Spanish Armada, July 28, 1588. National Maritime Museum, London. (John Philpin)
Armada Maps. *Expeditionis Hispanorum in Angliam vera Descriptio*, by Augustine Ryther after Robert Adams, 1588. Courtesy, Trustees, British Museum. (John Philpin)
138* Queen Elizabeth. National Portrait Gallery, London. (Studio Sun Ltd.)
139 Sir Walter Raleigh. Collection of Preston Davie, New York. Reproduction from Museum of Fine Arts, Boston.
Commissioners to Ratify a Treaty, 1604, MARCUS GHEERAERTS THE YOUNGER (?) National Portrait Gallery, London. Reproduction from Museum of Fine Arts, Boston.
140-141 View of London, by Nicholas Visscher, 1616. British Museum. Reproduction from Museum of Fine Arts, Boston.
Sir Philip Sidney. National Portrait Gallery, London. Reproduction from Museum of Fine Arts, Boston.
Countess of Pembroke. National Portrait Gallery, London. Reproduction from Museum of Fine Arts, Boston.
Frontispiece of *The Roaring Girle*, by T. Middleton and T. Dekker. London, 1611. The Folger Shakespeare Library, Washington, D.C. (J. Waring Stinchcomb, Harris and Ewing)
Title Page to Francis Bacon's *Instauratio Magna*, by Simon van de Passe, London, 1620. Reproduction from Museum of Fine Arts, Boston.
Pocahontas. (Picture Post Library)
Tempest. *India Occidentalis*, by Theodorus De Bry, Frankfurt, 1590. Rare Book Room, New York Public Library. (Werner Wolff, Black Star)
142 Mask of Quetzalcoatl. British Museum.

VI THE PROTESTANT REFORMATION

144 The Martyrdome of William Gardiner in Portugall. *Ecclesiasticall History. . . . Actes and Monumentes of Martyrs*, by I. Foxe, London, 1576. Rare Book Room, New York Public Library.
145 Fight between Luther and Calvin. (The Bettmann Archive)
146-147 Woodcuts, by Lucas Cranach the Elder. *Passional Christi und Antichristi*. Wittenberg, 1521. The Pierpont Morgan Library. (Werner Wolff, Black Star)
149 Frontispiece. *Das Allte testament deutsch*, by Martin Luther, Wittenberg, 1524. Rare Book Room, New York Public Library. (Werner Wolff, Black Star)
The Burning of Luther's books before the Pope. *Wider den Nerven Abgot und alten Teufell*, by Martin Luther, Wittenberg, 1524. The Pierpont Morgan Library. (Werner Wolff, Black Star)
150 Doors of the Wittenberg Church. (Exclusive News Agency)
Martin Luther's Hideaway. (Culver Service)
151* *Luther and His Friends*, LUCAS CRANACH THE ELDER Toledo Museum of Art. (Jahn & Ollier Engraving Co.)
152-153* *Allegory on Conditions in the Low Countries.* Rijksmuseum, Amsterdam. (Studio Sun Ltd.)
The Fishers for Souls, ADRIAEN PIETERSZ VAN DE VENNE Musées Royaux des Beaux-Arts de Belgique. (Studio Sun Ltd.)
The Massacre of the Innocents, PIETER BRUEGEL THE YOUNGER. Rijksmuseum, Amsterdam. (Studio Sun Ltd.)
154* *Mary Stuart*. Courtesy Duke of Alba. (Frank Lerner)
155 *John Knox* Preaching, SIR DAVID WILKIE By courtesy of the Trustees of the Tate Gallery. (Studio Sun Ltd.)
156 Student Sketches of Calvin. *Iconographie calvinienne*, by Emile Doumergue, Lausanne, 1909. New York Public Library.
Pilgrim Fathers in Public Worship, JOHANN SCHWARTZE. Courtesy Pilgrim Society. (Fernand Bourges)
157 St. Paul's Cross. Widener Library, Harvard University. Reproduction from Museum of Fine Arts, Boston.
158-159 *La Fondation et la Propagation de la Compagnie de Jésus*, by Charles van Mallery. Print Room, The Metropolitan Museum of Art.
Council of Trent. *Speculum Romanae*, published by Antonio Lafreri, Rome, XVI Century. Print Room, The Metropolitan Museum of Art.
The Jesuit Martini as a Chinese Mandarin. *La Morale Pratique des Jésuites*, by Du Cambout, Cologne, 1682. Rare Book Room, New York Public Library. (Werner Wolff, Black Star)
The Martyrdom of the Jesuits Brébeuf and Lalement. *Historiae Canadensis*, Libri Decem, by François du Creux, 1664. Rare Book Room, New York Public Library. (Werner Wolff, Black Star)

204* *A Fête at Rambouillet*, JEAN-HONORÉ FRAGONARD
National Gallery of Art, Washington, D.C.
Gulbenkian Collection (Loan). (Henry Beville)
205* *The Swing*, JEAN-HONORÉ FRAGONARD
From the Original in the Wallace Collection,
by Permission. (Walter A. Curtin)
206* *The Toilet of Venus*, FRANÇOIS BOUCHER.
The Metropolitan Museum of Art. (Fernand Bourges)
207 Jean Jacques Rousseau. (Historical Pictures Service)
L'Education de l'Homme Commence à la Naissance, by
C. N. Cochin. Bibliothèque Nationale, Paris.
Mill, Versailles. (Combine Photos, New York)
208-209 Voltaire. (The Bettmann Archive)
Frederick the Great. (The Bettmann Archive)
Four illustrations for Voltaire's *Candide*, by Jean-Michel Moreau le Jeune. Bibliothèque Nationale, Paris.
Taillanderie. *Dictionnaire des Sciences*, by Diderot,
Paris, 1751. Vol. IX of the Supplement, 1771.
New York Public Library. (Werner Wolff, Black Star)
Denis Diderot, by Henriquez. *Celebrités Françaises*,
Vol. III, Plate XXIV. The New York Public Library.
(Werner Wolff, Black Star)
Catherine the Great. (Alinari)
210 Perruques. *Dictionnaire des Sciences*, by Diderot,
Paris, 1751. Vol. VIII of the Supplement, 1771.
New York Public Library. (Werner Wolff, Black Star)

VIII EIGHTEENTH CENTURY ENGLAND

212 Chatsworth House. Courtesy *Country Life*.
213 A Modern Belle going to the Rooms at Bath. *The Caricatures of James Gillray*, Miscellaneous Series,
Vol. II, London, 1778–1811. Print Room, New York
Public Library. (Werner Wolff, Black Star)
214-215 Earl of Chesterfield. National Portrait
Gallery, London.
Duchess of Marlborough. (The Bettmann Archive)
William Blackstone. (Brown Brothers)
Captain James Cook. (Culver Service)
Lady Mary Montagu. (Culver Service)
Edward Gibbon. (Culver Service)
216-217 London Scenes, by Rowlandson and Pugin. *The Microcosm of London*, by R. A. Ackerman, London, 1810.
Print Room, New York Public Library.
(Werner Wolff, Black Star)
218-219 Badminton in the County of Gloucester, by I. Kip.
Nouveau Théâtre de la Grande Bretagne, London, 1724,
Vol. I, Plate IX. Art and Architecture Room,
New York Public Library. (Werner Wolff, Black Star)
220-221 Eighteenth Century Furniture.
The Gentleman and Cabinet Maker's Director. Supplement: A Gallery of Chippendale's Furniture,
by Walter Rendell Storey. Towse Publishing Co.,
New York, 1938. *The Cabinetmakers and Upholsterers Guide by Alice Hepplewhite. Supplement: A Gallery of Hepplewhite's Furniture*,
by Walter Rendell Storey. Towse Publishing Co.,
New York, 1942. *Thomas Sheraton's Complete Furniture Works. Supplement: A Gallery of Sheraton's Furniture*, by Walter Rendell Storey.
Towse Publishing Co., New York, 1946.
222 Silhouette of the Sitwell and Warneford Families.
Courtesy Sir Osbert Sitwell.
(Andrey Anderssen, Black Star)
A Side Box at the Opera. *A Collection of Political Caricatures, Broadsides, Portraits . . . 1642–1830, from the library of Sir Robert Peel, Bart.* Vol. V.
The Pierpont Morgan Library.
223* *The Honorable Mrs. Graham*, THOMAS GAINSBOROUGH
By courtesy of the Board of Trustees of the
National Galleries of Scotland. (Studio Sun Ltd.)
224-225* *The Mall.* Courtesy Marshall Field, New York.
(Fernand Bourges)
The Rotunda; Ranelagh Gardens, ANTONIO CANALETTO
Reproduced by courtesy of the Trustees,
The National Gallery, London. (Walter A. Curtin)
The Thames, ANTONIO CANALETTO. Courtesy His Grace
the Duke of Richmond and Gordon. (Walter A. Curtin)
226-227* *The Great Race Meeting*, JOHN WOOTTON
(Fernand Bourges)
The Wedgwood Family, GEORGE STUBBS
Courtesy Miss Phoebe Wedgwood. (Walter A. Curtin)
The Auriols (A Colonial Family), JOHN ZOFFANY
Courtesy M. G. Dashwood, Esq. (Studio Sun Ltd.)
228-229* *The Interior of a Coffeehouse.* Courtesy Trustees of
the British Museum (Walter A. Curtin)
The Tribuna, JOHN ZOFFANY
Copyright Reserved. (Studio Sun Ltd.)
230* *Samuel Johnson*, SIR JOSHUA REYNOLDS
National Portrait Gallery, London. (Walter A. Curtin)
231 Up the High Street; The Recovery, by William Hogarth.
Boswell's *Life of Johnson*, London, 1791. The Pierpont
Morgan Library. (Werner Wolff, Black Star)
David Garrick, by William Hogarth. *The Original and Genuine Works of William Hogarth*, London, 1795.
Print Room, New York Public Library.
(Werner Wolff, Black Star)
232-233 Sterne at Ranelagh. British Museum. Reproduction from
Johnson's England, by T. S. Turberville, Oxford, 1933.
New York Public Library. (Werner Wolff, Black Star)
Map of Robinson Crusoe's Island. *Serious Reflections during the Life and Surprising adventures of Robinson Crusoe*, by Daniel Defoe, London, 1720. The Pierpont
Morgan Library. (Werner Wolff, Black Star)
Tom Jones and Squire Weston. *Tom Jones*, by
Henry Fielding, London, 1831. Print Room,
New York Public Library. (Werner Wolff, Black Star)
Clarissa Harlowe.
Picture Collection, New York Public Library.
Gulliver, by Louis Rhead. *Gulliver's Travels*,
by Jonathan Swift. Copyright 1913 by Harper & Bros.
Copyright 1941 by Bertrand Rhead.
234-235 George Whitefield.
National Portrait Gallery, London. (Keystone View)
John Wesley.
National Portrait Gallery, London. (Keystone View)
John Wesley preaching on shipboard. (Methodist Prints)
John Wesley preaching at Bolton Cross. (Methodist Prints)
Methodist Tree of Life. *A Collection of Political Caricatures* . . . Vol. II. The Pierpont Morgan Library.
(Werner Wolff, Black Star)

THE RISE OF PARLIAMENTARY GOVERNMENT

236 Robert Walpole, J. B. VAN LOO. (The Bettmann Archive)
237 Walpole and his Cabinet. *A Collection of Political Caricatures* . . . Vol. II. The Pierpont Morgan Library.
(Werner Wolff, Black Star)
238 The Trial of Simon Lord Lovat. *A Collection of Political Caricatures* . . . Vol. II, The Pierpont Morgan Library.
(Werner Wolff, Black Star)
239 John Wilkes, by William Hogarth. *Op. cit.* London, 1795.
Print Room, New York Public Library.
(Werner Wolff, Black Star)
The Coalition Dance, by James Gillray. *Op. cit.*
Political Series, Vol. I, London, 1778–1811. Print Room,
New York Public Library. (Werner Wolff, Black Star)
240-241 Canvassing for Votes; The Polling; Chairing the

BIBLIOGRAPHY

When more than three books on this list are published by the same house, the publisher is identified by a symbol (as SS = Simon & Schuster). The symbols are explained at the end of the bibliography.

GENERAL

The Cambridge Medieval History. Cambridge University Press, Cambridge 1911–36.

The Cambridge Modern History. Cambridge University Press, Cambridge, second revised edition, 1924.

BARNES, H. E. *The History of Western Civilization*. Harcourt, Brace and Co., New York, 1935.

BECKER, C. L. *Everyman His Own Historian*. FSC, 1935.

DAVIS, W. S. *A History of France*. HM, 1919.

FERGUSON, W. K. AND BRUUN, G. *A Survey of European Civilization*. HM, 1947.

GREEN, J. R. *A Short History of the English People*. A. L. Burt Co., New York, n.d.

GUIGNEBERT, CHARLES. *A Short History of the French People*. M, 1930.

GUIZOT, FRANÇOIS P. *General History of the Civilization in Europe*. D. Appleton and Co., New York, 1896.

HASSALL, ARTHUR. *France, Medieval and Modern*. OUP, 1919.

HAYES, C.J.H. *A Political and Cultural History of Modern Europe*. M, 1932.

HAYES, C.J.H., BALDWIN, M. W. AND COLE, E. W. *History of Europe*. M, 1949.

PARRINGTON, V. L. *Main Currents in American Thought*. HB, 1930.

RANDALL, J. H., JR. *Making of the Modern Mind*. HM, 1926.

ROOS, FRANK J., JR. *An Illustrated Handbook of Art History*. M, 1937.

SEIGNOBOS, CHARLES. *The Rise of European Civilization*. AAK, 1938.

TAYLOR, H. F. *The Taste of Angels*. LB, 1947.

THORNDIKE, LYNN. *A Short History of Civilization*. FSC, 1948.

TOYNBEE, ARNOLD. *A Study of History*. OUP, 1934–39.

WELLS, H. G. *The Outline of History*. M, 1930.

WESTERN MAN'S ANCIENT HERITAGE

DURANT, WILL. *The Life of Greece*. SS, 1939.

———. *Caesar and Christ*. SS, 1944.

GIBBON, EDWARD. *The Decline and Fall of the Roman Empire*. ML, n.d.

HUGHES, PHILIP. *A History of the Catholic Church*. Sheed and Ward, New York, 1935–1947.

LIVY. *Books I, II, III, IV*. G. P. Putnam's Sons, New York, 1922.

PLUTARCH. *The Lives of the Noble Greeks and Romans*. ML, 1932.

SHOWERMAN, GRANT. *Eternal Rome*. Yale University Press, New Haven, Conn. 1925.

SMITH, WILLIAM (ed.). *Dictionary of Greek and Roman Antiquities*. H, 1886.

TACITUS. *Complete Works of Tacitus*. ML, 1942.

I THE SPIRIT OF THE MIDDLE AGES

II MEDIEVAL LIFE

ADAMS, G. B. *Civilization During the Middle Ages*. CSS, 1922.

ADAMS, HENRY. *Mont-Saint-Michel and Chartres*. HM, 1933.

COULTON, G. G. *Life in the Middle Ages*. Macmillan and Co., Ltd., London, 1930.

CRUMP, G. G. and JACOB, E. F. *The Legacy of the Middle Ages*. OUP, 1943.

DANTE. *Divine Comedy of Dante Alighieri*. ML, 1932.

D'ARCY, M. C. *Thomas Aquinas*. Newman Bookshop, Westminster, Md., 1944.

DAVIS, W. S. *Life on a Medieval Barony*. H, 1923

DURANT, WILL. *The Age of Faith*. SS, 1950.

FLETCHER, BANISTER. *A History of Architecture*. CSS, 1945.

FUNCK-BRENTANO, F. *The Middle Ages*. William Heinemann, London, 1922.

KELLY, AMY. *Eleanor of Aquitaine and the Four Kings*. Harvard University Press, Cambridge Mass., 1950.

PIRENNE, HENRI. *Economic and Social History of Medieval Europe*. Paul, Trench, Trübner and Co. Ltd., London, 1936.

ROSENBERG, MELRICH. *Eleanor of Aquitaine*. HM, 1937.

STEPHENSON, CARL. *Medieval History*. H, 1935.

STRAYER, J. R. AND MUNRO, D. C. *The Middle Ages 395–1500*. D. Appleton-Century, New York 1942.

TAYLOR, H. O. *The Medieval Mind*. Macmillan and Co., Ltd., London, 1938.

WADDELL, HELEN. *The Wandering Scholars*. HH, 1932.

III RENAISSANCE MAN

IV THE GLORY OF VENICE

BOCCACCIO, GIOVANNI. *The Decameron*. ML, 1931.

BURCKHARDT, JACOB. *The Civilization of the Renaissance in Italy*. P, 1947.

BURROUGHS, BETTY (ed.). *Vasari's Lives of the Artists*. SS, 1946.

CLARK, KENNETH. *Piero della Francesca*. P, 1950.

COTTERILL, H. B. *Italy from Dante to Tasso*. Harrap, London, 1929.

FATTORUSSO, JOSEPH. *Cities of Central Italy*. Medici Art Series, Florence 1937.

FATTORUSSO, J. and M. L. *Florence*. Medici Art Series, Florence 1937.

GOLDSCHEIDER, LUDWIG. *Ghiberti*. P, 1949.

MACHIAVELLI, NICCOLÒ. *The Prince and The Discourses*. ML, 1940.

MATHER, F. J., JR. *A History of Italian Painting*. HH, 1923.

OLIPHANT, MRS. *The Makers of Venice*. M, 1906.

PATER, WALTER. *The Renaissance*. Boni and Liveright, New York, 1919.

PETRARCH, FRANCESCO. *Sonnets and Songs*. Pantheon, New York, 1946.

PIUS II. *Commentaries*. Smith College Studies in History, Northampton, Mass. 1936–37.

POLO, MARCO. *The Travels of Marco Polo*. Boni and Liveright, New York 1926.

PREZZOLINI, G. *The Legacy of Italy*. Vanni, New York, 1948.

RICCI, CORRADO. *Art in Northern Italy*. CSS, 1930.

ROEDER, RALPH. *The Man of the Renaissance*. The Viking Press, New York 1933.

SALVATORELLI, LUIGI. *A Concise History of Italy*. OUP, 1940.

SELINCOURT, BASIL DE. *Giotto*. CSS, 1950.

SYMONDS, J. A. *Renaissance in Italy*. ML, 1935.

VENTURI, LIONELLO, SKIRA-VENTURI, ROSABIANCA. *Italian Painting*. Albert Skira, Geneva. 1950.

V THE AGE OF EXPLORATION

BELL, DOUGLAS. *Elizabethan Seamen*. J. B. Lippincott Co., Philadelphia, 1936.

GIBSON, C. E. *The Story of the Ship*. H. Schuman, New York, 1948.

HOLAND, H. R. *America, 1355–1364*. Duell, Sloan and Pearce, New York, 1946.

MALORY, THOMAS. *The Morte d'Arthur*. FSC, 1946.

MITCHELL, J. L. *Earth Conquerors*. SS, 1934.

MORISON, S. E. *Admiral of the Ocean Sea*. Little, Brown and Co., Boston, 1944.

ROWSE, A. L. *The England of Elizabeth*. M, 1951.

SANCEAU, ELAINE. *Henry the Navigator*. W. W. Norton and Co., New York, 1945.

SITWELL, EDITH. *Fanfare for Elizabeth*. M, 1946.

STEFANSSON, VILHJALMAR, *Great Adventures and Explorations*. The Dial Press, New York, 1947.

STRACHEY, LYTTON. *Elizabeth and Essex.* Harcourt, Brace and Co., New York, 1928.
SYKES, P. M. *A History of Exploration.* M, 1936.
TAYLOR, F. S. *The World of Science.* W. W. Norton and Co., New York, 1950
WOOD, C. H. W. *Elizabethan Sea-Dogs.* Yale University Press, New Haven, Conn., 1918.
WORTH, LAWRENCE. *The Way of a Ship.* Southworth-Anthoensen Press, Portland, Maine, 1937.

VI THE PROTESTANT REFORMATION

ACTON, J. E. E. D. *Lectures on Modern History.* Macmillan and Co., Ltd., London, 1930.
BAINTON, R. H. *Here I Stand, A Life of Martin Luther.* Abingdon-Cokesbury Press, Nashville, Tenn., 1950.
CHAMBERS, R. W. *Thomas More.* Jonathan Cape, London, 1935.
FISKE, JOHN. *The Beginnings of New England.* HM, 1902.
GRISAR, HARTMANN. *Luther.* Paul, Trench, Trübner and Co., Ltd., London, 1913–17.
HARNEY, M. P. *The Jesuits in History.* The America Press, New York, 1941.
LEA, H. C. *Inquisition in the Spanish Dependencies.* M, 1922.
MOTLEY, J. L. *The Rise of the Dutch Republic.* EPD, 1939–42.
PARRY, E. A. *The Persecution of Mary Stewart.* CSS, 1931.
SMITH, PRESERVED. *The Age of the Reformation.* HH, 1920.
STONE, J. M. *Reformation and Renaissance.* Duckworth and Co., London, 1904.
WILLISON, G. F. *Saints and Strangers.* Reynal and Hitchcock, Inc., New York, 1945.
ZWEIG, STEFAN. *Mary Queen of Scotland and the Isles.* The Viking Press, New York, 1935.

THE RISE OF BOURGEOIS MAN

BARBOUR, VIOLET. *Capitalism in Amsterdam in the Seventeenth Century.* The Johns Hopkins Press, Baltimore, 1950.
BARNOUW, A. *The Dutch.* Columbia University Press, New York, 1940.
BEARD, MIRIAM. *A History of the Business Man.* M, 1938.
BLOK, P. J. *History of the People of the Netherlands.* G. P. Putnam's Sons, New York, 1898–1912.
TAWNEY, R. H. *Religion and the Rise of Capitalism.* EPD, 1939–42.
TEMPLE, WILLIAM. *Observations.* (1693 edition available at Columbia University Library.)
VAN LOON, H. W. *Life and Times of Rembrandt.* Liveright, New York, 1930.
VLEKKE, B. H. M. *Evolution of the Dutch Nation.* Roy Publishers, New York, 1945.

THE DAWN OF MODERN SCIENCE

ANDRADE, E. N. *Isaac Newton.* Max Parrish, London, 1950.
BELL, E. T. *Men of Mathematics.* SS, 1937.
DAMPIER, WILLIAM. *A History of Science and Its Relations with Philosophy and Religion.* M, 1949.
HAGGARD, HOWARD. *Devils, Drugs and Doctors.* Blue Ribbon Books, New York, 1929.
JEANS, JAMES. *The Growth of Physical Science.* M, 1948.
LOEB, L. B. and ADAMS, A. S. *Development of Physical Thought.* John Wiley and Sons, New York, 1933.
PLEDGE, H.T. *Science Since 1500.* Ministry of Education, London, 1947.
SINGER, C. J. *A Short History of Science.* OUP, 1941.
———. *Isaac Newton, 1642-1727.* M, 1938.
SULLIVAN, J. W. N. *Isaac Newton, 1642–1727.* Macmillan and Co., Ltd., London, 1938.
WHITEHEAD, A. N. *Science and the Modern World.* New American Library, New York, 1939.
WOLF, ABRAHAM. *History of Science, Technology and Philosophy in the Sixteenth and Seventeenth Centuries.* M, 1935.

VII THE AGE OF ENLIGHTENMENT

ANTHONY, K. S. *Catherine the Great.* AAK, 1925.
ASHLEY, M. P. *Louis XIV and the Greatness of France.* M, 1948.
FERGUSON, WALLACE. *The Enlightened Despots.* FSC, n.d.
GALANTIÈRE, LEWIS (ed.). *The Goncourt Journals 1851–1870.* Doubleday and Co., New York, 1937
GAXOTTE, PIERRE. *Louis XV and His Times.* Jonathan Cape, London 1934.
DE GONCOURT, E. L. AND J. A. *The Woman of the Eighteenth Century.* Minton, Balch and Co., New York, 1927.
———. *French Eighteenth Century Painters.* P, 1948.
GORDON, DOUGLAS AND TORREY, NORMAN. *The Censoring of Diderot's "Encyclopédie."* Columbia University Press, New York, 1947.
LACROIX, PAUL. *The Eighteenth Century, Its Institutions, Costumes and Customs.* Bickers and Sons, London, n.d.
MONTESQUIEU. *Persian Letters.* Gibbings and Co., London, 1899.
PADOVER, SAUL K. *The Life and Death of Louis XVI.* D. Appleton-Century, New York, 1939.
PICARD, ROGER. *Les Salons Littéraires et la Société Française, 1610–1789.* Brentano's, New York, 1943.
REDMAN. BEN RAY (ed.). *The Portable Voltaire.* The Viking Press, New York, 1949.
SAINTSBURY, G. E. B. *French Literature and Its Masters.* AAK, 1946.
———. *A Short History of French Literature.* OUP, 1945.
SOKOLNIKOVA, HALINA. *Nine Women.* Cape and Smith, New York, 1932.
TAINE, HIPPOLYTE. *The Ancient Régime.* HH, 1876.
VOLTAIRE, F.M.A. de. *Candide.* ML, 1936.
———.*The Portable Voltaire.* The Viking Press, New York, 1949.
WILENSKI, R. H. *French Painting.* Hale Cushman and Flint, Boston, 1949.
WILLIAMS, H. N. *Madame de Pompadour.* CSS, 1902.
———. *Madame du Barry.* CSS, 1904.

VIII EIGHTEENTH CENTURY ENGLAND —THE RISE OF PARLIAMENTARY GOVERNMENT

D'ARBLAY, FRANCES. *The Diary and Letters of Fanny Burney.* R. Ingram, London, 1948.
BAGEHOT, WALTER. *The English Constitution.* D. Appleton-Century, New York, 1890.
BAILY, JOHN. *Johnson and His Circle.* OUP, 1945.
BIGHAM, CLIVE. *The Prime Ministers of Britain, 1721–1921.* EPD, 1922.
BOSWELL, JAMES. *The Life of Samuel Johnson.* ML, n.d.
BURKE, THOMAS. *English Night-Life.* BTB, 1941.
———. *The English Townsman.* BTB, 1946.
CECIL, DAVID. *The Young Melbourne.* The Bobbs-Merrill Co., New York, 1939.
CHANCELLOR, E. B. *The Eighteenth Century in London.* BTB, 1920.
CHURCHILL, WINSTON. *Marlborough.* CSS, 1933–38.
CUNNINGHAM, PETER. *Hand-Book of London.* John Murray, London, 1850.
DOBRÉE, BONAMY (ed.). *From Anne to Victoria.* Cassell and Co., ltd., London, 1937.
DUTTON, RALPH. *The English Garden.* BTB, 1937.
EDEN, GUY. *The Parliament Book.* Staples Press, New York, 1949.
FUNSTON, J. W. *The Wesleys in Picture and Story.* John Wesley Funston, Oak Park, Ill., 1939.
GUTTMACHER, M. S. *America's Last King.* CSS, 1941.
HOLE, CHRISTINA. *English Home-Life.* BTB, 1947.
JENNINGS, W. I. *Parliament.* Columbia University Press, New York, 1939.
KENT, WILLIAM (ed.). *An Encyclopedia of London.* EPD, 1937.
KRONENBERGER, LOUIS. *Kings and Desperate Men.* AAK, 1944.
KRUTCH, J. W. *Samuel Johnson.* HH, 1944.
MACAULEY, T. B. *Life of Samuel Johnson.* Ginn and Co., Boston, 1928.

MACKENZIE, KENNETH. *The English Parliament.* Penguin Books, Harmondsworth, Middlesex, 1950.
MITCHELL, R. J. and LEYS, M. D. R. *A History of the English People.* LG, 1950.
MORLEY, JOHN. *Burke.* H, 1902.
———. *Walpole.* M, 1889.
QUINTANA, RICARDO. *The Mind and Art of Jonathan Swift.* OUP, 1936.
ROBERTS, PENFIELD. *The Quest for Security, 1715–1740.* H, 1947.
ROBERTSON, C. G. *Chatham and the British Empire.* M, 1918.
SHELLABARGER, SAMUEL. *Lord Chesterfield.* Macmillan and Co., Ltd., London, 1935.
SITWELL, EDITH. *Bath.* Faber and Faber, London, 1932.
SITWELL, OSBERT AND BARTON, MARGARET. *Brighton.* HM, 1935.
SUMMERSON, JOHN. *Georgian London.* CSS, 1948.
TASWELL-LANGMEAD, T. P. *English Constitutional History.* Stevens and Haynes, London, 1875.
TREVELYAN, G. M. *England Under Queen Anne.* LG, 1930-34.
———. *English Social History.* LG, 1949.
TREVELYAN, G. O. *The Early History of Charles James Fox.* H, 1880.
TRUSLER, JOHN. *Hogarth Moralized.* Shakespeare Press, London, 1831.
TURBERVILLE, A. S. *English Men and Manners in the Eighteenth Century.* Clarendon Press, Oxford, 1929.
———. (ed.). *Johnson's England,* Clarendon Press, Oxford, 1933.
WILENSKI, R. H. *English Painting.* Hale, Cushman and Flint, Boston, 1937.
WILLEY, BASIL. *The Eighteenth Century Background.* Chatto and Windus, London, 1940.
WILLIAMS, BASIL. *The Whig Supremacy, 1714–1760.* Clarendon Press, Oxford, 1945.

IX THE AGE OF REVOLUTIONS

ANGAS, W. M. *Rivalry on the Atlantic.* Furman, New York, 1939.
BARZUN, JACQUES. *Marx, Darwin, Wagner.* Little, Brown and Co., Boston, 1941.
BOGART, E. L. *Economic History of Europe.* LG, 1942.
BOLITHO, HECTOR. *The Letters of Queen Victoria.* Yale University Press, New Haven, Conn., 1938.
———. *The Reign of Queen Victoria.* M, 1947.
BRINTON, CRANE. *Age of Revolutions.* H, 1934.
CLOUGH, S. B. AND COLE, C. W. *Economic History of Europe.* D. C. Heath, Boston, 1946.
DICKINSON, H. W. AND JENKINS, RHYS. *James Watt and the Steam Engine.* Clarendon Press, Oxford, 1927.
JONES, G. P. AND POOL, A. G. *A Hundred Years of Economic Development.* M, 1910.
KLINGENDER, F. D. *Art and the Industrial Revolution.* Carrington, London, 1947.
KNOWLES, L. C. A. *Industrial and Commercial Revolutions.* EPD, 1922.
LEFEBVRE, GEORGES. *Coming of the French Revolution, 1789.* Princeton University Press, Princeton, N. J., 1948.
LOWELL, E. J. *The Eve of the French Revolution.* HM, 1925.
LUDWIG, EMIL. *Napoleon.* ML, 1933.
MANTOUX, P. J. *The Industrial Revolution in the Eighteenth Century.* M, n.d.
MARX, KARL, AND ENGELS, FRIEDRICH. *The Communist Manifesto.* Kerr, Chicago, 1912.
NOCK, O. S. *The Railways of Great Britain, Past and Present.* BTB, 1948.
SMITH, E. W. *Trans-Atlantic Passenger Ships, Past and Present.* George H. Dean, Boston, 1947.
STRACHEY, LYTTON. *Queen Victoria.* Harcourt, Brace and Co., New York, 1939.
TOYNBEE, ARNOLD. *Lectures on the Industrial Revolution of the Eighteenth Century in England.* LG, 1937.

X THE AMERICAN IDEA

ADAMS, HENRY. *The Degradation of the Democratic Dogma.* M, 1919.
ADAMS, J. T. (ed.). *Album of American History.* CSS, 1940.
BEARD, C. A. AND M. R. *The Rise of American Civilization.* M, 1942.
BUTTERFIELD, R. R. *The American Past.* SS, 1947.
FAULKNER, H. U. *American Economic History.* H, 1938.
GABRIEL, R. H. *The Course of American Democratic Thought.* Ronald Press Co., New York, 1940.
GOSNELL, H. F. *Democracy, the Threshold of Freedom.* Ronald Press Co., New York, 1940.
GREENE, F. V. *The Revolutionary War.* CSS, 1911.
HACKER, L. M. *The Shaping of American Tradition.* Columbia University Press, New York, 1947.
HALE, W. H. *The March of Freedom.* H, 1947.
HANDLIN, OSCAR. *This Was America.* Harvard University Press, Cambridge, Mass., 1949.
HENRY, R. S. *Trains.* The Bobbs-Merrill Co., Indianapolis, 1934.
LEWIS, WYNDAM. *America and Cosmic Man.* Nicholson, London, 1948.
MELVILLE, HERMAN. *Moby Dick.* ML, 1926.
MILLER, J. C. *Triumph of Freedom.* Little, Brown and Co., Boston, 1948.
MORISON, S. E. and Commager, H. S. *The Growth of the American Republic.* OUP, 1930.
NORMANS, J. F. *The Spirit of American Economics.* The Committee on the Study of Economic Thought. John Day Co., New York, (dist.), 1943.
PARKES, H. B. *The American Experience.* AAK, 1947.
SMITH, ADAM. *The Wealth of Nations.* ML, 1937.
SMITH, H. N. *Virgin Land.* Harvard University Press, Cambridge, Mass., 1950.
STEIN, E. AND DAVIS, J. *Labor Problems in America.* Farrar and Rinehart, New York, 1940.
TURNER, F. J. *The Frontier in American History.* HH, 1937.
WHITMAN, WALT. *Complete Works of Walt Whitman.* Pellegrini and Cudahy, New York, 1948.

KEY TO PUBLISHERS

AAK	Alfred A. Knopf, New York
BTB	B. T. Batsford, ltd., London
CSS	Charles Scribner's Sons, New York
EPD	E. P. Dutton and Co., New York
FSC	F. S. Crofts and Co., New York
H	Harper and Brothers, New York
HH	Henry Holt and Co., New York
HM	Houghton Mifflin Co., Boston
LG	Longman's, Green and Co., New York
M	The Macmillan Co., New York
ML	The Modern Library, New York
OUP	Oxford University Press, London, New York.
P	Phaidon, Oxford
SS	Simon and Schuster, New York

INDEX

†This symbol under a subject indicates that an illustration, as well as mention, of the subject is to be found on the page thus marked.
††This symbol under an artist's name indicates that a reproduction of a work by the artist is to be found on the page thus marked.

PRINTED AND BOUND BY R. R. DONNELLEY & SONS COMPANY
CHICAGO, ILLINOIS AND CRAWFORDSVILLE, INDIANA.
PAPER BY THE MEAD CORPORATION, DAYTON, OHIO.